# THE DYNASTY

## THE
## NEHRU–GANDHI
### STORY

# THE DYNASTY
## THE
# NEHRU–GANDHI
### STORY

JAD ADAMS

AND

PHILLIP WHITEHEAD

TV Books • New York

Published by TV Books, Inc., 1619 Broadway, New York, NY 10019.

First published in the United Kingdom by Penguin Books Ltd., 1997.

10  9  8  7  6  5  4  3  2  1

**Publisher's Cataloging-in-Publication Data**

Adams, Jad.
    The dynasty: the Nehru-Gandhi rule over modern India/
Jad Adams and Philip Whitehead.—1st ed.
    p. cm.
    Includes index.
    ISBN: 1-57500-056-3

    1. Nehru, Jawaharlal, 1889–1964. 2. Gandhi, Indira, 1917–1984.
3. Gandhi. Rajiv, 1944–  4. Nehru family. 5. India—Politics and
government—1947– I. Whitehead, Philip. II. Title.

DS480.84.A43 1998               954.05
                           QBI97–41388

The publishers would like to thank the following for providing
photographs and for permission to reproduce copyright
material. While every effort has been made to trace and
acknowledge copyright holders, we would like to apologize
should there have been any errors or omissions.

Mark Anderson, London: 25
Brook Associates: 24
Indira Gandhi Memorial Trust, New Delhi: 12, 23
Hulton Getty, London: 9, 14, 20, 22
Magnum Photos: 11 © Cartier Bresson; 29 © Raghu Rai; 31 © Raghu Rai
The Nehru Memorial Museum and Library, New Delhi: 1, 2–5, 6–8, 10, 13, 15, 18–19
Nayantara Sahgal, Dehradun, India: 16, 21, 27, 28
SPI: 17, 26, 30

Design and production by Joe Gannon.
Printed and bound by Royal Book Manufacturing.

# Contents

# Acknowledgements

A book of this nature, associated with a television series, is invariably indebted to a large number of people. Material from the transcripts of recorded interviews and research interviews is clearly marked as such in the notes. Just as important, however, have been office discussions about the series and the referencing of source material. A significant contribution was made by assistant producer Miriam Joseph, who read and corrected the text and undertook additional research for the book.

We are also grateful to other members of the production team: Mark Anderson, Rosalind Bentley, Charles Bruce, Dan Carter, Mark Davis, Elaine Goodwin, Sallyann Kleibel, Polly Lansdowne, Emma Lysaght, Gemma North, Christine Pancott and production manager Jayne Rowe.

We also benefited from the advice of Judith Brown, Sunil Khilnani and James Manor.

Thanks are also due to Harold Hewitt and Julie Peakman, who read and corrected early drafts of the text.

"The Dynasty: The Nehru–Gandhi Story," a four-part series for television, was produced by Brook Associates for the BBC in the UK, WGBH in the U.S., and Canal Plus in France.

# India in the late 1980s

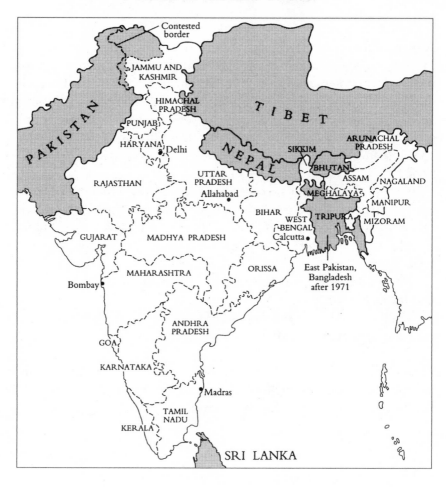

# The Nehru-Gandhi Family Tree (simplified)

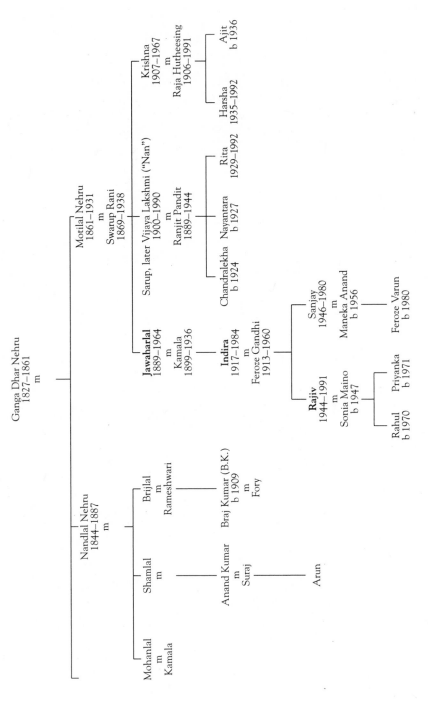

Ganga Dhar Nehru
1827–1861
m

Nandlal Nehru
1844–1887
m

Motilal Nehru
1861–1931
m
Swarup Rani
1869–1938

Mohanlal
m
Kamala

Shamlal
m

Brijlal
m
Rameshwari

**Jawaharlal**
1889–1964
m
Kamala
1899–1936

Sarup, later Vijaya Lakshmi ("Nan")
1900–1990
m
Ranjit Pandit
1889–1944

Krishna
1907–1967
m
Raja Hutheesing
1906–1991

Anand Kumar
m
Suraj

Braj Kumar (B.K.)
b 1909
m
Fory

**Indira**
1917–1984
m
Feroze Gandhi
1913–1960

Chandralekha
b 1924

Nayantara
b 1927

Rita
1929–1992

Harsha
1935–1992

Ajit
b 1936

Arun

**Rajiv**
1944–1991
m
Sonia Maino
b 1947

Sanjay
1946–1980
m
Maneka Anand
b 1956

Rahul
b 1970

Priyanka
b 1971

Feroze Varun
b 1980

# AWAKENING

# ONE

# GENESIS OF A RULING FAMILY

On Friday, June 15, 1945 a slight, serious-looking man stepped out of Almora District Jail into the brilliant Indian sunlight. He had spent nine of the last twenty-four years in prison, but his step showed no hesitancy. At the sight of the thin man in simple white homespun clothing, the crowds, who had waited for hours in the heat and dust, burst into tumultuous cheering and surged forward to greet him. They knew that he was the key to the destiny of India. He was an extraordinary son of an extraordinary family, a man of vision, of seductive charms which endeared him to men and women alike. He was born an Indian, but became a man of two worlds: the public school and college atmosphere of aristocratic England, and the high hills and dusty plains of India. His life was as deeply tied up with Britain and the British as with India.

Jawaharlal* Nehru had been groomed for greatness. He was born into a home of almost legendary wealth, surrounded by rich furnishings, a retinue of liveried servants, tennis courts, a swimming pool and lawns with sparkling fountains. He renounced this life, however, and took to hardship and agitation, down the winding roads of India, in front of the swarming crowds. If his hour had come, it was the culmination of a long journey both for himself and for India. In their remarkable lives, the Nehru family came to personify the struggles and triumphs of the entire nation, an identification with national life which they did everything to promote.

Jawaharlal was from a family of Brahmins, the highest caste in Indian society, traditionally destined to be priests or scholars, and who tended to intermarry to preserve their exclusivity. The Nehrus came from Kashmir, the beautiful region of mountains and lakes in northern India. The fair-skinned Kashmiri Brahmins, often given the honorary title "pandit," meaning learned person or teacher, were regarded as a particularly aristocratic race for their fine appearance and intellectual powers. The skills

---

* Jawaharlal himself was never entirely happy with his given name and suggested abbreviating it, but without success. It is generally pronounced with the third syllable elided: Jawarlal.

of the Nehrus as scholars had long been in demand for public duties. The family, originally named Kaul, migrated from Kashmir at the request of the Mogul emperor Farukh Siyyer around 1716, when he asked for the services of Raj Kaul, who had impressed him as a scholar of Sanskrit and Persian. Kaul and his family were given a house on the banks of a canal (*nahar* in Urdu), and the corruption of this word gave them a new family name. The Nehrus continued in public service, Lakshmi Narayan Nehru becoming the lawyer of the East India Company at the Mogul court, and his son, Ganga Dhar Nehru, becoming chief of police under the last Mogul emperor of Delhi, though this was really a position as a palace official for the puppet emperor. This life of courtly service was interrupted by the revolt against British rule, which is referred to as the Mutiny of 1857. When Delhi fell to the British and recriminations began, almost the entire Indian population of the city fled, including Ganga Dhar Nehru, his wife, and their two sons and two daughters. The family was almost put to death on account of one of the girls, who was so light of complexion that British soldiers took her for an English girl who had been abducted, but the sons' knowledge of English saved them.

Ganga Dhar, having lost his job, home and almost everything he possessed, began again in the city of Agra. Within a few years, however, he died, aged only thirty-four, leaving his wife Indrani pregnant with Motilal, who was born on May 6, 1861, three months after his father's death. The eldest son, Bansi Dhar Nehru, was on government service and liable to frequent transfers, so it fell to the next son, Nandlal Nehru, to support the family. This he did by working as a teacher, then a private secretary and finally as chief minister to the head of Khetri state in Rajasthan. He worked in this capacity until 1870, when he became a lawyer in Agra. When the High Court moved from Agra to Allahabad, the Nehru family moved with it.

Motilal grew up as more of a son than a brother to Nandlal. He was taught by the private tutor who taught the children of his brother's employer and his early education was confined entirely to Persian and Arabic. He then attended the government school at Cawnpore and began learning English at the age of twelve. While he was quick-witted and a good scholar, admired for his excellence in Persian, he was more interested in games, particularly wrestling, and in boyish adventures. He moved on to Muir Central College at Allahabad and was looked upon there as a leader of the rowdy element. When a local public figure of forty-five married an eighteen-year-old, Motilal wrote a satirical poem about it and had it published privately. Nandlal was furious when he found out, and insisted that all copies of it be burnt. Motilal's contact with British professors at the college strongly influenced him, and he took to wearing Western dress and copying Western ways when it was rare for Indians to do so except in the big cities. He got through his university examinations without any special distinction but failed to work for his finals. After the first paper he felt he had no chance of success, so he did not take the remaining exams and spent his time instead at the Taj Mahal, a popular gathering place as well as a tourist attraction. Subsequently, his professor sent for him, enraged that he had not completed the examination, for he had done the first paper fairly well. He never graduated, but had clearly learned his lesson. When he took the examinations to enter the legal profession in 1883, he gained top marks and received the prestigious Lumbsdon Medal.

Motilal first practiced in the district courts of Cawnpore, working hard and winning success, and moved to Allahabad to work in the High Court after three years. Soon after the move, in 1887, his brother Nandlal died at the age of forty-two, so Motilal, only twenty-five, was now called on to support the family. He set aside all other activities and devoted himself entirely to the law, becoming a great professional success but, as one of his sons later wrote, "more and more a slave to his jealous mistress—the law."[1] During this period Motilal also lost his wife, who had been weakened by childbirth, and their only child, his three-year-old son Ratanlal.

When Motilal married again it was to Swarup Rani, an exceptionally beautiful girl from a similar background to his own. She was fourteen years old and said to be petite "with a Dresden china perfection of complexion and features, hazel eyes, chestnut-brown hair and exquisitely shaped hands and feet."[2] She was her parents' youngest child and rather spoiled, so she found it difficult to fit into her husband's household, which was dominated by her formidable mother-in-law.

Motilal himself was handsome and well-built, with deep-set eyes and a large mustache. Photographs of him show a solidity and sense of purpose in his stance: indeed, his physical presence was said to be one reason for his great success in the courts. Motilal was a consummate cross-examiner, impressing everyone with his forensic performance, which was based more on keen perception and analysis than eloquence. In this way he would gradually build up a complete and unarguable case. "He loved a fight, a struggle against the odds," his son wrote.[3] While Motilal gave the impression that his legal brilliance was effortless, it was, in fact, based on a regime of rigorous hard work. For one day of which there is a record, November 9, 1905, he got up at four in the morning, worked at his briefs till eight, saw new clients till nine, was in court at ten and on his feet throughout the day. The secret of his success, he boomed, was simple: "I want money. I work for it and I get it. There are many people who want it perhaps more than I do, but they do not work and naturally enough do not get it."[4] In January 1896 Motilal was admitted to the Roll of Advocates at the Allahabad High Court, one of only four such appointments that year. The pinnacle of his career came in August 1909, when he was permitted to appear and plead at the Bar of the judicial committee of the Privy Council in Great Britain—in effect, the Empire's supreme court.

His work, largely in the complex field of Hindu land inheritance, was highly remunerative. In his early thirties Motilal was making nearly 2000 rupees a month (equivalent to around a million rupees or $32,000 a year in 1990s' figures) at a time when a teacher's salary was 10 rupees a month; by his early forties his monthly income was in five figures. Soon he was able to move to the smart suburbs of Allahabad, to 9 Elgin Road, an area largely populated by Europeans and Anglo-Indians. Motilal's Westernization even led him to decree that only English should be spoken in his house. This reduced the place to frequent silences, as most of the women and children could not speak it, so the idea was soon abandoned.

Jawaharlal said Motilal hated hoarding money because he thought this implied an inability to earn sufficient in an hour of need. But there was also something reckless in Motilal's character, probably derived from the terrible blows he had suffered—the death of his father, brother, wife and son all at an early age. Life was short, so why not enjoy what he had while he could? Nor was his largesse restricted to himself: Motilal paid for the foreign education of his nephews and was known to be generous to those in need. A story is told of how he was stopped on his way to court by a poor Brahmin who wanted help in preparing for his daughter's wedding. Asked how much was needed for the marriage, the man replied that it was 300 rupees. Motilal told his clerk to give the man the entire sum he received that day in fees, which in the end amounted to 1300 rupees.[5] There was an absurd story that Motilal sent his laundry to Paris. Although much of his wardrobe may have been bought in Europe, the laundry was actually dealt with by a local family.

Motilal and Swarup Rani's first child, a son, did not survive. A story was later told by the devout—or the credulous—that Motilal and some friends went to the holy city of Rishikesh in the Himalayas where he encountered a yogi who lived in a tree. Learning from one of Motilal's companions that all he desired was a son, the yogi volunteered that Motilal was not destined to have one. Another of Motilal's companions said that a great yogi could change destiny. The yogi was silent, then sprinkled water from his pot three times in front of Motilal and visibly paled. He told Motilal he had used the fruits of his penance of many life-times to pay for this boon, and the following day the yogi died. Ten months later, on November 14, 1889, Swarup Rani gave birth to Jawaharlal Nehru. The story of his miraculous conception was to gain in currency as Jawaharlal's prominence in life increased. What Motilal made of this tale is not recorded. He was famously secular in outlook, but was prepared to have the horoscope of the newborn baby cast by the court astrologer of Khetri state, where his brother had been influential.

Jawaharlal thus grew up as the only son—for the first eleven years of his life the only child—in a family which doted on him. His sister Sarup (on marriage renamed Vijaya but, confusingly, always known by her childhood nickname of Nan) was born on August 18, 1900, and another sister, Krishna, was born on November 2, 1907, but by this time he was away at school. A first son, and an only son, would be much treasured in any Indian family, but Motilal was particularly lavish in his affections, doubtless moved by the deaths of two previous sons. He also increasingly came to rely on Jawaharlal as a confidant and friend, as his letters to the boy show, and he found in his son a companionship missing in his marriage. For Swarup Rani too, Jawaharlal filled an aching need, for she had little to contribute to Motilal's Westernized life, and all her love and attention was lavished on her son. As a writer close to Jawaharlal once said, "the lack of companionship between husband and wife led to the mother building her life and affections round her son."[6]

In 1900, when Jawaharlal was about ten years old, the family moved to a huge house at 1 Church Road, Allahabad, which Motilal purchased from a High Court judge for 19,000 rupees. The price was low, but much renovation work was needed. Motilal was impressed by the size of the estate with its lawns, fruit gardens and swimming pool. He called it Anand Bhavan (Abode of Joy) and began turning it into a byword for luxury. The mansion would house several generations of Motilal's extended family, as well as an army of servants. Relatives would also come and stay at any time for as long as they wished. The rooms were huge and superbly equipped. It was the first house in Allahabad to have electricity and water installed; it also had flush toilets. Motilal used his frequent visits to Europe to buy furniture and fittings for his home.

Motilal often chided Swarup Rani about her pilgrimages to Hindu holy places: "Pilgrimages should lead to the West—to Europe, to America, in search of the key to progress so that we can open the door to a fuller, richer life for ourselves."[7] When he returned to India from Europe in late 1899, he failed to perform the *prayaschchit* or purification ceremony which was customary for a Kashmiri Brahmin after traveling abroad. Jawaharlal later remarked that the ceremony was "a bit of a farce and there was little of religion about it" but it was an outward manifestation of conformity to the group will.[8] Motilal alienated orthodox Kashmiris with his aggressive and disdainful attitude. He had already scandalized them by taking his midday meals in public at the High Court, in contempt of the strict dietary rules for a Brahmin. The family was thus isolated from the wave of Hindu revivalism which was sweeping India and which gave considerable impetus to nationalist feeling.

Motilal could be extremely blunt when talking about religion. During an election campaign in 1926 he said, ". . . I do not believe in Divine Revelation of any scripture whatsoever. Of course, as codes of moral guidance, almost all religious books are quite good. But to say that God speaks to men, is something beyond my grasp." Even more robustly, he mocked the Hindu adoration of "mother cow"; "People criticize me for not worshipping a cow. But I tell you quite frankly, whether you give me your vote or not, I can't bull my father by calling cow my mother."[9]

It was part of his Western secular approach that Motilal treated all his servants equally, whatever their religious background, and he showed his contempt for caste rules by keeping an untouchable as his personal valet. He was, however, said to respect the religious wishes of others, and high-caste Brahmin friends who could not eat communally had their food prepared and served separately when in his house. Those who felt uncomfortable with Western ways would eat in the kitchen, the Indian part of the house; others would join Motilal in the dining room. The demarcation was not rigid, however, and Motilal would often have dinner with all his family around him, whether they leaned to Western or Indian habits. His granddaughter Nayantara remarked, "It used to be said that wherever he sat became the head of the table because he was such a tremendous personality."[10]

The servants of the house were similarly divided, with Hindus on one side, speaking Urdu and Hindustani, and the European, Christian, Muslim and untouchable servants mainly speaking English on the other. Jawaharlal thus, like other educated Indians, lived in a variety of linguistic worlds: the family languages being Urdu, the language of the previous rulers; English, the language of the present rulers; and Hindustani, the language of that locality. This polyglot environment could lead to confusion for the children: Jawaharlal's sister Vijaya said she thought as a child that educated Indians spoke Urdu, and those employed by them spoke English.[11] All the servants had a form of familial relationship with Motilal; the English governess, Miss Hooper ("Toopie"), was even given away by him on her wedding day.

Motilal bought expensive novelties, like bicycles, in India, but imported his cars. In 1904 he had the first car in Allahabad, then bought another the following year, and two more in 1909. He also had carriages and a stable of fine Arabian horses. It was said that his children learned to ride almost as soon as they learned to walk, and Motilal was a hard taskmaster. When his daughter Krishna fell off her pony as a tiny girl, she expected to be comforted, but Motilal gave her two hard whacks: "No daughter of mine must show weakness of this sort," he said. "No matter how much you are hurt you are not supposed to cry."[12]

When age prevented him from wrestling, he would still enjoy watching bouts between the servants in a specially prepared arena in the garden. He employed an Anglo-Indian as superintendent of his garden and bought the best seeds from British firms. There were freshly cut flowers in the house every day. In summer there would be elaborate garden parties where the fountain in the courtyard was filled with ice and sweet-smelling flowers. In fact, the family entertained most days and some of Jawaharlal's earliest memories were of hiding behind a curtain to watch the gathering and try to make out what the big people were saying to each other. If caught, he would be dragged out and made to sit on his father's knee. Once he saw his father drinking blood from a glass and ran to tell his mother, who was able to reassure him it was only claret.

Jawaharlal adored his father whom he felt to be "the embodiment of strength and courage and cleverness." He remembered the house resounding with his father's "tremendous laughter."[13] He also remembered his father's overpowering rages, which frightened the child and filled him with resentment when he felt they were unfairly directed. Motilal once noticed a servant at a dinner party wipe a plate with the end of his sleeve. He beat up the man so violently that the other servants ran for their lives and the guests retired aghast. When Jawaharlal was five or six he was severely beaten for taking a fountain pen from his father's desk, and for not confessing to having done so when a search was being made for it throughout the house. Jawaharlal records himself as being "almost blind with pain and mortification at my disgrace," though he did not feel the punishment was unjust.[14]

Jawaharlal enjoyed the usual festivals, the Hindu Holi and Diwali, and the Muslim Id, which his father's steward Mubarak Ali introduced him to, but in general he felt religion to be "a woman's affair." Rather more interesting to him was his birthday, when he would be weighed in a huge balance against grain and other objects which were then distributed to the poor—an early example of the relationship between his physical being and the people of India, a theme which was developed throughout his life.

Jawaharlal's mother and aunt would tell him stories from the Hindu epics, the *Ramayana* and the *Mahabharata*, but intellectually the household was orientated towards the West. Motilal would read Dickens and books on homeopathy (which he practiced on family and friends), while Jawaharlal read books by Lewis Carroll and Kipling, then progressed to Scott, Dickens and Thackeray. The children had a British governess and between the ages of twelve and fifteen Jawaharlal had a resident British tutor, Ferdinand T. Brooks, who had been recommended to Motilal by Annie Besant, a leading socialist who was to play an important part in the early Indian independence movement.

Besant, who was born in 1847, had been tested in the fire of radical politics in Victorian London. She was a militant atheist, an advocate of birth control, and leader of the matchgirls' strike in 1888, which led the way for unionization of the unskilled. She became a prominent Fabian under the influence of George Bernard Shaw but later turned her attention to spiritual matters. Over 1889-91 she converted to theosophy, a Western philosophical system based on Indian religious principles. After a first visit to India in 1893, during which she made the self-discovery that she had often been incarnated there, she made the country her permanent home. She remained at the center of that part of Indian life which embraced both Western and Eastern thought, promoting both the Indian National Congress and the claims of her adopted son, Krishnamurti, to be the Messiah.

Interestingly, Jawaharlal's introduction to the mysticism of Indian religion came not through the religion of his mother and aunts, but through Besant and Brooks. It was largely through attending his tutor's weekly meetings of theosophists in his rooms that Jawaharlal came to reflect on such matters as reincarnation, the astral, auras and the doctrine of karma. When Annie Besant visited Allahabad and Jawaharlal attended her lectures, he was deeply moved, and returned from her speeches "dazed as if in a dream."[15] At the age of thirteen he went to ask his father's permission to join the Theosophical Society. Motilal laughingly gave it, as if it were a matter of no importance at all. His son felt hurt and inwardly lamented his father's lack of spirituality, though he later discovered that Motilal had once been a theosophist. Jawaharlal duly joined the society, his mystical initiation being performed by Annie Besant herself. On mature reflection, Jawaharlal judged his theosophical self harshly, considering that he had "developed the flat and insipid look which sometimes denotes piety." He was smug, assured that he was one of the elect, and "altogether must have been a thoroughly undesirable and unpleasant companion for any boy or girl of my age."[16]

The young Jawaharlal took a romantic interest in Indian nationalism: he dreamed of performing brave deeds and freeing his nation. By this token, the struggles of all Asian nations impressed him. He was particularly inspired by the victory of the Japanese in the Russo-Japanese war in 1905, the first time a great European power had been decisively beaten by an Asian one, and a portent of later turbulence in the twentieth century.

Jawaharlal's nationalistic feelings were fed by family conversations about the overbearing manner of the British in India and Anglo-Indian behavior, which was sometimes even more offensive. The offenses complained of ranged from petty rudeness and discrimination to institutionalized racism, such as park seats marked "For Europeans Only." The Nehru family used to visit the fashionable resort of Nainital, where the yacht club forbade membership by Indians. Motilal took his motor launch there and sailed it around to the inconvenience and annoyance of the yachting Europeans. On another occasion he and two of his nephews found their reserved first-class railway compartment occupied by a European who had locked the door. He refused to open it despite repeated knocking, so Motilal ordered his nephews to break the lock. He later paid for its repair, and refused to allow the European to share the compartment.

Such events did nothing to undermine Motilal's respect for his British friends and servants. Jawaharlal said of him, "He admired Englishmen and their ways. He had a feeling that his own countrymen had fallen low and almost deserved what they had got."[17] In fact, he admired the English to such an extent that he determined his son should have a public school education. Accordingly, in May 1905, when Jawaharlal was fifteen, the family set off for England, where he was destined for Harrow. Here he would rub shoulders with the sons of the political and military elite of the Empire.

Jawaharlal had received only six months of formal education, at the local St. Mary's Convent School. During his years of private tutoring he developed an interest in the sciences and set up a small laboratory at Anand Bhavan, but he needed further grounding in other subjects to prepare for college and a career. The Harrow headmaster advised tutoring before the term commenced, so Jawaharlal stayed in London with a tutor while the rest of the family visited spas in Europe.

They returned to England to bid farewell to Jawaharlal. Motilal was anguished at leaving him, and went through once more the reasons that forced the family to part from "the dearest treasure we have in this world, and perhaps in other worlds to come . . . I never thought I loved you so much as when I had to part with you." He could set his son up for life with just one year's income, but this would be selfish. Jawaharlal had to have an education to make a man of him. "I think I can without vanity say that I am the founder of the fortunes of the Nehru family. I look upon you, my dear son, as the man who will build upon the foundations I have laid and have the satisfaction of seeing a noble structure of renown rearing up its head to the skies . . . Be perfect in body and mind and this is the only return we seek for tearing ourselves from you."[18] It was with such high expectations of him that Jawaharlal entered one of the most venerable schools in England.

Jawaharlal had never before been alone among strangers and he confessed to feeling "lonely and homesick." Although he soon learned to get along in school and was rewarded with the nickname Joe, he later commented, "I was never an exact fit."[19] He had already developed the superior air which was to distinguish him throughout life, and wrote of his schoolmates, "I must confess, I cannot mix properly with English boys. My tastes and inclinations are quite different. Here, boys older than me and in higher grades than me, take great interest in things which appear to me childish . . . I almost wish sometimes that I had not come to Harrow, but gone straight to the Varsity. I have no doubt that public schools are excellent things and their training essential to every boy, but I have come there very late to really enjoy the life."[20] While his classmates chattered about games, Jawaharlal scoured *The Times* for news of India and asked Motilal to keep him supplied with Indian newspapers. In his first months Jawaharlal surprised his dean by being the only boy who knew anything about the new Liberal government, even to the extent of being able to name most members of the Cabinet.

Motilal urged his son to make friends, to entertain other boys on holidays and "try to be a general favorite." He gave detailed advice, that his son should "patronize the creameries . . . to entertain, specially the rowdier element of the school. Never mind the expense." He wanted to know everything, even if Jawaharlal got involved in fights. "Please do not suppress the information," he wrote, "even if you get the worse out of it. It will by no means be discouraging to me to hear about it." He urged Jawaharlal to play as many games as possible, offering to advance funds for him to engage a professional coach for any game.[21] Jawaharlal obliged and played football and rugby, as well as joining the Rifle Club and the Cadet Corps. He was also an excellent scholar, despite his early deficiencies in Latin, and won prizes for his work, including volume one of Trevelyan's life of Garibaldi, the Italian patriot who had freed Italy from the Austrian yoke. Jawaharlal quickly absorbed it, then bought the other two volumes, reading eagerly of national liberation.

In India, meanwhile, another son was born to Swarup Rani in 1905, but he did not survive a month. A second daughter, Krishna, was born on November 2, 1907. Swarup Rani kept Jawaharlal informed of family events in weekly letters in Hindustani; Motilal wrote in English. In the summer of 1906 Jawaharlal visited his parents at their summer home in Mussoorie. The following Christmas he went to Paris, where he visited the motor show, for he was already displaying the Nehru passion for cars and airplanes.

Jawaharlal eventually prevailed upon Motilal to allow him to leave Harrow early and go to Trinity College, Cambridge. In October 1907, and not yet 18, he began a natural sciences degree, taking chemistry, geology and botany. Jawaharlal records that his years at Cambridge were quiet and pleasant: he evidently did not become, as his energetic father urged, "the most popular young fellow and the most distinguished graduate."[22] He was rather self-conscious and shy, but proud that he had broken the shackles of boyhood.

There were more Indians at Cambridge than at Harrow, so Jawaharlal was able to mix with kindred spirits. He attended the Majlis Club, where Indian issues were debated, despite Motilal's warning him against it: he preferred his son to receive an exclusively British education. Jawaharlal went to the club frequently in his three years at Cambridge but rarely overcame his shyness and diffidence to speak there. He did, however, meet many people who were later to play a prominent part in Indian politics, the Indian Civil Service and the law. He attended a lecture on socialism by George Bernard Shaw, and spent time with other undergraduates discussing various thinkers such as Nietzsche, who was then in vogue. Jawaharlal describes how they would sit by the fireside on long winter evenings and talk unhurriedly deep into the night until the dying fire drove them shivering to their beds. It was in these discussions and his private reading rather than in his chosen subjects that Jawaharlal received a rounded education in literature, history, politics and economics. He described his student days as hedonistic, noting he was "superficial and did not go deep down into anything,"[23] but the British standards and values he honed here were to last him the rest of his life.

The students considered themselves very sophisticated in talking of sex and morality in a superior way as if it had little to do with them, quoting from Havelock Ellis and Krafft-Ebing. Despite their brave talk, Jawaharlal noted, most of them were rather timid, and his own sexual knowledge was confined to theory until after he left Cambridge. This was by no means because of a religious or moral inhibition—he attached no idea of sin to sex—but shyness, and a certain distaste for the "usual methods adopted (presumably prostitution)," kept him celibate.[24]

After completing his degree at the age of twenty, Jawaharlal had planned to take the examinations for the Indian Civil Service (ICS), which was his anticipated career. The minimum age for this, however, was twenty-two, so he would have to do something else for two years. As he pondered what to do, the ICS gradually lost its appeal. If he passed the exams, he would have to stay a further year in England. Moreover, when engaged in the service, he could be posted all over India, probably far from home. It was therefore agreed that he would follow his father's profession and study for the Bar. He seemed unconcerned that he would be working for the British Empire in its administration of Indian territory. His cousin Shridhar, son of Motilal's elder brother, had already gone into the ICS, buttressed by degrees from Cambridge and Heidelberg. Jawaharlal was not the scholar of the family.

Jawaharlal left Cambridge with a second-class honors degree in 1910 and joined the Inner Temple in London. He was not looking forward to "the technicalities and trivialities of the law" being his sole intellectual nourishment, but when he remarked on this to his father, Motilal replied: "Please do not judge the profession by the bad example of your father who is not even well-versed in law."[25] Though Motilal refused to allow him to enroll in the London School of Economics as well as the Inner Temple, Jawaharlal was nevertheless exposed to radical thinking, becoming interested in Fabian socialism, women's suffrage and the struggle for Irish independence. He visited Ireland in 1910 and wrote approvingly to his father about Sinn Fein: "Their policy is not to beg for favors but to wrest them. They do not want to fight England by arms, but 'to ignore her, boycott her and quietly assume the administration of Irish affairs.'"[26]

In contrast to these nationalistic and left-wing interests, Jawaharlal came across some old Harrow friends in London and developed expensive habits in their company, overspending the handsome allowance his father granted him. Sometimes a cable would arrive at Anand Bhavan with just one word on it: "Money." Jawaharlal later described this as a "soft and pointless existence" which did him no good at all.[27] When Motilal upbraided him for his extravagance and neglecting his studies, Jawaharlal wrote, "You ask me to send you an account of expenditure . . . May I know if I am supposed to keep you informed of every penny I spend on a bus fare or a stamp? Either you trust me or you do not. If you do, then surely no accounts are necessary. If you do not, then the accounts I send are not to be relied upon."[28]

Jawaharlal's reckless nature also showed itself in adventurous vacations, during one of which he nearly died. He and some friends were tramping across mountainous country in Norway in 1910 and stopped to bathe in a freezing, raging torrent. He slipped and fell, was numbed by the cold and swept away. An English companion ran alongside and eventually pulled him out before he went over a waterfall. Jawaharlal tended to find such experiences of danger exhilarating rather than chastening.

He was called to the Bar in the summer of 1912, and later described himself at that time as "a bit of a prig with nothing to commend me."[29] This was a harsh judgment on himself, written in a prison cell. He now had the education to go with his natural superiority, and had seen a great deal of the world, including the many entertainments of Edwardian London, so he would not be hankering after forbidden fruit. He was an aristocrat in a Bond Street suit, with abilities and aspirations, but with no goal. He was now twenty-three and already going prematurely bald when he sailed into Bombay harbor in August 1912. "I have become," he wrote, "a queer mixture of East and West, out of place everywhere, at home nowhere."[30]

# TWO

# WAITING FOR DESTINY

The entire household was "in a fever of excitement" making preparations for Jawaharlal's return, according to his sister Krishna,
who was then five. Motilal gave orders for the whole of Anand Bhavan to be redecorated and for two new rooms to be built on the first
floor to make the house even more palatial. Because of the heat in
India in August, the entire family had decamped to their house in the
hills of Mussoorie, along with about fifty servants (half the full com-
plement of Anand Bhavan). It was to the courtyard of this mansion
that Jawaharlal rode in on a horse, to the rapturous welcome of family and servants, after seven years away.

Little Krishna found her elder brother somewhat puzzling when
she was able to make his acquaintance. At times he was gentle and
very playful, but "at other times he teased me, handled me roughly to
'toughen me up,' played pranks on me and sometimes scared me badly.
If I gave way to tears there was the devil to pay. If I did not, he concluded that I had guts and immediately showered me with some of the
lovely gifts he had brought back from England and had kept stored
away to be brought out on just such an occasion."[1]

The long absence abroad had wrought a change in Jawaharlal
which the family took time to come to terms with. His nephew B. K.
Nehru said, "I don't think anybody quite realized that Jawaharlal, by
the time he came back from England, would be an Englishman in his
values, in his behavior, in his manner of living and the way he liked
things done."[2]

A major family issue, which was settled in a traditional way, was
that of finding him a wife. Jawaharlal Nehru was "one of the country's
most eligible bachelors."[3] While in London, he had shown himself a
dutiful son by leaving the matter of marriage entirely in his father's
hands, but he had grumbled about the process: "I am glad there is
some chance of my not becoming engaged to the girl of your choice
before I see her. I don't suppose my seeing her will make very much
difference. I am not likely to become passionately fond of her at first
sight, nor is there much chance of my disliking her violently. Still I

shall feel more satisfied if the engagement took place after we had seen each other . . . You express a hope that my marriage should be romantic. I should like it to be so but I fail to see how it is going to come about. There is not an atom of romance in the way you are searching girls [sic] for me and keeping them waiting till my arrival. The very idea is extremely unromantic. And you can hardly expect me to fall in love with a photograph."[4]

Writing in Hindustani to his mother, he had been more explicit. "Would you like me to marry a girl whom I may not like for the rest of my life and who may not like me? Rather than marry in that way, I would greatly prefer to remain unmarried. . . . I accept that any girl selected by you and father would be good in all respects, but still, I may not be able to get along with her. In my opinion, unless there is a degree of mutual understanding, marriage should not take place. I think it is unjust and cruel that a life should be wasted merely in producing children."[5] All of this probably struck a very personal chord with Swarup Rani.

It was usual for the far-flung Kashmiri Brahmin community to come together for weddings, which lasted several days and provided opportunities to arrange further matches. Kamala Kaul came to the attention of the Nehrus when she attended a Kashmiri wedding at the age of twelve. Negotiations between her family and that of Motilal Nehru started soon after, the opulent lifestyle at Anand Bhavan calming the Kauls' fears that such a traditionally educated girl could ever be comfortable in the home of the Westernized lawyer. B. K. Nehru remembered arguments in the family about "books versus looks": whether it was better to have an educated or beautiful bride. In the end, he said, "the looks won out against the books."[6] Motilal wrote to Jawaharlal in April 1912 to say that Kamala had been recommended as "a most desirable acquisition for the Nehru family" and after seeing her himself he, at least, was smitten with "the little beauty . . . So far as features go, there is no other girl to approach her. She seemed to be extremely intelligent."[7]

Jawaharlal was impressed with the photograph of "such a beautiful creature" but protested that because of her age he could not marry her until she was eighteen or nineteen. He was by no means committed, however: "I would not mind waiting as I am not in a matrimonial state of mind at present."[8]

Kamala had been born on August 1, 1899 in the Delhi house of her grandfather, who had been secretary to the Maharaja of Jaipur. She was the first child of Jawaharmul and Rajpati Kaul, who raised their family according to strict tradition: the boys were sent to school while the girls were given minimal education at home and spoke only Hindustani and Urdu. When they went to Jaipur, *purdah* was enforced on the girls. Kamala broke this by wearing her brothers' clothes, putting her hair in a turban and sneaking out to play with the boys. It may have been the freedom she experienced in male dress that often led her to dress her own daughter, Indira, in boys' clothes.

Kamala was slim, tall and beautiful, and wore simple cotton saris with no jewelry or makeup. She had a light complexion, her hair was dark brown and she had large brown eyes. She was said to be serious, intelligent and highly strung. Krishna Nehru wrote, "She was one of the most beautiful women I knew or ever have known . . . What made father like her, apart from her sweetness and beauty, was that she looked very healthy. My mother had been a semi-invalid most of her life, and though father treated her and taught us to treat her as a very delicate piece of china, he wanted a strong wife for his son."[9]

The engagement was agreed between the families and, at Motilal's request, Kamala went to live with her aunt in Allahabad a few months before the marriage, so that she could be tutored by the Nehru daughters' English governess. During this time she attended functions at Anand Bhavan, which is probably where she first met Jawaharlal. They sometimes went for a drive in the family car together, but always accompanied by a chaperone.

Jawaharlal joined the High Court and picked up work, probably because of his father's position. His first fee was an advance of 500 rupees from a client of his father's who wished to gain Motilal's favor. Motilal joked that his own first fee was five rupees, so Jawaharlal was obviously a hundred times better than he was. The young man worked hard on his briefs but lacked self-assurance in court. He settled into a routine of tennis, horseback riding, dinner parties and spending time at his club and the Bar Library, meeting the same people discussing the same things. He performed the social chore of calling at the homes of English judges and officials and leaving his card, and they called on him. His pocket diary for March 27, 1916 reads, "Called on eight English families"; the entry for three days later reads, "Called on nine English families."[10] He later wrote about this time: "I felt that I was being engulfed in a dull routine of a pointless and futile existence, a sense of the utter insipidity of life grew upon me."[11] His destiny still awaited him.

Independence, the liberation of India from the British, had been a boyhood dream of Jawaharlal's, but the state of Indian nationalist affairs just before the First World War made politics a turgid enterprise for a young man. India had long associations with the British Empire: there had been a British governor-general (later viceroy) since 1774, and Queen Victoria had been declared Empress of India, but only as recently as 1877. The British ruled three-fifths of India, the rest being controlled by 662 Indian princes, who accepted the British presence in return for a high degree of autonomy. The British supplanted the Mogul conquerors, who had ruled since the sixteenth century. It had been almost a thousand years since India had been controlled by rulers from the majority Hindu community. To the vast mass of the population, involved in subsistence farming, the religion and culture of the ruling class were matters of no great importance. The British tended to ignore the majority of Indians and their customs, with two exceptions—they suppressed *suttee* (the burning of a widow on the pyre of her husband) and outlawed *thuggee* (ritual murder and robbery in the name of the goddess Kali).

The old Indian aristocracy was conciliated by the British; the practice of appointing members of the British nobility as viceroys of India was felt to be appropriate in a country which had no shortage of nobility itself. Appointment according to ability, however, would certainly have been better for India.

This conciliation of the traditional ruling class, and the belief that India was a changeless, traditional culture, had far-reaching effects on British rule. They led to a neglect of the newly rising, Westernized middle class. The lawyers, teachers and other professionals who used English as their working language were the natural supporters of British rule and, like Motilal Nehru, consciously adopted the culture of their rulers. Indian nationalism was unwittingly fostered by Britain's failure to recognize the loyalty and devotion the Empire could receive from this new middle class.

Rules were deliberately set to make it difficult for Indians to improve themselves. The Indian Civil Service, for example, held its examinations in London; when Indians nevertheless began to compete in some numbers, the upper age limit for entry was lowered to nineteen making it virtually impossible for Indians to gain the relevant qualifications *and* travel to Britain before their twentieth birthday. The limit had been raised to twenty-four by the time Jawaharlal was in a position to apply, but the examination was still held in London. There was a widespread feeling that Britain was operating a colonial economy in India, with such measures as cotton tariffs favoring Lancashire goods, and that this treatment was responsible for perpetuating poverty and under-investment in industry.

When liberal measures were introduced, local Europeans did their best to sabotage them. Thus, when the Ilbert Bill proposed that Indian judges in Bengal could sit as the equal of Europeans in 1883, there was a furious campaign by Europeans, angry at the social implications of a white person being tried by an Indian judge without a jury. In this case a compromise was reached, allowing Europeans to opt for a European judge, but middle-class Indians, particularly those in the judiciary, had been deeply offended. Yet these protests by Europeans had shown the Indians, sometimes abetted by British radicals, how to organize themselves.

The Congress Party of India was started by Allan Hume, theosophist, formerly of the Indian Civil Service, who had been humiliated and denied promotion for being too pro-native. He retired in 1882 to devote himself to ornithology, theosophy and Indian issues. The first meeting of the Congress Party, in Bombay in 1885, began its proceedings with declarations of loyalty to Britain and a statement that its objective was not political independence but a better deal for the Indian middle class who were largely administering the colony for Britain, though never at the most senior levels. More than half of the seventy-two delegates at the first Congress were lawyers, and the party was an obvious home for the ideas which were common currency in the Nehru family. When Congress met at Allahabad in 1888, among the 1400 delegates was Motilal, who shared with his middle-class compatriots a sense of frustration with the Raj. The following year in Bombay he was elected to a committee position, and was secretary of the reception committee when Congress again met in Allahabad in 1892. This time there were 3500 delegates and visitors. Motilal was more concerned with his own work than with politics at this stage, however, though his intellectual interest shows in his correspondence with Jawaharlal when his son was in England. Jawaharlal attended his first Congress meeting in Bombay in 1904 at the age of fifteen.

Congress was largely divided between the Moderates under Gopal Krishna Gokhale and the Extremists under Bal Gangadhar Tilak. This division reflected not only their general approach to politics, but also a philosophical split between the Gladstonian liberals who admired the means and methods of the West, and those who looked back to the days of Maratha and Hindu glory. For Gokhale, social progress was an end in itself; for Tilak, Western institutions were a means to an end—independence and the reassertion of a Hindu national character. This mirrors the contemporary division in Irish politics, where the independence movement was split between those who felt independence should merely mean "home rule" and those who yearned towards a "Celtic twilight," a restoration of idealized ancient values and culture.

The goad to Indian radicalism was the partition of Bengal in July 1905, an administrative move, but one which ended up dividing a province of 78 million people along communal lines, with the east largely Muslim and the west largely Hindu. This was evidence, it was claimed, of a British "divide and rule" policy: dividing Bengal was a means of weakening the Bengali radicals. In fact, it was more a matter of political ignorance mixed with administrative flair on the part of the viceroy, Lord Curzon. Intellectuals, however, were outraged because their appeals, based on sound common sense about the linguistic and cultural composition of Bengal, had fallen on deaf ears. Congress matters, however, received a boost, and in 1906 at its Calcutta meeting the party made its first call for Swaraj (self rule), thus causing unease among the Moderates. There was also direct action for the first time: a boycott of British produce and a bonfire of Lancashire goods, coupled with vows to use only Indian cotton. More ominously, the hotbed of resistance in Bengal provided a breeding ground for a group of terrorists who considered political freedom a holy duty and assassination an offering to Kali.

Concurrent with the political storms caused by the partition of Bengal were elevated discussions on reform. It was the perennial theme of British government in India: clumsy mismanagement accompanied by reform. The history of India's transition to democracy can be seen as a slow process of the Empire releasing too little power too late to contain the unrest engendered by its own recalcitrance. To be fair to the British who did view India with foresight, it is as well to note that this was not so much a failure of overall planning as of policy changes wrought by changes of government at Westminster. Periods of Liberal or Labor rule in Britain were accompanied by democratic reform in India, Conservative rule by retrenchment. Local self-government in Indian towns and the countryside was introduced in 1884 under Gladstone (before the first meetings of Congress). The great Liberal landslide of 1906, in which the young Jawaharlal had taken such an interest in his first months at Harrow, promised democratic reforms under the Secretary of State for India John Morley and the new viceroy Lord Minto, but these were a long time under development. They were also much vitiated by the influence of the India Office and the Indian Civil Service. No policy promulgated in London was ever imposed directly on India; everything was filtered through the distorting prism of the ICS and local European sentiment. In contrast to the early period of imperialism, where British people served in India and then went home, the late nineteenth century saw English families begin to settle in India. This meant there was a preponderance of generally conservative-minded Europeans who tended to see reform in favor of Indians as an incursion on their own superior position.

Spurred on by the Bengal situation, Congress Moderates were feeling the pressure of radicalism and began to organize themselves. In January 1907 Motilal held a meeting of Moderates at Anand Bhavan, and a provincial conference for the United Provinces was arranged with Motilal as president. He wrote to Jawaharlal that he feared the open abuse from students which the Moderate leaders suffered: "I have so far escaped, but cannot be safe much longer as my views are even more moderate than those of the so-called Moderates." Jawaharlal hoped his father's presidential address "will not be too moderate. Indians are as a rule too much so, and require a little stirring up."[12] Motilal's address welcomed the promotion of home produce but criticized the boycott; he lambasted the Extremists for their "ill will and vindictiveness" and praised England, who had "fed us with the best food that her language, her literature, her science, her art and, above all, her free institutions could supply. We have lived and grown on that wholesome food for a century and are fast approaching the age of maturity. We have outgrown the baby garments supplied to us by England."[13]

Motilal was at the Congress session in Surat in 1907 when the Extremists were, as they saw it, again robbed of the presidency by the machinations of the Moderates: indeed, Motilal seconded the proposal for a Moderate president. The meeting broke up in disorder and fighting, with missiles thrown, turbans unrolled and chairs broken. The police had to be called to clear the hall. The net result was an increased polarization of opinion, with greater power for the Moderates within Congress, but also fiercer opposition, including that of Jawaharlal, who wrote to his father: "The manner in which some of them try to ignore and belittle all those who differ from them would be annoying, if it was not so ridiculous . . . I firmly believe that there will hardly be any so-called Moderates left in a very few years time." His father wrote back, stung by his son's evident contempt for his position. Jawaharlal, still only eighteen, wrote back superciliously that he was sorry if Motilal disapproved of his opinions, but "anyhow I have not the presumption of imagining that my opinions are infallible." He was then frankly insulting: "The government must be feeling very pleased with you at your attitude," and wondered if a mark of favor from the government, such as an honor, would make his father even less of a Moderate and, by implication, more of an Empire loyalist.

Motilal was furious, so angry that he did not mention the matter by letter, but talked of summoning Jawaharlal home. Word eventually reached his son by other means and a few months later Jawaharlal was begging to be forgiven. Motilal responded with an acceptance of their political differences, but said, "My love for you knows no bounds, and unless there is some very remarkable change in me, I do not see how it can be affected."[14] In the event, the future was to see that rare occurrence of a father taking political lessons from his son.

The watered-down nature of the Morley-Minto reforms, when they were eventually published in August 1909, appalled Motilal. Though they were made after consultation with Gokhale, Motilal said they were "just the opposite of reforms" and considered their object was "to destroy the influence of the educated classes."[15] They allowed Indians to be members of provincial executive councils, while also increasing the power of the councils and the number of representatives, but the Governor would always have a majority of appointed council members to rely on. Direct elections enfranchised a tiny proportion of the Indian population, who qualified to vote by having education and property. However, it was still a platform and in December 1909, Motilal successfully ran for election to the Legislative Council of the Lieutenant Governor of the United Provinces, being sworn in on February 7, 1910. This strengthened a long acquaintance with Sir Harcourt Butler, and between the two families. Harcourt's uncle, Henry Montagu Butler, had been headmaster of Harrow and was still the venerable Master of Trinity when Jawaharlal went up to Cambridge. Harcourt never lost his affection for Motilal, and his nephew R. A. Butler mischievously recollected that when "obliged to put him in jail," Harcourt sent Motilal a crate of champagne—a story "indignantly repudiated" by Jawaharlal.[16] Much later still, Jawaharlal's grandson, Rajiv, was in his final year at Trinity when R. A. Butler, in his turn, became Master of the college.

Motilal's frustrating experience of dealing with the Governor's officials and those whom he considered to be Indian sycophants on the council nudged him towards radicalism, a stimulation of his latent crusading spirit which was to bear fruit in the battle for independence.

One part of the Indian Councils' Act particularly disquieted Motilal and presaged the disaster of partition which was to befall India in forty years' time. This was the introduction of separate (or "communal") representation for Muslims, thus making religion the decisive factor in every political difference. Muslims had been angered by Hindu protests at the division of Bengal and formed the Muslim League to promote their interests which, as a minority in Hindu India, they considered to be under threat. This body, meeting at Dacca in December 1906, pledged loyalty to the British government and condemned the boycott movement. Motilal always correctly judged that there would be no solution to the problems of India until the relationship between the large Muslim minority and the Hindu majority was addressed. Other politicians acted as if the "communal" problem would be swept away in a surge of liberal reforms or would be submerged in a reborn Hindu "raj." The most promising progress on the Hindu-Muslim question came in 1916 with the Lucknow Agreement between Congress and the Muslim League drawn up at a meeting at Anand Bhavan. This stipulated that the League would support self-government for India in return for the protection of Muslim interests, which separate Muslim constituencies would afford.

Politics quieted as the Morley-Minto reforms settled into the Indian scene, and the British government took the occasion of the 1912 "durbar," or ruler's public appearance, to have King George V reverse the partitioning of Bengal which had caused so much unrest. One advantage of Jawaharlal's presence in London was that in 1911 he was able to buy for his father a full outfit of court dress, complete with sword, for the King's visit to India. Motilal had been commanded by His Gracious Majesty the King-Emperor "to be in attendance at Delhi." It was, Motilal said, "a funny way of inviting a gentleman," but it was an immense honor for an Indian to be presented to the King, and Motilal was far from being so radical a nationalist that he eschewed such an honor. He was still a servant of the Raj, even though one of its most vigorous critics.

For the duration of the durbar Motilal and Swarup Rani, one of only two Indian women to be presented to the King-Emperor, lived with their two daughters as guests of the Lieutenant-Governor of the United Provinces. His camp, a city of tents built outside Delhi on a site covering twenty square miles, housed nearly a quarter of a million people. It was served by railway stations, post offices, banks and bazaars, and was illuminated by electricity, which was then something of a novelty.

Motilal increasingly pondered social issues: the position of women and caste in Indian society. In 1909 he addressed a conference decrying "the two ugliest blots on our social system—caste and purdah. These are the two evils which have dragged us down the social scale and made us the laughingstock of modern civilization."[17]

On his return to India Jawaharlal found Congress politics stifling. He was a delegate to the Bankipore Congress in 1912 and found it "very much an English-knowing upper-class affair where morning coats and well-pressed trousers were greatly in evidence. Essentially it was a social gathering with no political excitement or tension."[18] Jawaharlal looked for his role in public service by working for the Red Cross and the St. John Ambulance Brigade, and seriously considered joining the Servants of India Society founded by Gokhale, but it would have meant his leaving the legal profession. He was involved in political agitation, such as that over the indenture system for Indian workers, whereby they surrendered all rights to their employers for five years in exchange for free passage to their country of employment. He was also involved in the South African Indian question, collecting money for the Indian passive resisters organized by Mohandas Gandhi. While Gandhi was later to transform the lives of all members of the Nehru family, at this stage his cause was one of many which Jawaharlal supported.

Nationalist politics became more exciting when the extremists, who had been expelled from Congress, failed to secure readmission, and Annie Besant and Bal Gangadhar Tilak set up Home Rule Leagues, each representing different geographical areas of the country. Jawaharlal was involved in both, but more particularly with the Nehru family's old friend Annie Besant. The First World War stimulated politics, as wars always do: they gave the participants the impression that everything was being stirred up and that prizes were available to those with the firmest grasp.

Indian nationalists did not oppose Britain during the First World War. Like the rest of their countrymen, they assumed that India would be rewarded for loyalty freely given. Gandhi returned from South Africa after his thrilling work to eliminate racial discrimination against Indians, and set about tramping India to recruit soldiers for the British Army. Swarup Rani and the other women of Anand Bhavan started knitting woollens and collecting warm clothing for soldiers. More than a million Indian troops served Britain in the First World War, but still the ordinary process of political debate was considered to be seditious. A series of government measures introduced under wartime emergency rules stimulated more unrest than would have been produced by government indifference to the agitations.

Jawaharlal was still diffident about public speaking and did not address a public gathering in India until 1916, at the age of twenty-seven, when he protested at the Press Act, a new piece of wartime legislation to muzzle the press. After the meeting was over, the veteran nationalist Dr. Tej Bahadur Sapru embraced him on the dais to his great embarrassment. When the seventy-year-old Annie Besant was interned by a shortsighted government in 1917, it revitalized interest in Home Rule and leading Moderates, including Motilal, joined the organization. Most of the Congress Moderates died away politically,

36

being insufficiently robust for the heady politics of the time and unwilling to fight their own corner. In contrast, Motilal went from strength to strength, though he mouthed the words of a Moderate with the ferocity of a radical. He was not without opposition, however: during a meeting in August 1917 when Motilal called on the audience to appeal to British democracy, a heckler called, "Question!" meaning that he wanted to ask one. Motilal angrily insisted he identify himself, to be greeted with silence; the heckler was Jawaharlal.[19] Krishna recalled "many domestic storms" at Anand Bhavan between Motilal and Jawaharlal over politics.[20]

Some optimism about Britain's intentions towards India during the war was fully justified under the wartime government (a coalition led by a Liberal, David Lloyd George). The Secretary of State for India, Edwin Montagu, told the House of Commons on August 20, 1917 that the British government's policy towards India was to be one of "gradual development of self-governing institutions" within the Empire. He and the new viceroy, Lord Chelmsford, toured India meeting politicians, including Motilal, and produced the Montagu-Chelmsford report of 1918, proposing "nationhood within the Empire" which consisted of joint rule or "dyarchy" where elected representatives would take over all matters in India, excepting those concerned with foreign relations, finance and law and order. Motilal considered its proposals too hedged in with provisions favoring British control and that they fell far short of the pledges implicit in the 1917 declaration. His attack on the report caused his final rift with the Moderates. It was a sign of his increasing radicalism that he launched a newspaper, *The Independent*, in February 1919, to campaign for independence. He was no great manager, or journalist, and he was to pour a great deal of money into the venture before he was finally obliged to admit defeat and close it, but not before Jawaharlal had gained considerable experience in writing quick pieces on current events.

At this time politics was still more a leisure interest than an all-consuming passion for the Nehrus, and anyone asked what the most important event of the war years was for them would certainly have said "Jawaharlal's wedding." This was one of the most magnificent occasions of the time, and the talk of the province long afterwards.

The appointed day was February 8, 1916, the festival of Vasant Panchami, which heralds the coming of spring; Jawaharlal was twenty-six and Kamala sixteen. Preparations had taken months: one room in Anand Bhavan was turned into a goldsmiths' studio to produce decorations, and a team of craftsmen worked continuously on the verandas creating Kamala's pearl-studded sari. Jawaharlal wore a pink turban and a brocade *sherwani*, a traditional three-quarter-length garment with a mandarin collar. He does not look markedly at ease in his wedding photographs. Kamala's family had approached a neighboring family in Delhi to borrow their huge, three-story house with large halls and courtyards to accommodate the bridegroom's party. Motilal chartered a special train to take 300 guests from Allahabad to Delhi, and many more guests joined them there. Further houses had to be requisitioned and a tent town was set up just outside the walled city of Delhi with the sign "Nehru Wedding Camp" written in flowers. B. K. Nehru later said, "It was to my childish eyes a whole city of white tents."[21] The festivities went on for seven days and nights, and continued even when the family returned to Allahabad, with a series of lunches, dinners, music recitals, poetry recitations and tennis matches at Anand Bhavan. As the weather became hot, Motilal took the family, including Jawaharlal and Kamala, on vacation to their beloved Kashmir, where they lived in a fleet of houseboats on Dal Lake.

Even after her lessons with the English governess, a narrowly brought up girl like Kamala can have given little companionship to an advanced thinker and traveller such as Jawaharlal. He was sometimes embarrassed that she was mistaken for his daughter. He does not even mention Kamala's name in the narrative of his autobiography until he has reached the year 1930, noting that "My marriage took place" in 1916, as if it had little to do with him, and rushing on to describe how he fell down a crevasse while walking in the mountains with a cousin (but not Kamala) soon after the wedding.

Jawaharlal returned to Allahabad on business while the family stayed in Kashmir. Kamala was clearly very unhappy, so Motilal wrote to his son that he needed to "strengthen her and make her feel so entirely at home with us as to get rid of all nervousness." He realized that the educational task he had set for Kamala and his daughters, of writing short descriptive essays or letters, was not conducive to her good health, so he desisted from "the constant nagging to which I subjected her" which he felt had contributed to her headaches.

Motilal also applied his diagnostic skills as an amateur homeo-pathic doctor: "I have been studying Kamala's case for some days and have come to the conclusion that it is eighty percent hysteria and twenty percent other minor causes which combine to give her a headache." He paints a vivid picture of a great, overpowering man questioning a fragile woman: "I spent the whole morning with her putting together the various indications of different remedies and tak-ing a nod of her head for reply on each point . . . Yesterday she was crying with pain." Some days later he wrote, "Kamala, I am sorry to say, has had another severe attack of headache. I gave her the reme-dies which were indicated by her symptoms as far as they were known to me. But it is always very difficult to get at all the symptoms of a young girl as so much depends on things she will never tell you about."[22]

Life did not improve for her when the family moved back to Allahabad and she and Jawaharlal were installed in the modern, self-contained apartment that Motilal had built for them at Anand Bha-van. Swarup Rani judged her by the exacting standards an Indian mother-in-law applies to the daughter of an only son, and Sarup, close in age to Kamala, held her in open contempt for her lack of sophisti-cation. She was a thoroughly Indian girl who hardly knew English and did not even know how to use a knife, fork and spoon. To enhance her misery, Sarup and Jawaharlal enjoyed a close relationship which excluded her completely. They would rise early to go riding together, returning after the rest of the family had finished breakfast, and would eat as if they were a separate entity, distinct from the family. "There was a complete sense of contentment in just being together," as Sarup later wrote.[23] Kamala also suffered other indignities, as a family friend noted: "If Kamala suggested a meal to the butler, it was liable to be countermanded on the grounds that the newcomer did not know [Jawaharlal's] tastes. If tickets were to be bought for an English movie, Kamala would be left out because Bhabhi [sister-in-law] could not be expected to follow it."[24] In contrast, Kamala became something of a favorite with Motilal (she was his choice of woman, after all) and this further irritated the other women in the family.

By her later account, Krishna had some sympathy with her sister-in-law's struggle to fit in at Anand Bhavan: "At first poor Kamala was completely confused and uncomfortable in a place so different from her home. The big dinners with crystal and china on the long table and rows of wine glasses at everyone's place, the strange food, and, most of all perhaps, the quick loud voices of our many British guests, made her feel lost and lonely."[25]

Kamala was soon pregnant and would by tradition have gone back to her mother's house in Delhi to have the baby, but Motilal wanted his first grandchild to be born under his own roof. He also argued that her health was too poor for her to travel. The entire extended family came from all over India to wait at Anand Bhavan while the labor took place, servants moving among them with soft drinks for the women and whiskey for the men. On November 19, 1917 a Scottish doctor delivered of Kamala a healthy girl. Though Jawaharlal was delighted, celebration among the gathered clan was muted. "It should have been a son," said Swarup Rani.

Motilal was angry. "Have we made any distinction between our son and two daughters in their upbringing?" he demanded. "Don't you love them equally? This daughter of Jawahar, for all we know, may prove better than a thousand sons."[26]

The child was named Indira, after Motilal's tough-minded mother, and a short time after her birth she was taken to the edge of the estate to the cottage of the retired steward, Mubarak Ali. He was loved as a family member, and now he was dying, they wished to fulfill his last request: to see Jawaharlal's child. He blessed the child joyfully as a son of the household: they had not the heart to tell him it was a girl.

# THREE

# A SON COMES OF AGE

At the end of the First World War the Nehrus, along with other Indians, confidently expected the restoration of civil liberties. The Indian contribution to the war effort had been immense: 1.2 million men had been recruited, many of whom served with distinction in all the theaters of war; India gave $160 million to Britain outright and contributed roughly the same amount in war expenses. Even those of no political bent at all considered that India deserved something from Britain for its sacrifices. The young Jawaharlal had chafed under wartime regulations, making one of his first speeches against the restrictions of the Press Act in 1916, and campaigning against the arrest of Annie Besant in the *Leader*, another newspaper owned by his father.

Wartime restrictions on political action were understandable, but now due process should recommence. There were, moreover, new winds blowing through the world: from the United States the right to self-determination was propounded by Woodrow Wilson; and from Russia the act of revolution showed the peril of government backwardness. The British Raj, however, acted as if the war had not happened, and everything must return to its prewar state forthwith: British civil servants returned to India to reclaim jobs, relegating the Indians who had held them during the war to their previous, inferior positions. Part of the government's response to nationalism in India came in a report on sedition—the fruits of a committee chaired by Sir Sidney Rowlatt. This recommended what was effectively a continuation of wartime restrictions, with draconian additions. The Anarchical and Revolutionary Crimes Bill, known as the Rowlatt Bill, proposed search and arrest powers without a warrant, the accused to be tried in a special court with three judges sitting in camera with no jury, with no right to legal representation and no right of appeal.

As a man who had made respect for the law his life, Motilal was appalled by the contempt shown for due process in the Rowlatt Bill and he argued vigorously against it in the United Provinces legislative council, but to no avail. The Viceroy's advisers insisted on the absolute necessity of the Rowlatt provisions and the supreme body, the Imperative Legislative Council, passed the Bill, which went on the statute books* (thus becoming an Act) on March 21, 1919. It was one of those rare cases in history where one side was completely right and the other completely wrong. The provisions of the Rowlatt Act were never used, and when the legislation came up for renewal, it was quietly allowed to expire. The unrest caused by the Rowlatt Act, however, and the government's responses to that unrest, made militants of the passive and ultimately made independence inevitable. Rarely has a government squandered so much for so little gain.

It was thanks to the Rowlatt Act that the whole Nehru family was plunged into direct political action. The catalyst for their dynamism was Mohandas Gandhi. Born in Kathiawar, modern-day Gujarat, into a merchant caste family of state functionaries, Gandhi was married as a boy and sent off to London to study for the Bar. Although exposed to two cultures, he remained true to the East and produced a personal philosophy that owed more to religion than politics. In London he eschewed wine, women and meat, and became a leading exponent of vegetarianism, which, incidentally, brought him into contract with such individuals as George Bernard Shaw and Annie Besant. In London, too, he first read the Hindu religious text *Bhagavad Gita*, but in English translation. He returned to India but was unsuccessful in practicing law, so he moved to South Africa, where he worked with an Indian trader in Natal. Here the ill treatment meted out to Indians, including himself, led him to take up their struggle. During this time he developed the concept of *satyagraha*, variously translated as "truth-force," "soul struggle," "fight for truth" and "soul-force," which incorporated the ideas of defiance in the face of injustice, the acceptance of suffering, and non-violence. His twenty-year campaign brought him to prominence in India and Britain.

When Gandhi returned to India, he had an all-embracing personal philosophy which combined Indian thinking from the *Bhagavad Gita* with its message of struggle and renunciation; elements of Christianity; non-violence from Jainism; communal living from Tolstoy; and militancy in the name of justice, which he had learned in South Africa.

---

* There was another, interim, Act introduced at the same time, so the legislative package is sometimes referred to as the Rowlatt Acts, though only the one referred to here introduced new legislation.

When Jawaharlal met Gandhi for the first time at the Lucknow Congress of 1916 it was for the "heroic fight" in South Africa that he praised the older man, but he remarked that Gandhi "seemed very distant and different and unpolitical to many of us young men."[1] He refused to take part in Congress politics at this time and confined himself to the South African question. An admirer of his work, the poet Rabindranath Tagore, gave him the title Mahatma, meaning "great soul." The Nehrus, however, never used this title, preferring to call him Gandhiji, the suffix "ji" being a common token of respect.

Although outside mainstream politics, Gandhi began agitating against the indentured labor system (effectively a form of licensed slavery) and, his arguments being unanswerable, the Viceroy agreed to end it. Gandhi's tours of the country in third-class railway compartments made him a hero of the peasants, and Jawaharlal, too, observed his progress with wonder and admiration. Here was someone who could reach the classes and castes which the young Jawaharlal could not. Gandhi, however, was still involved in localized peasant problems rather than national political issues. He had pledged ungrudging support to Britain in the war and, as a matter of principle, was obliged to do nothing that would take advantage of the Empire when it was in difficulties. The Rowlatt proposals, however, were a postwar outrage, and though Gandhi was seriously ill, having suffered from dysentery and undergone an operation, he pleaded with the Viceroy to quash the legislation, and traveled the country laying the foundations for civil disobedience, though he was so weak his speeches had to be read out for him. He drew up a satyagraha pledge in which the signatories vowed to disobey unjust laws by passive resistance. Jawaharlal was one of the signatories, in early April 1919, and was a member of the Allahabad satyagraha committee.

B. K. Nehru observed the transformation: "Jawaharlal, being a young man and being much more emotional than his father, took the pledge. His dress changed, his food changed, his language changed, just about everything changed."[2] This caused overwhelming unrest in the Nehru household. Jawaharlal wrote, "Here at last was a way out of the tangle, a method which was straight and open and possibly effective. I was afire with enthusiasm."[3] But Motilal urged caution: he was not in the habit of being swept away by new proposals. Breaking the law was anathema to him, even if it were a bad law. Motilal also had no concept of collective action: everything he had seen achieved in his life had been done by hardworking individuals. How could the imprisonment of a number of people, even a large number of people, effect a change in government thinking?

Night after night, Jawaharlal recorded, he wandered about alone, tortured in mind and trying to grope his way out. Motilal also spent nights in torment, sometimes sleeping on the floor to experience what he thought would be his beloved son's lot in prison. The idea that his son should suffer the indignity of prison was the hardest thing to bear: it was as if everything he had done to make Jawaharlal a respected man in the community would be thrown away in a gesture. "The heart is a fool, the only safe guide is the head," he would say.[4] Jawaharlal restricted himself to provocative gestures, like eating his dinner, which he now insisted should be only bread and milk, from a steel bowl in preparation for jail, a deliberately incongruous sight in front of the silver and crystal from which the rest of the family were eating.

Father and son knew this was the biggest issue in their relationship, and could be the biggest in their lives, so though their household debates on the matter were vigorous, they tried to be considerate to one another. Eventually Motilal turned to the only man whom he felt Jawaharlal would trust: Gandhi himself, who visited Anand Bhavan in the second week of March 1919 and had long talks with Motilal to which Jawaharlal was not invited. The family was rather embarrassed at inviting the acetic into a house with glittering chandeliers, rich carpets, masses of flowers and servants in red and gold livery, so they accommodated the great man in Swarup Rani's sitting room, which was furnished in a simpler, Indian style. He was served food in his own tin utensils by Swarup Rani and Kamala. It was the first of many visits to Anand Bhavan, which became a home for Gandhi when he was in Allahabad. The sage counseled caution, and emerged from his meetings with Motilal to tell Jawaharlal to be patient and not to do anything that would upset his father. Gandhi had judged the situation well: had he sided with Jawaharlal and urged immediate action, he would have forfeited Motilal's trust. This way he was to retain the trust of both.

When Gandhi left he was accompanied by Sarup, who the family thought would benefit from a spell in his ashram. She had developed an affection for Syed Hussain, the editor of her father's newspaper, the

*Independent*, but even in the famously secular Nehru household it was not felt proper that she should marry a Muslim. She was talked out of it, though not without resentment, and Hussain left India for the USA. The sojourn with Gandhi was supposed to introduce Sarup to the joys of traditional living, but she found life there appalling, "austere beyond belief." The day began with prayers at 4 A.M., the food was awful, there was no tea or coffee, and the regime was based not so much on morality as abstinence. She came to love Gandhi, as many did, without ever accepting the more forbidding aspects of his character. She wrote that "any sexual aberration was a heinous sin to him. At one time he used to advise young married couples not to have intercourse, and this led to many forms of frustration among his followers."[5] Stories abounded of his stringency to those who transgressed his sexual code.

While *satyagraha* pledgees were committed to passive resistance, the form that resistance should take had not been decided. On the eve of the Rowlatt Bill's passing into law, Gandhi saw what he was to do in a dream (other Congress leaders would have to adapt to this style of politics): he would call a general *hartal*—an Indian village concept where, as an expression of anger or mourning, business was suspended and people would fast or pray.

The *hartal* started badly, with a riot in Delhi directed against the Indians who made their living selling food, tea and other items at the station, who had refused to join, presumably because they could not afford the loss of their meager earnings. The police were called out to protect them, and when they were unable to restore order, troops were called and they opened fire. The worst violence, however, was in Punjab, where supporters of the *hartal* attempted to bring all government to a halt. Anger was directed at Europeans, and troops with machine guns narrowly prevented a vast crowd from moving in on the European district of Lahore. At Amritsar five Europeans were savagely murdered and an English woman missionary was assaulted and left for dead.

It was in such an atmosphere that the Amritsar massacre took place on April 13, 1919, the single event which ultimately ensured the British could not stay in India, for it utterly undermined their moral authority. It began with a meeting in Jallianwala Bagh, an open space enclosed on all sides in the holy city of Amritsar. Although

45

there was a government ban on meetings in Amritsar, it had not been widely publicized. There were perhaps 10,000 gathered there when Brigadier General Reginald Dyer, giving no warning, blocked access to the narrow entrance with fifty Indian troops and gave the order to fire. There were 1650 rounds fired into the unarmed crowd over a period of minutes, and when the ammunition was exhausted, the troops retired, leaving 379 dead and 1137 wounded. Martial law in Punjab soon followed and made it difficult for outsiders to know what was happening as travel was not permitted into the territory. Jawaharlal wrote that those outside "waited for scraps of news and bitterness filled our hearts."[6]

Dyer continued "restoring order" with humiliating instructions to Indians, such as ordering them to crawl past the spot where the European missionary was molested. Though the order had apparently been applied to only one Indian before it was cancelled, the stupid and brutal thinking which informed it further poisoned the relationship of trust between ruler and ruled.

Gandhi was appalled at the level of violence he had unleashed and declared his entire *satyagraha* campaign had been "a Himalayan miscalculation," his precise error being his failure to train his followers in civil disobedience and particularly the importance of non-violence. He fasted for three days in penance. One of Motilal's friends, Lala Harkishanlal, a Congress member, was arrested under martial law provisions and Motilal was refused permission to enter Punjab to defend him. Motilal immediately telegraphed the Secretary of State for India in London, over the heads of the Viceroy and the provincial Governor, and thereby probably curtailed martial law, which was called off soon after his intervention.

The government ordered a Committee of Inquiry into the Amritsar shootings under Lord Hunter but, concerned at its perceived partiality, Congress called its own inquiry under Motilal, Gandhi, C. R. Das, Abbas Tyabi and Fazlul Haq, with Jawaharlal collecting a great deal of the information laid before it. As soon as martial law was lifted, Congress workers poured into Punjab to do relief and inquisitorial work. Jawaharlal interviewed witnesses and survivors, counted the bullet holes in the walls of the Bagh and estimated the direction of fire, which was into the thickest part of the trapped crowd. When the committee began its sitting, the Nehrus witnessed the consistent strength of Gandhi's conviction and the force of his logic, and now Motilal, as well as Jawaharlal, became a devotee.

The historian Bipan Chandra said, "Motilal Nehru was affected much more by the massacre than Jawaharlal because Jawaharlal had already come across radical ideas and therefore had a certain notion about imperialism. But Motilal Nehru was one of the people who had argued with Jawaharlal that the British were genuine, though one may disagree with them as to how India is going to be prepared for freedom, but that the British were gradually preparing India for freedom. Well he was disillusioned. And that is why he now readily agreed with the politics of his son."[7]

Had the massacre been roundly condemned on all sides, British rule might have been saved. Even arch imperialists such as Winston Churchill, the Secretary for War, recognized that rulers must have both justice and mercy on their side. Dyer himself considered his action fully justified, an attitude Jawaharlal recounted that he was able to witness first hand when he traveled from Delhi to Amritsar by night train and entered a compartment where most of the berths were occupied by sleeping passengers. Jawaharlal took a vacant one. According to his account, "In the morning I discovered that all my fellow passengers were military officers. They conversed with each other in loud voices, which I could not help overhearing. One of them was holding forth in an aggressive and triumphant tone and soon I discovered that he was Dyer, the hero of Jallianwala Bagh, and he was describing his Amritsar experiences. He pointed out how he had the whole town at his mercy and he had felt like reducing the rebellious city to a heap of ashes, but he took pity on it and refrained. He was evidently coming back from Lahore after giving his evidence before the Hunter Committee of Inquiry. I was greatly shocked to hear his conversation and to observe his callous manner. He descended at Delhi station in pajamas with bright pink stripes, and a dressing gown."[8]

The Hunter report delivered a rebuke to Dyer, and he was asked to retire from the army, but in many places he was feted, and the House of Lords passed a motion congratulating him. A generous fund was subscribed by British sympathizers in respect of his services and he was presented with a jeweled sword inscribed, "Savior of the Punjab." It was this attitude towards the massacre by many British people which outraged Jawaharlal. "This cold-blooded approval of that deed shocked me greatly. It seemed absolutely immoral, indecent; to use public school language, it was the height of bad form. I realized then, more vividly than I ever had done before, how brutal and immoral imperialism was and how it had eaten into the soul of the British upper classes."[9]

Motilal was president of Amritsar Congress at the end of 1919, a Congress held shortly after the passing of the Government of India Act (whose provisions were not to come into effect until 1921), which increased the Indian electorate and Indian self-government along the lines of the Montagu-Chelmsford reforms. That same year northern and southern Ireland began to elect separate parliaments, a final step towards independence in the south, but also making for a partition of the country. For Jawaharlal, whose youth had been filled with romantic examples of independence from foreign domination, particularly Italy and Greece, it was clear that history was on his side.

Indian history had its own very specific course, however, and communal interests were part of them. Gandhi sought Hindu-Muslim unity in his support for the *khilafat* (caliphate) movement, which was an attempt by some Muslims to link themselves with the Sultan of Turkey, whom they considered to be their caliph—spiritual leader and guardian of the holy places of Islam. This had placed them in an ambivalent position during the First World War when Britain was fighting Turkey, and after the war when surrender terms imposed on the Sultan were unacceptable to Indian Muslims.

Gandhi was sympathetic with people who principally defined themselves in religious terms rather than those of class, nationality, region or language. To him it seemed sensible to link the Muslim concern for the overlordship of their holy shrines (in countries other than India) with the struggle for national identity. Bewitched by his commanding personality, most people in the independence movement tried to come to terms with the *khilafat*, and articles were written in the nationalist press trying to justify it as a political question. The effect of *khilafat* agitation taking place at the same time as *satyagraha* agitation against the Rowlatt Act was to give the impression of an entire nation up in arms against British rule—a true Hindu-Muslim unity. Eventually both the Khilafat Committee and Congress accepted Gandhi's next stage for anti-British agitation—non-cooperation, though

Gandhi led from the front as usual and announced the policy long before he had the agreement of his colleagues on it.

Jawaharlal had largely ceased to practice law in order to devote himself to politics. He was spending more time with Gandhi, learning not only from his ideas, but also from his approach to people and meetings. Gandhi was a man of many convictions and turned them into an awesome certainty. Jawaharlal described the master as he saw him addressing one gathering: "He spoke well in his best dictatorial vein. He was humble but also clearcut and hard as a diamond, pleasant and soft-spoken but inflexible and terribly earnest. His eyes were mild and deep, yet out of them blazed a fierce energy and determination. 'This is going to be a great struggle,' he said, 'with a very powerful adversary. If you want to take it up, you must be prepared to lose everything, and you must subject yourself to the strictest non-violence and discipline.'"[10]

Gandhi's subtle—even subversive—influence on the Nehrus was shown by their progressive unease with the comfortable lifestyle they had previously enjoyed. This began as early as 1919, before they formally renounced Western ways. Motilal went to the special Calcutta session following the atrocities in Punjab in his usual style—traveling first class in a compartment reserved entirely for himself. On a later journey to Bombay, Rajendra Prasad, another Congress leader, met Motilal traveling second class and was urged to join him: "Let us come to a compromise. I have come down from the first to the second class, you come up from the third to the second and let us travel together." As they shared a carriage they saw Jawaharlal on the platform. Motilal turned to his companion and said with tears in his eyes, "Look at this boy: he is traveling third like you. This is a time when he should be enjoying himself but he has given up everything and become a *sadhu* [mendicant holy man]."[11] At other times he was less positive, writing tetchily to Jawaharlal about a homeopathic prescription his son had said was hard to decipher, "There is nothing very complicated about Dr. Ray's letter if you will only read it carefully after divesting your mind of the Khilafat and Satyagraha."[12]

Jawaharlal's first brush with the law came as a result of family illness, in May 1920. His mother and his wife fell ill, Kamala with a persistent though slight rise in temperature which was feared to be an early indication of tuberculosis. On the advice of doctors they went to Mussoorie, where they took rooms in the Savoy Hotel. British intelligence officers were keeping an eye on Jawaharlal, as an up and coming young radical, and they believed this trip to Mussoorie was a covert move to make contact with the Afghans, with whom the British had lately fought a brief war, and who they feared would sweep south into India in support of the khilafat movement. The superintendent of police called on Jawaharlal and demanded an assurance that he would not meet with Afghan diplomats staying in the same hotel. He had no intention of doing so but neither, on principle, would he give the desired assurance. He left for Allahabad, rather than risk imprisonment, leaving the women of the family unattended, much to Motilal's distress. Motilal pulled strings, writing to the lieutenant-governor, Sir Harcourt Butler, who was still a family friend. Sir Harcourt had the order against Jawaharlal rescinded. In the interim, however, at loose ends at Anand Bhavan, Jawaharlal went out to meet a few hundred peasants who had marched to Allahabad in search of Gandhi, hoping to draw his attention to the state of affairs in their villages.

Gandhi was not there, but the peasants were directed to the son of the great Motilal. Their specific grievance was vicious landlordism under the pro-British taluqdars. The law controlled rents, so these landlords had instituted taxes or nazarana on properties which peasants had to borrow money to pay, often from the landlords themselves. Crippling debt and eviction were the common lot of peasants, but the situation was particularly critical in Pratapgarh district, from which had come the peasants whom Jawaharlal met squatting on the riverbanks in June 1920.

Jawaharlal and some colleagues went home with the villagers, to places far from the nearest railway lines, and found the countryside afire with enthusiasm and strange excitement. Enormous gatherings would take place at the briefest notice by word of mouth, one village communicating with the next, or with the cry "Sita Ram," which would be called out in all directions and quickly echoed back. Immediately people would appear, running as fast as they could. They were in miserable rags, but their faces were full of excitement as they looked to the visitors who had come to them to lead them out of bondage. Jawaharlal and his colleagues traveled in a light car, and the peasants were so eager that they should visit the interior where there

50

were no roads that hundreds of them, working overnight, built temporary roads across the fields. When the car became stuck it was lifted out by scores of willing hands.

Jawaharlal recollected, "They showered their affection on us and looked on us with loving and hopeful eyes, as if we were the bearers of good tidings, the guides who would lead us to the promised land. Looking at them and their misery and overflowing gratitude, I was filled with shame and sorrow, shame at my own easygoing and comfortable life and our petty politics of the city which ignored this vast multitude of semi-naked sons and daughters of India, sorrow at the degradation and overwhelming poverty of India. A new picture of India started to rise before me, naked, starving, crushed, and utterly miserable. And their faith in us, casual visitors from the distant city, embarrassed me and filled me with a new responsibility that frightened me."[13]

He listened to the tales of sorrow, of crippling rent, beatings, extortion, eviction and hunger, and committed himself to return. Jawaharlal Nehru, son of wealth, had been a sybarite dabbling in politics, a thirty-one-year-old who had enjoyed a very long childhood, who was frankly not even a very likable character. He had discovered India and come of age. From that time, the future was his.

On future treks Jawaharlal left the car and walked through the scorching sun, which he had always been taught would injure him, but he found he could stand the heat, spending the whole day with no protection on his head but a small towel, the only effect being that his light Brahmin skin was tanned to a rich brown. Language, however, was a problem. He was diffident about addressing meetings in Hindustani, in which he was not sufficiently fluent for oratorical devices, so he developed a conversational mode of speaking, whether he was addressing a few people or a crowd of 10,000. "I spoke to them man to man," he wrote, "and told them what I had in my mind and in my heart."[14]

Jawaharlal remained, in his dealings with urban Congress activists, courteous, aloof, very much the product of his upbringing. "He would speak in a very English manner. He disliked anyone fawning on him in the usual Hindu reverent manner . . . Towards anyone who had the Hindu or Bengali accent in his English he would almost behave like an Englishman to a 'native'," recollected Nirad C. Chauduri. But this otherness proved a strength as he began to put away European things. "Nobody really minded the residual Anglicism in him. They knew what a sacrifice he had made of it in order to become a disciple of Gandhi."[15]

Jawaharlal had many adventures among the peasants, which helped him develop fearless self-control in the face of adversity. He was once banned from addressing a meeting, so he marched the entire crowd four and a half miles to the next district where there was no ban, and held the meeting there. On another occasion, he was summoned by telegram to Rae Bareli, where some peasant leaders had been imprisoned and their followers had marched to the town to free them. The government was terrified of a Bolshevik-type uprising among the peasants and sent out troops which started firing on the demonstrators. Jawaharlal addressed the crowd to lessen the fear and excitement of the villagers, but some were killed nevertheless.

Thanks to his words and their own solidarity, matters began to improve for the peasants, despite many setbacks. Their improved self-confidence lessened their fear of landlords' agents and the police; peasants refused to rent land made vacant by the eviction of fellow tenants; illegal evictions and violence were monitored and, for the first time, questioned. Under the moral pressure of the agrarian movement, landlords demured and the provincial government promised an amendment of tenancy law.

Jawaharlal was sometimes accompanied on his travels by his sister Krishna and wife Kamala. "Slowly," Krishna recalled, "he grasped the psychology of the masses and began to feel a thrill at being able to influence vast crowds."[16] By taking family members on these rigorous trips he was (consciously or not) building on the Nehru legend that the family in some mystical way had a unique relationship with India. The mystique applied not to just one gifted individual, but the Nehrus as a whole, like the families in the Hindu epics from which many peasants knew hundreds of verses by heart.

It was in this period of their life together that the troubled Kamala came into her own. From the first time she met Gandhi she came under his spell, even more forcibly than Jawaharlal had done. Kamala backed her husband in his desire to be more militant, encouraging his radicalism and urging him to change his way of life. Her support for action which might lead to imprisonment and disgrace was a further cause of friction with Swarup Rani and Sarup, though the latter now tended to ignore her.

Sarup, who was twenty in 1920 and outstandingly beautiful, had her own concerns, for she was to marry. A lawyer called Ranjit Pandit came to consult Motilal on a legal matter and stayed with the family, Motilal's intention being for Ranjit and Sarup to converse. When they did, Ranjit's first questions were whether she liked Sanskrit poetry and whether she sang. She knew very little poetry and the Nehrus were an unmusical family, so he recited poetry to her in the garden and she took him riding. He asked to marry her within two days. When he left, he gave her a tiny copy of the *Bhagavad Gita* that his father had always read from, the most precious thing he possessed. Swarup Rani was horrified at the tattered gift and wanted to know where the diamond ring was. She secretly had the couple's horoscopes matched—she knew Motilal would not approve, but when he found out, he said they were both pleased, "I for my ability to judge human beings and my wife for her faith in the stars."[17]

Ranjit Pandit was from a wealthy family, and in his spare time was a Sanskrit scholar whose translations of ancient texts have enduring merit. The Kashmiri community, however, boycotted the wedding because, though the Nehrus were from the same Brahmin stock as Ranjit, they were considered to be outside the close community (of Uttar Pradesh Kashmiri Brahmins) in which acceptable mates could be found. Sarup's earlier relationship with Syed Hussain may also have been considered improper among the more conservative Brahmins.

Soon, outside events were to sweep away many of the more petty social restrictions and replace them with others. This manifested itself in Gandhi's insistence that Sarup should be married in homespun cloth with no jewelry—an interference in private matters considered outrageous by Swarup Rani, but he had his way. Gandhi vested an almost mythical importance in the handspinning and weaving of cloth for clothes: "I regard the spinning wheel as a gateway to my spiritual salvation," he said.[18] There were, however, more prosaic economic reasons for the encouragement of homespun or *khadi*: the development of a peasant, home-based industry stimulated village economies while increasing the self-respect of the poor. It also reduced India's reliance on British imports. It was a longterm source of resentment that raw materials for cotton goods were sent to Britain to be made into cloth and sold back to India. The wearing of khadi by all members of society also emphasized the unity of the nation while identifying nationalists. Jawaharlal called it "the livery of our freedom."[19] It was at Gandhi's suggestion in 1921 that the national (Congress) flag of India was embellished with the charkra, or spinning wheel.

Sarup's wedding took place on May 10, 1921, a day chosen as auspicious by an astrologer, but the British nervously noticed that it was the anniversary of the 1857 Mutiny. They feared that the arrival of such a large group of Congress supporters in Allahabad would be the precursor of an armed uprising, which gave great amusement to the wedding guests. It was at her marriage, in accordance with custom, that the Nehrus' eldest daughter was given a new name, in this case Vijaya Lakshmi, which was as well for her as she had never liked her earlier name. After the wedding the couple went to Gandhi for his blessing and he gave them a lecture about national duty, responsibility and the sacrifice of chastity in married life. The young bride was frightened lest her husband would give a pledge to the guru, and the Nehru spirit asserted itself: "Why did you give your permission to our marriage if you thought it was wrong for us to live together as husband and wife?" she demanded. "I want a normal married life." The Mahatma relented.[20]

Gandhi retained the initiative in politics and declared non-cooperation from August 1, 1920, coincidentally on the day that Tilak, the old hero of radical nationalism, died, leaving Gandhi the pre-eminent nationalist leader. Living as simply as he did, Gandhi had little left to renounce, but as a gesture he sent to the Viceroy the medals the British had given him for his service in the Zulu uprising and Boer War and for his humanitarian work in South Africa. Many Indians similarly sent back British medals and decorations.

Motilal's response to non-cooperation was characteristically cautious: he questioned whether Congress would be prepared to bind itself to the policy, feared it would mean breaking the law and imprisonment, and ranged himself with other powerful opponents of the policy, such as Muhammad Ali Jinnah—the Anglicized lawyer who was already the leading Muslim in Congress, C. R. Das, Annie Besant and Madan Malaviya. They agreed on the eve of the Calcutta Congress in September 1920 that they would accept non-cooperation in principle, but they would not agree to Gandhi's program. In Spring 1920 Motilal had been planning the election campaign for the councils and seeking out a constituency for Jawaharlal—hardly the action of someone preparing for non-cooperation with the government.

Gandhi's program had not then been drawn up, but it was widely understood to be extreme, and when he did write it down, it incorporated withdrawal from the courts, elections, legislatures, schools and colleges, and the boycott of official functions and foreign goods. He argued his case with Congress leaders in the Subjects Committee, making it clear that if he did not win, he would go ahead with his policy anyway as conscience demanded. Congress realized they needed Gandhi; if he left, he would take the most vigorous nationalists with him. Gandhi won the final vote in the Subjects Committee by 144 votes to 132, the most important single factor in his victory being the last minute defection of Motilal, who had brought enough minor defectors to swing the vote. In the open session that followed, Gandhi won by two to one.

The reason for the dramatic change must have been in part the strength of Gandhi's argument in committee, his clarity and directness of purpose, coupled with the political strength he had gained by embracing the *khilafat* and thereby carrying the Muslims with him. These factors had been present before, but seeing them in force must have made Motilal realize that this time his own influence on Jawaharlal was insufficient to tip the balance: Gandhi would win and it would split the family. Motilal voted to be on the same side as his son when the battle started.

B. K. Nehru, Motilal's grandnephew, said, "Motilal followed Gandhiji but he did not agree with any of his idiosyncrasies, with his teetotalism nor with his vegetarianism nor non-violence. I remember Motilal saying to me once, "I do not agree with anything that Gandhiji says, and he knows it, but he still has more respect for me than for those half-witted disciples of his." "[21]

Motilal's decision to throw in his lot with Gandhi was not without misgiving, more for his family than himself. He wrote to Jawaharlal in evident distress a few days after the Calcutta Congress: "Have you had any time to attend to the poor cows in Anand Bhavan? Not that they are really cows but [they] have been reduced to the position of cows by nothing short of culpable negligence on your part and mine—I mean your mother, your wife, your child and your sisters. I do not know with what grace and reason we can claim to be working for the good of the masses—the country at large—when we fail egregiously to minister to the most urgent requirements of our own flesh and blood and those whose flesh and blood we are."[22]

Motilal treated politics as he did the law: when he had a problem, he came to a decision after analyzing all aspects of it, then seized on his solution and pursued it doggedly. Once he had changed his allegiance, he obeyed Gandhi in more than full measure. Indeed, the extent of his renunciation was as great as his former extravagance had been. The sixty-year-old lawyer wound down his practice, resigned from the provincial council and withdrew Krishna from school; she was to write later of "those short gay years before Mahatma Gandhi came to change all our lives."[23]

This much renunciation of Britain would have satisfied the needs of non-cooperation, but Motilal went further: the Western kitchen and the wine cellar at Anand Bhavan were abolished: henceforth meals at home would be largely vegetarian and Indian. Motilal refused, however, to bow to Gandhi's teetotalism, and continued to enjoy his whiskey and sodas. The horses, carriages, crystal, china and Western wardrobes disappeared; the staff was drastically reduced. Leisure, too, underwent a change. Motilal wrote to Gandhi in the summer of 1921, "The shikar [hunt] has given place to long walks, and rifles and guns to books, magazines and newspapers (the favorite book being Edwin Arnold's *Song Celestial*, which is undergoing its third reading). "What a fall, my countrymen!" But, really, I have never enjoyed life better."[24]

All the family began to wear clothes made of homespun yarn. Motilal would wear a white cap, a long shirt and a Kashmiri shawl. His granddaughter Chandralekha Mehta said, "I remember him in that shawl that was always over one shoulder, making him look like a Roman senator in a toga."[25] A journalist, Sant Nihal Singh, described him at this time: "The homespun in which he was clad was coarse. It seemed to add distinction to his handsome face and figure. It certainly did not detract from them. The pure white of the khaddar [cotton] harmonized exceedingly well with his hair and mustache that had gone gray during the interval between our two meetings [twelve years]. The years had left a few marks upon his face, but he looked robust." Sant Nihal Singh commented aloud on the great change. "Only in the externals I hope," said Motilal. The journalist thought there must have been mental change too but his host demurred: "Hardly, I have been a rebel all my life. I must have been born a rebel."[26]

The most public demonstration of the Nehrus' commitment to nationalism was when they had a bonfire of their Western clothes. In fact, it was Indira's earliest memory: "I can still feel the excitement of the day," she wrote, thirty-six years later. "What rich materials, what lovely colors! What fun for a toddler to jump on, play hide and seek in the heaps of velvets and satins, silks and chiffons!" Indira also remembered this day as the time she discovered her power of manipulation as a child. Her parents had forbidden her to go to the bonfire as it was past her bedtime. She appealed directly to her grandfather, who overruled Jawaharlal and Kamala and carried her to the bonfire himself, where she promptly fell asleep.[27]

A more testing experience for the young Indira came a year or so later when she was four or five. She was playing alone, as she usually did, but within sight and sound of her mother who had a visitor—a relative returning from Paris. She had brought Indira an exquisite embroidered dress. Kamala thanked her but returned the gift, saying they wore only homespun material. The visitor was angry and pointed out that the rough fabric had chafed Kamala's skin red: she snapped that Kamala might make herself ill, but she had no right to make Indira suffer. Kamala called her daughter over and said, "Auntie has brought you a foreign frock. It is very pretty and you can wear it if you like but first think of the big fire where we burnt our foreign things. Would you like to wear this dainty thing when the rest of us are wearing *khadi*?"

Indira recounted the event: "The temptation was very strong—my eyes shone with desire—I stretched out a small hand to touch the dress but even before my hand reached it I found myself saying, 'Take it away—I shan't ever wear it.' 'But why not, don't you like nice things?' the visitor teased. 'I do . . . I do . . . but . . .' and I repeated all the arguments I had overheard from the elders' talk, when she said, 'All right, Miss Saint, how is it that you have a foreign doll?'" This deeply affected Indira, for she loved her doll, and for a long while after she struggled with her conscience about it, "overwhelmed by the burden of indecision." She stopped eating and sleep came only with exhaustion. At last the decision was made and, quivering with tension, she took the doll to the roof terrace and set fire to it. The tears came as if they would never stop and she was ill for days, but she had served her country. The legacy of this event was that for the rest of her life she hated striking a match.[28]

Although there must have been traumatic moments in the lives of everyone at Anand Bhavan, the women of the house adapted easily to the change, and this was particularly so of Kamala: the increasingly simple and Indian lifestyle tilted the balance of influence in the house away from sophisticated Westerners like her visitor from Paris, and towards her own preferences.

The family's new simple lifestyle won the admiration and affection of the people and struck a significant chord. Renunciation of worldly things is a mystical longing embedded deep in the Indian psyche: it is the message of the *Bhagavad Gita* and the life of Buddha, but is also one of the themes of the epic *Ramayana*. Indeed, Allahabad is a holy city because it was there that Rama re-met his brother Bharata after wandering the land for fourteen years. The meeting was said to have taken place at exactly the spot on the Anand Bhavan land where their fountain played. Rama had been tricked out of his inheritance, but Bharata had refused to perpetuate injustice by usurping the throne, and Rama was restored to his rightful place to inaugurate the Rama Raj, the mythical Hindu golden age. The stories told of the Nehrus' wealth were often wildly exaggerated, as were the tales of how low they had abased themselves (they still lived very comfortably by Indian standards) in order that the mythic element of renunciation could shine through. Their destiny was not thrust upon the Nehrus, it was fashioned by them.

Some commentators have seen a conscious element of long-term planning in the Nehrus' decision to go with Gandhi. Journalist Khushwant Singh said, "Gandhi felt the pulse of the country much more than [Jawaharlal] Nehru did. Nehru after all was a product of Harrow and Cambridge, a bit of a brown sahib, going on holidays skiing and this kind of thing. I think he sensed when he arrived on the scene that if he had any future in politics it had to be with Gandhi. He had to ride Gandhi's wagon and he could achieve his goal."[29]

The *Independent* newspaper, into which Motilal had poured money, had to fold now that he was no longer earning vast amounts, and Jawaharlal began to feel more guilty at living on his father's generosity. Motilal was supporting his son and his family while Jawaharlal was working full time for the Congress. Jawaharlal said he would ask Congress for a salary but Motilal refused, saying he should not take public funds and if the need arose he could take up "chamber practice" to earn money for the family. Motilal wrote, "Swaraj or no swaraj, the one thing which I will not willingly permit is the possibility of any child or grandchild of mine having to depend for maintenance on any other person in the world however near or dear, or that of their being a charge on the nation."[30]

Jawaharlal, now given free rein, plunged headlong into the movement, giving up all his old associations and contacts, old friends, books and even newspapers, except where they dealt with the political work at hand. He lived for meetings and the committee room. In spite of strong family bonds, he wrote, "I almost forgot my family, my wife, my daughter." It was only afterwards that he realized what a burden he must have been to his loved ones "and what amazing patience and tolerance my wife had shown towards me."[31] The work at hand was to "go to the villages" to mold a national, all-Indian movement from what Congress had been: a weekend of nationalist talk for the educated class. It was this work with the peasants into which Jawaharlal now threw himself with tireless enthusiasm. He undertook a tour of the districts in the United Provinces to strengthen the Congress and *khilafat* movements, traveling by car, train and horse carriage, and even, on one occasion, running between two locations in order to make his timetable.

The principal political question was whether Congress would contest the elections to be held under the Government of India Act 1919 (coming into effect in 1921). Having achieved some measure of reform, the old Congress leaders argued, it was incumbent upon nationalist politicians to work within the system to fit India for self-government. A number of Congress veterans resigned and joined the Indian Liberal Federation, some of them taking over provincial administrations which they ran with distinction. Their departure stemmed not only from their desire to wield administrative responsibility, but because they were out of alignment with the direction in which Gandhi was leading Congress. The independence movement was becoming a mass movement aimed at political freedom, but it also involved a very Gandhian remodeling of India. It had taken on a character which was rural, Spartan, self-sufficient and (as it was to prove), disastrously, Hindu.

The most important defector at this time was Muhammad Ali Jinnah, another London-educated lawyer, who, while in England, had worked for the election of the first Indian in the House of Commons, Dadabhai Naoroji. Jinnah entered Indian politics when he attended the 1906 Congress, but he also joined the Muslim League in 1913. He was a secular Muslim who became known as the "ambassador of Hindu-Muslim unity" for his work in bringing the Muslim League nearer to the Congress. But the Congress he now encountered was not the one he had joined. The European clothes he regarded as a mark of his sophistication were frowned upon; a new type of delegate emerged, often from the lower middle class; Hindustani, not English, became more commonly the conference language; or sometimes it would use the language of the province where the conference was held. He saw much of Gandhian policy as mere rhetoric or worthless gestures, and he accused Gandhi of being a perpetual cause of disunity. In that Gandhi's policy had an objective, it tended towards a restoration of Hindu village society, which was anathema to Jinnah. Jawaharlal commented on him, "The enthusiasm of the people outside struck him as mob hysteria. There was as much difference between him and the Indian masses as between Savile Row and Bond Street and the Indian village with its mud huts."[32] For his part, Jinnah felt abandoned by Motilal and those who had fallen in line with Gandhi at Calcutta for a program which "struck the imagination mostly of the inexperienced youth and the ignorant and the illiterate." At the next Congress at Nagpur he was booed off the platform. He never returned. Congress's failure to accommodate educated Muslims like Jinnah had dire consequences in the future.

Gandhi was also playing his own tune to a startling extent. At the height of agitation in 1921 he contacted the Viceroy to say that if the government would promote home spinning and weaving and suppress alcohol and opium in India, he would call off non-cooperation. The government did not reply (and thus lost a golden opportunity to split the Congress). Gandhi's emphatic moralizing and abrupt changes of direction antagonized opponents and supporters alike.

By September 1921, Gandhi was facing the problem of a localized breakdown in Hindu-Muslim unity in southern India, involving massacres and the forced conversion of Hindus. Spinning now became to him what even his sympathetic biographer describes as an "obsession."[33] He discarded his previous garb of cap, sleeveless jacket and loose trousers, and took to wearing nothing but a loincloth. The rational explanation was that such evident poverty brought him closer to the peasants, but it was as if, having encouraged everyone else to wear homespun, he just had to go one better.

Such behavior stimulated "dismay and amusement"[34] in his colleagues, not least Jawaharlal, who said that having recognized Gandhi as a "great and unique man and a glorious leader," they had effectively given him a blank check to do as he wished. Jawaharlal and his colleagues often joked about Gandhi's fads among themselves and said that "when swaraj [self-government] came, these fads must not be encouraged"[35]—tantamount to saying that when Gandhi's methods won freedom, it would be hard-headed politicians who would operate the state.

It was not these peccadilloes that troubled Jawaharlal the most, however, but the growth of a religious element in politics, both Hindu and Muslim. However much he tried to reconcile himself to it, he could not help concluding that religion prevented clear political thinking. He wrote, "Even some of Gandhiji's phrases sometimes jarred upon me—thus his frequent reference to Rama Raj as a golden age which was to return. But I was powerless to intervene, and I consoled myself with the thought that Gandhiji used the words because they were well known and understood by the masses. He had an amazing knack of reaching the heart of the people."[36]

In truth, the revolts of the immediate postwar years were held in the name of diverse interests. Peasants thought Swaraj meant "cloth at four annas [a quarter of a rupee] a yard"; and in Urdu-speaking areas, khilafat was thought to relate to the word khilaf meaning "against," so people who chanted it were simply against the government. As a movement, khilafat was already doomed, regardless. While the reassertion of Turkish national identity had given the khilafat some hope, soon Turkey became a secular state under Ataturk; the Sultan was expelled and the caliphate was officially abolished. The khilafat movement into which Gandhi had urged everyone to put so much effort was dead.

Nor was the collective non-cooperation movement so successful, despite Gandhi's claim there would be Swaraj by the end of 1921. Courts, schools and colleges continued, few officials resigned, and there was a reasonable turnout to the elections, with a third of the electorate going to the polls. To inject new momentum into the movement, forty-five Indian leaders, including Gandhi, Motilal and Jawaharlal, issued a manifesto declaring it was "contrary to the national dignity" for any Indian to serve as a soldier under the present Indian government. This was an open challenge to military disaffection but the government stayed its hand until after a visit by the Prince of Wales in November 1921.

This supposedly gala event revived the non-cooperation movement, with the future King Edward VIII finding himself being led in splendor through deserted streets in areas where Congress had organized an effective protest. Motilal himself arranged the *hartal* in Allahabad when the royal visitor was paraded through what seemed to be "a city of the dead."[37] B. K. Nehru described the scene: ". . . there was a complete hartal, a complete strike in Allahabad: the streets were vacant, there was no traffic, all the shops were closed, and the Prince of Wales' procession went along with nobody to see it."[38] In some areas, though, there was violence: in Bombay, for example, supporters of the boycott attacked those who had come to welcome the Prince and more than fifty were killed.

As a footnote to this visit, one of the people in the Prince of Wales' entourage was a young relative of the future king, Louis Mountbatten. On this trip he proposed marriage to Edwina Ashley, who had come to India to be near him. Twenty-five years later they were to return as the last viceroy and vicereine. At this stage in Mountbatten's life, however, he was a typical British aristocrat who, when he gave them any thought, had no respect for the nationalist demonstrators. "Rude young cubs," he called the students demonstrating at Benares.[39]

Government officials were outraged at the boycott: they felt the situation was getting out of control and that they must reassert themselves. They began by arresting individual Congress leaders, then followed with mass arrests of defiant Congress workers. Jawaharlal was in his Congress office at Allahabad when an excited clerk announced that the police had surrounded the building. Jawaharlal insisted on precise self-control. He ordered a clerk to witness the police search of the building, while everyone else continued with their normal work, ignoring the police. When they arrested a colleague who came to say goodbye, Jawaharlal made him and his police escort wait until he had finished a letter before he spoke to them.

At home there was a similar story. The police had arrived at Anand Bhavan, and a very nervous officer told Motilal they wished to search the house. Motilal told them it would take six months to do it justice, and didn't the policeman have something else to say, he coaxed, didn't he want to arrest Motilal under clause two, section seventeen of the Criminal Law Amendment Act? Well, the policeman said, there was that too. He also had a warrant for Jawaharlal's arrest, and when he arrived home both father and son were arrested and taken through the throng of friends and admirers who had gathered in the grounds of Anand Bhavan. They were driven away, watched by Swarup Rani and Kamala, holding back tears, then a magisterial Swarup Rani gave an interview to a journalist in which she "rejoiced in the great privilege of sending my dear husband and my only son to jail."[40]

Motilal's trial began the following day, December 7, 1921, before a magistrate who had been Jawaharlal's colleague in the administration of the St. John Ambulance Brigade. The government prosecutor was an old friend of Motilal's and very ill at ease. Motilal cradled the four-year-old Indira on his knee throughout the trial, which he described as a "farce" but refused further participation. The charge was of having signed up as a Congress volunteer, which was true, though the case was hardly strengthened by the government's producing an illiterate witness to verify Motilal's signature in Hindi, who held the document upside down. Motilal was sentenced to six months' imprisonment and a 500 rupees fine, and Jawaharlal received a similar sentence for distributing Congress leaflets supporting the boycott of the Prince of Wales. They went to the district jail at Lucknow where they were placed together, and in the company of two of Motilal's nephews, Shamlal and Mohanlal, the sons of his brother, Nandlal. B. K. Nehru, who visited them, said, "The first thing I heard when we were near them was the laughter of Motilal, who had a very loud and very peculiar laugh recognizable by anybody because it came right from the belly. So I realized that he couldn't have been tortured or ill-treated, he must be alright, because it was a thought that terrified me that my great respected grandfather [actually granduncle] and uncles were in jail."[41]

As the Nehru father and son refused to pay their fines on principle, the police raided Anand Bhavan and carried off carpets and furniture in lieu, though they were worth a great deal more than the amount of the fines. The women of the house maintained a stoical silence at this injustice, except Indira, who railed against the police, her first overtly political act.

The District Jail at Lucknow was the headquarters of Motilal's friend of thirty years, Sir Harcourt Butler, formerly lieutenant-governor of the United Provinces (now designated governor, since the Government of India Act had come into force in 1921). Sir Harcourt did his best to make their stay tolerable by relaxing regulations so Motilal could receive food sent from outside, write letters and obtain newspapers and books. If he sent champagne, as the Butler family believe, the Nehrus felt obliged to deny it, Motilal with good humor, Jawaharlal more testily. Motilal maintained his physical strength by exercise, including walking round the exercise ground on his toes—his asthma notwithstanding. Jawaharlal embraced the prison experience with vigor; he cleaned their barracks, washed his and his father's clothes, and spun yarn on a spinning wheel. He read and discussed energetically and conducted evening classes for other prisoners. Prison was not so much a punishment as a vast, enthusiastic camp for Congress supporters, particularly when the government turned to mass arrests. Far from striking fear into the hearts of non-cooperators, the punishment was one they embraced. Jawaharlal wrote, "Young men and boys would crowd inside the prison trucks and refuse to come out. Every evening we could hear from inside the jail, truck after truck arriving outside heralded by our slogans and shouts."[42] The jail was crowded but still they came, happy martyrs to the cause; prison trucks would arrive with more prisoners than were covered in the warrants of arrest, and officials looked in vain at the rule book for guidance. Between December and January 1922, an estimated 30,000 were imprisoned in connection with the non-cooperation movement. Gandhi now planned to test a more active civil disobedience program in Bardoli.

Suddenly, and with no prior warning, Gandhi gave instructions to call off non-cooperation, to the utter astonishment of Motilal, Jawaharlal and other Congress leaders who had not been consulted. The immediate cause was an event in the village of Chauri Chaura in the district of Gorakhpur in the United Provinces. A procession through the village of Chaura in support of Gandhi broke into taunts then scuffles with constables guarding the local police station. When members of the procession went to help their comrades, the constables became frightened and opened fire into the crowd. Not having been prepared for trouble, their ammunition soon gave out and they took shelter in the police station. The enraged crowd set light to it and twenty-two policemen were either burned to death or hacked to pieces as they tried to flee. Gandhi instantly saw that, in contrast to the British ambivalence about Jallianwala Bagh, he had to keep the moral high ground.

In the light of this event, and the general tendency towards violence in non-cooperation protests, Gandhi had felt obliged to call a unilateral halt to the movement. Gandhi's new line was accepted by the Congress Working Committee and non-cooperation was replaced with a program of spinning, temperance, education and reform. Motilal was beside himself with rage: all his sacrifices had been for naught, and he must now sit in jail tasting the ashes of defeat. Jawaharlal took it differently but no less deeply: he felt utterly betrayed. It was the first reverse he had faced in his entire life and he struggled in his bitterness to comprehend it. "Were a remote village and a mob of excited peasants in an out-of-the-way place going to put an end . . . to our national struggle for freedom?"[43] For the time being the answer was "yes": the government's hard line had worked.

FOUR

# FATHER, SON AND HOLY GHOST

Jawaharlal wrote an angry letter to Gandhi which the recipient described as a "freezing dose." The immediate reply was read to Jawaharlal by Swarup Rani at visiting time. In it Gandhi gave the background against which the decision to stop non-cooperation was made: Chauri Chaura had not been an isolated incident; from all over India, Gandhi was receiving information that his own supporters were becoming aggressive, violent and threatening. "I assure you," he wrote, "that if the thing had not been suspended we would have been leading not a non-violent struggle but essentially a violent struggle." He implored Jawaharlal to allow the people outside prison, who were in full possession of the facts, to direct the movement, without burdening himself with worry. He further urged him to keep spinning: ". . . we shall never have the slightest cause for regret that we have pinned our faith to the spinning wheel or that we have spun so much good yarn per day in the name of the motherland."[1]

Jawaharlal was out of prison sooner than expected, as a review committee had realized he was improperly sentenced (having been sentenced under a different law from that under which he was convicted). He immediately went to see Gandhi, who was now himself in jail awaiting trial, more at the insistence of the government in Britain than because the Viceroy felt his incarceration would have any value in India. The bemused magistrate summed up: "The law is no respecter of persons. Nevertheless, it will be impossible to ignore the fact that you are in a different category from any person I have ever tried or am likely to try . . ." Jawaharlal was present to hear Gandhi sentenced to six years' imprisonment, a term from which he was released early. Six weeks after Jawaharlal was released he was again imprisoned, this time for eighteen months, on various counts of sedition, the primary cause being his encouragement of Allahabad merchants to boycott foreign cloth. He did not defend himself, in accordance with Congress practice, but used his court appearance to make a bitter denunciation of the way in which Britain had betrayed India, and a passionate statement of nationalism. His education in England

66

had left him "as much prejudiced in favor of England and the English as it was possible for an Indian to be," but he had been disillusioned by the way the rulers had fallen short of their own best standards. Now he welcomed the chance to undergo imprisonment for the freedom of his nation, "to suffer for the dear country." It was a histrionic speech, but, for the first time, it secured Jawaharlal a national audience, particularly among the young, and received high praise from Motilal: "On reading your statement I felt I was the proudest father in the world."[2] It was from this point that his son's fame began to eclipse his own. Formerly, Jawaharlal had been known as the son of Motilal: now, to Motilal's delight, the crowds began to hail him and Swarup Rani as the parents of the great Jawaharlal.

Motilal had publicly reconciled himself to the abandonment of non-cooperation. Soon after his release, in June 1922, he made a speech deploring the indiscipline of the movement which had made Gandhi change strategy, but claimed it was only an alteration of course to avoid destruction: ". . . there can be no question of our changing our destination or our good ship which we have chartered for the voyage."[3] So much for diplomacy. Privately, Motilal was making sure that the future of the movement would be in a wider range of hands than those of Gandhi alone, and that no decisions would be taken as to its direction without his involvement.

The first move was to reverse the policy of not running in council elections. The Congress had set up a Civil Disobedience Inquiry Committee to conduct a nationwide inquiry on how the movement could be revived. Its first sittings were at Anand Bhavan and they led inevitably towards the formation of the Swaraj Party within Congress, which aimed at putting parliamentary methods of obstruction into effect. Their inspiration was Parnell who, in the cause of Irish nationalism, won election to the House of Commons, then used his position to cause disruption. The Congress at Gaya in 1923 supported Motilal and C. R. Das in deciding to contest the next elections, directly contrary to the line Gandhi had argued.

Motilal campaigned ferociously during the election, traveling incessantly by road and rail, addressing vast meetings, and thus setting the standard of electioneering vigor which his descendants were to follow. At the end of 1923 Swaraj won forty-two out of 101 seats in the Central Legislative Assembly where Motilal led the party, and was for the next six years a formidable leader of the opposition to the Viceroy's government. Swaraj also won an absolute majority in the Central Provinces Council; it was the largest party in Bengal, where C. R. Das assumed control of it, and the second largest party in the United Provinces and Assam; it made no headway, however, in Punjab and Madras. As often happens, the radicalism of the Swaraj Party became progressively attenuated over the years by the compromises of office.

Motilal's colleagues in the new party had an opportunity of seeing his energetic working methods at first hand. Once, in 1923, when he had the executive council of Swaraj staying with him, he surprised them by having completed a huge correspondence and drawn up a detailed agenda by 8 A.M. He said to his colleagues, "This is the way to work. I scribbled this down nearly two hours before you were out of your beds. And have you brought your notes?" To those who stuck to their guns in argument he would "lash out with stinging irony" but would then present them with their own views reformulated.[4]

Indira said her grandfather's influence on her was much stronger than her father's, which came later, perhaps because her father was so often away working or in prison. Her earliest memories were of childhood in a house which was "sternly governed" by Motilal, with "his awe-inspiring temper softened by quick forgiveness and infectious laughter."[5] He seems to have been a most indulgent grandfather, who allowed Indira's pet deer, Mira Beau, to roam at will. It would enter the front veranda and nibble books and important papers on his desk, but Motilal did not try to get rid of the animal.

Indira later described herself as a "large-eyed and solemn child"— photographs testify to this, and to her spindly figure: she was forever being told to eat more to put on weight. As a small child her favorite game was to gather together as many servants as she could, stand on a table and deliver "speeches" consisting of political phrases picked up from her elders. She would arrange her dolls as "armies" of police and freedom fighters and have them act out street battles. Her aunt Krishna once found her on a veranda, striking a pose with her arm outstretched and muttering valiantly. Krishna asked what she was doing and Indira said she was practicing at being Joan of Arc: "Someday I am going to lead my people to freedom as Joan of Arc did."[6] No one could claim Indira lacked a sense of destiny. She was a dreamer, however, and showed no more willingness to get down to school work than her grandfather had done. When she was five, Jawaharlal wrote that he had heard from Kamala that Indira was becoming "more and more intractable and pays no heed to any kind of study" and insisted Motilal do something about Indira's schooling.[7] She was sent first to Allahabad's Modern School, which was found to be unsatisfactory, and then to St. Cecilia's, which angered Jawaharlal because he considered it a British school run by English women. Ultimately, Indira was tutored at home, which did nothing for her social skills.

Her aunt Vijaya described Indira as always "withdrawn by nature and not really close to anyone . . . a lonely person, unable easily to confide, unable to have close friends when she was a little girl. She developed all the faults of an only child." Vijaya admittedly was writing this from a standpoint of outright opposition to Indira as a mature woman, but her comments bear scrutiny—that Indira's upbringing with an absent father and frequently ailing mother bred in her a sense of insecurity. Vijaya comments on Indira's "degree of obstinacy and insistence on having her own way and believing she was always right."[8] Indira must have recognized the deficiencies in her childhood, for at an early age she resolved that she would not have an only child when she grew up.[9]

It was not true that Indira was friendless, but her only close companion for the first part of her life was Kamala, whom the glamorous Vijaya despised. Kamala would spend long hours in her room, away from the jibes of her husband's family, with only Indira for company. Indira said of her mother, "We were very close to each other. I loved her deeply and when I thought that she was being wronged, I fought for her and quarreled with people."[10]

Kamala poured both her love and her frustration into little Indira. While it was said that Kamala had never in her life raised her voice, she had a toughness that belied her physical frailty. "She counseled courage and dedication," her biographer writes. "To Indira, her advice was to stand firm by her convictions."[11] Indira thought of her mother as a saint: "There was something," she said as an adult, "a kind of little radiance which emanated from her."[12] It was this spiritual aspect of her makeup that endeared her to Gandhi. To the child Indira, the Mahatma was not a great leader so much as a family elder to whom she would go with her childish problems, which he would treat with great seriousness. Later, she wrote, "I disagreed with many of his ideas and had long discussions with the usual dogmatism of the very young who think they have all the answers."[13]

Jawaharlal's letters to her as a young child show how limited family communication had to be, and how it pained her father to be away from her, "To dear Indu, love from her Papu. You must get well quickly, learn to write letters and come and see me in jail. I am longing to see you. Have you plied the new spinning wheel which Dadu [Motilal] has brought for you? Send me some of your yarn. Do you join your mother in prayers every day?"[14]

Jawaharlal's second prison term was less hectic and exciting than the first: the area in which he was incarcerated was more overcrowded and there were no privileges for senior figures like himself. Prisoners received one meeting with family and one letter per month, though they stopped seeing visitors for many months in protest at the petty indignities to which their visitors were subjected. He and his fellow inmates bathed and washed their clothes in public and ran round and round the barracks for exercise. Jawaharlal wrote how he "often yearned for solitude" and would sit outside the barracks, braving the heat and the monsoon rain, watching the sky. He and five others were eventually separated out as "troublemakers." They were confined together and settled down to a routine of spinning, tending their vegetable garden, exercise and reading. It was not that Jawaharlal actually enjoyed prison, but sacrifice came easy to him, and he appreciated the chance to read and think. His preferred reading was mainly history, travel and poetry. A favorite poet was Byron, with whom he sensed an affinity because both had been to Harrow and Trinity, and Byron had fought for Greek independence (which led to his death).

Jawaharlal and other political prisoners in the United Provinces were freed as part of a state government amnesty early in 1923. Gandhi was released the following year, it being deemed hardly worthwhile detaining Congress leaders: the movement as it was had virtually died, the Congress Party was split and *khilafat* was no more. Gandhi's only contribution to Congress politics in the five years after his arrest was an attempt to change its constitution so membership would be limited to people who would spin a specified amount of yarn. This was so fiercely resisted by Motilal and C. R. Das, who organized a walkout of "Swarajists" at the Congress that discussed it, that Gandhi withdrew the resolution, even though it had been passed.

Jawaharlal found Congress politics unexciting; his general feeling was that his father's line on contesting elections was wrong, but he himself had no proposal for alternative action. For all his other leadership qualities, Jawaharlal did lack the "big idea" which could inspire followers. He waited for other leaders, like Gandhi, to have the ideas and he would follow. This is a key not only to his behavior towards Gandhi (his need for a great man) but of Gandhi's behavior towards him: Gandhi needed a devotee with every leadership potential except big ideas; Gandhi had more than enough of those himself.

Still, Gandhi was now concentrating his efforts on Indian spiritual development, on Hindu-Muslim unity, the removal of untouchability, and the inevitable spinning wheel. Jawaharlal applied himself assiduously to day-to-day political work: in 1923 he was elected chairman of the Allahabad Municipal Board, where he was to serve with distinction for two years until his restless nature and impatience with bureaucracy asserted themselves and he resigned. Also in 1923 he became a general secretary of Congress for two years, and it was in this capacity that he visited Nabha state in Punjab to observe the work of activists in the Akali movement, whose aim was the protection of Sikh shrines.

There, Jawaharlal and his two companions were arrested by the police, marched through the street in handcuffs and thrown in jail. Motilal knew the conditions in Punjab jails and hurried to Nabha, but he was denied permission to see and represent his son until he had appealed to the Viceroy over the head of the state administrator. Motilal was disappointed when he was finally able to see Jawaharlal, however, for his son refused to be defended. It seemed as if Jawaharlal accepted injustice as his lot, even if it had no direct relation to any cause he had espoused. Motilal wrote to him, "I was pained to find that, instead of affording you any relief, my visit of yesterday only had the effect of disturbing the even tenor of your happy jail life . . ." and he returned to Allahabad.[15] Jawaharlal apologized to his father, but showed he was reconciled to a jail term in Nabha: "It will be a new experience and in this blasé world it is something to have a new experience."[16] Jawaharlal certainly had a new experience: he contracted typhus from lice in the jail and was ill for weeks.

Jawaharlal and his two colleagues were tried and each sentenced to two and a half years' imprisonment but, in a very British compromise immediately afterwards, an "executive order" suspended the sentences and expelled the men from the state. It was Jawaharlal's first experience of the rule of law in princely states, as overseen by the British, and it cannot have improved his view of the princes with whom, twenty years later, he would have to negotiate.

Meanwhile, Anand Bhavan had been growing shabby because of goods seized by police (always fiercely resisted by Indira, who once almost injured a policeman) and because there were fewer staff to clean the house and tend the garden. Motilal therefore recommended legal practice, once again refusing to allow Jawaharlal to work on anything except politics, insisting he would keep his son and his family. Jawaharlal was surprised anyway at how little he spent: ". . . *khadi* clothes and third class railway traveling demand little money."[17]

Domestic concerns now began to preoccupy Jawaharlal. Anand Bhavan became a house of sadness: Vijaya had a baby girl in 1923 but she died after nine months; Kamala gave birth to a son prematurely in 1924, but he survived only two days. These were not the family's only worries: Kamala had been unwell for some time and was finally diagnosed in November 1925 as having tuberculosis. She was treated in a hospital in Lucknow and, as the Congress was held at Cawnpore, Jawaharlal had to spend his time rushing between these cities. When treatment in Switzerland was recommended, Jawaharlal welcomed the idea, not only for medical reasons but to get away from India where there was no clear path for future action.

Jawaharlal, Kamala and Indira sailed from Bombay for Venice in March 1926, along with Vijaya and Ranjit who had planned their visit to Europe long before. They were joined in the summer by Krishna, who arrived in Geneva to find that Kamala's treatment was having no great effect. That trip was the only long period in Indira's childhood when the family was together. She was enrolled in the Ecole Nouvelle at Bex between the ages of nine and ten, and learned French, which was to stand her in good stead for the future. Jawaharlal divided his time in Switzerland between taking Indira to and from school, nursing Kamala, learning French, reading widely and attending courses and lectures. Indira said that when the three of them were together, the family would read the *Bhagavad Gita* in the morning and the *Ramayana* in the evening.

Jawaharlal attended the Congress of Oppressed Nationalities in

Brussels in 1927 and was elected to the nine-person executive committee of the League Against Imperialism, in the company of George Lansbury, Madame Sun Yat Sen, Albert Einstein and Romain Rolland, though Jawaharlal was later to break with the League because of its attempt to impose socialist dogma on the complexities of Indian politics. The Congress of Oppressed Nationalities, though it contained many individual spirits, was something of a Soviet "front" organization, through which the Soviets made contact with those who were expected to be valuable to them in the future. Clearly Jawaharlal was considered a potential recruit, for he was invited to visit Moscow in 1927 for the tenth anniversary celebration of the Russian Revolution.

Motilal was, of course, paying for his family's travel, schooling and medical treatment, so it was fortunate that he was at this time called to plead before the judicial committee of the Privy Council in London, for which the fees were handsome. In September 1927 Motilal joined his son and they traveled in Italy, Britain, France and Germany, staying in the best hotels, as in the old days. They continued to the Soviet Union, where they were generously welcomed. In his four days there Jawaharlal was impressed with Soviet planning, the stress on health and education for all, and the push towards industrialization rather than backward-looking peasant culture. He felt India had a great deal to learn from communism, but was not interested in importing a political philosophy wholesale. He was often considered a socialist, but was not doctrinaire, and if socialist thinking was not producing results, he would try something else. His experience of the new European political systems of communism and fascism reinforced his view that Gandhi's ideas offered the only real way forward for India.

Kamala's health improved, probably more because of rest and nursing care in different parts of Switzerland than the experimental "Spahlinger" treatment of vaccines she had received, and the family returned to India at the end of 1927, having been in Europe for a year and nine months. Another pregnancy followed in 1928 but it resulted in a miscarriage.

Jawaharlal plunged straight back into politics, becoming general secretary of Congress for a second two-year period. Gandhi re-entered political activism by giving direction and support to a peasant movement. A new *satyagraha* directed by a rising lieutenant of Gandhi's,

another London-educated lawyer known as Sardar Patel, began in
Bardoli in Gujarat on February 12, 1928, when peasants refused to pay
taxes in protest at a 22 percent tax increase. Government collectors
took what possessions the peasants had and imprisoned protesters till
no more could be imprisoned. Finally, after six months, the government gave in, released the political prisoners, agreed to return con-
fiscated goods and reduced the taxes to their previous levels. Patel, a
sternly moralistic man of strong Hindu convictions, emerged from
Bardoli as one of the few leaders with a status to rival that of Jawaharlal. Jawaharlal, meanwhile, was involved with trade union and
labor leaders who were carrying on more conventional agitations,
such as strikes, across the whole of India.

It was again the crass behavior of the British that stimulated a resurgence of nationalist feeling. The Government of India Act of 1919
had made provision for a ten-year constitutional survey of India, so the
British government set up the Simon Commission, a group of six peers
and MPs (one of them Clement Attlee) headed by Sir John Simon.
They did not, apparently, consider having any Indian input to the pro-
cedure. All India was outraged, including those who knew nothing of
constitutional law but could understand an insult well enough. A
movement to boycott the Commission sprang up spontaneously, rallying support from the usually loyalist Liberal Party, and also from M. A.
Jinnah, representing the Muslims. Jawaharlal organized and coordinated the nationwide boycott movement. Everywhere the Simon
Commission went, it was greeted with black flags and "Go back,
Simon" slogans.

The police responded to these peaceful demonstrations by charges
with *lathis*, long, thick sticks which could inflict serious damage. In
fact, Lajpat Rai, a veteran Congress leader from Punjab, died shortly
after such a beating, which inflamed popular sentiment. Later the
same month, on November 29, 1928, Jawaharlal was attending a
demonstration that was charged by the police. His colleagues dis-
persed and he began to move to the side of the road to be less con-
spicuous, but then he stopped "and had a little argument with myself,
and decided that it would be unbecoming for me to move away."[18] So
he stayed, and received two blows from a mounted policeman. The
next day, he was further tested when he was part of a massive demonstration in Lucknow waiting near the station for the arrival of Simon

and his colleagues. Mounted police carried out a cavalry charge using *lathis* and spears, beating and trampling hundreds. Jawaharlal was standing his ground, receiving blows on his back, shoulders and legs, until a group of students carried him away to save him from further punishment, "to my great annoyance," as he later wrote. Gandhi wrote to him, ". . . my love to you. It was all done bravely. You have braver things to do. May God spare you for many a long year to come, and make you His chosen instrument for freeing India from the yoke"—a clear statement of succession.[19]

Often government hospitals were not willing to take victims of the frequent shootings and *lathi* charges. One night several young boys were brought into Anand Bhavan with bullet wounds. Kamala saw them and persuaded Motilal to allow her to keep them in the house, so from September 1929 several rooms were turned into a makeshift hospital. At first, doctors came only at dead of night and the women of the house, including Kamala and Indira, acted as nurses. The temporary setup was later staffed and equipped as a proper hospital.

Lord Birkenhead, Secretary of State for India, who was responsible for the Simon Commission, scorned Indian politicians, claiming they were unable to make constructive suggestions and were divided among themselves. The Madras Congress in December 1927 had already called for a "Swaraj constitution" to cut through the verbiage obfuscating Congress demands for *swaraj*, which seemed to mean a different thing every time it was called for. Motilal chaired the working committee that produced what became known as the Nehru Report, although it was also the work of Sir Tej Bahadur Sapru and representatives of other political parties. It was a draft constitution for an India under dominion status, like that enjoyed by Australia, New Zealand, Canada and South Africa, and it attempted to solve the problem of the Muslim minority by offering reserved seats for Muslims. Motilal considered the influence of religion in politics to be detestable, that religion had "come to signify bigotry and fanaticism, intolerance and narrow mindedness," and he advised the separation of religion and politics.[20]

The Nehru Report was the subject of a major difference of opinion within Congress, with Jawaharlal and Subhas Chandra Bose arguing from the radical side that complete independence should be demanded: not for them some intermediate situation within the

British Empire. Motilal and his supporters were arguing for dominion status, but the issue was evenly balanced in Congress as a whole. Jawaharlal's time in Europe had left him impatient with the pace of Indian politics. He called for a declaration of independence followed by civil disobedience to achieve the aim.

Under dominion status India would have remained part of the Empire, with a constitution that could only be changed with the permission of Britain, and with armed forces having allegiance to the Crown. There was also another problem—one of motivation. As the historian Bipan Chandra said, "Jawaharlal Nehru and the young felt that the freedom struggle required a sacrifice, that you cannot inspire people by saying 'Fight for dominion status.' If you say fight for independence, then it will give you a psychological feeling of uplift; psychologically you cannot make people go to jail and sacrifice their all for dominion status."[21]

The exemplar of all Nehru rages, which was referred to in awe down the family line, happened over this issue. Motilal was boasting of his son's achievement to guests at a dinner party at Anand Bhavan. He recited some Persian couplets and asked Jawaharlal to translate them. Jawaharlal was not fluent in Persian and declined, but when Motilal insisted he reluctantly made a poor translation. Motilal chided him for not knowing the difference between two similar Persian words. The angry Jawaharlal said, "At least I know the difference between dominion status and independence!" Motilal jumped up in fury and overturned the entire table in front of the horrified guests.[22]

Motilal feared losing the vote in Congress full session, which he was chairing as president that year, but he also feared losing his son. He called on the magician, Gandhi, who came to the 1928 Congress at Calcutta despite his ill health and proposed a compromise: Congress should adopt the Nehru Report, but if the government did not accept it in two years, Congress should opt for full independence. Jawaharlal pressed for the period to be reduced and it was finally agreed that if India had not achieved freedom under dominion status by December 31, 1929, Gandhi would throw in his lot with those demanding independence. The differences between Motilal and Jawaharlal were upsetting, but Motilal consoled himself, as he confided in his nephew B. K. Nehru, "Jawahar would not be my son if he did not stick to his guns."[23]

Labor came to power in Britain in June 1929 and the new Secretary of State for India, William Wedgwood Benn, promoted the idea of a round table conference to discuss a dominion status constitution for India. This was rejected as inadequate at a meeting with the Viceroy attended by Gandhi, Motilal, M. A. Jinnah and other Indian leaders late in 1929. The Viceroy, Lord Irwin (better known to history as the appeasement Foreign Secretary Lord Halifax), accommodated—too late—the changed mood in London. Shaken by an assassination attempt on the day of the meeting, he still could not bridge the gap of imagination to understand what Gandhi and Motilal were plainly saying, and his advisers could point out that already Jinnah was using different language for different ends. Whether this was one of the great lost opportunities of Indian history, or another gesture of goodwill which would have turned out to be illusory, the British impetus for reform was soon lost as the minority Labor government became enmeshed in an economic crisis.

Gandhi had put Jawaharlal's name forward for the presidency of the 1929 Congress at Lahore, a vitally important occasion. Jawaharlal was somewhat embarrassed and tried to refuse the honor, but Motilal was overjoyed, quoting the Persian adage, "What the father is unable to accomplish, the son achieves." Indira, now aged twelve, was present to see the transfer of power from father to son. There were vast, cheering crowds for Jawaharlal's ride through Lahore on a white charger, with people casting flower petals on him from balconies and rooftops. Pran Chopra, a young Congress supporter who was later a distinguished journalist, said, "When Nehru came to Lahore he was already in the eyes of many of us a very romantic figure. He was handsome, he was dedicated. He inspired a kind of response which I don't think anyone other than Gandhi has inspired among the people."[24] Others remarked grudgingly that the nationalist movement was now being run by a triumvirate of father, son and holy ghost.

The fundamental decision at the tense Lahore Congress was that henceforth Swaraj should mean "complete independence," whatever it had meant in the past. The bid for dominion status had lapsed. Motilal and Indira were with Jawaharlal at midnight on the eve of 1930 when the flag of independence was unfurled amid scenes of wild enthusiasm, with Jawaharlal dancing, rather stiffly, round the flagpole. Jawaharlal organized Independence Day for January 26, when everyone was called upon to take the independence pledge drafted by himself and Gandhi. Not everyone, however, was impressed by the independence movement. G. D. Khosla, later a judge but at this time a member of the Indian Civil Service, said, "The Congress did not really have that much power, that's what we felt. The British were ruling the country and had a complete hold, and there seemed to me at that time no prospect at all of India becoming independent."[25] Most Congress leaders, too, felt independence would not come in their lifetime.

Motilal renamed his house Swaraj Bhavan (Abode of Freedom) and donated it to the nation in April 1930. The family moved to another house he had built in its grounds: it was to be smaller and simpler, but gradually came to be as well appointed as the old house. It was given the old name of Anand Bhavan. In those vital years of 1929 to 1931 the Nehrus' homes, always central to the life of the family, began to assume a similar role in the life of the nation. Crowds of devotees would gather outside anxious to catch a glimpse of Motilal or Jawaharlal Nehru. "The verandas of the house were full of these visitors of ours," wrote Jawaharlal, "each door and window had a collection of prying eyes. It was impossible to walk or talk or feed or, indeed, do anything. This was not only embarrassing, it was annoying and irritating. Yet there they were, these people looking up with shining eyes full of affection, with generations of poverty and suffering behind them, still pouring out their gratitude and love and asking for little in return, except for fellow feeling and sympathy."[26]

Gandhi's plan for the future was as simple as it was spectacular: he would oppose the salt tax and challenge the British government salt monopoly by making his own salt. The salt tax, though slight, was punitive in a hot climate, and particularly hit those doing arduous outdoor work—the poor. The argument was one both the government and the simplest peasant could understand. It was also an easy tax to disobey, so Gandhi made his challenge as dramatic and public as possible: he announced that he and his followers were going to march 200 miles across India until they reached the sea at Dandi, where they would break the salt laws by making salt from sea water. Jawaharlal went some distance with Gandhi and had never admired him more.

Once Gandhi had broken the salt laws, Jawaharlal's job was to ensure the activity was duplicated all over India. Congress organizations were detailed to make and sell salt (despite the dubious quality of salt manufactured by untrained hands) and to court arrest. If the entire Congress committee in an area were arrested, the future conduct of the campaign could be conducted by a nominated individual or "dictator." The government fell into the trap and made mass arrests, which stimulated further demonstrations and further arrests—perhaps 100,000 during the whole campaign.

Jawaharlal wrote about Kamala at this time as if he were making an emotional voyage of discovery: "She wanted to play her own part in the national struggle and not be merely a hanger-on and a shadow of her husband. She wanted to justify herself to her own self as well as to the world. Nothing in the world could have pleased me more than this, but I was far too busy to see beneath the surface, and I was blind to what she looked for and so ardently desired . . . But she did not say this to me in so many words, and it was only gradually that I read the message in her eyes . . . In the early months of 1930 I sensed her desire and we worked together and I found in this experience a new delight. We lived together for a while on the edge of life, as it were, for the clouds were gathering and a national upheaval was coming."[27]

The absurdity of the laws led to absurd acts of disobedience: making salt from earth brought into Allahabad at some cost specifically for this illegal purpose and selling the salt from stalls in the street. Eventually, on April 14, 1930, Jawaharlal was arrested and charged with the crime of filtering saline earth and water through a tin and wrapping the finished salt in paper. He was tried on the same day as his arrest and sentenced to six months under the Salt Acts. Motilal, as had been previously agreed, took over as president of Congress, until he too was arrested. He was now unwell, with fibrosis of the lungs and perhaps the beginnings of the tumor that would kill him, and was nursed in jail by his son, with whom he shared a cell.

The imprisonment of so many men, and the widespread nature of the protests, stimulated women to come to the fore. Swarup Rani and her daughters went on picket duty under the hot summer sun, urging a boycott of foreign cloth shops. Krishna and Kamala had become Congress volunteers, helping to steward the large crowds involved in demonstrations, and donned male clothes for the purpose. Jawaharlal was moved by the women's sacrifice but particularly by Kamala's approach to the crisis. He wrote of how she threw herself into the movement "with an energy and determination which amazed me, who thought I had known her so well for so many years. She forgot her ill health and rushed about the whole day in the sun, and showed remarkable powers of organization."[28] Enormous processions of women took place, and women who were otherwise unused to public activity took the lead and became Congress "dictators." Kamala became president of the Allahabad District Congress.

The effect on family life was devastating. On one famous occasion Indira was obliged to tell a visitor to the house, "I'm sorry but my grandfather, father and mummy are all in prison."[29] Indira was now attending St. Mary's Convent School, her father having apparently relaxed his ban. She excelled at English and history, and was proficient at French, which she had learned in Switzerland. At twelve years of age she made her contribution to the highly charged climate by rallying the children of the neighborhood to a meeting in the garden of Anand Bhavan. She addressed the several hundred who turned up like a seasoned orator, calling on them to serve the motherland whatever the dangers, and organized what she called a *vanar sena* (monkey army), whose members helped Congress by running messages, putting up posters, making flags, doing simple office tasks and running messages past unsuspecting policemen. She was often dressed in boy's clothing and her father would sometimes call her "Indu-boy." The poet and Congress leader Sarojini Naidu described the developing girl as like "Atalanta, fleet of foot with sunrise in her eyes."[30] Her monkey army grew to several thousand children.

A project Jawaharlal now resumed, and continued through imprisonment in future years, was a history of the world from prehistory to the present, which he intended for Indira's edification. He had started this in 1927 and published the result as *Letters from a Father to His Daughter* in 1929, the publication again underlining the way the family, their relationships, literally their world view, was being made public property. The next book of letters from this project, *Glimpses of World History*, running to over 1000 pages, was published in 1934, still containing what Jawaharlal called "many intimate touches . . . which were meant for my daughter alone."[31] The first letter in this series, written for Indira's thirteenth birthday, reads, "What present can I send you from Naini Prison? My presents cannot be very material or solid. They can only be of the air and of the mind and spirit, such as a good fairy might have bestowed on you—things that even the high

walls of a prison cannot stop." He gave advice on how she should conduct herself in this great movement. "Never do anything in secret or
anything that you would wish to hide. For the desire to hide anything
means that you are afraid, and fear is a bad thing and unworthy of you.
Be brave and all the rest follows. If you are brave you will not fear and
will not do anything of which you are ashamed."[32] What Indira
thought of letters to her being published is unrecorded, but she doubtless found it unremarkable—the Nehrus were unused to privacy.

The Viceroy tried to see a way through the political morass and
asked if Gandhi wanted to negotiate. He said he could do so only after
discussions with his colleagues, so Motilal, Jawaharlal and other leaders were transported by train from their jail to Gandhi's home in
Poona. After two days of discussions, they finally agreed that the gap
between their position and the government's was unbridgeable. The
Secretary of State, William Wedgwood Benn, confessed himself
"depressed" by Jawaharlal's "apparent pride" in what the nationalists
had achieved and his faith in non-violence: "it did not show the spirit
of a beaten man."[33] Motilal was released on grounds of ill health after
just over two months in Naini Jail. He was coughing up blood: clearly
his days were numbered.

When Jawaharlal's term was up and he was freed in October, he
and Kamala went to Mussoorie and for three days the Nehru family
spent their last, happy time together. Motilal seemed a little better in
health, Indira was present, as were Vijaya's three daughters, the
youngest of which now aged three or four. Jawaharlal would be marching round the house with them in a stately procession, bearing the
national flag and singing a nationalist song. The children would later
remember how he would announce, "Now we will stand on our
heads," and one by one he would tip them upside down. He once took
out the book of his Harrow school songs and they all sang the songs,
"Jerry, You Duffer and Dunce," and "When Grandpapa's Grandpapa
Was in the Lower Lower First."[34]

Jawaharlal immediately resumed the Congress presidency, courting
re-arrest as it was now a banned organization, and again began agitating for the manufacture of salt, the boycott of British goods and for
peasants to stop paying rents. After ten days out of prison, he was re-
arrested and sent back to Naini Jail, which he jokingly called his "second home," this time for two years, plus five months for non-payment

of fines. Jawaharlal's niece Chandralekha remembered, "Departures for jail were always very exciting in the sense that word usually got around and there were about a hundred people in the garden waiting with garlands and shouting slogans so it was always an occasion of excitement. You were brought up to feel that going to jail was something wonderful. We were doing it for a goal, and you had to go with a glad heart as the ones in our family did, that we saw going off: uncle, father, mother, grandmother, everybody . . . We didn't consider ourselves in an abnormal situation. We felt that we were in a normal situation, that we were privileged to be in that situation."[35]

Motilal was distressed when Kamala came to tell him of his son's re-arrest but he pulled himself together and banged a table in front of him, saying that he had made up his mind to be an invalid no longer. He was going to be well and do a man's work. For some days his resolve proved miraculous and he managed to work with his old energy at his last, great public act. Jawaharlal had been convicted for making a speech, so Motilal designated his son's forty-first birthday in November 1930 as "Jawahar Day" and distributed copies of the speech all over India. On the appointed day, crowds assembled all over the country and the illegal parts of the speech were read out. Kamala gave the whole speech in Allahabad to a huge meeting, including her mother-in-law and sisters-in-law, which must have been a vindication of her sterling qualities. There were police *lathi* charges in many areas against these demonstrations, and 5000 were arrested. Motilal had succeeded in rendering the interests of the nation identical to those of his family.

Despite Motilal's illness, thousands assembled at the gates of Anand Bhavan "to have *darshan* [sight] of their revered leader." Motilal would go through with these public appearances but would say to his aides, "Oh, here I am present as if at a fancy dress competition."[36]

With Motilal's health worsening, Krishna determined to look after her father and tried to keep out of politics. She did get arrested but was released after twelve hours in detention when a friend paid her fine, much to Motilal's annoyance, as it was against policy to concede that the British had any right to fine protesters. Kamala was arrested on January 1, 1931, which delighted her for she too was now suffering for freedom. She gave a bold statement to the court: "I am happy beyond measure and proud to follow in the footsteps of my husband," which amused Jawaharlal no end as he had come to know Kamala as "a champion of woman's rights over the tyranny of man"; she was going her own way and certainly not following him. Kamala would frequently address groups of women, speaking of "women's struggle for freedom against man-made laws" and urging women not to be too submissive to their menfolk.[37]

The first round table conference, with no Congress delegates, had been proceeding in London without result. By the end it was recognized that Congress involvement was essential for progress, so the government sent a covert message to India, which led to Gandhi, Jawaharlal and other Congress leaders, plus Vijaya's husband Ranjit Pandit, and Kamala, being freed unconditionally on January 26, 1931. The family assembled around Motilal, whose condition had deteriorated seriously. He faced death with the same robust self-confidence with which he had faced life. He told his family not to pray for him after his death—if he could not get to heaven by his own good deeds he was not interested in getting a seat there on the recommendation of others. When Gandhi visited, he asked the Mahatma for a drink. Gandhi said Motilal should be reciting the *Gita* and trying to think of spiritual things. Motilal said, "I leave unworldly things to you and my wife. While I'm still on earth, I will be earthy."[38] He insisted on meeting Congress leaders, even though he was too ill to participate in discussions. He did, however, manage humorous asides while propped up in his chair. Soon the constriction in his throat rendered conversation too painful and he wrote on slips of paper. He died in the early hours of February 6, 1931 with Swarup Rani and Jawaharlal at his bedside, his son holding Motilal's head in his lap.

Jawaharlal, looking ten years older overnight, stood by the body as Motilal lay in state with the national flag draped around him, while thousands of people from near and far, high and low came to pay their respects. Gandhi and Swarup Rani sat silently by the body. There was a huge funeral procession from Anand Bhavan and a constant shower of flowers and petals around the cortège as it made its way towards the banks of the Ganges, where Motilal's remains were cremated, Jawaharlal lighting the pyre of sandalwood with a flaming torch.

Political events now began to move rapidly, just at the time when Jawaharlal was least emotionally equipped to deal with them. The Viceroy, Lord Irwin, was finally ready to speak to Gandhi, if not to

Congress as a whole, later that February. Gandhi, plus the Congress Working Committee including Jawaharlal, went to Delhi where Gandhi had almost daily meetings with the Viceroy, then returned to consult with his committee. Jawaharlal, however, took little part in the proceedings. Gandhi had a touching faith in the ability of two individuals to get together, realize the good in each other and come to an agreement. He did not seem to appreciate that he was not dealing with an individual, good or bad, but with an imperial power structure in which Lord Irwin held nothing but a four-year appointment. The mere fact of negotiation was a significant achievement, but, as Jawaharlal had written to Motilal some months before, "The British Government are past masters in the art of political chicanery and fraud, and we are babes at their game."[39]

Gandhi accepted what came to be called the Gandhi-Irwin truce, in which he agreed that civil disobedience would be called off in return for the right of those who lived near the coast to make salt, but not to sell it; the release of civil disobedience prisoners but not all other political prisoners; and the right of peaceful picketing. Other demands, relating to an investigation into police brutality and the payment of extortionate rates of tax by peasants, were not conceded. Gandhi was to represent Congress at the following year's round table conference, which would be based on a program which disconcerted Jawaharlal considerably when he saw it for the first time. It fell far short of independence or even dominion status, reserving a host of rights to Britain even before the conference started. Jawaharlal was physically and emotionally exhausted and the other members of the Working Committee were not in much better shape. The country was waiting for a settlement and Gandhi had already agreed it. What could they do?

Jawaharlal wept bitterly and told Gandhi such a settlement would never have been reached had his father been alive and at his full power. Gandhi was very offended, doubtless realizing the truth of the statement. "Was it for this that our people had behaved so gallantly for a year? Were all our brave words and deeds to end in this?" wrote Jawaharlal. "So I lay and pondered on that March night, and in my heart there was a great emptiness as of something precious gone, almost beyond recall." Gandhi had let him down again, and with Motilal dead, there was no one left to turn to.

# FIVE

# DEATH, WAR AND IMPRISONMENT

India put a good face on the pact, releasing civil disobedience prisoners who, to the irritation of the British, returned triumphantly to villages decorated with bunting. Breaches of the Gandhi-Irwin pact began almost immediately it was agreed, and their severity worsened throughout the year, though not before Gandhi persuaded Jawaharlal to move a resolution supporting settlement at the Karachi Congress. At the same meeting, as if to reciprocate, Gandhi approved Jawaharlal's social charter—Fundamental Rights and Economic and Social Changes—which, for the first time, gave Congress policies a distinctly socialist character.

Jawaharlal was exhausted, and on the advice of his doctor traveled to Ceylon for a long vacation with Kamala and Indira, but the hospitality lavished on such celebrated guests as themselves left little room for privacy. On his return Jawaharlal busied himself with supporting the peasants against their landlords in renewed agrarian agitation. Back at home Anand Bhavan was silent without Motilal. As Indira said, "His resounding voice no longer echoed in the rooms or along the verandas."[1]

By the time the round table conference was held in London, the Labor government which had sponsored it was no longer in power, and Gandhi came away with nothing. Jawaharlal was arrested in December 1931 for his involvement with the peasants, and returned to Naini Central Prison, eventually to suffer a two-year sentence. Early in January 1932, soon after returning from the London conference, Gandhi was also arrested, along with a host of other Congress leaders. Their renewed civil disobedience provoked a far more draconian response from the government than had been the case the previous year. Swaraj Bhavan was seized and all the hospital equipment taken, along with cars belonging to Jawaharlal and Ranjit Pandit. The hospital doctor continued treating outpatients under a large tree in nearby Bharadwaj Park. The government stopped short of seizing Anand Bhavan, perhaps fearing that this would stimulate rather than quell civil disobedience, and they were doubtless right. Jawaharlal wrote that he was "attracted to the idea of losing the house. I felt that this would bring me nearer to the peasantry, who were being dispossessed, and would hearten them."[2] The thought of national flags being hauled down caused him more pain.

Congress and all its organizations were declared unlawful and some 80,000 Congress workers were arrested, including Vijaya and Krishna Nehru, who was secretary of the Congress Youth League. Vijaya's husband Ranjit Pandit and Jawaharlal's cousin Mohanlal were also arrested and shared a cell block with Jawaharlal. The last of the Nehru women were now plunged into the conflict. Swarup Rani was in a procession which was charged by police, and the elderly woman was thrown to the ground and repeatedly hit on the head. A rumor spread in Allahabad that she had been killed and an anti-police riot broke out, during which some protesters were killed. Jawaharlal, listening to the rumors in his cell, had never felt more impotent: ". . . the thought of my frail old mother lying bleeding on the dusty road obsessed me."[3] Swarup Rani slowly recovered, proud that she had shared suffering with the best of them: ". . . had it been a gun I would have bared my chest," she wrote defiantly to her son.[4]

These years in prison were among Jawaharlal's worst. His father's death weighed heavily upon him, as did the failure of civil disobedience and the virtual destruction of Congress as an effective organization. Civil disobedience was eventually called off by Gandhi as a dead letter in 1934, to Jawaharlal's utter misery. Now his general health began to suffer and his teeth troubled him, but throughout all adversities his relationship with Kamala seemed to strengthen and deepen; it was as if, for the first time, they were falling in love. He wrote, "We grew ever nearer to each other. Our rare meetings became precious, and we looked forward to them and counted the days that intervened. We could not get tired of each other or stale, for there was always a freshness and novelty about our meetings and brief periods together. Each of us was continually making fresh discoveries in the other, though sometimes perhaps the new discoveries were not to our liking. Even our grown-up disagreements had something boyish and girlish about them."[5] He yearned to see her: "I am much too fond of her!" he wrote in his prison diary.[6]

Nevertheless, when a jailer insulted Swarup Rani and Kamala at an interview with Ranjit Pandit, Jawaharlal forbade them to come again, saying he was not prepared to take the slightest risk of their being further insulted. He went without their visits for eight months, but Gandhi persuaded him to relent.

When they had completed their terms of imprisonment, the two sisters, Vijaya and Krishna, joined their mother in a house at Mussoorie, supposed to be the "gayest hill station in northern India," full of nightclubs and enlivened by fabulous parties held by the maharajas. As agitators against the British, the Nehrus were not invited to those parties, and people who had been friends or clients of Motilal avoided them. "We were mere spectators of the life and doings of others," remarked Krishna, who was struck by the contrast between the life Jawaharlal lived in prison and that of the people surrounding them.[7]

Indira, inured through repeated experience, probably found this round of imprisonments easier to take than did Vijaya's three little girls, the eldest of whom, Chandralekha, was only eight. Vijaya and Ranjit showed some imagination in impressing on the children that a spell in prison was something to be proud of. One afternoon, while the children were eating a rich, dark chocolate cake, the police came to arrest their father, but Vijaya explained it was nothing to worry about because he wanted to go. So the children kissed him goodbye and watched him leave. Nayantara said, "We ate our chocolate cake and, in our infant minds, prison became in some mysterious way associated with chocolate cake." They longed to be old enough to go to prison too.[8]

For Indira there were no such happy associations: her childhood was one of loneliness because of her father's absence and her mother's illness. When she overheard her aunt Vijaya describing her as "ugly and stupid," the thirteen-year-old was cut to the soul, so much so that more than fifty years later Indira was still repeating the words with bitterness.[9] One effect of her childhood isolation was to make her retreat even further into her own shell: it appeared that she wanted to avoid too much affection and was fearful that the object of her love would be withdrawn. Pupul Jayakar, a family friend the same age as Indira, described her withdrawn behavior: "She merged into the background, became invisible, had to be drawn out."[10] One of her school friends recalled how she would come upon Indira crying behind a tree or in some other secluded place, unable to share her grief with another.[11] Jawaharlal complained about Indira's coldness towards him, saying she wrote only once in three or four months and the letters seemed to have been written out of a mere sense of duty. "Indu does not write to me and I get very angry," he wrote in his diary. "I know that Indu is fond of me and of Kamala. Yet she ignores us and others completely. Why is this so?" he lamented to Vijaya.[12]

Indira's unsettled education had continued with three years (her longest period of continuous schooling) at the Pupils' Own School at Poona, where she was occasionally able to visit Mahatma Gandhi in Yeravada Jail. She looked after him during his fast to protest against a government proposal for separate electorates for untouchables: he felt the Hindus themselves should eradicate the concept of untouchability, rather than have government recognize it constitutionally. Jawaharlal was irritated at Gandhi's "religious and sentimental approach"[13] to a political question, but Indira joined the campaign in a practical way, persuading her school to help out a local untouchable colony, and herself taking responsibility for an untouchable child adopted by the school.

When Jawaharlal was released, he went to see Indira and she was then sent to Shantiniketan, an institution presided over by the poet Rabindranath Tagore. On her way to school after a visit home she poured out her anger to Jawaharlal for failing to understand why she wanted a relative of her own choosing to live in the house and look after her mother: "Do you know anything about what happens at home when you are absent? Do you know that when Mummie was in a very bad condition the house was full of people, but not one of them even went to see her or sit a while with her, that when she was in agony there was no one to help her?"[14]

Indira wrote of herself that as a child she had wanted to be a boy, "but at sixteen the delight of being a woman began to unfold itself and almost overnight, the long-legged tomboy in frocks changed into a sari-clad young lady."[15] She was still thin, however, remaining at just seventy-five pounds for a long time. This prompted the well-meaning to encourage her to eat, but she simply became irritated as, like her father, she had little interest in food.

Indira discovered the beauty of nature, of dance and the visual arts during her months at Shantiniketan, and also had her first brush with romance, when she was desired by an older man, a German called

Frank Oberdorf, who taught her French. They remained friends after she left the school and corresponded for years, but she was irritated by his amorous intentions. When he said she was beautiful, she had thought he was making fun of her. "I was so sure that I had nothing in me to be admired," she confided to Pupul Jayakar many years later.[16]

Kamala's illness again interrupted her daughter's education when she was admitted to a sanatorium in the Himalayan foothills in October 1934 and Indira accompanied her. By this time, however, Jawaharlal was back in prison for another two years for making seditious speeches, his seventh term in jail after only six months of freedom. He had been allowed out for twelve days on compassionate grounds to see Kamala, and would have been released permanently if he had been prepared to eschew politics, but Kamala explicitly forbade him to give any such assurance to the government.

Kamala became increasingly spiritual during her last illness, reading the *Gita*, meditating on Lord Krishna and rejecting all jewelry and decoration. "For me it is criminal," she said, "to walk on the streets exhibiting my jewelry while the people of my country do not have enough food to satisfy their hunger."[17]

At the beginning of 1935 Jawaharlal was allowed to visit her for a couple of days and found her estranged from him: "Somehow things went wrong . . . I felt there was a psychological change. She seemed reserved," he wrote in his diary. Jawaharlal continued talking to her, reading some of the things he had written, reciting some favorite poems, then she said "she wanted to realize God and give her thoughts to this, and as a preparation for this our relations should undergo some change. Apparently I was not to come in the way of God." Jawaharlal was bemused, and felt this to be less a search for God than a type of hysteria. He had struggled to draw closer to her but now felt his efforts had been wholly in vain, "She was further away than ever from me and an almost unbridgeable chasm stretched out between us." He left her in the early evening; she had nothing to say to him anyway, and he wandered around outside the house in a cold, moonless landscape. "In politics I was an unhappy, lonely figure," he wrote, "and now even my home life was ending for me. Loneliness everywhere."[18]

His youngest sister was now ready to make her own life. Krishna had sought from Jawaharlal, as the male head of the household, permission to marry Raja Hutheesing, yet another English-educated lawyer, whom she had met in Bombay. Jawaharlal consulted Gandhi (he was unable to make the most straightforward decision on his own authority) and he eventually consented. They were married on October 20, 1933 at Anand Bhavan in a civil ceremony; Raja was a Jain and Krishna a Brahmin, so a religious marriage was not possible. Krishna wrote that Vijaya "had a hundred and one saris in her trousseau; I had thirteen. She had diamonds, emeralds and pearls in matched sets of necklaces, rings, bangles and earrings: I had the scraps that my mother and Kamala's kindness found for me."[19] How the fortunes of the Nehrus had changed. Fortunately for Krishna, when she went to the Hutheesings' house later that day, her in-laws loaded her with jewels, even more than her sister had. The marriage prospered in other ways too: her sons Harsha and Ajit were born in 1935 and 1936.

In 1937 Jawaharlal persuaded Raja to stop practicing law and go into politics as "no self-respecting Indian should concentrate on earning a livelihood when a struggle for freedom was being fought." Krishna opposed the change: of all the Nehrus, she seems to have gained least from the independence movement, and to have felt that, in personal terms at least, the sacrifices were not worth it. Family loyalty, however, prevented her from saying so explicitly.

Krishna's marriage in 1933 had made Swarup Rani eager to have Indira married. There had been a proposal from a stranger but Indira, with Kamala's support, managed to resist it. At the age of sixteen she received another proposal (the first of several) from Feroze Gandhi, a Parsi some five years older than Indira. He was a stocky, ruddy-faced man, the gregarious and exuberant son of an officer in the merchant navy, whose family were now shopkeepers, and therefore of a much lower class than the Nehrus. This had not prevented him, however, from becoming Kamala's constant companion.

Feroze (no relation to Mahatma Gandhi) had been a student at a government college in Allahabad when he first saw Kamala, just twelve years older than him, leading a demonstration urging students to boycott the college. Feroze and his fellow students watched the beautiful, frail woman with amused interest until she suddenly fainted, the heat and exertion overcoming her. Feroze rushed to her aid and took her back to Anand Bhavan. His life was transformed by this meeting. The next day he left college, enlisted as a Congress volunteer and became a permanent fixture at Anand Bhavan, attending to Kamala's every need, both personal and public (she was then president of the Allahabad District Congress committee). Relatives avoided tending Kamala because of the contagious nature of her illness, but Feroze showed no such concern. "He would not hesitate to do for her such unpleasant tasks as cleaning her spittoon, a chore that even Anand Bhavan sweepers performed reluctantly and with unconcealed distaste."[20] Feroze would follow as she traveled to villages around Allahabad, walking just behind Kamala and carrying her lunchbox. He also agitated for civil disobedience himself, and received a six-month sentence in Fyzabad jail, where the high-spirited young man made himself a nuisance to the prison authorities.

When Kamala went to a sanatorium in Bhowali, Feroze traveled constantly to see her and help her in whatever way he could, spending a considerable part of the year there. His family never approved of his political work and a relative proposed to remove him from India by paying for his education at the London School of Economics. Feroze readily agreed to this, as Kamala was to stay in a German sanatorium in May 1935 and Indira was to attend a school nearby. Feroze would be able to visit them frequently. Shortly before their departure, Jawaharlal let Indira know by letter that he was handing Anand Bhavan over to Vijaya and Ranjit, and her room would also be made available to them. This was utterly insensitive: all her childhood treasures would be handed over to Vijaya, whom she saw as her mother's bitter enemy. It was a blow she never forgot.

In September 1935 Jawaharlal joined his wife and daughter in Germany now, to his disgust, run by the Nazis. He made a point of shopping in Jewish-owned stores whenever possible. When Kamala moved to another sanatorium in Lausanne, Switzerland, four months later, Indira returned to her old school at Bex. It was to be the family's last time together. After a few months with his ailing wife, politics recalled Jawaharlal, as he had been elected president of Congress in his absence. Doctors, however, advised him to postpone his departure for India, as Kamala was fading fast. She died on the morning of February 28, 1936, at the age of thirty-six, with Jawaharlal and a cousin who was also a doctor beside her. Indira was in another room.

Kamala was cremated in Lausanne, "and all our bright dreams were also dead and turned to ashes,"[21] wrote Jawaharlal. He returned with the urn of ashes to India. On a stopover in Rome, Mussolini conveyed a message that he would like to see Nehru to convey his condolences. Jawaharlal, deeply mistrustful of fascism, refused. During another stopover, in Baghdad, he cabled his publishers in London and gave them the dedication to his autobiography: "To Kamala, who is no more." He immersed most of Kamala's ashes at the point where the Ganges meets the Yamuna at Allahabad, but he retained a portion of them for the rest of his life: they were always beside him. He wrote later of what his wife meant to him and of how she fitted in with the image he had of his family's relationship with India: "She became a symbol of Indian women or of woman herself. Sometimes she grew curiously mixed up with my ideas of India, that land of ours so dear to us, with all her faults and weaknesses, so elusive and so full of mystery."[22] She too had become part of the Nehru legend: not a person so much as a personification of the nation. Among pictures of gods and Indian heroes, the bazaars sold pictures of Jawaharlal and Kamala with the inscription *Adarsha jori*, "the ideal couple," rather ironically considering their less than ideal married life. Kamala's death was now woven into the living myth of the Nehrus, a myth very consciously promoted by Jawaharlal's autobiography, a book which was as much a political statement as a personal testimony.

Indira was left at school in Bex. Her emotional isolation was almost complete. "I saw her being hurt," she said of her mother, "and I was determined not to be hurt."[23] Whatever warmth she had shown in life had been directed to her mother; she hoped never again to experience the pain of loss, but sadly this awaited her with her own children and grandchildren.

Jawaharlal, now president of Congress, again submerged himself in politics, but Gandhi's influence helped create an atmosphere in which Jawaharlal's socialist ideas failed to gain widespread support. Jawaharlal was a left-wing president held in check by his right-wing party. The elimination of Congress militancy meant the government was now prepared to lift the ban on most Congress organizations and allow them to fight elections. The 1935 Government of India Act, coming into effect in 1937, had been pushed through a British parliament distracted by its own problems of unemployment and the rising threat of fascism. The Act gave Indian provinces self-rule with their own governments. There was much debate as to whether Congress should fight the elections, as this would be to cooperate with a government system they considered intrinsically oppressive. Jawaharlal was against such cooperation and threatened to resign, but in the event he went along with the Congress decision to support it, and turned powerful electioneering into one of his great assets as a leader. He went on a national campaign, traveling 50,000 miles by plane, train, car, bicycle, cart, steamer, paddleboat, canoe, horse, elephant, camel and on foot. On one occasion the crowd to see him was so great that he had to walk on their shoulders to reach the front. He is said to have addressed 10 million people and been seen by many more.

Congress won almost half the seats in that election; it had a clear majority in six of the eleven provinces and was the largest single party in three others. Even having won, Jawaharlal was reluctant to see Congress accept office, but the weight of opinion was against him, and Congress ministries were formed in six provinces. Among the new ministers was his sister Vijaya, Health Minister of the United Provinces, and the first woman in India to hold such a senior public appointment. Jawaharlal became more disgruntled as Congress leaders settled into their posts. He wrote to Gandhi in disgust, ". . . we are losing the high position that we have built up, with so much labor, in the hearts of the people. We are sinking to the level of ordinary politicians."[24]

Still, this period of the "Congress Raj" was known as a time of reform and social progress, although there was a widening split between Muslims and Hindus, and bloody rioting in many cities, including Allahabad. Jawaharlal had tried to remain on good terms with M. A. Jinnah, who had resumed leadership of the Muslim League in 1936, but their relationship descended to mutual personal attacks in the press. The main source of conflict was that the Muslim League claimed to be committed to all the same ideals of freedom as Congress, but represented only Muslims. Congress represented all Indians, including Muslims, though Gandhi certainly gave the party an overtly Hindu image. Jawaharlal rejected Jinnah's request after the election for power sharing with the Muslim League, an important moment on the road to partition, but he also made specific efforts to attract Muslims to Congress.

Jawaharlal came to the end of his period as president and wrote an anonymous article for the *Modern Review* on the dangers of giving

Jawaharlal Nehru too much power: "Let us not spoil Jawaharlal by too much adulation and praise. His conceit is already formidable. It must be checked. We want no Caesars!"[25] Only Indira knew that he was the author. Jawaharlal had had an almost unprecedented second period of presidency, covering 1936 and 1937. Subhas Chandra Bose, his rival on the radical side of the party, followed him in 1938. Bose was a former Indian Civil Service officer who had resigned to devote himself to nationalist politics, though in the 1930s he became increasingly attracted to European fascism as a model for India. This inevitably distanced him from Jawaharlal and others of a more left-wing persuasion, and from those who followed Gandhi along the path of non-violence. When Bose ran for a second term as Congress president, Gandhi refused to back him. Although Bose won the vote, he found it impossible to run Congress without Gandhi's support, so he resigned and founded a radical group within the party called Forward Bloc. From this point onwards, Bose drifted further and further away from Congress high command, never to return.

Jawaharlal at this time, according to his own testimony, was "partly bald and my hair was gray, lines and furrows crossed my face and dark shadows surrounded my eyes."[26] A more sympathetic observer, a British official, wrote that he "looked a thorough gentleman and an impressive figure. He is about the only good-looking Indian I have seen in a Congress cap and appears sturdy and vigorous . . . It is easy for a European to follow his Hindustani, partly because he uses simple words and phrases, and partly because he talks it with what I can only describe as an English accent."[27] One thing that did not change about Jawaharlal was his notoriously short temper. It became worse after Kamala's death but his flare-ups were brief and good feeling quickly returned.

Swarup Rani suffered a stroke and died in January 1938. After the funeral, her elder sister Bibima, who had lived with her at Anand Bhavan, lay on the floor wrapped in her shawl. When Jawaharlal went to wake her, he found her dead: she had simply died of grief.

Now loneliness haunted Jawaharlal. His wife's death, his mother's death and Indira's absence in Europe took away all the closest members of his family. His sisters were preoccupied with their own families. He wrote, "I would return to my home from my wanderings almost unwillingly, and sit in that deserted house all by myself, trying even to avoid interviews there." He wrote pathetically to Indira, ". . . at night, and sometimes in the daytime too, I go to your room and have a look round and say goodnight to it."[28] His loneliness was obvious to everyone. His niece Nayantara, Vijaya's daughter, wrote how she would sometimes run ahead of him and switch on the light so he should not have to walk alone into a dark, empty room. Even in political work he felt isolated, as though he did not fit in with his closest colleagues. "I became a solitary figure in public life," he wrote, "though vast crowds came to hear me and enthusiasm surrounded me."[29] This was not mere self-pity: others had long commented on Jawaharlal's isolation, including Gandhi, who called Jawaharlal "one of the loneliest young men of my acquaintance in India."[30] Nirad Chaudhuri, meeting him in the 1930s, was always struck by the "ineradicable sadness in all his expression."[31]

While he never lost his sense of isolation and being out of place, Jawaharlal did find comfort in his relationships with women. Sarvepalli Gopal, a biographer who later worked for him, wrote that women, "drawn by his charm or driven by snobbery, made claims on him and, especially after Kamala's death, sought to thrust themselves into his life; and he did not always firmly resist their gross ardors."[32] One woman who was close to him, and almost certainly a lover, was Padmaja Naidu, eleven years younger than Jawaharlal, daughter of the veteran nationalist Sarojini Naidu. Padmaja had long had an affectionate relationship with Jawaharlal and spent a great deal of time at Anand Bhavan in the 1930s.

In April 1938 Jawaharlal left India for Europe, saying he wanted to "freshen up his tired and puzzled mind."[33] He was now a truly international figure, thanks to the positive reception his autobiography had received, despite its prolixity. He was to visit England, France, Germany, Czechoslovakia, Switzerland and Republican Spain, witnessing with foreboding the slide towards war in Europe. He traveled with Vijaya and, for part of the journey, with Indira, who had been studying for Oxford entrance examinations at Badminton School in Bristol. He went to Spain with Krishna Menon, the waspish leader of the London-based India League, which sought to influence British opinion on Indian issues. Menon was perhaps the only man who could be considered a close friend of Jawaharlal, someone with whom he could laugh and confide. Jawaharlal addressed Republican meetings and witnessed bombs falling nightly. He wrote, ". . . there, in the midst of want and destruction and ever-impending disaster, I felt more at peace with myself than anywhere else in Europe. There was light there, the light of courage and determination and of doing something worthwhile."[34]

In England Jawaharlal, along with Indira and Krishna Menon, spent a weekend at Filkins, the country house of the Labor politician Stafford Cripps. There he also met Clement Attlee, Aneurin Bevan and other members of the Labor leadership, who reassured him that a Labor government would support independence for India.

In London, Jawaharlal spoke at a Spanish Civil War meeting with the young socialist Michael Foot, who recalled, ". . . there were wonderful speakers at that platform, but none to beat him. He was absolutely quiet about what his case was, but it was overwhelming in strength. He was furiously anti-fascist on Spain, Germany, Italy . . . he was a natural democrat."[35]

Indira and Feroze, like all nationalist students in England, saw a good deal of Krishna Menon at the India League offices. Indira also raised funds for the Spanish Aid Committee and the China Aid Committee, and met such socialist luminaries as Fenner Brockway and Harold Laski, but she was shy and does not appear to have impressed them unduly. Although Feroze had been funded by his aunt to study at the LSE, he attended for only seven months, until April 1938. As late as 1939, however, his aunt was writing to the LSE authorities about him. Doubtless he felt that Europe in the 1930s offered more immediately exciting things to do than go to college. Feroze was passionately anti-fascist and was treasurer of an action committee to raise funds for the International Brigade, which he had applied unsuccessfully to join. (The British government had retained his passport, presumably to keep a check on potentially subversive Indian nationalists.) Indira also helped to raise funds for the Spanish Republican cause, so she and Feroze spent much time in each other's company. He would buy her flowers, take her to the theater and to restaurants, but to observers their relationship seemed friendly rather than romantic. They would have been surprised to know that in 1937, the year following Kamala's death, Indira had accepted one of Feroze's many proposals of marriage on the steps of Sacré-Coeur in Paris. It may have been discussed with Jawaharlal, but was not announced for another four years, so the engagement may have been a private rather than official understanding between the couple. Indira later wrote of him, ". . . we quarreled over every conceivable subject, but the strong bond of affection never weakened." His loyalty was a tremendously important factor for her: ". . . when my mother died and at all times of stress and difficulty, he was by my side even if he had to travel across continents to get there."[36] Perhaps her consent to marry him was a reward for his loyalty; people have married for worse reasons. Asked how he had managed to ensnare Indira, Feroze replied, "In life, if you try for anything long enough, you get it."[37] Her aunt Krishna made a virtue of Indira's lack of apparent affection in her biography of her niece, writing that "Indira, like a true Nehru, does not show her feelings."[38]

Indira went on to Somerville College, Oxford, and loved the town. She was remembered as being shy and aloof, "very unhappy, very lonely, intensely worried about her father and her country and thoroughly uncertain about the future,"[39] according to Iris Murdoch, the novelist who was at school and college with her. She nonetheless noted that Indira had a certain sense of "destiny" about her. She read modern history, though she was not very academic and twice failed the obligatory Latin examination. It may have been for this reason that she left Oxford, or because of her generally poor health at this time: she had fallen ill with pleurisy and had been to Switzerland for treatment. Or it may have been a wish to be with her father. Whatever the reason, she returned to India early in 1941, despite the dangers of traveling by sea when so many ships were being sunk by submarines. As Jawaharlal wrote in typical Nehru vein, "There are all manner of risks and dangers of course, but it is better to face them than to feel isolated and miserable."[40]

Feroze returned to India with Indira. When the ship docked at Durban, South Africa, the Indian community heard that the great Jawaharlal Nehru's daughter was in town and invited her to a public reception. She was unwilling to go, but after she had seen the conditions in which black South Africans lived, she addressed a meeting where she scourged the Indians for their failure to oppose the racial segregation policy, for their servility before Europeans, and for their refusal to find common cause with the Africans. This was a telling incident, for only a short time before she had sworn never to speak in public again; this was after an India-China League meeting in London where she had

97

been unprepared when Krishna Menon asked her to speak, and been much embarrassed in front of the audience. In South Africa, however, her anger at the poverty and injustice she had seen made her overcome her disinclination to speak in public, and she stood unafraid before an increasingly hostile meeting. It was an early sign of Indira's forceful character.

When Indira returned to Anand Bhavan, she found that family expenses—Jawaharlal's traveling, Kamala's medical bills and her own education—had placed great strains on Nehru family resources. Contemporary accounts record Jawaharlal's parsimony in small matters, such as walking long distances rather than taking a taxi. He had fought with Kamala to sell her few jewels, but she was reluctant to do so because they were the only legacy she could pass on to her daughter. This seems to have been resolved with the sale of the jewels but with some of the resulting money going into a trust fund for Indira, which paid for her education abroad. Jawaharlal's writing, particularly the great success of his autobiography, was another source of income, but the affluence of former times was past.

Jawaharlal was in prison again by the time Indira returned, as a result of the crisis caused by the Viceroy's committing India to the British war effort in 1939 without consulting Indian leaders. The constitution had been rapidly amended and all power was concentrated in the hands of the Viceroy. In response, the Congress Party withdrew its members from ministries. The Congress position was that they wanted nothing to do with a war being fought to defend the Empire: they would, however, back a war being fought for democracy, not least democracy in India. Indians should not fight for liberties abroad which they did not enjoy at home. When Congress failed to receive the assurance that independence would be granted, a largely symbolic program of mass civil disobedience was launched. Notice of intent was given to the local magistrate, and Jawaharlal was arrested a week before his scheduled act of civil disobedience: he planned to address a meeting advising people not to cooperate with the war effort. On October 31, 1940 he began his eighth term of imprisonment. Vijaya and Ranjit were also arrested before they had performed their act of civil disobedience.

During this time it became increasingly clear that there was to be war with Japan, and the British authorities hoped that if India herself were threatened, nationalists would begin to see the war in a different light. Jawaharlal was released on December 4, 1941, followed by all the other civil disobedience prisoners. The Japanese attacked Pearl Harbor on December 7, then made a lightning sweep through Southeast Asia towards India's borders. Europe and Asia were now both faced with aggressive conquest by different imperialists. India was threatened with conquest by Japan, which, if Manchuria's experience were anything to go by, would be infinitely more brutal than rule by Britain. An early sign that nationalists would not support the war effort came when Subhas Chandra Bose escaped from India and made his way to Japan to organize the "Indian National Army" against the British.

Jawaharlal, meanwhile, was involved in family affairs, for on July 8, Indira had visited him in prison and asked for permission to marry Feroze. Jawaharlal later wrote to say that her question "rather surprised me in the manner it was put and the impatience that lay behind it." But in the same letter he also wrote, "If you want to marry Feroze, well go ahead and do it. No one will stop you."[41]

Jawaharlal's relationship with Feroze was complicated. He had tolerated the young man's presence in his house, no doubt grateful for his support of Kamala. He had a father's suspicion of his only daughter's first suitor, and he had little in common with the ebullient Parsi. Jawaharlal also felt Feroze's background and upbringing were too different from those of the Nehrus. It was not religion that divided them so much as class: Feroze's family were comparatively poor. Jawaharlal also felt Indira's time abroad meant she had met too few Indian young men to make a reasoned decision.

Indira discussed her father's opposition with Krishna, arguing, "I have known Feroze for a number of years and know him well. I have met many other Indian young men abroad, and I do not see why I should go out of my way to meet some more now. Besides, I wish to marry Feroze."[42] Her words had the merit of logic, if not romance. When news of their engagement leaked out, however, there was a storm among both orthodox Hindus and Parsis. "The whole nation seemed to be against my marriage," Indira said.[43] Once again, the ups and downs of Nehru family life were seen as turning points in the history of the nation. Public opposition to his daughter's marriage spurred the protective instinct in Jawaharlal: he made a public statement supporting Feroze, but also declared, ". . . on whomsoever my daughter's choice might have fallen, I would have accepted it or been false to the principles I have held."[44]

One cannot help thinking that it was Kamala whom Feroze loved, and that Indira was a substitute. What *did* he mean to her? She never had a great interest in young men and it may just be that he was available, well known to her and willing. She was twenty-four, which was not young for an Indian bride; she had had pleurisy, which it was feared presaged tuberculosis, and this may have given her an incentive to secure the future of the Nehru dynasty quickly. She certainly wanted children, as she told Vijaya when her aunt impertinently asked why Indira wanted to marry. It may have been another source of conflict between them that Vijaya resented Indira's being permitted to marry a Parsi when she had not been allowed to marry a Muslim. The aunts also looked down on Feroze's humble origins, and scoffed at Mrs. Commissariat, the aunt who had helped to raise Feroze, calling her Mrs. Commissariat wallah.

Gandhi (who had been consulted about whether the marriage should take place) had suggested the wedding should be a large affair or it would seem that Jawaharlal was not standing by her. He had no more than his usual success in urging celibacy on the bride and groom. The ceremony was by Vedic rites, as a concession to Hindu convention, and took an hour and a half. Indira wore a shell pink sari of cloth spun by her father in prison, embroidered with silver flowers. She wore fresh flowers in lieu of jewelry. An empty place was reserved in memory of Kamala. Krishna later described the bride: "She was tall and rather frail, ethereal looking, with very black hair that fell down to her shoulders. She had large dark eyes in an aquiline face, and a complexion like the golden color of ripe wheat. In profile Indu looked like the head on a Greek coin."[45] Jawaharlal added a Sanskrit verse to the traditional nuptials so that Indira pledged, "If there are any people in the four quarters of the earth, who venture to deprive us of our freedom, mark! Here I am, sword in hand, prepared to resist them to the last. I pray for the spreading light of freedom; may it envelop us on all sides."[46]

The couple honeymooned in Srinagar, Kashmir, then returned and rented a house near Anand Bhavan. Feroze, who had a flair for designing furniture, made things for the house and gardened. He worked as an insurance agent and wrote for illustrated journals, using photographs he himself had taken in Europe.

One guest at the wedding was Stafford Cripps, an old family friend and now a Cabinet minister in Churchill's coalition government. The Labor MP had come at the government's behest to attempt a solution to the independence puzzle. Indira's cousin Nayantara said, "It was quite usual in our family for a very personal, private event to be somehow involved with matters that were happening in the world and in the country. So we took it for granted that the Cripps Mission should be somehow mixed up with Indira's wedding."[47] Cripps had been given a rigid brief to put to Congress: after the war India would have dominion status and a constituent assembly to frame a constitution, with the right of provinces to opt out of whatever constitutional arrangement was reached. This latter clause meant that the princely states, for example, could choose to stay under British authority. Cripps had no freedom to negotiate—it was a take-it-or-leave-it offer. A great problem was Britain's wish to control India's defense policy, which was totally unacceptable. It was, like all British offers in the independence struggle, too little too late. Ten years earlier it would have been the basis for an agreement. Gandhi is said to have called it "a post-dated check on a failing bank."

Gandhi now took the initiative. He famously wrote in his newspaper, "You have sat too long here for any good you have been doing. Depart and let us have done with you. In the name of God, go." In August 1942 Congress met in Bombay and agreed what came to be called the "Quit India Resolution." So the Gandhi who had supported Britain in the Boer War, the Zulu uprising and the First World War now felt unable to do so, and had additionally lost his scruples about attacking an enemy who was suffering unconnected misfortunes. Jawaharlal was reluctant to embarrass the British while they were fighting fascism, but went with Gandhi.

The Quit India Resolution was passed late on the night of August 8. In the early hours of the next morning all members of the Congress Working Committee were arrested; this included Jawaharlal and Raja Hutheesing in Krishna's flat in Bombay, and Vijaya at Anand Bhavan. At the time, Vijaya was hiding the future prime minister, Lal Bahadur Shastri, a fact unknown even to the servants.

A warrant was issued for Feroze, but he went underground, making it hard for Indira to know how he was. He grew a mustache and dressed in khaki, his light coloring allowing him to pass for an Anglo-Indian soldier. When Indira was invited by a local college to attend the hoisting of the Congress flag, she arrived to find the police already beating the demonstrators and one student on the floor still holding the precious flag. Indira took it and held it up, becoming a rallying point for the students and a target for the police, who attacked her with *lathis*.

Feroze heard of the attack and came secretly to see her that night. Some days later she called a meeting, but after she had been speaking for ten minutes, a large contingent of armed British soldiers appeared and a sergeant threatened to shoot Indira, holding a gun a yard from her head. Suddenly Feroze rushed up and thrust himself between the gun and her. When the sergeant tried to lead her off to prison, the crowd surged forward. No shots were fired, but rifle butts were used to disperse the crowd. A large number were arrested, including Indira and Feroze, who spent their first wedding anniversary in prison. Indira was in a barracks with her cousin Chandralekha and her aunt Vijaya. This period of imprisonment may have been the only time when Indira and Vijaya got on together. At the end of 1942 Indira again developed pleurisy. She was seen by a civil doctor, who prescribed a tonic and a special diet. Scarcely was his back turned when the superintendent of the prison took the prescription and tore it up: "If you think you are getting any of this you are mistaken," he said.[48] She was eventually released on May 8, 1943 on grounds of ill health. When she visited Feroze, she found he had been placed in solitary confinement and was himself unwell, which led to his release on July 8. To mark his release, Jawaharlal arranged for Feroze to receive a Schick electric razor—Jawaharlal was always fond of technological gadgets. The young couple then moved to Anand Bhavan, a measure prompted by economy as well as practicality.

In 1943 Vijaya's daughters Nayantara and Chandralekha were sent to the United States for their education (the third daughter, Rita, was to follow) because India was "a vast concentration camp."[49] They visited Ranjit in prison before they left and he refused to let them look unhappy: "We mustn't let these people see us cry," he said, and led them in a song. He had no advice for them but, "See that you have the best time possible."[50] These were virtually the last words they heard from their father, for shortly afterwards he fell ill with pneumonia and died in 1944 when they were still abroad. Injustice was added to grief, for in the absence of a will, Ranjit's family insisted on the Hindu law of inheritance being applied, which meant that as Vijaya had no "issue" (girls did not count), she and her children were virtually disinherited.

Indira became aware she was pregnant in January 1944, and because of her poor health went to Bombay to be with Krishna and close to advanced medical facilities. Rajiv Gandhi was born on August 20, news which Jawaharlal was to celebrate in prison. He wrote that he was concerned to have a "proper horoscope made by a competent person" for the child.[51] Indira and Feroze waited in the hot darkness one night outside Naini Jail in Allahabad, while Jawaharlal was being moved from one prison to another, and when he was walked to the prison van, they held up baby Rajiv so he could see his first grandson in the glow of a dim roadside light. The family started a baby book to chart Rajiv's development, in which the happy mother's name was entered as "Indira Nehru." Sarojini Naidu was already plotting the destiny of the baby, writing to him, "My little greatnephew, you inherit a famous ancestry and a high tradition . . . In a free India which will be, you know, you will achieve a splendid manhood and be a leader among those who dedicate their talents, their time, their hope and their faith and service to the redeeming of humanity from evil," so he already had rather a lot to live up to.[52]

There was more reason for joy: with the war in Europe over and victory in the Pacific in sight, Congress leaders were freed. Jawaharlal left Almora Jail on June 15, 1945 to a reception by cheering crowds, and an immediate return to politics and *darshan*. He wrote prophetically to Indira, "I doubt if I shall ever be able to go out for a walk because of the crowds following, except at dead of night."[53]

Jawaharlal had spent his last imprisonment writing *The Discovery of India*, a lengthy account of Indian history from the Indus Valley civilization through British rule and the independence struggle to the present, including biographical material such as the death of Kamala, which could not be included in his autobiography. If anyone ever wrote himself into history it was Jawaharlal Nehru.

The month following Jawaharlal's release, Labor won a landslide election victory in Britain, led by the much underestimated Clement

Attlee. Having been a member of the Simon Committee, he knew India and understood the strength of feeling against continued British rule. He had also been chairman of the India Committee, which had sent Cripps to resolve the independence dispute in 1942. It was said that India was one of the few subjects on which the normally phlegmatic Attlee would become emotional. At last there was the will in Britain to concede independence to India, plus the power to do it.

# SIX

# FREEDOM AND DISASTER

In 1945, Jawaharlal plunged into action on the most important event in his life: the creation of an independent India complete and undivided. Two-fifths of India was in the hands of princes, whose lands would have to be compounded in one great state to create a modern nation. That state would also have to be united, and multi-cultural to satisfy the long-held dream of secular Indian nationalists.

Jawaharlal had been working for years to ensure that nationalist agitation covered the whole of India, not just the areas directly ruled by the British, and in 1942 he had brought together Congress and All India States' People's Conference leaders (representing nationalism in princely India) to ensure that their objectives were as one.

The question of multiculturalism was a far greater problem. The Muslim League came out of the war with great credibility in the eyes of the British. Many Muslims had helped the war effort, earning the approval of the Viceroy, Lord Wavell. The fact that so many had taken up arms in support of Britain also influenced a wider range of British people than merely those in the government of India. By contrast, many nationalists had sympathized with Subhas Chandra Bose's Indian National Army, recruited from Indian prisoners of war to fight on the side of the Japanese, although it did little fighting.

Domestically, Muslims had taken control of a number of ministries after Congress members withdrew from them. They were more prepared for elections, and for government, than was Congress. The Muslim League had moved on from the days when it was a small elitist group and become more a mass movement. Jawaharlal, with his instinctive lack of sympathy with communal thinking, refused to recognize the strength of Muslim feeling. When independence approached, he believed, cultural and religious divisions would recede in importance and a united India would be free.

Jinnah, however, had been calling for the creation of an independent Muslim state throughout the Second World War. The proposed state would be called Pakistan, taking its name from letters of its constituent Muslim provinces: Punjab, Afghan province (the Northwest

Frontier Province), Kashmir, Sind and Baluchistan. While Jawahar-lal's objective was unity, he had been realistic enough to consider the possibility of losing several provinces, but could not countenance the loss of Kashmir: for a Kashmiri Brahmin like himself, the notion of losing the homeland was terrible beyond belief.

While plans were laid for elections, India steadily became more ungovernable. There was a naval mutiny in February 1946, which Jawaharlal tried to calm down, and considerable unrest over the tri-als of Indian National Army (INA) members. They had been charged with treason for fighting with the Japanese against the British, but they had hardly made a free choice: they had been taken prisoner by the Japanese and offered the opportunity to fight against their imperial foe. Subhas Chandra Bose was missing, pre-sumed dead, in an air crash, so he was not going to come back to argue the case in his bid for Congress leadership. Jawaharlal had no sympathy, Japanese imperialism being no more attractive to him than British imperialism, but the men were the focus of national sympathy. Continued irritation with the British transmuted itself into support for the three officers on trial. With maladroit symbol-ism, the Commander-in-Chief had selected a Hindu, a Muslim and a Sikh officer, thus uniting sentimental opinion in their favor. In these circumstances, Jawaharlal saw the advantage of associating with them and ostentatiously appeared among their barristers in 1945 during their trial at the Red Fort, Delhi. The men were cashiered, but no more.

Jawaharlal was now to meet the man who further shaped his des-tiny—Lord Louis Mountbatten. Out of the chaos of liberated South-east Asia, the Supreme Commander, Lord Mountbatten, was maneu-vering with skill between independence movements and returned but enfeebled colonial rulers. His command included over 120 million people of many races—Burma, Singapore, Malaysia, Indo-China and the Dutch East Indies. He revealed early an instinctive understanding of the new nationalists, even when, like the charismatic Aung San in Burma, they had initially taken advantage of Japanese support. There were substantial Indian communities (and troops of the Indian Empire) in many of them.

Congress wished to re-establish contact with this Indian diaspora, so in March 1946 Jawaharlal landed at Singapore to begin a tour of them. The British authorities had generally been obstructive until Lord Mountbatten, Allied Supreme Commander, an urbane and open-spirited man, ordered that Jawaharlal's reception should be appropriate for a prime minister-in-waiting and even made his own car available.

Jawaharlal was received at Government House by Mountbatten and the two drove to a canteen for Indian soldiers where he was introduced to Edwina, Lady Mountbatten, on the porch. As they entered the hall, a rush of Indian soldiers and other people surged forward and Lady Mountbatten disappeared from view. Jawaharlal got up on a chair to look for her and saw the rather disheveled countess crawling out of the crowd, having been knocked down by the rush.

Edwina was from a wealthy family which had made money in "trade," and in customary fashion it was deemed appropriate that new wealth should marry impoverished aristocracy, in this case a cousin of the king. That "Dickie" Mountbatten and Edwina were fond of each other is beyond doubt, but it is unlikely they were in love past the first weeks of courtship. In 1946 Edwina was distraught over the recent marriage of her longtime lover Bunny Phillips, a relationship always tolerated by Mountbatten. By the time Edwina first met Jawaharlal, age and wartime had taken their toll on the once-sparkling debutante. She had worked tirelessly in the war for the St. John Ambulance Brigade and the Red Cross, and after the war was working to repatriate prisoners. Now very thin, she generally wore a uniform, her glamorous pre-war clothes being dated and too big. Both the Mountbattens were left-wing, Edwina more so than her husband, and generally sympathetic to nationalist movements. Edwina had even read Jawaharlal's autobiography. Jawaharlal got on well with Mountbatten, but with Edwina, who at forty-four was thirteen years his junior, Jawaharlal had an instant rapport which promised to ripen, given time.

Elections were held in 1946 to choose an interim legislature which would bridge the gap between British and independent Indian rule. This election was virtually a straightforward battle between Congress and the Muslim League, with the League winning almost all the seats reserved for Muslims, but Congress sweeping the board to become the largest single party. Jawaharlal continued to underestimate the strength of the League. He started a fifth term as Congress president in May and was selected as head of the interim government in August.

The British government's last effort at an imposed settlement was a Cabinet mission including Sir Stafford Cripps, who again stayed with the Nehrus. He was by far the most dominant member of the mission, but the titular head was the new Secretary of State for India, Lord Pethick-Lawrence. Cripps proposed an ingenious plan for a three-tier system of government, the lowest tier being groups of Hindu and Muslim-majority provinces, but it came to nothing when he could not obtain all-party agreement. A solution was almost reached, but Jawaharlal circumscribed his acceptance with so many conditions that it was no longer an agreement. Jinnah, who had for once been prepared to cooperate, consequently withdrew his agreement on the part of the Muslim League. Jawaharlal's colleague Sardar Patel criticized his leader's "acts of emotional insanity . . . it puts tremendous strain on us to set matters right. His mind has been exhausted by overwork and strain. He feels lonely and he acts emotionally and we have to bear with him in the circumstances."[1] Jinnah now announced that the only option left was Pakistan.

It was at this time that Indira virtually became Jawaharlal's full-time consort. Temperamental differences meant that neither she nor her husband found married life easy. They had been living at Anand Bhavan for economy's sake and so that Indira could look after her father. Jawaharlal's possessiveness was a further strain. A perceptive Allahabad neighbor watched the three at a domestic reception: "When Indira got up to leave the room, his eyes followed her, and they never left the door through which she went out until she returned through it. When Nehru took his leave, Indira immediately went with him. Feroze was left wandering around the room, picking up her shawls and bags. As he left he murmured, 'Look at me. I am the husband of Indira Nehru.'"[2] This arrangement was altered in 1946 when Jawaharlal asked Feroze to join the *National Herald*, a newspaper Jawaharlal had founded in 1937, but which had ceased publication rather than submit to wartime censorship. Now it was to be relaunched and Feroze took on a post more managerial than journalistic in Lucknow, where it was published. He was a popular character, good with both people and machines, and made a success of increasing the income and reducing the liabilities of Associated Journals which published the *Herald*.

Feroze, Indira and Rajiv moved to Lucknow, but Indira spent so much time in Delhi at 17 York Road, a residence made available for Jawaharlal in his role as interim prime minister, that in April 1946 she moved in. She was already pregnant with Sanjay. It was as if marriage had supplied her with what she required, two children, and she now had no further need of a husband. If she was a substitute for her mother for Feroze, he was a substitute for her father for her. She was to look after Jawaharlal's house, acting as his host and consort, from now until the day he died. How badly Feroze felt about this is in some doubt. He had always enjoyed female companionship: now he had more freedom to spend time with women, a long way from his wife and family.

At the birth of Sanjay, on December 14, 1946, a large number of family and friends gathered at 17 York Road. Among them were Sir Stafford Cripps and his wife Isobel, who was out shopping with Indira when she felt the labor pains. There were, in fact, so many guests that there was no room for Feroze: he had to stay in a tent pitched in the garden with other "overspill" guests. Sanjay's was a difficult birth for Indira and she lost a great deal of blood; when Krishna first saw her after the birth she thought her niece was dead. Sanjay's premature arrival was later seen as astrologically auspicious and "patent proof of his ability to get things done quickly and before the target dates."[3] The enlarged family remained very close and shortly after independence Jawaharlal, Indira and her children moved to Teen Murti House, which became the official residence of the prime minister.

By the time Jawaharlal was in post, however, Jinnah had already declared a day of "direct action" for August 16. In Calcutta this degenerated into the Great Calcutta Killing, in which 5000 people were slaughtered in three days. Hindus in Bihar then turned on Muslims and there were further outbreaks of rioting elsewhere. Congress took office in September, to be joined by the Muslim League in October, but the League went on to boycott the Constituent Assembly. They had learned the Congress lesson of obstruction and non-cooperation very well. The nation was heading for disaster, and now the British were not holding the country together for themselves, they had lost interest in holding it together at all. Jawaharlal was so overwrought by the disintegration of the country and by divisions in his own party and the government that the Viceroy, Lord Wavell, thought he was "not far from a nervous breakdown." Jawaharlal offered his resignation three times in five minutes until Wavell calmed him down.[4]

There was no doubt that India would be free: the questions were what India would look like and when independence would take place. India was already behaving as an independent nation: in October 1946, at the first session of the United Nations in New York, the Indian delegation was led by Vijaya, thus reinforcing her family's close relationship with the USA, and paralleling Jawaharlal's relationship with Britain. Vijaya, now a widow, was to meet her old boyfriend Syed Hussain in the US, where he had settled in exile after their ill-fated romance, and they resumed their relationship. He later became Indian ambassador to Egypt.

The British prime minister Clement Attlee decided to speed events by imposing a deadline, and on February 20, 1947 told parliament that power would be transferred "into responsible Indian hands by a date not later than June 1948," even if that meant transferring power to provincial governments. He further announced the appointment of Mountbatten as viceroy, replacing Lord Wavell before his term was up. Wavell had limited diplomatic skills and was tainted by the cruelties of the wartime emergency, so he was not the right person to negotiate an agreement. He was also too evidently without the flair and imagination a viceroy would need to help heal a fractured nation and steer it towards independence.

It has been speculated that Jawaharlal had Krishna Menon suggest Mountbatten's name as the next viceroy to Attlee's colleague Stafford Cripps. Whether he did or not, Mountbatten's credentials as an aristocrat and war leader in Asia ensured he was on the list of candidates anyway. If the contender Jawaharlal happened to favor was chosen, that does not mean he caused the choice to be made.

The Mountbattens arrived in March 1947 in a country seething with communal violence. Punjab was virtually in a state of civil war and there was serious unrest in Bombay, Amritsar and the province of Bihar. Mountbatten immediately set about making himself known to the chief players. He re-established his rapport with Jawaharlal, who at their first meeting suggested an Anglo-Indian union involving common citizenship of the two countries. This would have created a closer relationship than membership of the Commonwealth, another indication of how deeply Anglophile Jawaharlal was, despite his many years of incarceration in the prisons of the Raj. Mountbatten's daughter Pamela later said, "My father formed a really deep and sincere friendship with Pandit Nehru. They liked each other enormously, respected each other and got on extremely well."[5] Jawaharlal succinctly assessed Jinnah to the new Viceroy as a man to whom success had come very late in life. He almost certainly did not know that Jinnah was dying from tuberculosis, and that part of the doomed man's desperation stemmed from his desire to create Pakistan before his death. When Mountbatten met Jinnah he found him cold: "It took most of the interview to unfreeze him," but by April 19, 1947, after a month in India, Mountbatten was beginning to think the creation of Pakistan was inevitable. Gandhi's solution to the problem of partition—to appoint an all-Muslim administration—was characteristically creative but sank among the proposals of more pragmatic politicians.[6]

Jinnah's family had converted to Islam only in the recent past. He was a pork-eating, alcohol-drinking, secular Muslim who knew little of the *Koran*, whose Urdu was poor and who married a Parsi. He made an interesting pair with Jawaharlal, who was criticized as "English by education, Muslim by culture, and Hindu by an accident of birth."[7] Both were London-qualified lawyers who had spent a great deal of time away from India. While Jawaharlal discarded the trappings of religion and disdained its use as a political force, Jinnah embraced the revolutionary potential of Islam with a vengeance.

Edwina Mountbatten as Vicereine played a major role in entertaining guests and putting them at their ease, and particularly in making friends with the womenfolk of prominent Indians. The effort was wasted on Fatima Jinnah, Ali Jinnah's sister, who was as cold and fanatical as he was. By contrast, Vijaya became an ally and supporter of Edwina, Indira visited at least once, and Jawaharlal called in regularly to talk to Mountbatten and socialize with Edwina. Despite his age, for he was fifty-eight in 1947, Jawaharlal had stayed trim and fit, doubtless aided by the yoga he had practiced in prison. He still wore a homespun tunic with a rose in the buttonhole, and a Gandhi cap covered his bald head. He was, according to Edwina's biographer, "never at a loss for the right phrase or gesture."[8]

The story of the following months in 1947, full of jolting attempts at diplomacy, was of words and maps which established the dissection of India. Jawaharlal finally conceded the creation of Pakistan as a solution to the problems of communal violence. The decisive shift was when Sardar Patel, the only Congress leader who could approach Jawaharlal in stature, broke ranks and conceded, in characteristically hostile terms about Muslims, that it was "better if a gangrenous arm is cut off and thrown away, rather than the whole body get gangrenous."[9] Patel was a hardline Hindu who saw the Muslims as a problem to be contained or discarded rather than as fellow Indians.

To add to the difficulties of the negotiators over India's future, by May they had to face the blistering heat of summer. The Mountbattens, in time-honored fashion, took to the hills, to the viceregal lodge in Simla. The whole entourage, including servants, meant moving around 333 people. Jawaharlal, Indira and Krishna Menon were invited as guests, and the Mountbattens had the opportunity to see Jawaharlal at his most informal. Pamela Mountbatten knocked on Jawaharlal's door one morning and received an impatient call to enter: "So I burst in and found the Prime Minister of India standing on his head, because he used to do yoga every morning. He said, 'Come on, don't be silly, what do you want to say?' so we had a long conversation with him standing on his head."[10]

Mountbatten noted that he had "made real friends with Nehru during his stay here."[11] After dinner, and over a glass of port in the Viceroy's study, Mountbatten felt so moved with warmth and friendship that he simply passed to Jawaharlal a copy of the secret plan, just approved by London, on the final settlement of the Indian question. Jawaharlal, accepting that he saw it unofficially and that he would make no mention or use of his prior knowledge, was duly grateful, and they continued their gentlemanly conversation. When he read the file in his bedroom later that night, he flew into one of his rages and burst into Krishna Menon's room at 2 A.M., beside himself with fury at what he saw as a betrayal.

The plan was, to Jawaharlal's mind, the negation of the agreement he had been working on, which provided for just two governments, with strong central control, to which power would be transferred. This plan, now approved by the government in London, was for the "Balkanization" of India, allowing the nation to fragment by transferring power locally, with a weak central government in Delhi.

Jawaharlal sent an immediate and at times incoherent handwritten note to Mountbatten, then a more considered typewritten letter the following day. He was at pains to stress that his India was the successor to British India, and that Pakistan was a seceder from it. There had to be a continuity: partition was barely tolerable, dismemberment was certainly not.

Mountbatten postponed the meeting soon to take place to announce the agreement, and there was time for reflection. He had taken Jawaharlal's good nature for acceptance, while Jawaharlal still had such personal faith in the Viceroy that he thought the undesirable parts of the plan had been inserted in London. In fact, both men had probably been deluding themselves about the nature of the settlement up to this point—Mountbatten believing he was closer to the desired agreement than he actually was, and Jawaharlal convincing himself that the plan under discussion was what he wanted until he saw it in print and had to confront the truth.

Mountbatten visited London and, with a heavy heart, obtained permission for a straight partition of India. His daughter Patricia (later Countess Mountbatten) said, "My father was deeply disappointed that there was no way that partition could be avoided. I think he'd gone out to India with the thought that India could be handed over as a complete country. When it became apparent that Mr. Jinnah was quite intransigent about that, it disappointed him very much."[12]

Mountbatten accommodated Jawaharlal's main objections, and Jawaharlal, desperate to reach a solution, made several concessions, including the acceptance of dominion status rather than full independence. Jinnah had spent so long saying "no" he seemed to some observers to have lost the capacity to say "yes." Mountbatten's press secretary, Alan Campbell-Johnson, recalled, "There was one historic meeting when they were having a meeting and Jinnah took the point, but he said to Mountbatten, 'I don't agree.' Mountbatten said, 'I thought I'd got your agreement.' Jinnah said, 'No, I accept, but I don't agree.' This exasperated Mountbatten."[13]

After all the discussions, the parading of conscience and the territory deals, Mountbatten's plan was published to the world at large on June 3, 1947. Two states, India and Pakistan, were to be set up, to which the British government would hand its assets, and they would draw up their own constitutions. The princely states would be encouraged to accede to either India or Pakistan, and provincial governments would decide their allegiance by a vote of their legislature. This could work well for states which were overwhelmingly one religion or the other. The problems would come where there was a more mixed population, as in Bengal and Punjab, where it was envisaged there would be a division by a boundary commission. Other problems were caused by the Indian princes, who were dithering about whether to go in with India or Pakistan or attempt independence, and the Northwest Frontier Province which, though Muslim, had a Congress leadership.

Jinnah was in a state of impotent rage, for he wanted the provinces to go intact into the new Pakistan, yet now Punjab and Bengal would be partitioned to give Pakistan only the areas with Muslim majorities. On June 3, with the Indian leaders assembled around the table, Mountbatten called for them all to affirm their agreement. Alan Campbell-Johnson recalled, "Mountbatten looked at Jinnah and said, 'Today we have a meeting that's going to affect the transfer of power to a fifth of the human race. I don't expect anybody to agree with it, only to accept it,' so he nursed that little remark of Jinnah's." He had previously agreed with Jinnah that he would accept his assent in any form he wished to give it: in the event, it was a barely perceptible nod of the head, but that was enough, agreement was reached.[14]

Neither were Congress Muslims happy with the agreement: they had made great sacrifices for a united India and felt betrayed by the creation of Pakistan. The Sikhs were also deeply dissatisfied, arguing for their own state to be carved out of Punjab. However, agreement to the plan was stimulated by the horror Jawaharlal and others had of the entire nation descending into violence. "We are at present living in the midst of crises and the situation is volcanic," he wrote.[15] Efforts at peace-making came from different quarters: Gandhi went to Bengal to attempt a reconciliation between the Muslims and Hindus; Edwina Mountbatten toured riot-stricken areas, visiting hospitals and refugee centers.

Jawaharlal welcomed the plan in a historic broadcast to the nation, saying, "We are little men serving a great cause, but because the cause is great, something of that greatness falls upon us also." He believed communal violence would die down and cease now that agreement had been reached. He also believed that partition would be a temporary matter, after which India would be restored to wholeness. In the summer of 1947, the opposite looked the case, with many of the princely states agitating for sovereignty and building up their independent armies.

At a press conference on June 4, 1947 Mountbatten almost casually announced the date of British withdrawal from government: August 15. It was ten weeks away: ten weeks to dismantle an empire and create two new states out of it. Mountbatten had a tear-off calendar printed which showed how many days were left to the transfer of power. Politicians and officials worked to it as they dissected the Indian Civil Service, the railway and telegraph system, the police and the army. One problem of some significance for India was that astrologers said August 15 was a most inauspicious day, so with due diplomacy, the final minutes of August 14 were chosen for the announcement of freedom. Independence came into effect at midnight.

Most of the princes were persuaded to accede to India or Pakistan thanks to the diplomatic efforts of Mountbatten and threats from Sardar Patel, who was in charge of negotiations. There were three exceptions: Hyderabad, Kashmir and Junagadh. Jawaharlal had no sympathy for the feudal autocracies which were the princely states, and on Patel's advice he was to send the Indian Army into Junagadh in November 1947, and into Hyderabad in September 1948, ensuring that these states acceded swiftly. Clearly non-violence had limited use in such situations. Kashmir was another problem: its Hindu leader ruled a Muslim population which would almost certainly vote to go with Pakistan, given the chance. Jawaharlal let this princely state stay as it was for a while.

A huge celebration was planned for August 15, but not everyone was coming to the party: Gandhi had returned, saddened, from his work of reconciliation in Bengal, unwilling to partake of a celebration when he felt he had nothing to celebrate. Jawaharlal made the ringing speech, which will always be associated with his name, to the legislative assembly at midnight: "Long years ago we made a tryst with destiny, and now the time comes when we shall redeem our pledge, not wholly or in full measure, but very substantially. At the stroke of the midnight hour, when the world sleeps, India will awake to life and freedom. A moment comes, which comes but rarely in history, when we step out from the old to the new, when an age ends, and when the soul of a nation, long suppressed, finds utterance. It is fitting that at this solemn moment, we take the pledge of dedication to the service of India and her people, and to the still larger cause of humanity."

Soon after midnight, Jawaharlal made his way through the celebrating crowds and arrived at the viceregal palace to issue Mountbatten with a formal invitation to become governor-general. Jawaharlal gave him an envelope which he said contained the names and posts of members of his first ministry. In fact it was empty: in all the excitement the person whose job it was to put the list in the envelope had sealed it up empty.

Jawaharlal's deputy prime minister was Sardar (Vallabhbhai) Patel, longtime associate of Gandhi and a hardline Hindu. Third in command was Maulana Azad, whom Jinnah had resented as a Muslim in the Congress Party. Rajendra Prasad, a right-winger and former associate of Motilal's, was President of the Constituent Assembly. Other members of the Cabinet were Baldev Singh, a Sikh, and Dr. John Matthai, a Christian. It was indeed an attempt at a ministry of national unity.

Mountbatten agreed to remain, temporarily, as Governor-General of the newly independent Commonwealth state. He had hoped for a similar offer from Pakistan, but none was forthcoming.

The Indian flag was unfurled in Princes Park, Delhi, on August 15 in front of a massive crowd. Some 30,000 had been expected to attend; in the event, 300,000 cheerful people came, swamping the dignitaries. An eyewitness in the specially constructed arena said, ". . . the crowd became like some gigantic ocean, remorselessly converging on a tiny island and liable at any moment to convulse it."[16] Pamela Mountbatten was trapped in the crowd and Jawaharlal fought his way through to rescue her. She later described the scene: "There was just a living sea of human beings. I mean, you could not see an inch. I remember getting out of the car and standing with my mouth agape looking at this, of course dressed in my best clothes. In those days it was white gloves, high-heeled shoes and a hat, very correct." Jawaharlal shouted and beckoned to her, then eventually reached her by walking on a human platform created by people holding up their hands. "Of course," Pamela later said, "he was very nimble and quick with his sandals. When he arrived he said, 'Come on' and started to drag me by the hand. I said, 'I can't, I've got high heels on.' He said,

'Well, take them off.' I took off my high heels and had them in one hand and he dragged me with him as we were handed over this sea of people, all of them laughing."[17]

Mountbatten and his entourage were excitedly welcomed by the crowd: whatever hate there was in India, it was not directed against the British. It had been planned to lower the Union flag before raising the saffron, white and green of the Indian flag, but Jawaharlal canceled this part of the ceremony because he did not want to hurt British feelings. On the return trip Jawaharlal was unable to get back to his car, so Mountbatten pulled him into the open-topped state carriage, where he sat on the hood.

The national flag was hoisted over the Red Fort in Delhi the following day, the spinning wheel symbol beloved of Gandhi having been replaced in the run-up to independence by the wheel symbol of Ashoka, the last indigenous emperor before the foreign invasions. Jawaharlal addressed a meeting of half a million people, but at this point rejoicing stopped, for the Radcliffe Award—the decision of the boundary commission for the division of Bengal and Punjab—was given to Indian and Pakistani leaders that afternoon. The process of partition, already steeped in blood, was now ready to degenerate into one of the great horrors of the twentieth century. The boundary commission had an easier task in Bengal where there were two communities to be divided. In Punjab there were more or less equal numbers of Hindus, Muslims and Sikhs. Within days of the award, announced on August 17, Sikhs and Hindus attacked the Muslims of eastern Punjab, and Muslims attacked Sikhs in the west. The slaughter stimulated a further exodus of refugees until there were literally millions of people on the move. It was estimated 11 million people crossed the India-Pakistan border in either direction.

No one realized how bad the violence would be, though Jawaharlal's shock was compounded by his complete and long-standing misreading of the communal situation. He genuinely believed that "when the British go, there will be no more communal trouble in India."[18] Partition, supposed to end the communal problem once and for all, in fact brought hatred to a head.

In an orgy of slaughter, thousands upon thousands were killed, mutilated, raped. Huge marching convoys with their carts and bundles were attacked with almost unimaginable savagery. Refugee trains

117

would arrive with all their passengers dead: everyone, down to the smallest child, had been killed. The Boundary Force of 50,000 soldiers was entirely inadequate to deal with the level of violence, and was rendered less effective by the units themselves being partisan.

Jawaharlal toured Punjab twice with the Prime Minister of Pakistan, Liaquat Ali Khan (Jinnah had become governor-general). Jawaharlal was beside himself with anguish, weeping with victims and threatening assailants. He visited one village where he heard a group was going to attack a nearby Muslim settlement. He ordered his bodyguards to shoot these men if they attempted it. In Delhi a young journalist, Kuldip Nayar, witnessed Jawaharlal in action. He later recounted, "Connaught Circus had lots of shops owned by Muslims, and Hindus were ransacking them. The police were just spectators. Nehru rushed in just with his small baton saying, 'Get out, get out, get out!' People did say, 'Look here, how can the Prime Minister do this kind of thing?' but he was a man."[19]

In vain did Nehru broadcast that "India is not a communal state but a democratic state," for it was a position that even some of his closest colleagues did not acknowledge. Jawaharlal found that while he had taken Gandhi's message of freedom and discarded the religious element, other Congress leaders, including Prasad and Patel, had taken the Hindu message and discarded the element of universal love. They wanted not a secular but a Hindu state, and were unwilling to intervene to help Muslims while Hindus were being attacked in Pakistan.

Gandhi had tried intervening on the side of peace in Punjab, but had not been well received by the Sikhs. He went to Calcutta, a powder keg of communal feelings since the "Calcutta killings" of the previous year. There the seventy-eight-year-old man threatened to fast to death unless there was peace. As the days passed and news of the fast spread, religious leaders came to him, then ordinary people. Finally, the fighters laid down their weapons before him and there was peace.

Another dangerous situation was now developing: many of the half a million refugees from East Pakistan had gone to Delhi. The presence of large numbers of angry and bewildered people heightened an already tense atmosphere and attacks, largely by Hindu and Sikh refugees, began on the remaining Muslim minority. The victims were hacked, stabbed, raped and their shops looted. Jawaharlal lamented not only the horrors of the violence, but the effect it had on India's image abroad: "Every ambassador's house has been visited by gangs in search of Muslim servants," he wrote to Prasad.[20]

The slaughter came close to home, with killers stalking the prosperous suburbs of New Delhi. The Nehrus' next-door neighbor, Quenna Hunt, recalled the terrible scenes enacted in their neighborhood. "That night Sikhs rounded up all the Muslim villagers in [the area] and drove them into my garden and there was a battle all night. There was screaming and shouting—it was terrifying. I sat on the edge of my bed all night with a little hammer in my hand waiting for the first beard to come over the windowsill. When it got light, I walked out on to the verandah feeling relieved and wondering if my driver had got away. Suddenly, somebody ran down the drive and across the lawn followed by four Sikhs and they hacked him to bits in front of my eyes on my lawn. He had been hiding overnight in a little mosque."[21]

Jawaharlal was out among the people at all times, showing great physical courage in trying to quell rioters. He made his home a safe haven—refugees filled the house and crowded tents in the garden; many had nothing in the world but the clothes they wore. His niece Nayantara recalled a drive with her uncle: ". . . the road was lined at intervals with people who signaled the car to a halt. Some talked, some quietly cried. Some were agitated, some beseeching. They, too, were now a part of [his] daily routine. In the office there was work and more work. Outside it there was the sharing of a different burden, the pall of heavy-heartedness that lay over the people. Frequently he repeated to those who stopped him, 'I know, I know, *mere bhai* (my brother), it is my sorrow too.'"[22]

Gandhi had come to Delhi from Calcutta, where he did what work of pacification he could, and gave spiritual comfort to leaders such as Jawaharlal, who visited him every evening. Edwina Mountbatten also frequently visited the Mahatma. She toured the refugee camps, organizing such things as sanitation facilities and cholera vaccines. To the horror of her staff, she would stop in the midst of sniping attacks to pick up bodies to take them to the infirmary. Despite the chaos all around, she managed to coordinate fifteen organizations under the banner of the United Council of Relief and Welfare.

One night in September, Edwina called on Gandhi's former secretary, now Minister of Health, Amrit Kaur, to discuss the riots in Delhi. During the evening they heard that Jawaharlal had gone out to investigate and had disappeared. She and Kaur scoured the dark and dangerous streets looking for him and found him standing by the roadside, calming a group of angry men armed with knives. "Brought him back!" Edwina wrote in her diary.[23]

After independence, Indira had gone to Mussoorie with her two small sons. Feroze cabled her to say that on no account should she return to Delhi. She telephoned and, learning of the violence on the streets there, picked up the boys and took the next train back. Indira had many faults, which became increasingly hard to overlook, but her sheer physical courage, her unhesitating determination to head for the greatest danger where she could be useful is a source of continuing wonderment. Her train stopped at a Delhi suburb, Shahdara, where she saw on the platform that a mob was preparing to lynch a Muslim. She leapt out, furious, and addressed the mob, shaming them into letting the man go. Clearly the Nehru temper had its uses. She said she would have done more but had been putting her clothes on in her carriage when saw the outrage, and was not fully dressed.[24]

Once asked where she found such fearlessness in the face of danger, she said, "I found that if one wasn't afraid in crowds, nothing went wrong. I can't say I was brave, I simply went ahead."[25] Indira did what she could with the refugees camped out around her father's house, then Gandhi asked her to work in the camps where Muslims were taking refuge. "I am not feeling well," Indira said, for she was still anemic and had not fully recovered from Sanjay's birth, "but if you want me to do it, I will." But who, she asked, would go with her? She did not even know where the Muslim areas of Delhi were. "My dear girl," said Gandhi, "if I had someone else to go, I wouldn't ask you."[26] For months Indira spent over twelve hours a day in the worst trouble spots, racing a Jeep into riot-torn areas to rescue Muslim families, and improving sanitation in the camps and surrounding areas by such expedients as providing two guards for each street cleaner so the health hazard of accumulated rubbish could be cleared away. She reported back to Gandhi each day or, if there was no time, he would send her a flower or a message.

Every day she sat for hours interviewing refugees who poured in. "For the majority there was not much one could do except listen to their tale of woe," she confessed, "but even this apparently gave peace of mind and there were always just enough cases which were within one's power to help or keep up hope."[27] She was particularly proud of having persuaded the defense minister to allow a mutilated orphan girl, Satya Danphi, to have artificial limbs from the institution which provided them exclusively to the military. This breakthrough eventually led to the institution's being permanently opened to civilians.

With time the violent disturbances died down, if only because in many places there was no one left to kill. Some 500,000 had been slaughtered in more than a month-long orgy of killing, which would have had more impact on the world's imagination had it not come at the end of the war and the Holocaust which between them had sated the imagination for horror.

Paradoxically, the dreadful events of partition strengthened Jawaharlal's position because they made his compassion and courage so evident: he was truly the father of his nation. Alan Campbell-Johnson, Mountbatten's press secretary, had not been impressed with Jawaharlal's moodiness and outbursts of exasperation during the negotiations for transfer of power, but during partition, he wrote, ". . . to see Nehru at close range during this ordeal is an inspiring experience. He vindicates one's faith in the humanist and the civilized intellect. Almost alone in the turmoil of communalism, with all its variations, from individual intrigue to mass madness, he speaks with the voice of reason and charity . . . he is shown at his full stature—passionate and courageous, yet objective and serene: one of the enlightened elect of our time."[28]

Kashmir continued to be a problem. It had a three-quarters Muslim majority, a long border with both India and Pakistan, all-weather road contact with Pakistan only, and contained the headwaters of Pakistan's major rivers. Muslims in Kashmir had, however, been closer to Congress than the Muslim League. They were led by Sheikh Abdullah, a personal friend of Jawaharlal and in favor of a government composed of Muslims, Hindus and Sikhs, but the reactionary Maharaja had him imprisoned. Jawaharlal was cautious about Kashmir, fearing an enforced accession would stimulate further communal violence. If there were an invasion by Pakistan, however, he declared he would "throw up his prime ministership and take a rifle himself, and lead the men of India against the invasion."[29] A visit by Mount-

batten to Kashmir did not improve the situation, which was in stale-
mate until October 22, 1947, when thousands of "irregulars" invaded
Kashmir from the Pakistan border. Pakistan denied responsibility for
the tribesmen, but their arms certainly came from Pakistan, and Pakistani army officers, supposedly in a non-official capacity, led the
contingents that went killing and burning across Kashmir, not spar-
ing their Muslim co-religionists, until they were twenty-five miles
from the capital, Srinagar. Emissaries were sent to the Maharaja to
persuade him to accede. Eventually, with the tribesmen only a few
miles from the capital, the Maharaja (who was packing to leave)
agreed to accession.

The invaders were closing in when, instead of moving on to take
the airport and thus denying India the opportunity of intervention
(the roads were impassable), they stopped in order to loot a town
called Baramula. This gave the Indian leaders time, though some of
those around Jawaharlal did not think he was prepared to use it effectively. Director of Military Operations Sam Manekshaw said, "Nehru
had a large perspective on life and he talked about the United
Nations, he talked about America, he talked about Russia, he talked
about everything until Sardar Patel said, 'Do we want Kashmir or
don't we?' And Nehru said, 'Of course we want Kashmir.' So Patel
said, 'Will you give your orders?' and he turned to me and said, 'You
have your orders.'" [30] It was one way of getting a decision out of Jawaharlal. Indian troops were quickly flown to Kashmir in a hundred aircraft. They secured the airport and beat back the invaders in two
weeks, though Pakistani troops then moved in along the border.

India's action had been facilitated by Sheikh Abdullah, who had
been released from prison and was in Delhi when the invasion took
place. Jawaharlal had also relied a great deal on Mountbatten who was
assisting as Governor-General during India's first year of independence. Unfortunately, despite his administrative skill, Mountbatten,
was weak at international relations, and he now persuaded Jawaharlal
to refer the matter of Kashmir to the United Nations. This made the
situation far worse, as the UN Security Council felt that India and
Pakistan had an equal interest in Kashmir, and even wanted to act
equably towards the invading tribesmen. Jawaharlal had made a serious error of judgment that prevented a solution to the Kashmir issue,
because referral to the UN legitimized Pakistan's claim. The UN

called for a ceasefire, the withdrawal of Pakistani troops occupying part of Kashmir, followed by the withdrawal of Indian troops, and a plebiscite so that the population could decide whether to join India or Pakistan. A ceasefire was established in the sporadic fighting between Pakistan and India at the end of December 1948, but Pakistan did not withdraw from Kashmiri territory, so no plebiscite took place. The ceasefire line became the *de facto* border between India and Pakistan. Fifty years later the problem of Kashmir still remained; Jawaharlal's failure to solve it was his first foreign policy disaster, but by no means his last.

In the meantime, at the beginning of 1948, Jawaharlal had learned what it was like to have a saint, not as a friend but as an opponent, challenging him to righteousness. In January 1948 Gandhi fasted to demand the restoration of peace in Delhi, to be achieved by generous treatment of Muslims, and for Pakistan to be immediately given the 55 crores (550 million rupees) owed to her from the Indian exchequer as the agreed portion of assets from the old India. Jawaharlal had been withholding it pending settlement of the Kashmir question, but he was no more willing than any of the viceroys to have a dead Gandhi on his hands, so five days into the fast he paid up.

There were bad omens, however, that Gandhi had enemies who would not be placated: opponents picketed Birla House, where he was living during the fast, with banners saying, "Let Gandhi Die." Hindu fanatics hated Gandhi for placating the Muslims: for them the dream of a united, Hindu India had been betrayed and he was responsible for partition. They were prepared to go to any lengths to attack him: a bomb exploded (without causing injury) at his regular prayer meeting in January 1948. Gandhi also attracted the usual types of lunatics overwhelmed by religion: one lay in the road outside Birla House, calling himself "the voice of Krishna" and stopping all the traffic until Jawaharlal, exasperated, picked the man up bodily and threw him to one side.

All the Nehrus were frequent visitors to Gandhi. On January 29, 1948, Gandhi sent for Indira, who went with Padmaja Naidu, Krishna and Rajiv, then three years old. The small boy played happily with a flower garland Indira had brought, slipping it on Gandhi's ankle or hanging it on his big toe. They laughed and joked and talked about films. The following afternoon, as Gandhi made his way to prayers, a man stepped out of the crowd and fired three shots into him at point blank range: he died immediately.

When Jawaharlal was told that Gandhi had been shot, his composure suggests that he did not realize the Mahatma was dead. As the crowds parted to let Jawaharlal through, he saw Gandhi's small body stretched out in its bloody white shawl and realized the truth. He fell to his knees beside the body and wept uncontrollably. His niece, who was present, said that when he rose to his feet "he had regained complete self-control, and through the ordeal of loneliness and personal loss which was to follow in the days to come, he was never again going to show a vestige of it. Those who could bear to look at his face during those days saw a strained white mask through which only the eyes revealed stark anguish."[31]

The Cabinet and Mountbatten gathered in a side room near the body. Mountbatten said that at his last meeting with Gandhi, the Mahatma had said his dearest wish was to bring about a full reconciliation between Jawaharlal and Sardar Patel. On hearing this they dramatically embraced each other. Mountbatten told them they must both broadcast to the nation that night and they both recognized the importance of defusing tension at this time of national crisis. The assassin had been a Hindu fanatic: had he been a Muslim, there would certainly have been pogroms.

Jawaharlal, in an attempt to organize the crowds who were crushing in on Birla House, climbed up on the wrought-iron gates to tell the people not to push: he would make sure they had a chance to view the body. Mountbatten begged him to desist: "You come down, you're a sitting target, standing up on that post," he said. "I must see that nothing goes wrong," said Jawaharlal. When he came down, journalist Pran Chopra, standing close to him, noticed that the Prime Minister was shaking.[32]

So many people came to have a last sight of Gandhi that the body was placed in an inclined position on the roof of Birla House overnight and a searchlight played on it. Jawaharlal's voice rang out in his broadcast, sharing a very private grief: ". . . we will not see him again as we have seen him these many years. We will not run to him for advice and seek solace from him." Moving on to a grander theme, he declared, "the light that has illuminated this country for these many years will illuminate this country for many more years, and a thousand years later that light will still be seen in this country, and the world will see it and it will give solace to innumerable hearts." Yet whatever verbal consolation there was, the man Jawaharlal Nehru had called Bapu—father—was dead. Although the Prime Minister ruled over hundreds of millions of souls, he was as alone as he had ever been.

# TRYST WITH POWER

# SEVEN

# THE LAST ENGLISHMAN

Jawaharlal truly loved Gandhi: to the end of his life he kept a small bronze statue of him in his office, along with a cast of the hand of Abraham Lincoln. However, personal affection aside, the death of Gandhi strengthened Jawaharlal's position in India as it removed the only world-class statesman to whom he had to defer, and to whom he was undoubtedly heir. The assassination also discredited Jawaharlal's main rival, Sardar Patel, who, as Home Minister, was responsible for Gandhi's security. The plotter who actually killed Gandhi was one of a gang which had attempted assassination by bomb a short time earlier. Despite the fact that one of the bombers had been caught and had betrayed his colleagues, the future assassin had not been arrested. As a man of the Hindu right, Patel's career never recovered but, more importantly, the hopes of hardline Hindus were also dealt a bitter blow, full recovery from which took fifty years. When the assassination was linked to the fundamentalist right, it strengthened the secular model of development for which Nehru had always campaigned.

The disappearance (and presumably death) of Subhas Chandra Bose had removed Jawaharlal's radical rival on the political right, leaving him virtually without opposition. The Muslim League no longer existed in India as an effective force, and the politicians of the former princely states were either effete or had been rendered ineffectual by their severance from power.

Particularly after Patel's health began to fail (he was to die in 1950) Jawaharlal had unchallenged and virtually unlimited powers within the parliamentary framework. He was prime minister, foreign minister, chairman of the planning committee, head of the atomic energy commission and, for a time, minister of defense. Jawaharlal Nehru in 1948 had more power in India than anyone since the Mogul emperors. He was not, however, well-equipped to use it. The previous government experience of the man now running the world's largest democracy had been two years on Allahabad's borough council. The years of obstruction and non-cooperation had won freedom, but left their perpetrators with precious little experience of government. Jawaharlal recognized this and only days after partition asked Mountbatten to take over the running of the emergency committee set up to deal with the crisis. He agreed on condition that no one outside the committee knew about it. After Jawaharlal's death Mountbatten would talk about his period as governor-general to Nehru when he "gave him a course in administration."[1]

The Prime Minister had also isolated himself from those equipped to give him advice, such as Vijaya and Krishna Menon, who were sent to Moscow and London as ambassador and high commissioner respectively. Sending his sister in this capacity was an indication of the importance he placed on links with the Soviet Union, but also showed that he favored having her at arm's length, familial love notwithstanding. Krishna Menon, on the other hand, like many former exiles, was probably more comfortable in London than in the new state for which he had fought.

Jawaharlal evolved a rather distant form of leadership, relying on the moral authority he had built up over the years. J. K. Galbraith commented, "I am not entirely at home in his presence and I rather wonder if anyone is," adding his opinion that a strong political leader is one who "raises a certain moral threshold against disagreement," which was certainly Jawaharlal's style.[2] Personalizing his political decisions in such a way could lead to petulance, however, and into repeated threats to resign unless he got his own way: he did this on at least seven recorded occasions.[3]

Marie Seton, a visitor to him in the mid-1950s, found him a shy man when separated from the crowds. She was given an introduction to Jawaharlal by a mutual acquaintance, but her courtesy call was treated more like an interview. She sat opposite him, across a large, modern desk while he asked her questions about herself and took notes. She felt awkward and uncomfortable, later writing, "I was taken aback that any meeting could turn out so nebulous with one whose sincerity I did not doubt. His lack of personal identity in his office left an impression of vacuum, and some sort of enigma. Nehru, the intellectual, seemed to be having his individuality extinguished by the exigency of prime ministership."[4]

Though diffident to the point of rudeness when he was alone with someone, his niece Nayantara said that the Prime Minister's "most rewarding moments, his relaxation and greatest fulfillment, came when he faced a crowd. The huge brown blur that assembled whenever he spoke, the men and women who lined the roads when his car drove past, the people he did not know by name but whose needs washed up against him in his daily work were his sustenance. Contact with them transcended fatigue and discouragement, kindled a lambent optimism."[5] She described her exhausted uncle on an election tour: ". . . because he loved his people better than his party or his policies, [the tour] was, for him, one more expression of his belief in them. They, in turn, shouldered the responsibility they were given and came out to vote." It was indeed a curious democracy which was vested in one man's love for an anonymous people, and their reciprocation.[6]

His bad temper was more than tolerated. His rages were considered to be Himalayan visitations from the gods, rather than the outbursts of a spoiled child. He would frequently leap into audiences and assail dissenters. An American journalist, Phillips Talbot, witnessed such an event during a conference at which there were disturbances in the aisles and it was difficult to get people to be quiet. "Finally Nehru, in considerable irritation after his pleas and demands for people to be quiet and sit down, jumped out into the crowd and began pushing people out of the aisles, and finally he picked up one of these folding chairs and lifted it over his head and brought it down. And that got some attention."[7] Only Indira was known to murmur "control yourself" to him, as she was heard to do at an international conference where, purple with rage, he was beginning to stalk out of one session.[8]

The acute problems of 1947 receded in time: gradually the refugee crisis subsided, stalls and shops sprang up in Delhi and the refugees founded new townships. A new constitution was developed along Western lines, borrowing in places from the American and Irish constitutions, and thus recognizing their precedence in gaining freedom from the British Empire. One objective of the constitution was to abandon dominion status, which Jawaharlal had never favored, and to achieve full independence. India became a republic in 1950. The constitution acknowledged the fundamental human rights of all, ignored caste distinctions, specifically abolished untouchability and outlawed its practice, but ancient Indian traditions were not to die so easily. Another outbreak of communal massacres, in East Pakistan and Calcutta, led Jawaharlal and Liaquat Ali Khan to sign an agreement in

1950 guaranteeing the status of minorities. Ali Khan was assassinated the following year.

Jawaharlal's India was moving towards a secular, socially equitable society which was to some extent socialist. There was undoubtedly centralized planning, ostensibly in the public good, but it is questionable whether Jawaharlal's "post-office socialism" as J. K. Galbraith called it, had anything to do with the Soviet Union; it was more a commitment to public enterprises operated at no profit, preferably with no loss, with no particular efficiency and with no other clear purpose in mind.[9] Jawaharlal was more of a nationalist, interested in Indian self-sufficiency, than a socialist with a primary economic objective. His government restricted public ownership to munitions, atomic energy and railways, and promised there would be no nationalization of existing industries for ten years, though the government might start new ones in essential areas. The authority of Hindu big business, represented by such industrial giants as textile magnate G. D. Birla, was a crucial factor in Congress policy, as it had given much support to Congress, and the party, while committed to social welfare, was never socialist.

The first national plan, launched in 1951, emphasized the importance of industrial production as a means of reducing reliance on imported food. Feeding the nation was a passion for Jawaharlal. T. N. Kaul, then a young civil servant, told how he was taught a lesson by the Prime Minister. "I remember I was with him in the Waldorf Towers, where he was staying as a guest of the U.S. government. I said, 'Sir, we're short of food. They're willing to offer us a million tons of food. Why don't we take it?' He literally hit me and said, 'Sit down, young man. Do you know that I am sitting on an explosive situation? Any country in Asia which cannot feed its people cannot be stable, can't last long. So we have got to be self-sufficient in food grains in the next two or three years, and we must depend on ourselves and not depend on others, particularly when there are strings attached.'"[10] The policy was a great success, increasing agricultural production by a quarter over a five-year period. Jawaharlal also urged large building and technology projects, including dams for power and irrigation schemes and new steel plants. A second five-year plan began in 1956, aimed at large-scale industrialization. Jawaharlal believed it was possible to raise India's standard of living to match that of European nations. Surveying the new Bhakra-Nangal dam he said, ". . . these are the new temples of India where I worship."[11] When the first Indian-made jets took to the air, he stood on the airfield with shining eyes murmuring, "Gazelles of the sky!"[12]

There was acrimonious disagreement as to which of India's many languages should be the official language. More Indians spoke Hindi than any other language, but it was not rooted in the south and could not be presented as the preeminent national language. Any choice would discriminate against vast numbers of people, so Jawaharlal referred the question of an official language to a committee of scholars. In the meantime, English and Hindi were accepted as the official languages, but the matter was never finally resolved. Jawaharlal said he was embarrassed at addressing parliament in the language of the former conquerors, but one wonders at his sincerity in saying this, as he would confess whimsically, "Well, you know that I am the last Englishman to rule in India."[13] His Englishness was not merely a residue of youth; he continued to adopt new English ways. The first time he dined at Buckingham Palace he noticed the serving arrangements and decreed that in his own house milk and sugar should be placed in the cups before the coffee. This was often bewildering to the guests, Indira said, and they would "look around furtively to see if they have somehow mislaid, or forgotten to take, the coffee."[14]

Nehru's reception at the palace of the former king-emperor probably took place in September 1948, when Jawaharlal attended the Commonwealth prime ministers' meeting and agreed that India would remain in the Commonwealth so long as there was no obligation to pledge allegiance to the King. Instead, a form of words was arrived at in which India swore "acceptance" of the King as head of the Commonwealth. The left in India considered this a great betrayal, but Jawaharlal was concerned at India's isolation, particularly from such an important economic partner as Britain, if she stayed outside the Commonwealth. He also enjoyed the world stage which Commonwealth membership gave him.

It was not the left, in fact, which caused Jawaharlal the most problems; he was much more constrained by powerful figures on the right. The perennial battle within Congress always revolved around the extent to which India was a Hindu nation. Jawaharlal's secular faction was aided by youth and idealism, while Hindu big business backed Patel and Prasad and demanded that political priority be given to such issues as banning the slaughter of cows. When the fervently anti-Muslim Purushottam Das Tandon was elected president of Congress, Jawaharlal publicly denounced the success of a candidate cheered by "communal and reactionary forces" and undermined him by declining to serve on the working committee formed by the new Congress president.[15] Eventually Tandon stepped down and Jawaharlal was elected in his place, acting as Congress president and prime minister until 1955.

He was less successful in promoting his own nominee as president of India. Jawaharlal wanted Mountbatten's successor as governor-general, Chakravarti Rajagopalachari, to continue as president after full independence, but Sardar Patel maneuvered behind the scenes to ensure the success of his candidate, Rajendra Prasad, who therefore took up the post on January 26, 1950 when the nation became a republic.

Although the leader of an Indian republic, Jawaharlal remained an Englishman at heart. Further evidence of this lay in the fact that his closest relationship was with an Englishwoman. The love which was to develop between Jawaharlal and Edwina Mountbatten was not evident until near the end of the Mountbattens' stay. On May 13, 1948 Jawaharlal went with the Mountbattens up to the viceregal lodge at Simla. "Suddenly I realized (and perhaps you did also)," Jawaharlal later wrote to Edwina, "that there was a deeper attachment between us, that some uncontrollable force, of which I was only dimly aware, drew us to one another. I was overwhelmed and at the same time exhilarated by this new discovery. We talked more intimately, as if some veil had been removed, and we could look into each other's eyes without fear or embarrassment."[16] As soon as Jawaharlal left Simla, the letters started, with Edwina writing, ". . . you have left me with a strange sense of peace and happiness. Perhaps I have brought you the same?"[17]

Mountbatten noticed the change in his wife, and wrote to his daughter, "Please keep this to yourself, but she and Jawahalal" [he never pronounced or spelled Jawaharlal's name correctly] "are so sweet together. They really dote on each other in the nicest way and Pammy and I are doing everything we can to be tactful and help. Mummy has been incredibly sweet lately and we've been such a happy family."[18]

The last sentence gives the main reason for Mountbatten's heroic tolerance: Edwina's temper tantrums were such that an affair with someone trusted to be discreet was a small price to pay for peace and quiet. Edwina was in a sense not unlike Kamala, engaging in public work to the point of exhaustion, while privately nursing neuroses: a life full of tearful scenes and resentments at imagined or unintended slights.

Edwina had had affairs from early in her marriage, perhaps in compensation for Mountbatten's sexual shortcomings, or just because she needed more sexual attention than one man could supply. Mountbatten was constantly comparing himself unfavorably with the flashy, vapid men who were her lovers. His attempts to console Edwina after one of these characters announced his engagement were often pathetic.[19]

With Jawaharlal, however, it was true love, and the love of equals. They had enjoyed a similar, privileged background, but had a deep humanity and shared an intolerance of traditional constraints. Their relationship was passionate but also intellectual, it was deep but also lighthearted, their conversations full of giggles and sidelong glances. They hypnotized each other. Patricia, later Countess Mountbatten, said, "Mr. Nehru was obviously a lonely man, his wife had died many years before, and my mother was somebody who had not been able to communicate or make easy relationships with anybody, even with her own husband. I think the fact that these two had this similar lack in their lives, which the other person fulfilled, gave them a very strong relationship to each other. And I'm quite sure it didn't go beyond that."[20]

They had little time to be together, for the Mountbattens were due to leave on June 24, but they met as frequently as they could, and when they were not together they were writing. "The more one talks, the more there is to say," wrote Jawaharlal to her after they had parted following one of their latenight conversations in the Viceroy's palace, "and there is so much that it is difficult to put it into words. I have a feeling that I did not say the right thing or did not put it in the right way."[21]

They had one last long period together, when they went to Barelli so Edwina could say goodbye to Sarojini Naidu who had been a friend of her mother. They rode in the mountains the following day and talked about their future together—or apart. Edwina later wrote to

Jawaharlal, "This was the only promise we ever made, on the road to Naini Tal—that nothing we did or felt would ever be allowed to come between you and your work and me and mine—because that would spoil everything."[22]

On the Mountbattens' last night in India the Cabinet gave them a farewell banquet. Edwina wept when Jawaharlal and Mountbatten spoke, and Jawaharlal was too upset to take in any of what she said in her farewell speech. They exchanged gifts: she gave him a silver St. Christopher medallion which her mother had once given her father; he gave her an ancient Indian coin which she attached to a bracelet. Jawaharlal walked through her now-deserted rooms at the Viceroy's palace, scenting her presence there, "a fragrance on the air." He would read her letters again and again, and "lose myself in dreamland" he confessed.[23]

In the autumn, when Jawaharlal traveled to London for the Commonwealth conference, he visited Broadlands, the Mountbattens' country house, for the first time. During the visit they enjoyed their life of dinner parties, riding and games on the lawn. Within a few months, however, Edwina was back in India. Jawaharlal and she went on vacation together to Orissa to walk on the white sand beaches and visit the great Sun Temple with its erotic sculptures at Konark. They were accompanied by Edwina's daughter Pamela, by Indira, Krishna and Jawaharlal's niece Rita. Much of their relationship was conducted in front of others, members of their family and servants, and there was no secret about their physical closeness: they would hug, and he would take her arm and press her hands as he spoke.

Every year Edwina made a special trip to Delhi to see Jawaharlal, and whenever she was traveling near India on her trips for the St. John Ambulance Brigade or the Red Cross, she would visit him on the way out and the way back. She loved Jawaharlal but she also loved India: for her they were inseparable, and his gifts were the essence of India: "pressed flowers from Kashmir, dried ferns from Sikkim, saffron, tea, orchids, mangoes, a sandalwood box, a crocodile skin . . ."[24] Jawaharlal wrote, "I have been absorbed in and have passionately pursued the love of India and her people and sought to give them such service as I could. But you came to add to it and not come in its way."[25] He also visited England often, staying at Broadlands, the Mountbattens' home, eight times between 1950 and 1957. Pamela Hicks later said,

"My father very much respected their friendship and trusted them. I think occasionally when she went out on a tour and was going to be stopping off in India he would rather prudently say, 'Maybe you shouldn't go to some of Panditji's public things and be photographed the whole time. You know you ought to be a little bit discreet because maybe the papers would read far too much into it.'"[26]

In the first six months of the relationship they wrote to each other daily. The letters went via the diplomatic bag, and were sent on by hand through Krishna Menon in his capacity as high commissioner. Each letter was in a double cover and numbered so that they would know if any letters had gone astray and fallen into the hands of ill-wishers. On days when there were no letters from him, she telephoned, an exercise in patience, for the call would have to be routed through several switchboards and the line was so indistinct that telephone operators would sometimes have to repeat Edwina's words to Jawaharlal.

Their letters became less frequent as the years passed, though there would always be at least one every three weeks. Edwina was concerned about the eventual fate of these letters, even when she herself was in danger. She had been taken to the hospital with severe hemorrhaging in 1952, and while waiting to be taken to the operating theater, she wrote to Mountbatten telling him about the correspondence: "Some of them have no 'personal' remarks at all. Others are love letters in a sense, though you yourself well realize the strange relationship—most of it spiritual—which exists between us. J. has obviously meant a great deal in my life, in these last years, and I think I in his too. Our meetings have been rare and always fleeting, but I think I understand him, and perhaps he me, as well as any human beings can ever understand each other."[27] It was indeed strange that her valedictory letter to her husband should almost entirely consist of references to another man, but Mountbatten was simply pleased she survived the operation. He wrote that he would always treasure her letter: "I'm glad you realize that I know and have always understood the very special relationship between Jawaha and you—made the easier by my fondness and admiration for him and by the remarkably lucky fact that among my many defects God did not add jealousy."[28]

Rather too much time has been spent on the question of whether Jawaharlal and Edwina actually had sex. It is unremarkable that "evidence" of personal activities should be lacking from the record: the answer is to be found in the personalities of the individuals. Given Edwina Mountbatten's sexual behavior as an adult, she would have found it peculiar to the point of insult if Jawaharlal had not wanted to have sex with her. His views on sexual pleasure, unrestricted by conventional morality, were public knowledge at least from the publication of his autobiography in 1936. The onus of proof would seem to be with those who question whether there was a sexual element: why should there not have been?

Krishna noted that visits from Edwina were the only times her brother recovered his youthful gaiety. "Nothing Edwina did was wrong," Krishna recorded, but he was not so tolerant with his sisters. Krishna remembered how Jawaharlal once flared up at her, saying, "Do you have to wear so much jewelry and flashy diamonds around the house, especially in the morning?" Krishna angrily responded, "You don't get angry with Edwina, in fact you keep admiring her jewelry, all the different sets she wears. No matter what time of the day or night she wears them you think it's wonderful. Why do you scold me?" Jawaharlal looked puzzled and said it was not quite the same thing, but could not think why. He never again commented on Krishna's jewels.[29]

It quickly became apparent that 17 York Road, designated as the Prime Minister's residence, was too small for Jawaharlal's family and state entertaining needs. In its place he was given Teen Murti House, a former residence of the commander-in-chief of the British Indian armed forces. It was a huge, gloomy, red sandstone building with long corridors and large rooms, which Indira struggled to make a little more homey.

The writer John Grigg, who made several visits to the family over a long period, considered that Jawaharlal's making Indira his closest companion and confidante was his compensation for leaving her during her childhood to look after her sick mother alone. "Sensitive as he was, and always prone to soul-searching, he was well aware that his long absences in prison might have been due as much to self-indulgence as to patriotism," Grigg commented.[30] The main reason, however, seems to have been an imperious selfishness: Jawaharlal's needs, which were also the needs of India, were simply more important than the needs of his daughter's family, and he needed a hostess.

When Indira was away, his sister Krishna was summoned from Bombay, away from her husband and children, to do the job.

Being the Prime Minister's hostess meant coordinating the visits of such notables as the Shah of Iran, King Ibn Saud, Ho Chi Minh, Khrushchev, Eisenhower, Tito and Nasser. Indira did not enjoy being a hostess, but as it was her duty, she resigned herself to do it well. She was reserved and shy when she started this work, always ducking out with the excuse that she was seeing to "the arrangements." It was the more creative aspects of keeping house, like interior decoration and flower arranging, that delighted Indira.

She learned to negotiate the minefield of protocol with the additional complication of the dietary restrictions of Indian culture. It was not only a matter of the dietary taboos of Muslims avoiding pork and Hindus beef, but "there are meat-eaters who are vegetarians on certain days of the week—there are vegetarians who eat eggs, others eat fish as well, and one distinguished guest, who declared himself a vegetarian, ended up eating everything except chicken!"[31]

The British novelist Barbara Cartland became a friend of Indira's after a visit in the company of Edwina Mountbatten in 1959. She later remembered Indira at that first meeting "wearing a blue sari, [she] was very quiet and gentle. She was overshadowed by the overwhelming personality of her father . . . She always looked deeply beneath the surface. In all my conversations with her I was aware that she was not satisfied with what she had been told or what she had seen, she knew instinctively there was more to be discovered."[32] In viewing newsreels of Indira and her father at this time it is remarkable how Indira, so often seen as a withdrawn person, comes alive as an assertive individual when she is by Jawaharlal's side greeting foreign dignitaries, where she is constantly on hand to give advice and guidance, to smooth the diplomatic process.

The leading journalist Arun Shourie considered that taking the position of official hostess was decisive in Indira's development. He said, "Mrs. Gandhi's coming of age is as the person in charge of Pandit Nehru's household as prime minister. That's where she acquires an imperiousness, a feeling that they are the ruling family, here forever."[33]

Indira's role as hostess extended to organizing all domestic arrangements at Teen Murti House, including the Nehru menagerie accommodated in the large gardens. Jawaharlal had always loved animals. He had spent many hours of imprisonment watching birds and other small animals, and had even made pets of some insects. Now he had what amounted to a private zoo. There were dogs, including pedigrees and some strays rescued from the street, parrots, pigeons, squirrels, deer and other small animals. There were also a Himalayan panda and three tiger cubs. Indira once had to sit up five nights in succession with one of these cubs when it was unwell. Eventually they grew up and had to be given to Lucknow Zoo, except one which was so admired by Marshal Tito of Yugoslavia that Jawaharlal made him a present of it. The panda and the mate eventually found for him were particular favorites of Jawaharlal, who visited them morning and evening. Sanjay had a baby crocodile, which was given to a zoo after it bit Indira.

There was a keen emphasis on health in the Nehru household. He had written to Indira, "Not to be physically fit seems to me one of the major sins that a person can be guilty of."[34] He continued to practice yoga and his staff would still come upon him standing on his head while he was in his seventies. Jawaharlal and Indira at some time in the 1950s engaged the services of a yogi called Brahmachari who was known for braving Delhi's winter wearing nothing more than a thin dhoti (a cloth tied around the waist). Indira wrote to a friend in 1958, "I get up early these days to do a special set of exercises. It is a system (part of yoga) that was taught us by an exceedingly good-looking yogi. In fact, it was his looks, especially his magnificent body, which attracted everyone to his system."[35]

Many rooms in the house were powerfully air-conditioned but Jawaharlal did not use his machine: Krishna remarked he never seemed to feel the cold or the heat. He slept in a plain wooden bed with no springs, just a plank with a mattress on it. His room had book-cases around the walls and pictures of Kamala, Indira and the rest of the family. There was a high level of security around the house but it was treated with no great seriousness by Jawaharlal or most of his guests. Prince Philip was once found walking across the lawns in the morning, having climbed out of his bathroom window to leave his security men guarding an empty room.

In the right company, Jawaharlal would revert to moods of merriment, as one visitor said at meeting the sixty-eight-year-old premier:

"Nehru was positively gleeful. He bounced happily from one foot to the other. He became gay beyond measure, and smiling."[36] He also had the happy knack, most fortuitously for a leader, of being able to cast off care: "In the final analysis," he said, "I am not worried about the future of India, about the things that I care for. Having done my best, I have a good sound sleep and I get up refreshed in the morning, whatever may happen."[37]

Jawaharlal had an English-style breakfast, copying those of English country houses, where food was arranged in heated dishes so that guests could help themselves and not be bothered by servants fussing around. Despite his privileged upbringing, Jawaharlal would generally rather do things for himself than call servants, and he was highly intolerant of sycophancy. He was a soft touch for a hardluck story, however, and when he made his daily personal appearances on the lawn of Teen Murti House, he would be flooded with needs and requests. Indira complained that "much of his time is taken by people's personal problems and by matters which could be dealt with by the people in charge of departments more directly concerned."[38] Others would claim that Indira kept too close a rein on Jawaharlal's schedule, even planning what friends he met. Vijaya complained angrily that she was not being allowed to see her own brother.

Indira had her own interests which tended, in the first half of the 1950s, towards welfare work. She set up Bal Sahyog, a training center for teaching destitute children useful trades, after she was pestered in the street by a child trying to sell her a comb. When she angrily asked why he was not in school, he said his family needed the money he earned, so Indira went with him to the slum where he lived to meet the family and discuss what could be done for children like him. Indira later became president of the Indian Council of Child Welfare, and she also fostered the establishment of organizations for the development of Indian music, dance and film. She never forgot her own miserable childhood and kept her priorities in mind. She said, "I don't think I ever allowed public activities to interfere with anything that was important on the domestic side on any day or any occasion. I was always there if the children needed me."[39] Sanjay himself testified to the truth of this when a society woman visiting Indira commented that with all her public work she could have little time for her children. Sanjay was angry and rushed to his mother's defense: "My mother does lots of important work yet she plays with me more than you do with your little boy," he said.[40]

Rajiv and Sanjay first went to a kindergarten school opened by Elizabeth Gauba, the German wife of a Lahore businessman, whom Indira had met when they were doing refugee work during partition. Later the boys attended the Doon School in the Himalayas, but Indira made sure that her trips abroad and around India coincided with term time so she was with them in the holidays.

Despite her undoubtedly deep love for them, Indira's manner towards her sons and Jawaharlal was always cool; she was unable to demonstrate love openly. When questioned about her lack of openness she said, "One does not wear one's heart on one's sleeve."[41] She also consciously passed emotional reservation on to the children. When Rajiv was three, the birth of Sanjay coincided with their move from Allahabad, and the little boy expressed his discomfort in tantrums which irritated Indira. She tried scolding him and reasoning with him to no effect, then told him to go to a fountain in the garden and cry there. "After that," she wrote, "at the first sign of tears I would whisper "fountain" and away he went."[42] There were also lessons in sacrifice. Rajiv needed an operation as a boy, and the surgeon assured .him it would not hurt. Indira interrupted to say there would be considerable pain and discomfort and he must be prepared to bear it— weeping or complaining would make no difference. He bore the pain without complaint.

A letter from Indira to Rajiv in 1955 when he fractured his arm shows the spirit of defiance she tried to instill in her children: "One must not be afraid of being hurt. The world is full of all kinds of hurts and it is only by facing them that we can become strong and hardy and able to do great things . . . You know how much I want both of you to be courageous in mind and body. There are millions of people in the world, but most of them just drift along, afraid of death and even more afraid of life."[43]

Feroze made frequent visits to Delhi; he constructed wooden fretwork toys for the children and encouraged them to find out how machines worked but, inescapably, when he walked out of Teen Murti House, it was as if he were a divorced husband. Inevitably, the children saw more of their grandfather than their father, and Indira had a much closer relationship with the boys. Feroze was given a parliamentary seat at Rae Bareli, Uttar Pradesh, in January 1950, when appointments were made pending clarification of the voters' lists, which were still being compiled under the new constitution. At the first general election, held between 1951 and 1952, he ran for the seat and won it on his own merits. These were the first elections in free India, with 150 million votes cast. The slogan was "A Vote for Congress is a Vote for Nehru"—indeed, Jawaharlal himself had written the Congress manifesto. Indira often campaigned with her father, this time addressing an election meeting alone for the first time, and also devoted considerable energy to Feroze's campaign. The State Congress Committee of Uttar Pradesh asked Indira to run for election to the state legislature but she refused, wanting to devote herself to children and social welfare work.

Feroze, as an MP, now had his own house in Delhi, where he received guests and petitioners, but he lived in Teen Murti House with Indira and the boys. Feroze disliked his subordinate position, as "son-in-law of the nation," and attended only functions to which he was invited as an MP, and not those where he was invited as Indira's husband. He was, anyway, the sort of man who was much more at ease at children's parties than at formal receptions, particularly when the seating plan at formal events put him in a markedly inferior seat to that enjoyed by his wife. Feroze also stood apart from the Nehrus because he was coarse and outspoken, particularly when offended. On one occasion when Jawaharlal was admonishing a Congress meeting because so many delegates had brought their wives and children, Feroze interrupted, "I did not bring my wife here."[44] Witnesses to mealtimes in the Nehru household noted an atmosphere of intense irritation, with Feroze contradicting Jawaharlal on every topic and Jawaharlal struggling to keep his temper.

Indira later denied that she had left Feroze, though she said, "It wasn't an ideally happy marriage. We were very happy at times. We quarreled tremendously at times. It was partly because both of us were so headstrong, and partly circumstances." She said that he particularly disliked being asked how it felt to be her husband: ". . . it would take me weeks to win him over. To hurt the male ego is, of course, the biggest sin in marriage."[45] One of Indira's friends reported that in 1957, as Indira was becoming more successful in Congress politics, Feroze was flaunting his relationships with other women to humiliate her.[46]

Divorce was certainly considered, for years later, when Nayantara went to Jawaharlal with problems in her own marriage, he said "For God's sake, whatever you do, don't make the mistake Indu did. She couldn't make up her mind one way or the other, and it only caused more suffering all round."[47] When the Hindu Succession and Hindu Marriage Acts were passed in 1955 and 1956 respectively, gossip said it was to prepare the way for Indira's divorce, but this was fanciful, for laws giving women inheritance and divorce rights were clearly matters of human rights. The Acts were social reforms which Jawaharlal believed to be the most important changes made under his leadership.

Domestic problems notwithstanding, Feroze quickly began to show his merits as a parliamentary crusader. His meticulous research and attention to detail contrasted with the approach of many of his colleagues, who made self-important speeches containing nothing. Feroze first campaigned against the misuse of funds by the Bharat Insurance Company. His denunciation of the corruption led to the appointment of a commission of inquiry, the conviction of the company chief Rama Krishna Dalmia, and ultimately to the nationalization of the life insurance business. Feroze was also always available to work on the unglamorous problems of the poor, who came to his small house for help.

Feroze was returned in the elections of 1957, after which he started to campaign against the Finance Ministry, which had sanctioned a large loan to a businessman. The Finance Minister, T. T. Krishnamachari, was one Jawaharlal's ablest ministers and the Prime Minister was angry at the charges, but he agreed to a judicial inquiry at which Feroze was the chief witness. The report of the inquiry was an extreme embarrassment to Jawaharlal, as it implicated a number of government officials in corruption. Krishnamachari was obliged to resign amid widespread criticism of the government. Feroze was alarmed at the way the investigation had spread and undermined the government: "Oh where did I aim, and where did I hit?" he said.[48]

The fact that Jawaharlal found it impossible to establish a rapport with Feroze was a loss to both of them, and to democracy in India. Had it been possible for them to work together, Feroze's attacks on backsliding Congress grandees and exposure of corruption in high places would have given a radical edge to Jawaharlal's governments, something they undoubtedly required. The problem was that Jawaharlal was very poor at choosing colleagues. John Grigg said, ". . . his habit of introspection made him a better judge of himself than of others" and ". . . his solitariness made him vulnerable to anybody who could win his confidence and seemed to be protecting him against the outside world."[49]

This was forcibly brought home in the affair of M. O. Mathai. Jawaharlal received up to 2000 letters and telegrams a day, and spent four to five hours every night dictating replies. Obviously, some sifting mechanism had to be operated. The person who decided which papers Jawaharlal would actually see and which would be dealt with routinely or passed to particular departments occupied a very important post, and it was this post that Mathai created for himself.

M. O. Mathai was Jawaharlal's special assistant and confidant, effectively Jawaharlal's guardian, so only those who had the favor of Mathai could have the ear of the Prime Minister. He passed on gossip about those he did not favor and regularly gave Jawaharlal his opinions. Ministers sought his advice, Indira was grateful that he protected Jawaharlal from the world, and even the Mountbattens and Padmaja Naidu treated him with affection. None of them seemed to recognize that he was concentrating power in his own hands. Feroze, however, collected enough details on Mathai's arrogant abuse of power to force his resignation. From personal loyalty, Jawaharlal would not allow either police investigations or a departmental inquiry, so, to the dismay of Feroze, Mathai was never finally brought to account for the great wealth he had accumulated during his government employ. Such was his wealth, that he was widely believed to have been the CIA's man in Jawaharlal's office.

Another unwise association was Jawaharlal's excessively close relationship with Krishna Menon, one of his few real friends. When Krishna Menon returned from London where he had been high commissioner from 1947 to 1952, Jawaharlal invited him to live at Teen Murti House. He was "glum and rather sinister" according to Jawaharlal's sister Krishna: "the only person I saw him smile at and talk with in an animated way was my brother, but the minute someone else entered the room he would fall silent . . . they spoke the same language, understood each other's jokes based on English slang or customs; and they delighted in reminiscences of the English days."[50] Menon was a difficult, unsettled character who exemplified the isolation of the nationalist exile. He had studied at the LSE in London and was called to the Bar at the Middle Temple. Since 1929, he had promoted the ideas of Indian independence through the India League, but he also participated in local politics. From 1934 to 1947, he served as a Labor member of St. Pancras Council. By the time independence was achieved, England was his home, and when he returned to India in 1952 he had virtually no Indian languages. Menon was fond of Indira, perhaps detecting a kindred spirit, but he hated Vijaya, with whom he served at the United Nations. Later, in 1956, Jawaharlal made him a minister without portfolio, then defense minister, against the opposition of the whole of the Cabinet. Indira insisted he move out, as it was not seemly for the Prime Minister to live with one of his ministers. Menon did so, but still visited on a daily basis. Indira had a far from tranquil relationship with Menon, but they backed each other publicly: she stood up for him against his detractors, while he promoted her cause with the Congress left. He was as far left as one could be in the Congress Party, and had many communist friends.

Elsewhere Jawaharlal's exhortations to public morality merely formed an oratorical ornament to a corrupt system, where Congress politics rapidly became an ingenious variety of avenues for corruption. The goodwill built up in the long struggle for freedom was being squandered in the scramble for graft.

There was also significantly less national unity in India in 1957 than in 1947. Part of the problem was that many states wished to have their boundaries redrawn on linguistic lines. This would inevitably lead to greater local power, and therefore less centralized, national authority. It would also lead to a multiplication of linguistic minorities in the new states, whose rights it would be difficult to safeguard. Allied to this was the renewed anxiety over the proposal to use Hindi as a national language, a move opposed by southern Indian states which feared non-Hindi speakers in the public services would suffer discrimination. In most cases state boundaries *were* redrawn along linguistic lines in 1957, which left some problems, notably in Punjab, where Sikhs wanted a Punjabi-speaking state.

Jawaharlal's failure to deal decisively with problems, disguised though it was as a willingness to hear all sides of an argument, was now tending to allow the disintegration of the Indian body politic. He recognized this and talked of resignation, saying, "I feel now that I must have a period when I can free myself from this burden and can think of myself as an individual citizen of India and not as prime minister."[51] However, an announcement like this to the Congress parliamentary party was little but an invitation for them to beg him to stay, which they did. India needed him. His resignation threats were not only a political ploy—they expressed a real need to be free from the burden of responsibility. He told a house guest in 1957, "I haven't been out alone for twelve years. It's a long time never to have been free to do what I like." He mentioned a time when he had tried to go to a book shop, but a crowd had gathered and the police had to be called.[52] He had become a prisoner of his own legend.

# EIGHT

# JAWAHARLAL LECTURES
# THE WORLD

Increasing failure and skepticism about Nehru's policies at home led him to engage ever more deeply in the luxuriously inspiring area of foreign affairs. To some extent, these started at home because small areas of the country were still occupied by foreign powers—Goa by the Portuguese and Pondicherry by the French. An honorable way for the French to hand over Pondicherry was arrived at in 1954, but the Portuguese resisted persuasion to the extent of imprisoning nationalists and shooting Indians who attempted to cross the border. Eventually, in 1961, and contrary to his principles of non-violence, Jawaharlal sent in troops, but there was no international sympathy for the Salazar dictatorship in Portugal. Goa capitulated without a single death.

Kashmir never did calm down, and the dispute gained an international dimension, because the USSR supported India while the USA supported Pakistan to the point of supplying arms. In the election of 1951, Sheikh Abdullah became Chief Minister of Kashmir, but proved something of a disappointment to the Congress Party by keeping to the letter of his agreement: that the central government had rights only over defense, external affairs and communications—in other respects, Kashmir was autonomous. An uneasy situation ensued, with communal tensions again coming to the fore and Sheikh Abdullah moving towards a demand that the Indian Army leave Kashmir. Behind the scenes, Congress Party insiders manipulated Abdullah's fall from power in 1953, and his deputy, Bakshi Ghulam Mohammed, more sympathetic to Delhi's position, took over. Almost the first act of the new regime was to arrest Abdullah, who was in detention until 1957. It hurt Jawaharlal desperately that his old friend, an elected prime minister, was imprisoned; but with the political situation as it was, and seeing all sides of it as he was wont to do, he abdicated responsibility and left matters to the local Congress leaders and his ministers. By way of recompense, he personally paid for Abdullah's son to be educated in England. In 1958, Abdullah was again arrested, after four months of liberty. A woman who was an old friend of both the Nehrus and

Abdullah could not contain her anger. She stormed into Teen Murti House, found Indira ill in bed, and slapped her across the face, presumably thinking she was to some extent responsible for Jawaharlal's Kashmiri policy. Indira apparently managed to maintain her dignity.

In his foreign policy Jawaharlal had always yearned for complete independence from any outside influence. When he became minister for external affairs in the interim government in 1946, he declared, "India will follow an independent policy, keeping away from power politics of groupings aligned one against the others."[1] This was easier to say than to achieve, though it was to develop into what was represented as a policy of "nonalignment" with the communist or capitalist power blocs. The objective was, from an idealistic point of view, to serve as a bridge and bring about a measure of understanding between powerful antagonists. A more cynical approach would be to say it was nonalignment aimed at receiving economic aid from both power blocs while owing allegiance to neither.

At the risk of alienating the United States, Jawaharlal spoke up for China to join the United Nations, which the U.S. was preventing with its "non-recognition" policy. He explained his view of the American position: "It was to me completely opposed to the very conception of the United Nations for China not to be in it. It is not a question of liking the Chinese people's government or not. It is a question of recognizing a fact of reality. If you don't, well, it is the United Nations that suffers."[2]

His sympathy for China was misplaced, however, when in 1950 he condoned China's invasion of Tibet, an independent state between the borders of China and India. In 1954, he compounded his error by formally recognizing Tibet as part of China without receiving any assurances in return about India's borders with Tibet. The Chinese later allowed the two religious leaders of Tibet, the Dalai and Panchen Lamas, to visit India for the 2500th anniversary celebration of Buddha's birth, but this was no guarantee of continued good will.

It was during discussions with the Chinese premier Chou En-lai to regulate trade and pilgrims from India to Tibet that Jawaharlal enunciated his principle of *panchsheel* (co-existence) in which Asia was supposedly offering the world a different approach from that of either West or East. Based on the centuries-old Indian practice of many different religions and philosophies co-existing, the principle sounded fine and humanistic, but the Chinese found it hard to understand, as their foreign policy was based entirely on pragmatic considerations about what was best for China.

Chou En-lai visited India in 1954 and was met with calls of "Hindi, Chini, bhai bhai" ("Indians and Chinese are brothers"), though he later said, "I have never met a more arrogant man than Nehru."[3] Jawaharlal and Indira visited China later that year to an enthusiastic welcome. Sympathy for China and the USSR may have given him a warm moral glow, but there was no material gain, and Jawaharlal risked sacrificing United States support and aid.

The apotheosis of *panchsheel* was the Bandung conference, held in Indonesia in 1955, in which twenty-nine Afro-Asian nations "proclaimed the political emergence in world affairs of over half the world's population," as Jawaharlal put it.[4] Jawaharlal was on his way to Indonesia when news reached him that a plane scheduled to carry Chou En-lai to the conference had been sabotaged, reportedly by agents of the British government. Chou En-lai had in fact taken another plane, but Jawaharlal was furious and penned an angry telegram to the Prime Minister Anthony Eden. B. K. Nehru, who was traveling with him said, "In his usual boyish, enthusiastic manner he got up from his seat and was going to the pilot to give the telegram to him to radio it. One of Jawaharlal's most lovable characteristics was that he did everything himself, he couldn't be bothered, didn't have the patience to wait for things to be done through the proper channels, he did things on the spot. Indira, who was sitting next to him, stopped him and said, 'What are you doing?' She read the telegram and generally cooled him down and said, 'There's no proof, you must wait until you get some kind of proof, there's just an allegation and you can't send that kind of thing to the British prime minister.'" Not for the first or last time, Indira's good sense prevailed over Jawaharlal's impetuousness.[5]

Bandung was largely a platform for high sentiments. It produced no organization, seeming to suggest that principles should be enough. It also tended to define nonalignment in a way that allowed alignment, so communist countries of all persuasions were well represented. Still, by the next nonaligned conference, in Belgrade in 1961, twenty-four countries had publicly declared themselves for nonalignment and peaceful co-existence.

Jawaharlal was first and foremost an anti-imperialist, a stance which had served him well in his early political career. But as imperialism became less important internationally, his position became less relevant and more difficult to justify. In 1956 he was quick to condemn Britain's invasion of Egypt, but tardy in condemning the Soviet Union's invasion of Hungary, despite the fact that both were examples of aggression by powerful countries against weak ones.

The Anglo-French invasion of Egypt and the secret agreement with Israel which preceded it caused serious alarm to Mountbatten, now First Sea Lord, who feared the effect British behavior would have on the Commonwealth. Jawaharlal in a despairing letter confirmed his worst fears: "I would never have conceived of a government of the United Kingdom functioning as the present one has done. . . . Whatever the future may bring, I fear that respect for the UK has vanished utterly from Asia and Africa."[6] This came as further torment for Mountbatten's troubled soul. Already bowed down by the pressure of the ill-conceived Suez enterprise, he was also at odds with Edwina because, as a serving officer, he was obliged to take part in starting the unjust war. He drafted a letter of resignation to Prime Minister Anthony Eden, writing of the risk of provoking a nuclear war and of Britain's "retrograde and absolutely indefensible step" in flouting the principles of the United Nations.[7] He balked at submitting his resignation to Eden, however, and instead sent it to his immediate superior, the First Lord of the Admiralty, who rejected it. Mountbatten stayed on to mitigate some of the worst aspects of the original plan.

Nehru was highly suspicious of the USA in what he saw as its policy of encouraging divisions in the Third World, supporting one side against the other. For their part, Americans showed little understanding of India. As B. K. Nehru, a diplomat and later Indian ambassador to the US, said, "The people of the United States knew absolutely nothing about India except what they had read in Rudyard Kipling. They didn't realize that India had existed for a fairly long time, they assumed that India having been a British colony, that all India was a creation of the British. Therefore the Indians would rather be with them in the cold war than with anyone else."[8]

The economist J. K. Galbraith referred to a suspicion of Nehru among American public and official opinion for not being prepared to side with them in the cold war: "But on the other hand, here was a man who had brought a great country from imperial control to independence, and one had to attend to the concerns of that country."[9]

There was ample room for distance between Jawaharlal's view and that of the Americans, however. B. K. Nehru said, "His way of looking at the United States was that of an upper-class Englishman of the early nineteen hundreds—that they were just a country of upstarts who had a lot of money. They had no manners; they had no behavior; they had no knowledge; they had no culture. That was the prejudice that Jawaharlal came back with from Harrow."[10] During Jawaharlal's state visit to the U.S. in 1949, George McGhee, later an ambassador but at that time a U.S. State Department official, guessed that he thought of the country as being "low on the intellectual and social scale. We were a new country, we didn't have the traditions that England or India had, and he didn't conceal this reaction very well."[11] In his first address to the Congress and the Senate, Jawaharlal, without great subtlety, underlined what he saw as India's moral superiority: ". . . like you, we have achieved our freedom through a revolution, though our methods were different from yours."[12]

At the state banquet Jawaharlal did not find particularly elevating the argument that President Truman and Vice-President Alben Barkley had on the respective merits of Kentucky and Missouri bourbon. Phillips Talbot accompanied him for some of his visit and found Nehru interested in the Science Museum and in a visit to a farm, but "taking him to a drug store turned out not to be very successful."[13]

Indira accompanied him on this visit, but the old family rivalry came out when Vijaya, now Indian Ambassador to the USA, did not include her name as part of the Prime Minister's official party, so she did not receive invitations to official functions. She was largely left to her own devices, or to non-official meetings, but this turned out well, for at one of these meetings she met Dorothy Norman, a writer and political campaigner who was to be a friend and correspondent for the rest of Indira's life. According to Norman, they had an immediate rapport, and met over the years to go clothes shopping or to the theater. In her letters Indira shows herself to be girlishly enthusiastic about the pleasures of life, but quick to take offense. The preoccupations of the two women were similar: they shared interests in nature, art, dance, architecture and music; both had children; in politics they were both committed to democratic freedoms, social welfare programs, the eradication of poverty and non-violence. Norman considered that although Indira lived surrounded by the powerful and the trappings of power, "she was not herself drawn to power."[14]

There was certainly part of Indira that resisted political posts, for she had refused them before. By 1955, however, perhaps because her sons were now growing up, she was prepared to take official roles. Two Congress dignitaries, U. N. Dhebar and Lal Bahadur Shastri, made a surprise visit to Indira in 1955 and asked her to join the Congress Working Committee (national executive). She came out of her room to see them, though she was in bed with flu and "all wrapped up in woollies"[15], but she said they insisted and she did not resist too much. Her elevation, which strengthened Nehru loyalists against hardline Hindus, provoked little surprise as she was no novice to politics.

The Working Committee put Indira in charge of the Women's Department in 1955, which involved traveling the country organizing local units of women. She was markedly less radical than her mother, who was a feminist urging women to rebel against male authority and the dead weight of tradition. Indira liked to emphasize women's role as wives and mothers. She talked to them of household savings and balanced diets and declared "to a woman, motherhood is the highest fulfillment."[16]

In 1957 she campaigned for Jawaharlal in Phulpur, visiting almost every one of the 1100 villages in the constituency and receiving praise more for her tireless determination than her oratory. Jawaharlal described her thus: "Hardly eating and often carrying on with a handful of peanuts and a banana, she has been constantly on the move, returning at midnight, slightly gaunt but full of spirit and with flashing eyes."[17] It was an election in which some of the Nehru magic was beginning to wear off. Although Congress won with no difficulty, there were unusual results, such as a low vote for Congress in the south, where the language issue was paramount, and a communist government was elected in the state of Kerala.

Having acquired political experience, Indira was drafted in to deal with the problem of the Congress presidency. The Nehru loyalist U. N. Dhebar had held the post since 1955, but in 1958 Indira was proposed as president. To avoid accusations of partiality Jawaharlal made an ostentatious display of not doing anything to encourage her candidature, although he had always been deeply involved in the choice of the Congress president. Indira was in two minds about taking the job and leaning towards retraction, until reminded that this would vindicate media comment which said she would not be competent. She therefore became Congress president around the age of forty. Her father and her son Rajiv were also Congress presidents in their fortieth year. In each case it was a fair criticism that their parentage gave them an advantage over other candidates.

Feroze had moved to his own house permanently in 1958, though he continued to visit Teen Murti House for meals and to see his children. Shortly after the move he suffered a heart attack. Indira was in Nepal but she traveled to Delhi immediately in order to take over his nursing care herself. The two, with Rajiv and Sanjay, then went to the family province of Kashmir, where Feroze recuperated amid the mountains and the lakes. It was to be the last time they were together as a family.

Despite their reconciliation during his illness, Feroze found the proposed elevation of his wife to Congress president too much to bear and it became a major source of conflict between them. "He exudes such hostility that it seems to poison the air," Indira wrote to Dorothy Norman.[18] When she assumed the presidency in February 1959, she turned her attention to what was seen as the problem of Kerala. This state, which had the highest rate of literacy in India, had a balanced mix of Hindus, Muslims and Christians, with a large Communist Party contingent in its elected government. The Communist Party of India was tolerated by the Congress bosses until it became an effective challenger. There was horror (particularly in the United States) when Kerala went communist that it would start an infection which would ravage the whole of India like a plague. Indira observed with hostility some of the consequences of the Kerala government's program of reforms. This included putting party men in administrative agencies and the police, interfering with judicial appointments, and modifying the education syllabus which now allegedly lauded Lenin and Mao Tse-tung while ignoring Gandhi. Indira accused the Kerala communists of fomenting strikes and agitations in other parts of the country. Communists had long opposed Jawaharlal and the Congress, and had supported the British during the war when they were allies of the Soviet Union, so there was no love lost between the parties. On the other hand, Indira and Feroze had known many Indian communists in London during the 1930s and Feroze was still friendly with the parliamentary communists. He became Indira's fiercest critic in her efforts to overthrow the government of Kerala in what was the couple's last public battle.

As a democrat, Jawaharlal felt nothing should be done to unseat a democratically elected government, and Indira argued with him, but with his characteristic indecisiveness, he made no firm statement on the matter. "Operation Overthrow," as it was called, had militant bands of Congress supporters taking to the streets to oppose the Kerala government. Funding for opposition to the Kerala communists, channeled through the churches, poured in from the USA. The United States' Central Intelligence Agency (CIA), funding anti-communists throughout the world, also became involved. This was rather ironic, given Indira's later tendency to see CIA interference in every aspect of Indian political life. As Dennis Kux, historian of Indo-American relations, said, ". . . the one occasion when we had become involved was after the elections in 1957 in Kerala, when we provided money to help the Congress Party, whose president at the time was Indira Gandhi. She received money from the United States to help the Congress Party in their efforts to oust the communists."[19]

Krishna Iyer, communist Home Minister of Kerala, went to Jawaharlal to protest about Congress violence in his state. Jawaharlal listened with concern and summoned Indira, telling her she must speak with Iyer. He recalled ". . . for three days I waited, she couldn't find time to meet me. Then the third day I went and told [Jawaharlal] I was going back. 'But Indu, what about Indu, has she met you?' he said. I said, 'She doesn't find the time.' He called her and rebuked her and said, 'Indu, please meet Krishna Iyer. He has been here three days. You please meet him.' So I told her, and she ritualistically heard me and said, 'Yes, yes, yes, we'll consider about that.'"[20] There was, of course, no relaxation of the pressure Indira was putting on the Kerala government.

Indira toured Kerala organizing opposition to the communists and, on her return to Delhi, persuaded India's president, Rajendra Prasad, a staunch traditionalist, to oust the Kerala government and return control to central government. The constitution of India gave the nation's president the right to take control in cases of emergency, though it is questionable whether this was the type of emergency the framers of the constitution had in mind.

Fresh elections were proclaimed, for which Indira constructed an alliance between Congress and a renewed Muslim League. She campaigned ferociously for this unlikely alliance, and in February 1960 it won with a big majority, though the communists increased their proportion of the vote. Indira had thus shown the powers of the Congress Party her worth as a tough operator who did not shrink from difficult tasks: she could act to protect Congress bosses if they were threatened. This experience also gave her an intimate acquaintance with emergency powers.

Indira had been elected for a two-year term, but by the end of her first year she was ill with kidney stones which required an operation, so she resigned as Congress president before officiating at the annual conference. Political disagreements notwithstanding, it was now Feroze's time to help Indira; he was with her at the time of the operation and helped nurse her back to health.

The illness was as much of an excuse as a reason for her not staying in the post, however. One night, tormented by uncertainty about her future and her father's refusal to be more decisive, Indira rose at 3:45 A.M. to write to Jawaharlal about the pressure the veteran Congressman Govind Pant was putting on her to stay on as Congress president: "Since earliest childhood I have been surrounded by exceptional people and have participated in exceptional events. This has given me a somewhat unusual attitude. I am not terribly concerned with public acclamation or the reverse, nor do I feel any honor in holding a high position. Some people are attaching importance to my presiding over a Congress session and delivering the address. To me that has no special meaning or attraction.

"The circumstances in which I passed my girlhood—both the domestic and public spheres—were not easy. The world is a cruel place for the best of us and specially for the sensitive. We are apt to guard ourselves with whatever armor we can lay our minds on . . . I felt a burden on me and these last eight years or so, I have worked harder and harder as the years went by, always feeling that I could never do enough. Last year there suddenly came a moment of lightness, as if the last of the debt had been paid off. By the time I became president, I just was not in the mood for this sort of work and I have felt like a bird in a very small cage, my wings hitting against the bars whichever way I move.

"The time has come for me to live my own life. What will it be? I don't know at all. For the moment, I just want to be free as a piece of flotsam waiting for the waves to wash me up on some shore, from where I shall arise and find my own direction."[21]

In 1960 both father and daughter had to face devastating loss. Edwina Mountbatten had suffered various ailments during the 1950s and had been warned by her doctor not to overtax herself. Nevertheless, she determined to "rise above it" as she often said of any difficulty, and went on a tour of Malaya and Borneo in early 1960, making her usual stop in Delhi to see Jawaharlal. The Soviet president Marshal Voroshilov was visiting India at the time, so she was invited to the reception for him. She continued with her grueling work of inspection, speeches and administration, ending in North Borneo, where she was found dead in bed on the morning of February 21. She had suffered a heart attack at the age of fifty-seven. Beside her bed was a sheaf of Jawaharlal's letters, her nightly reading.

Jawaharlal was told of the death while on his way to the Indian Council for International Affairs, and he decided to proceed with the engagement. Marie Seton watched him arrive: ". . . his face was expressionless and self-contained . . . he took no notice of anyone."[22] The following day, the Indian parliament stood in silence for two minutes in Edwina's memory. She was buried at sea from the British ship *Wakeful* off the coast of Plymouth. Jawaharlal sent the Indian ship *Trishul*, from which his wreath of marigolds was cast on to the spot where her body had been committed to the waves. Mountbatten asked his daughter Pamela to go through Jawaharlal's letters before he did, lest he might find something too disturbing for him.

Feroze had gone straight back to work after his heart attack, and straight into conflict with Indira over her Kerala policy as Congress president. He suffered a second heart attack on September 7, 1960, having ignored the symptoms for two days, and drove himself to a nursing home. Indira was summoned from Kerala and stayed by his bedside until he died, holding her hand, on the morning of September 8, at the age of forty-eight. Indira was later to recount the last moments to Dorothy Norman: "'He really loved me, after all,' she said, with a youthful wistfulness that revealed a touching vulnerability behind the disciplined public mask."[23]

Indira later said: "The most important death in my life was my husband's. I could see my grandfather dying, though I was a child, I could see my mother dying, and my father dying, but my husband's death was so sudden. My whole mental and physical life changed so suddenly, my bodily functions changed."[24]

Though a Parsi, Feroze had said he wished to be cremated in the Hindu manner. Thousands of laborers and poor people whom Feroze had helped followed the funeral procession to the cremation grounds where Rajiv lit the pyre. Indira locked herself away alone, unwilling to allow anyone to see her grief. She wrote, "Will I ever be free from this burden or be able to touch and see without feeling 'the heartbreak in the heart of things'?"[25] Rajiv, then sixteen, and Sanjay, two years younger, are reported to have shown no great sympathy for their mother, feeling that she had ignored Feroze.[26] Rajiv later said, "I went through a very difficult period, but we had been brought up to be perhaps a bit stoic, and I kept it all inside, I did not let it come out or show in any way."[27]

Krishna went to Jawaharlal's room on the day of the funeral and found him staring into space. He was upset about the speed of Feroze's death, its effect on Indira and how young his son-in-law had been to die. He was impressed by the number of ordinary people who had gathered to pay their respects. He said mournfully, "I did not know he was so popular."[28]

NINE

# THE LAND AND THE KING

India and China had continued with the jargon of brotherhood and peaceful co-existence through the second half of the 1950s, when China's strategy for invasion was already well under way. In March 1956 the Chinese began laying a 750-mile road through Aksai Chin, an inhospitable mountainous part of what had long been recognized as northern India, which jutted into Tibet. Through all the years of *bonhomie* between Chou and Jawaharlal, the road was never mentioned.

When the existence of the road was discovered, only after its completion, Jawaharlal took the betrayal personally. As his sister Krishna said, ". . . it rocked the innermost foundation of his belief in the essential goodness and honor of human beings."[1] He had thought it was only European imperialists who could be duplicitous. Feelings in India ran high, and for the first time in his prime ministership there was widespread criticism of Jawaharlal, which pained him deeply.

Jawaharlal had been poorly advised by Sardar Panikkar, Indian Ambassador to China, who admired the current Chinese regime but had been equally enthusiastic about the previous regime of Chiang Kai-shek: this alone should have alerted Jawaharlal to his ambassador's lack of credibility. He was also warned against the Chinese by his brother-in-law, Raja Hutheesing, who had discussed the situation with him. A book he subsequently wrote about what he had seen in China mentioned the suspicion with which the Chinese leadership viewed India.

In March 1959 Jawaharlal granted political asylum to the Dalai Lama, a decision urged on him by Indira, who was involved in setting up an all-party Central Relief Committee for Tibetan refugees. This was amid a period of worsening relations with China, because Jawaharlal was demanding that Chou En-lai withdraw maps that placed many thousands of square miles of Indian territory on the Chinese side of the border. China considered the whole of her border with India as a subject for discussion, and regarded the previous boundaries as unjustly imposed by the British along the so-called McMahon line.

Jawaharlal sent patrols into the border areas and there was sporadic fighting.

Defense matters were the responsibility of Krishna Menon from 1957, Jawaharlal as usual having put loyalty above good sense and promoted his old friend who was frustrated at being a minister without portfolio. Menon had turned his brilliant, inventive mind to making defense establishments useful in a day-to-day sense, so when war loomed with the most powerful nation in the area, munitions factories were manufacturing hairclips, pressure cookers and were gearing up to make mechanical toys. Menon's political wisdom told him the Chinese would never invade, a certainty he reiterated to his troops at every opportunity. In order to have a military figure he could rely on, Menon began to promote an officer, by common consent of no outstanding ability, Brij Mohan Kaul, to lieutenant, then major-general, while also giving him direct access to Jawaharlal. He was given military command of the northeast frontier, the contested border area.

B. K. Nehru tried in vain to warn Jawaharlal about the danger of over-reliance on Menon. He said, "It was just impossible to get him to disagree with Krishna Menon, or to believe all the things that Krishna Menon was actually doing. So that when Krishna Menon told him that there was no danger and that the army was quite prepared to handle the Chinese he took it for granted."[2]

Sarvepalli Gopal, one of Jawaharlal's civil servants and later his biographer, received a lesson in Nehru insouciance when he had an urgent message to go to the Prime Minister's office. "I thought, 'Oh, God, what has happened? Have the Chinese attacked?'" he said. He rushed over and Jawaharlal said, "I've been waiting for you. This has been worrying me the whole of last night. Tell me, do you think Danton was a better man than Robespierre?" The thunderstruck civil servant then had to go through a potted history of the French Revolution, which Jawaharlal asked him to repeat to the Cabinet, who were at that time assembling for a meeting. Gopal obliged, to no great enthusiasm from the ministers: "Krishna Menon looking sour; Morarji Desai looking dumb; Lal Bahadur Shastri looking acquiescent, et cetera," then he was allowed to go and the Cabinet meeting proceeded. Gopal explained the event, "Nehru was not diverted by Chinese attacks or anything. The regions of the mind, those were the most important thing to him."[3]

1. An Edwardian family. The close affection between Vijaya and Jawaharlal was lifelong. Swarup Rani, holding the baby Krishna, habitually wore Indian dress.

2–5. Four faces of Motilal: a successful lawyer; a freemason; in court dress attending the king-emperor; in homespun clothes fighting for Indian independence.

6-9. Four faces of Jawaharlal: a schoolboy at Harrow; a student at Trinity, Cambridge; an imprisoned freedom-fighter; the hero of the masses.

10. (*above*) The wedding of Jawaharlal and Kamala. He was twenty-six, she was sixteen.
11. (*opposite*) Jawaharlal and Edwina Mountbatten share a joke.

12. (*top*) Feroze Gandhi and Indira return from England in 1941 already engaged, on the way to tell her father the news.
13. (*bottom*) Congress volunteers; Kamala and Jawaharlal are in the center of the middle row.

14. *(top)* Jawaharlal the urbane prime minister.
15 *(bottom)* The old warrior in 1963, broken by a year of defeats.

16. Three future prime ministers: Indira, Rajiv, and Jawaharlal pictured in 1946.

17. Indira in front of the family home, Anand Bhavan.

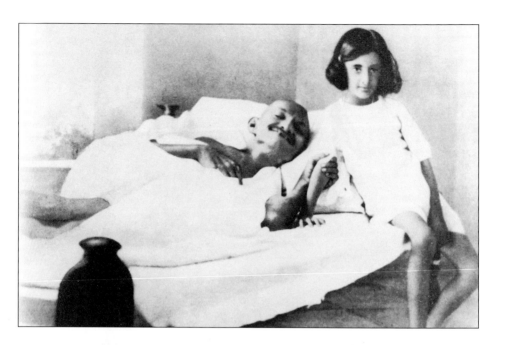

18. *(top)* Indira as a child with Mahatma Gandhi on one of his fasts.
19. *(bottom left)* Indira, the glamorous hostess.
20. *(bottom right)* Mother Indira.

21. *(top)* The Queen with Vijaya ("Nan") Pandit, India's top diplomat.
22. *(bottom)* Close friends, prime ministers Indira Gandhi
and Margaret Thatcher.

23. Mother and sons: Rajiv, Indira and Sanjay.

24. (*top*) Arun Nehru, political ally of his cousin Rajiv, before their feud.
25. (*bottom*) B.K. Nehru, senior diplomat and elder statesman of the
Nehru–Gandhi clan.

26. (*top left*) Sonia and Rajiv after their engagement.
27. (*top right*) Krishna Nehru Hutheesing, aunt and affectionate
supporter of Indira.
28. (*bottom*) Nayantara Sahgal, cousin and fierce critic of Indira.

29. (*top*) Indira and the dead Sanjay's only child, Feroze Varun.
30. (*bottom*) Indira and family. Back row: Sanjay, Rajiv and Maneka;
Front row: Rahul, Priyanka and Sonia.

31. Prime minister Rajiv meets the people.

Jawaharlal's foreign policy breezed on unrealistically, with a non-aligned meeting in Belgrade on September 1, 1961, and a visit to the United States in November 1961, when he and President Kennedy did not get on so well as commentators had predicted. Jawaharlal found Kennedy a brash young man, while Kennedy found Nehru a pompous old one. Kennedy tried deferentially to encourage Jawaharlal to talk, asking for advice on how he should handle the developing problem in Vietnam. As former journalist and then U.S. assistant secretary of state Phillips Talbot said, "Nehru remained silent, and Kennedy came back to the issue again, and Nehru remained silent and he came back to it again and he could never get Nehru to talk about the issue. Nehru had one of his moody silences. It was said that the only time his eyes lit up was when Jackie Kennedy came into the room."[4] J. K. Galbraith, Kennedy's newly appointed ambassador, said that after the meeting the President asked, "How does one communicate with him? He doesn't respond."[5]

Galbraith, a Canadian-born, Cambridge-educated academic, who had long been a friend of India and Indian art, became used to Jawaharlal's Delphic manner. Once the ambassador had kept the scrupulously punctual Nehru waiting for a meeting at which the Prime Minister said without sarcasm, "I always imagine that you have something more important to do, such as looking at pictures."[6] When Galbraith went to Jawaharlal to give him the message that President Kennedy had marked him down for a billion dollars' worth of aid, the Ambassador was met with a typical Nehru reaction: "I could not be sure whether he was embarrassed or touched—he made almost no comment," Galbraith said.[7] He felt Nehru's personal pride was closely engaged with that of India: he hated to see his country as a beneficiary of charity. Nor was this trait peculiar to dealings with the USA. On a trip to the USSR Indira had to ask for help with some measures of industrial production after Jawaharlal had let several opportunities slip.[8]

The election of 1962 resulted in a Congress victory, though with a reduced majority. The seventy-two-year-old Prime Minister was unwell with a kidney disease, pyelonephritis. Jawaharlal must have felt the chill winds of mortality, the more so because his devoted valet, Hari Lal, an untouchable who had served him since he was a child, died at that time. Two ministers who were also Congress colleagues of many years, Maulana Azad and Govind Pant, had also died recently.

The geographical nature of the border territory being contested between China and India was easier for China to attack than for India to defend. Additionally, years of preparation meant that the Chinese had excellent supply lines, while many Indian areas could be supplied only by air. Each side now knew that the other operated with different maps and different strategies. Nehru concurred with a "forward strategy" popular with his parliamentarians but militarily unsupportable. Forward patrols pushed up to the disputed border but had no buildup of arms and logistics behind them. For a period, while the Chinese were preoccupied around 1960 by the fear that they might face simultaneous attack on several sides, they did not respond. Then things changed. As other pressures eased, Mao became more belligerent on the border issues, and Nehru, unwisely, engaged in tough talk in reply. The Chinese motives remain inscrutable, but some time in early October 1962 they resolved to teach Nehru a lesson, using his rasher statements about pushing them back as an excuse. Early on the morning of October 20, 1962, thousands of Chinese troops crossed the border and attacked Indian positions. Despite isolated examples of extreme bravery by Indian troops, they soon fell back in this one-sided conflict, under fire from Chinese heavy mortars and mountain artillery.

Jawaharlal offered brave words, ". . . we shall build up our strength, both military and economic, to win this battle of Indian freedom,"[9] though many would ask, now and later, why India's strength had not already been built up for this easily foreseeable event. Jawaharlal advised the Indian people to be ready for further reverses, which can hardly have been encouraging to the troops in the field. On the day of the invasion, finance minister Morarji Desai launched an appeal for gold and silver ornaments to help raise foreign exchange to buy arms and equipment for the forces which he himself had kept starved of resources. Indira led the donations, giving all her gold jewelry, including even the little trinkets she had used for the weddings of her dolls as a child.

Jawaharlal had blundered into the war by not sending the right signals to the Chinese, or by not understanding the signals the Chinese were clearly sending to him. To lose part of the land entrusted to him is the worst disaster that can befall a national leader. For Jawaharlal, the shame was redoubled because the Himalayas were venerated as the abode of the gods, the source of the holy River Ganges: their importance was far in excess of their value as territory which was, frankly, slight.

Galbraith described Nehru's speech on November 9 in the crowded parliamentary chamber as "less than Churchillian. It was long, at times vague, a little repetitious and not inspiring . . . Nehru defended Indian border claims, alluded at length to the perfidy of the Chinese and explained away the shortcomings of the Defense Ministry. This last effort was interrupted many times and occasionally the Speaker had to call for order. There was also an uproar when he defended General Kaul."[10]

Jawaharlal was forced to sack Menon, though even at this time of national crisis and personal disgrace he was trying to save his friend by making him minister of defense production. There was a massive revolt against this by Menon's many enemies (in fact, he may have had no friends, except Jawaharlal and Indira), so he was obliged to relinquish even this position. Vijaya reported how Jawaharlal "felt the world had turned against him in forcing him to reject Krishna Menon, his friend of thirty years."[11]

Work now started on reinforcing and equipping the armed forces, who were even inadequately clothed for fighting in freezing conditions. A Citizens' Defense Committee was set up, headed by Indira, who arranged for a plane to be stripped of its seats and loaded with warm clothing, food and drugs. As usual with Indira, she called on all her resources: Dorothy Norman received a letter asking for plasma drying and freezing machines to be dispatched.

Family life of a sort continued. It was Indira's forty-fifth birthday on November 19, 1962, and many relatives and friends came early in the morning for breakfast, as was the tradition at Teen Murti House. Presents and a big birthday cake gave the table a festive air. Indira came in, according to her aunt Krishna, "like a stone sculpture of herself . . . making a tremendous effort at self-control." She was shortly followed by Jawaharlal, whose appearance shocked his sister. "He had aged twenty years since I had kissed him goodnight, his hair seemed whiter, his face more deeply carved with wrinkles; catastrophe was plainly written on it."

The cheerful chatter stopped as he went to his chair without speaking and sat down. Krishna put her arms around him and asked how he was.

"Haven't you put your radio on this morning?" he snarled.

"No darling," she said, "what happened?"

"The Chinese," he said wearily, "have broken through the Se-La Pass."[12]

The silence was almost palpable. The Se-La Pass through the mountains was supposed to be impregnable. Once through, the entire province of Assam, and then the rest of India, lay exposed to the Chinese advance. Indian batteries had been picked off one by one with the latest Russian equipment, leaving only the infantry with their First World War Lee-Enfield rifles and machine guns to hold back the "human wave" of 20,000 Chinese troops.

Indira rushed by plane and helicopter to Tezpur, the military and civil headquarters of the Indian forces on the northeast frontier, just thirty miles from the Chinese lines. The Indian military had already retreated, and Indira was left to reassure the terrified civilian population. Pupul Jayakar, who had seen her that morning, wrote, "She was in a raging temper. I could hardly get a word in. The news that the district authorities had abandoned the people outraged her. An instinctive response had awakened in her that the Assamese must be assured that someone cared." She promised the terrified people she would not leave till the crisis passed, arranged for emergency rations, and ensured that some of the officials returned to duty.[13]

When Jawaharlal addressed parliament, the Indian Army had been routed and the Chinese occupied 50,000 square miles of Indian territory. He said he was endeavoring to get help from friendly countries, but what countries were these? Jawaharlal's foreign policy had disintegrated at this first test. The nonaligned stayed nonaligned, one of the unforeseen consequences of basing a foreign policy on what a country was not rather than on what it was: they had no commitments to each other. The USSR showed that it placed more value on China's friendship than that of India by urging Jawaharlal to settle on China's terms. The United States, however, was more than willing to give assistance.

This was where Galbraith's personal prestige and genuinely cordial relations with Jawaharlal came into play. He promised massive military aid and advice. Galbraith had considerable freedom because the war coincided with the Cuban missile crisis. This was hardly coincidence: the Chinese had been testing the border, waiting for a suitable moment to attack, and had done so when international attention was distracted from Asia. Jawaharlal asked the United States for twelve squadrons of supersonic all-weather fighters, a radar communication network and two B-47 bomber squadrons. Kennedy assured Jawaharlal of as much help as possible, and began American airlifts of arms and supplies to beleaguered Indian units in the Himalayas. The warship *Enterprise* was sent to India. In the streets of India the fickle crowd was chanting "Yankees bhai bhai" (Americans are brothers).

Not all nonaligned friends were perfidious. Tito of Yugoslavia and Nasser of Egypt were sympathetic but in no position to give practical aid. Britain airlifted 150 tons of arms, and Canada and Australia were also quick to give help: the despised Commonwealth, which Jawaharlal was so loath to enter, proved more supportive than all his new friends. France and Belgium also provided supplies.

The lifting of the naval blockade of Cuba on November 20 allowed the United States to pay full attention to the Indo-Chinese war, and on the following day the Chinese withdrew, to a line further back than the one at which they started. This was partly out of respect for American firmness, but probably because the exercise had been a success: they had humiliated India, shown the world they were the Asian superpower, and demonstrated that they could defend their claim to the disputed territory. Actually holding the land was unnecessary. Jawaharlal's personal vanity, in strutting the world stage like a powerful leader, had encouraged the Chinese to teach him a lesson. If a war can ever be an individual's responsibility, this was his.

For India the result was not entirely negative: Indians rediscovered nationalism, an emotional closeness to the united country, not just their linguistic, territorial or religious segment of it. It also prompted a long-overdue reassessment of military equipment and preparedness, now India realized that almost all her borders could be threatened, and not just those with Pakistan, which had been a source of anxiety since Independence.

Galbraith had a meeting with Jawaharlal on December 10 and found that he had weathered the pressures and "looked much younger and more vigorous than at any time in recent months and told me that the tension of the crisis agreed with him,"[14] The writer Marie Seton, with whom Jawaharlal was prepared to be more relaxed, recorded soon after the war, "There was an air of sad, sorrowing desolation about him. He sat crumpled. Never before had I seen such an expression of stunned, muted, searing misery on anybody's face."[15]

His nephew B. K Nehru said, "I used to say to him, 'You think the world consists of Jawaharlals. It doesn't.' He said, 'No, no, no, I'm not such a fool. I don't.' But actually he did. And I think his whole trust in humanity was broken by that, and he never really lived after 1962."[16]

A pressing need, given Jawaharlal's age, was to make some provision for a successor. It was believed he had been grooming Menon for the succession, which was why he had brought him into the Cabinet despite opposition. Menon's disgrace over China rendered further preferment out of the question, which was another beneficial aspect of the defeat. Still, Jawaharlal had no obvious protégé. S. K. Patil, his minister of food and agriculture, said, "The prime minister is like the great banyan tree. Thousands shelter beneath it but nothing grows."[17]

Too late, Jawaharlal came to understand that what was not stale in the Congress Party was corrupt, an impression intensified by the loss of three by-elections in the summer of 1963 and a well-argued (though unsuccessful) no-confidence motion in the Lok Sabha (people's assembly). Perhaps it was just that only now, in Jawaharlal's weakened state, could Congress president Kumaraswamy Kamaraj force the prime minister to clean up the party. Kamaraj was the party strongman of southern India, uneducated and of low-caste stock, but possessed of great dignity and political skill. Kamaraj proposed that a number of cabinet ministers and chief ministers of states should resign and work full time to rebuild the party. In 1963, the Kamaraj Plan was put into effect, with six cabinet ministers and six chief ministers resigning. Among the ministers were the puritanical Morarji Desai, who considered himself Jawaharlal's natural successor, Lal Bahadur Shastri and Kamaraj himself. Kamaraj also, however, organized a secret caucus of five regional party chiefs, called the Syndicate, to determine Jawaharlal's successor.

Indira was not considered an obvious runner. In fact, she had even thought of leaving India in 1963. She had been so depressed with the lack of privacy, with the relentless stream of people "presenting their cards and their problems" that she considered moving to London and identified a house she might buy, planning to take in lodgers to keep herself. Rajiv was already in Cambridge and Sanjay would finish school that year, and she hoped he would go to England too, but nothing came of this idea. She did not have the money to buy the house, and it was sold to someone else.[18] This was not a passing fancy: a year later, on May 8, 1964, she was writing to Dorothy Norman that she "must settle outside India for at least a year" and was looking for ways of earning the foreign currency to do so.[19] Her feelings may have had something to do with the continuing emptiness of bereavement. It was not until three years after his death that she said she felt she had ceased to mourn Feroze, and again wanted to wear bright colors, always one of her joys.[20]

Despite her uncertainties, she was never discounted from the leadership race. "No public figure in India disclaims political ambition so insistently," wrote the political commentator Welles Hangen, who interviewed her in the summer of 1962, "and none is more disbelieved."[21] Hangen was clearly a fan, finding Indira "more attractive than her sinister-looking newspaper pictures," though feeling there was "something forbiddingly regal" about her. "She enters the little sitting room where visitors are received so swiftly and noiselessly that I am always startled and slightly flustered. It is as if a queenly apparition has suddenly materialized on the couch beside me. But her imperial aura and my confusion vanish as soon as she greets me in a voice so soft that I must strain to hear. Her smile is disarming, almost girlish. The dark eyes are reflective and a bit melancholy. Her white embroidered sari is immaculate. She dresses simply, with little jewelry. Her hair, beginning to turn gray noticeably, is cut short and waved softly . . . If she is bored or annoyed, her natural reserve can become glacial. But her most striking quality is a passionate sincerity that makes her seem more candid and outspoken than she really is. She has her father's knack for appearing to be modest while saying consistently immodest things about herself."[22]

Near the end of this interview she made one of those statements that showed she was hardly a political shrinking violet: "I have an idea of what India should become," she said, "anything I do I regard as a step toward ensuring what I want India to become."[23] The question, improbably enough considering the resounding answer, had simply been whether she regarded her welfare or political work as more important.

Jawaharlal was not grooming her for the succession; had he been doing so, he would not have supported her in rejecting offers of parliamentary seats. It was this failure to prepare her for a future without him which was the key to his plans for her: he had none. His attitude towards Indira was the same as his attitude towards other female members of his family: they were there to serve him. Had he given the least thought to the future of Indira, a widow with two children to see into manhood, he would have supported her in obtaining at least parliamentary, if not ministerial, experience, or some other form of public office. She was suited to nothing but politics and would need a home and an income after his death, but he made no plans for her.

Justifiable criticism of Jawaharlal's foreign policy in the wake of the China debacle had opened the gates to criticism of his economic policies. He defended himself against attacks at the Congress session at Bhuvaneshwar, Orissa, in January 1964, urging that only a socialist program could provide economic advance. As he was bringing his speech to a close, he suffered a stroke and pitched forward into Indira's arms. Although paralyzed and unable to speak clearly, he made a remarkable recovery and angrily refused to take the long convalescence that doctors advised: "If I lie down in bed even for a week, I know I will not get up."[24] He broadcast to the nation in English and Hindi on March 26, appealing for an end to the communal violence which had again flared up following the theft of a relic—a hair from the Prophet's beard—from a shrine in Srinagar. It had been replaced, but massacres and retaliations continued.

The Syndicate now asked Jawaharlal to take Shastri back into the Cabinet to relieve him of some of the burden and allow him to function effectively as deputy prime minister. Shastri complained that Indira kept him from seeing Jawaharlal, and many claims have been made that it was Indira, not he, who was running the country by controlling access to Jawaharlal and making decisions herself.

Following India's military humiliation by China, Pakistan began pushing again at Kashmir. Jawaharlal wanted one last attempt at regaining the whole of Kashmir for India, and he put pressure on the Kashmiri State Government to release Abdullah, which they did in April 1964. The two men spent many hours talking about old times and trying to reach some workable agreement over Kashmir, but Abdullah still wanted an independent state. He was later to resume his role as chief minister of Kashmir, from 1975 until his death in 1982.

Jawaharlal had become more religious in his latter years, consulting with astrologers and allowing "death conquering" Hindu rites and fire ceremonies to be performed at a temple on his behalf. If they had any value, it came too late. At a press conference on May 22, when a reporter asked if he would solve the problem of succession, Jawaharlal answered after a long silence, "My life is not ending so very soon," and received a standing ovation (unusual and inappropriate at a press conference).[25] On May 26, he discussed the forthcoming Commonwealth prime ministers' conference with Shastri and worked on papers, going to bed at 11 P.M. At six the following morning he called a servant to say he was in pain. A doctor arrived within fifteen minutes and diagnosed a burst aorta. Jawaharlal, who preferred not to make a fuss, had been bleeding internally for some time and needed an immediate transfusion, so Indira's blood was used.

His sisters were brought to Delhi on a government plane, and the Cabinet waited in a room next to the sick man. He lapsed into a coma and died shortly before 2 P.M. on May 27, at the age of seventy-four. When Vijaya and Krishna arrived, they drove through huge crowds which the police were struggling to hold back. When they got through the gates of Teen Murti House, there were groups of people, mainly from the household, standing in the driveway. In the house there were more crowds: cabinet ministers, members of parliament and diplomats. Inside Jawaharlal's bedroom they found Indira sitting on the floor beside the bed with an agonized expression on her face. Death had removed the stress from Jawaharlal, and he looked much younger than he had in life. Indira did not move as people crowded into the room, so the sisters imposed order, allowing only those closest to Jawaharlal into the room.

The crowd outside burst through the gates and tried to enter the house, but one of the ministers called for calm and promised that Jawaharlal's body would be brought out for them to see. It was placed on a catafalque and draped in the national flag, which was covered in lilies, roses and marigolds. Just behind the body, electric fans blew over huge blocks of ice placed on trestle tables to prevent putrefaction setting in. All night people walked past the body, and the next morning the foreign dignitaries arrived, including Mountbatten and his daughter Pamela. He said, "I have come to attend the funeral of one of the greatest friends of my life and one of the greatest men the world has known."[26]

Indira stayed by the body as thousands passed to pay their last respects. She cried only the next morning in the arms of her aunt Krishna, when they were alone. Then she regained control of herself and began giving orders to prepare breakfast for the many guests staying at the house, and telling the staff, who had been up all night, that they should shave and change their clothes, for her father had not tolerated slovenliness in his life and "would not like it after his death."[27]

Jawaharlal, who spurned religious ceremonies during his life, had explicitly requested that none mark his death. Indira tried to keep to his wishes, but as Hindus, Muslims, Christians, Buddhists and Jews insisted on holding services, she allowed them to do so. The government organized a traditional funeral, which involved the body being taken on a gun carriage to the Shanti Vana (abode of peace), the cremation grounds. It moved slowly through masses of mourners and showers of flowers, with Indira and Sanjay following in an open car. Rajiv was on his way back from Cambridge, but there was no time to wait for him before the cremation took place, which by tradition had to be as soon as possible after the death. Only the first few cars in a huge cortège passed through the crowd, which numbered over a million. Officials and dignitaries in the other vehicles had to get out and reach the cremation grounds by the Jamuna River on foot. Jawaharlal's body was placed on a sandalwood pyre, the honor guard fired three volleys, bugles sounded the *Last Post* and Sanjay thrust a flaming brand into the pyre. As the crimson flames leapt up, the crowd surged forward and the whole scene descended into hysteria.

In his will Jawaharlal made explicit plans for the disposal of his remains. As a gesture towards Hindu tradition, he wanted a small handful of his ashes to be thrown into the Ganges. Most of his ashes, however, should "be carried high up into the air in an airplane and scattered from that height over the fields where the peasants of India toil, so that they might mingle with the dust and soil of India and become an indistinguishable part of India."[28]

The urn containing the smaller part of the ashes was taken in an open car on a special train to Allahabad, with Indira sitting beside it all the way as millions lined the route to get a glimpse. Indira's personal secretary, Usha Bhagat, described the scene: "The train would stop at almost all important stations, and Mrs. Gandhi would be near the window so that she could receive their homage . . . I can't tell you the amount of people on the platform wanting to pay their respects. The pressure of people was so much at Kanpur [formerly Cawnpore] that the plate glass cracked.

"In the middle of the night we were going to be between two stations, so Mrs. Gandhi told me she was going to rest, and that when the next station comes, to wake her up. When the next station came I saw she was asleep and I was really in two minds because I knew she had had such a long day, should I wake her up or not? But I knew her and knew I had to do it. So I did, and told her I didn't want to, so she said, 'No, if I'd not been there when people came, I would not have forgiven myself.'"[29] She was still, at this time of grief, thinking of her duty to India.

The urn was placed on a platform at Anand Bhavan so that people could come to see it and place flowers. Later, Indira, her aunts and sons all entered the boat which took the urn far out into the river. There, Rajiv and Sanjay poured the ashes into the Ganges, and Indira added the small amount of her mother's ashes which had stayed with Jawaharlal, in prison cell or bedroom, in all the years since Kamala's death.

Indira completed her father's last wishes by scattering some ashes from a plane over the mountains of his beloved Kashmir. At the same time a number of other planes scattered the remaining ashes over different parts of India. At last the land and the king were one.

# TEN

# PASSING THE TORCH

The Congress Working Committee authorized Kamaraj, as president of Congress, to make a recommendation on the choice for Nehru's successor. He chose Lal Bahadur Shastri rather than Morarji Desai, the hardline Hindu candidate who was unpopular and divisive. No one disliked Shastri enough to render his candidature untenable, and as a longtime assistant to Jawaharlal from the days of the independence movement, he was a link with the glorious past. Kamaraj talked and bullied Desai out of standing, so Shastri was elected unopposed.

There had been an unseemly discussion between Congress leaders in the room where Jawaharlal's body was lying. "None of them had the decency to keep their mouths shut until he was cremated," said Krishna Menon, who was present.[1] Morarji Desai's behavior, acting as if he were the obvious successor, was particularly offensive to Indira, and was a major factor in his not becoming prime minister: she vowed that anyone else, even herself, should get the job rather than him.

Shastri was therefore elected by parliament on June 2, 1964, as the sole candidate. He was a diminutive man from a poor, low-caste family, but an old Congress fighter, who had joined the civil disobedience movement in 1920 at the age of sixteen and was a longtime friend of the Nehru family. He was one of the few people who had ever bothered to play with Indira during her lonely childhood, and she had hidden him at Anand Bhavan in 1942 when the British were out to arrest him.

He begged Indira to accept a cabinet post, saying that her presence would lend his Cabinet prestige. He is said to have offered her the foreign ministry and others, but she declined, saying that she wanted to devote herself to establishing a memorial to her father. He went back each day, sometimes twice a day, to encourage her, and finally persuaded her to accept a minor post as minister of information and broadcasting. As all cabinet ministers had to be members of parliament, she was nominated to the upper house, the Rajya Sabha, becoming a minister at the age of forty-six.

Losing her father also meant losing her home, as Teen Murti House (which later became the Nehru Museum) went with the job of prime minister. Even Feroze's former small house was a perk of his job as an MP, so she faced the upheaval of removal as well as bereavement. She had inherited Anand Bhavan in Allahabad, but Delhi was now her home. She inherited little else from her father but some personal possessions and the royalties from his books. "I was not interested in making financial provision for the future," he wrote in his will, and he had never taken out life insurance.[2] His salary as prime minister had not been enough to run his household, so he had drawn on his capital when time prevented him from adding to his income by writing. Indira was thus left with almost nothing.

As a minister, however, Indira did receive a salary and a government-owned house, 1 Safdarjung Road, which had four bedrooms, two of which were converted for use as an office and a reception room. Following her move to this house, a strange phenomenon occurred; the crowds who had gathered outside Teen Murti House to observe Jawaharlal now began coming for Indira, as if she had inherited her father's power. She met people, listened to their grievances and showed sympathy with their hardships. Indira herself, always at her best in a crowd that needed her, gained strength from them.

She approached her work as a minister with customary vigor, improving the quality of government radio broadcasts and encouraging the manufacture of cheap transistor radios, an essential medium of information where more than half the population was illiterate. She planned to get two million low cost radios out to rural programs so that family planning and other information could be broadcast direct to the villages. Television was also used for propagating better farming and family planning methods with sets which were in schools or community television clubs. She also encouraged democracy by opening the airwaves to the opposition parties and independent commentators.

Indira was bigger than the job, however, and needed other challenges. When riots broke out in Madras over renewed proposals to make Hindi the official language of India, Indira suggested national leaders should visit to calm the situation. No one responded, so she flew there herself to reassure Tamils that their interests were not being overlooked by national politicians: she for one would not allow Hindi to be imposed on them and said the matter would be reconsidered. It was a favor for which the non-Hindi-speaking Kamaraj would be grateful. Shastri later had parliament agree to a measure retaining English as an "associate official language."

Shastri had no experience of foreign affairs: he had never been out of India, except to Nepal. When the Soviet premier and party leader Nikita Khrushchev was dismissed in October 1964, Indira's first reaction was to fly to the USSR to meet the new leaders. She was the first important foreign visitor to be received by the Russians, who believed she had been sent by the government, which in fact was uncertain of what action to take. Either by instinct or good judgment, Indira knew that it was right to create a relationship with the new Soviet hierarchy: if a *rapprochement* with China followed their taking office, India's interests as a friend of the Soviet Union would not be overlooked.

In June 1965 she was in London for an exhibition commemorating her father. Rajiv was studying technical engineering at Cambridge and took his eighteen-year-old Italian girlfriend, Sonia Maino, to meet his mother. Sonia was so terrified at the prospect of meeting the formidable Mrs. Gandhi that she panicked on the drive to London and Rajiv had to cancel the arrangement. Another meeting was set up and Sonia was relieved to find how "warm and welcoming" Indira was. She spoke in French because Sonia's English was still poor, and as Sonia later remembered, "She told me that I need not be frightened because she herself had been young, extremely shy, and in love, and she understood me perfectly."[3]

Not everyone saw the warm and reassuring side of Indira's nature. She left London shortly before the arrival of Shastri for the Commonwealth Prime Ministers' Conference, fearing that she would upstage him and give him further cause for grievance, as their relationship had rapidly deteriorated. Shastri found Indira's independence as a minister as irritating as she found his slow, conservative government. She toured the country speaking of her father's ideal of a socialist India and how Congress had fallen from its formerly exalted role—a rather selective view of recent history. For his part, Shastri failed to appoint Indira to major committees and found no time for her when she wished to recruit his support on certain issues. She felt "slighted and ignored" by the prime minister.[4]

With Jawaharlal gone, there was no barrier to soften the relationship between Indira and Vijaya, who had resigned the governorship of Maharashtra in 1964 to contest Jawaharlal's old seat of Phulpur. She had done this after conferring with the party hierarchy and with Indira, who had reassured her that she did not want the seat herself. Vijaya then set about lobbying for a ministerial job, but Shastri, though he sent her abroad on government business, gave her no work at home. She eventually challenged him on the matter and he said he had been "discussing the possibility with Indiraji," meaning that Indira's opposition had blocked her aunt's chances of preferment.

Vijaya tried to resolve the matter by writing to Indira: "I have a feeling that you are not happy about my being in Phulpur. I am conscious of the fact that this seat should have been yours by right. It is yours today should you wish to have it. Nothing would give me greater pleasure now or in 1967 [the election year] to retire from this particular constituency for you and work elsewhere."[5]

Indira replied immediately: "I do not know who has been talking to you but there is absolutely no foundation in the remark that I am not happy at your being in Phulpur . . . It may seem strange that a person in politics should be wholly without political ambition but I am afraid that I am that sort of a freak . . . I did not want to come either to Parliament or to be in Government. However, there were certain compelling reasons at the time for my acceptance of this portfolio. Now there are so many crises one after another that every time seems to be the wrong time for getting out."[6]

This correspondence, however, was far from the end of the matter. Eight months later, when papers were being entered for constituencies in the 1967 election, Vijaya was still offering Indira the seat and Indira was still refusing amid persistent rumors that she really wanted it. Vijaya was being coy (or extraordinarily dense) in her public presentation of this case. It was not that Indira wanted the seat for herself (she eventually ran for Feroze's old seat of Rae Bareli), but that she did not want Vijaya to have it.

Near the end of 1964, there was a Pakistani incursion into the Rann of Kutch, something of a wasteland border area, which was quickly and successfully resisted. The problem of Kashmir was no nearer solution than it had been in the late 1940s, though Jawaharlal had dealt with the problem of the rivers to which each side wanted exclusive access. It was agreed that the three western rivers should be for Pakistan's use and the eastern ones for India's.

In August 1965, Indira went on vacation to Kashmir. While there, she received information that Pakistani-trained tribesmen and troops disguised as civilian volunteers had raided the Kashmiri border. She went straight to the local chief minister to help organize the defense of the province, then flew to the Haji Pir Pass, where some of the heaviest fighting had taken place and land had been gained at great cost to India. Pakistan faced a very different Indian army from the one defeated ignominiously by the Chinese: rather than fighting defensively, the Indian army struck across the Pakistani border in five places, with great success.

In response, Pakistan invaded Punjab in September. Indira was the first minister to go to the battle zone, arriving even before the defense minister. She visited the hospital and frontline troops, and received the popular accolade, "the only man in a cabinet of old women." If destiny beckoned for Indira Gandhi, it was not because she had manipulated the situation, or that others had done so on her behalf, but because time and again she had shown herself as the only person with an instinctive understanding of how to run the country.

In a bid to end the war (and in one of the few successful episodes in Soviet diplomacy) the Soviet prime minister Alexei Kosygin invited Shastri and President Ayub of Pakistan to Tashkent in Uzbekistan to see if a settlement could be reached. Among the points agreed were a ceasefire line which India and Pakistan agreed to respect, what amounted to a non-aggression pact, and a resumption of normal trade relations. Shastri was feted: the Indian army had been vindicated and he had achieved a just and honorable peace, though Indira was concerned that the Haji Pir Pass had been handed back to Pakistan.

The night he signed the treaty Shastri suffered a massive heart attack and died. His government had lasted only from June 9, 1964 to January 11, 1966. Morarji Desai again thought his time had come, as did a number of other ministers, and even Vijaya rushed back from a lecture tour of the United States, eager to be considered. Kamaraj himself could have taken the post but would not do so for he spoke only Tamil, and a prime minister with neither Hindi nor English could not, he felt, be effective.

Kamaraj flew to Delhi, with two more or less equally important objectives: to stop Desai and to select the new prime minister. He later said he was still thinking about the question of who should be prime minister on the plane, and only at the end of the flight had he come to the conclusion that it must be Indira. Despite her lack of experience, she had positive qualities as a politician, one of which the party man Kamaraj found overwhelming: "In 1967, she can win the election."[7]

The news of Shastri's death reached Indira at 2 A.M. and she began conferring with her personal advisers immediately. Within hours of the death a senior minister, Gulzarilal Nanda, his ambitions inflated by the predictions of his astrologers, arrived at Indira's door to canvas support for his bid to be premier. Indira was noncommittal, but later said with glee, "No one can be prime minister without my support."[8] Meanwhile, Kamaraj was on his way to see her to promise his support.

In the days that followed Congress politicians had to weigh up the qualities of Indira Gandhi. Of course there was the magic of the Nehru family, but that was one factor among many. Indira had shown herself to be a tough national politician as Congress president, and had been a good minister, though her parliamentary performance had been poor. She showed willingness to travel great distances and grapple tirelessly with the problems of village India. She was not a regional politician with loyalty to a particular locality, as was the case with most other contenders. As Krishna said, "Just as my brother had belonged to all of India, she too was considered as belonging to the nation."[9] She was also not implacably devoted to one particular religion. She had a wide range of contacts with foreign governments, and her education (however limited) in England, Switzerland and Germany had given her a world view: other Indian politicians had been mainly absorbed with regional and national problems. India therefore did not have a large number of world-class leaders to choose from.

It must also be said that Kamaraj and the rest of the Syndicate, demonstrating a lapse of judgment, felt Indira, with her limited experience, would be pliable and compliant to their wishes. Kamaraj had convinced himself that Indira should be prime minister; convincing her was more difficult. Krishna believed that Indira's reluctance was based on the fear that if she were not up to the job, it might tarnish her father's memory. Eventually, Kamaraj prevailed and she agreed to run, while he used his ample powers of persuasion to encourage support for her and to make all the candidates withdraw, except Morarji Desai, who this time would not be denied a contest. He would not step aside, he said, for this *chokri* (little girl).[10]

On the morning of the vote, January 19, 1966, Indira went to Shantivana, where Jawaharlal had been cremated. She thought of what her father had written to her on her thirteenth birthday: "Be brave, and all the rest follows."[11] She also went to Teen Murti House and stood in the room where her father had died, in recognition that she had reached her own tryst with destiny.

Krishna described her niece during the vote of parliament: "She looked very beautiful with her black hair streaked with gray and her soft brown eyes in her pale classic face." She wore a brown shawl over her white sari with a rosebud pinned on it in memory of her father, who always wore a rose.[12] The atmosphere was tense as the ballot took place; it was by no means a foregone conclusion that Indira would win, but when the votes were counted she received 355 votes to Desai's 169. To have fought a contest and won a resounding victory was no bad thing for Indira, as it was clear she had not simply been handed the job by party manipulators.

Vijaya left immediately the announcement was made, in very bad humor. She remarked to journalists, "My niece is frail of health and not strong enough to carry on the duties of a prime minister," surely one of the great miscalculations of modern politics. Indira responded, also in print, "I am neither frail nor weak when it is my job to carry out tasks entrusted to me."[13]

Her personal secretary, Usha Bhagat, said, "I went to congratulate her, and when I entered I saw a quite different Mrs. Gandhi. Sometimes she used to have an irritable or bad look, and here she was glowing with a kind of inner radiance. I think it was that for the first time she had her own personal fulfillment."[14] She accepted the garlands of those who had supported her, and those who had not, and the cheers of the crowd, through which she drove in triumph to the presidential palace, where she was invited to form a government.

At the age of forty-eight Indira, who only three years before had been thinking of leaving India altogether to set up as a landlady in London, had become the most powerful woman in the world, ruler of 500 million people.

# MOTHER INDIRA

# ELEVEN

# CALL ME "SIR"

The rest of the world found the election of a woman as prime minister remarkable, but India had a long tradition of great women leaders, such as Razia Sultana, Queen Noorejehan and the Rani of Jhansi. Annie Besant and Sarojini Naidu had been leading figures in the independence movement; and independence had given the franchise equally to men and women, a development still awaited in some Western countries. Indira was asked about gender to the point of irritation, and always answered in similar terms: "I don't think a person who is head of state should think in terms of himself or herself as belonging to any group—whether it is sex, religion or caste. If the people accept you as leader of the nation, that is all that matters."[1] Self-image also matters a great deal, as Indira knew consciously or otherwise, for she was not head of state (the President of India held that post) but head of the government.

She was sworn in on January 25, choosing to affirm her allegiance to the constitution rather than swear in the name of God. Among the spectators were her aunts Vijaya and Krishna. Indira had responded to Vijaya's barbed criticisms of her health by saying to reporters, "Those who have watched me grow know that I am frail and hardy at the same time," which sounds more threatening than defensive.[2]

The principal problem for India at the time of Indira's accession was drought and a consequent food shortage. The rains failed in 1965 and there was a particularly bad harvest in Bihar and Gujarat. In normal circumstances, when famine threatened, the state's resources could be used, but military spending on the Indo-Chinese war and the Indo-Pakistan war left the national coffers short.

The famine was more a problem of distribution than availability: grain-poor states were linked with grain-rich ones in "food zones" but this attempt to ensure fairness was not entirely successful. There was agitation in Kerala, where rice was in short supply, a serious matter in a state where rice was the staple diet. Shortages were compounded by the people who, hidebound by tradition, were unwilling to eat alternative foods. Indira urged people to change their habits and eat whatever food was available, pledging herself not to eat or serve rice until supplies to Kerala were adequate.

There were insistent calls for the abolition of the food zone policy at the Congress annual session in Jaipur in February. Indira was pushed to the microphone and obliged to back her food minister. She had been briefed for this well-anticipated storm, but her voice was too quiet, she forgot her prepared answers. Unable to control the angry meeting, she had to step down. She was no better at handling parliament, where her political inexperience was exposed to the aggressive sneers of the Opposition. At her first appearance she read a speech, badly, to constant interruptions, and the Speaker had to come to her aid. She sounded like a backbench MP still finding her feet, not the leader of the government. A socialist MP called Ram Manohar Lohia called her "goongi gudiya"—the dumb doll—during one of these stumbling performances. The nickname was to stick for several years, until Indira gained the experience necessary to silence her critics, but she never forgave parliament its discourtesy, and in future showed the institution little respect.

It was a paradox that such a courageous and determined woman could fail so frequently and so visibly. She told her friend Pupul Jayakar that her lack of confidence in such situations related to her past and the spiteful treatment she received from her aunt Vijaya. She said, "From my childhood she did everything to destroy my confidence; she called me ugly, stupid. This shattered something within me. Faced with hostility, however well prepared I am, I get tongue-tied and withdraw."[3]

A matter she was more adept at dealing with was that of Punjab and the Sikhs' demand for a Punjabi-speaking state. Congress policy, and that of Jawaharlal, had always been opposed to linguistic states. Indira, however, faced with continuing agitation by the Akali Dal, the party of militant Sikh nationalism, could see no other way out of the Punjab problem. She therefore promoted the idea of redrawing Punjab's boundaries along linguistic lines, which in this case also made it a religious state, as almost all Sikhs were Punjabi speakers and Punjab was their historic homeland. The boundary changes created two new states, Punjab and Haryana, which shared a capital at Chandigarh, a city designed by the French architect Le Corbusier.

Sikhs predominated in Punjab, while Haryana was a Hindu state. The political result of the division was that the Sikhs' nationalist party, the Akali Dal, which had been a minority party, became top dog. The Hindus, who would now be a minority in the new state, rose in anger and rioting broke out. In Delhi a Hindu mob threatened to sack the main Sikh temple, at which the ceremonial guards were obliged to draw their swords. Indira faced crowds with a righteous anger absent from her parliamentary performances: ". . . there are no tears in my eyes, there is anger in my heart," she stormed. "Is it for this that so many freedom fighters and martyrs have sacrificed their lives?"[4]

A trip to the United States had been planned for Shastri, which the new prime minister took in March 1966. She asked Pupul Jayakar to help her to prepare. She read her speeches out to her friend, corrected them and timed them. Pupul then helped choose clothes for each occasion on her U.S. schedule. Indira's gray hair was dyed black, but she left a streak at the front, which became whiter as the years passed. Her makeup was improved to lessen the shadows under her eyes and make her nose seem less prominent.

Indira flew to the USA via Paris, picking up Rajiv and Sanjay who came over from England where they were both now studying. While in France, Indira took the time to see President Charles de Gaulle, who was delighted to meet a world leader who spoke to him in French, though purists noted she spoke it with a Swiss accent. It is much to her credit that the formidable French leader, who had no respect for women in politics, was able to admire her strength of character.

Indira's cousin B. K. Nehru was now Indian ambassador to the United States and therefore went to meet her plane when she landed. He found her tired and ill-tempered, "snapping at everybody" after her long flight. B. K. had to pass on a diplomatic enquiry: what should the President call her? Indira said, "He can call me Madam Prime Minister, he can call me Prime Minister, he can call me Mr. Prime Minister if he wants," and added, "you can tell him that my cabinet colleagues call me 'Sir'."[5]

Indira charmed Lyndon Johnson, who had taken over after Kennedy's assassination; it was an agreeable surprise for diplomats on both sides to observe such a successful visit. One evening Johnson called at the Indian Embassy for a thirty-minute talk, as protocol dictated, but stayed while dinner guests arrived and waited to sit down. Eventually, throwing protocol to the wind, Johnson had to be asked to stay. "The dinner party then instead of being an official banquet with written speeches and whatnot, turned into a real friendly jamboree," B. K. Nehru recollected.[6]

Johnson was hooked: "What a nice girl, and how beautiful," he said to B. K. the next day. "We must get her elected. You tell me what to do. Send her food? Attack her? I'll do whatever you say."[7]

Indira made impressive speeches, feeding off the enthusiasm of the audience and the crowds who came to see her. When she returned to India, far from being exhausted by her international journey, she seemed rested and reinvigorated by diplomatic success. She brought home American promises of $900 million in aid and 3.5 million tons of food, plus an agreement that Indian debts to the United States could be repaid by setting up an American college in India.

However, as Krishna Menon said in parliament, a "personal success is not the same as policy." He felt that she had abandoned nonalignment and the other foundations of Jawaharlal's policy.[8] This was true: she had, or events had destroyed them, for nonalignment hardly existed after the Indo-Chinese war. To placate the left she had stopped in Moscow on her way back to Delhi and met Soviet leaders, justifying her position by saying, "I do not divide the world into communist and non-communist."[9] Nevertheless, the cold war had created great dangers for India. Pakistan had become a regional member of CENTO, the US-backed anti-Soviet alliance for Asia, which qualified Pakistan for massive U.S. military aid. When India protested, the United States told Pakistan not to use the arms against India, as empty an injunction as ever uttered, even in the language of diplomacy. Cold war balance of power considerations propelled Pakistan towards the United States, and India towards its enemy's perceived enemy the Soviet Union. China remained the enigma in this equation, though the invasion in 1962 left Indo-Chinese relations with a legacy of ill will.

Indira did not have a firm grasp of the mechanics of government, or even the language of it. When asked at a press briefing what were India's greatest problems, she replied, "inflation and rising prices."[10] Still, she could recognize a politically necessary decision when she saw one. The United States and the World Bank had refused to underwrite the country's debts unless the depreciation of the rupee was recognized by a devaluation of the currency. This was the situation impressed upon Indira in Washington, and led to a devaluation of the rupee on June 6, 1966 by 35.5 percent. Indira moved swiftly and imposed the decision on reluctant colleagues, earning grudging admiration for decisive action where her father would have dithered. There was, however, a united tirade of denunciation from the Opposition.

In fact, the devaluation did not bring about the hoped-for miracle, as the government did not want to cut spending or reduce imports, which were necessary concomitants for its success. A more experienced prime minister would have appreciated this. Indira was also politically vulnerable for having a food policy so dependent on imports and on the United States, but at least some food was coming through. It was more than necessary: a second failure of the rains in 1966 extended the threat of famine, while grain hoarding and poor distribution exacerbated the problem.

The United States and the Soviet Union had both advised Indira to forget the heavy industrialization which had enchanted her father, and get on with developing agriculture. This, rather than any other issue, was the area on which Indira stamped her mark. Jawaharlal had imagined an industrialized India competing in the world with European nations, the rolling wheels of industry creating an endless source of wealth. Indira had a different vision: an India where everyone had enough to eat and no family had more children than they could provide for.

Indira approached the resolution of this ideal in a manner typical of her: with a small group of advisers, but otherwise acting independently, she flew to every state to discuss agriculture, talking to experts in the plane on the way. They briefed her on local conditions so that when she landed she was fully in command of the situation. She would take decisions there and then, with the state government, encouraging the use of high-yield seed and collaboration with fertilizer firms. It was the inauguration of the Green Revolution, which would make India self-sufficient in food within three years. One result of this was to make northwest India the granary of the whole country, with the energetic Sikh farmers of Punjab becoming disproportionately successful in relation to their numbers.

Agricultural changes took time to show results, however, and meanwhile there were food riots, strikers protesting at the increased cost of living caused by inflation, and a general discontent which focused on the leader of the government. What could you expect, people grumbled, when there was a widow as prime minister, for widows were considered inauspicious.

Against this background there was a resurgence of interest in militant Hinduism, typified by increased support for the RSS, whose supporters had been involved in the assassination of Mahatma Gandhi. The Jana Sangh, a Hindu chauvinist party, started a vigorous campaign for the prohibition of cow slaughter. Cows were sacred to them and, as a result, 230 million wandered unfettered around the country. As a source of cheap protein for low-caste Hindus and non-Hindus, it was unacceptable for the government to ban the killing of cows, and secular Indians like Indira and her family had no sympathy with "cow-savers" when the nation had serious problems to deal with. Many of their compatriots disagreed, however, and there were riots in Delhi when 100,000 naked or partially clad *sadhus* (holy men) marched on Parliament House. Gulzarilal Nanda, Home Minister in charge of law and order, was sympathetic to these people, whom many considered to be nothing but charlatans preying on the credulous, and he was unwilling to use the full force of the law on them. The mob, wielding tridents, axes and knives, caused considerable damage; cars were torched and a minister's house was burned down. Even Kamaraj, the Congress president, was threatened.

The fortunate result of these scenes was that Indira could get rid of Nanda, whom she had not trusted and had not wanted as home minister; he had held out, canvassing support from other Congress figures, until he was given the job he wanted. Indira replaced Nanda with Y. B. Chavan, but was unable to reshuffle the Cabinet further, as she wished, and replace two other unsupportive colleagues. Kamaraj and the Syndicate would not permit her to make such major changes with a general election so close.

Other changes, however, were forced on her. The United States had been particularly eager to help India, a major Asian nation which might stand against Communism. Unfortunately, the goodwill foundered, as did so much otherwise valuable U.S. policy in the 1960s, on the disaster of the Vietnam War. No one, friend or enemy, could uncritically support American policy in Vietnam; Indira's stance was to declare that "India understood America's agony over Vietnam," which was taken as support.

This was seen by Indira's old left-wing allies, including the particularly virulent Krishna Menon, as a sellout. The Indo-American Educational Foundation, the college to be built with the money India owed to the United States, was also denounced as a form of cultural imperialism and Indira had to repudiate the gift. Her natural instincts were for the political left, so she was stung by the attacks on her. After months of silence on Vietnam, she finally issued a statement "deploring" American bombings of Hanoi and Haiphong in July 1966, and repeated these denunciations on a trip to Egypt, Yugoslavia and the Soviet Union. President Johnson was outraged, which he demonstrated by delaying authorization for each American shipment of food aid to India. Indira said, "We were frantic because we didn't have wheat for the next week . . . but every time we asked the Americans, we were told that the papers were on the president's table."[11] In response to this behavior Indira became more outspoken, to the applause of her erstwhile critics, who now urged her to reject all American food. She reminded them that in such an event it would not be they who starve "but millions of poor people."[12]

When criticized for deviating from past Congress policies, Indira declared that she certainly would deviate, and pursue policies in the interests of the country: "the Congress is big, but India is bigger."[13] This was effectively the message of her election campaign: to rely on her own popularity with the people, going over the heads of the party chiefs.

This was her style in the 1967 election, when she traveled over 15,000 miles and addressed 160 public meetings in two months. She spoke to audiences in homey metaphors which they easily understood, but because they came from her, an aristocratic Brahmin and Jawaharlal's daughter, they were invested with almost spiritual significance. This election campaign was the first in which she was addressed as "Mother Indira," a role she expanded herself: "My burden is manifold because crores [tens of millions] of my family members are poverty-stricken and I have to look after them. Since they belong to different castes and creeds, they sometimes fight among themselves, and I have to intervene, especially to look after the weaker members of my family, so that the stronger ones do not take advantage of them."[14]

Election united the normally fragmented Congress Party. The opposition consisted of the Socialists: the Communists who came in both Moscow and Peking-line organizations; Jana Sangh, the Hindu fundamentalists; and the Swatantra Party, which united big business conservatives, princes and former civil servants. The election year of 1967 began with rowdy election meetings in which opposition groups tried to disrupt meetings, overturned cars and burned them.

Indira was always at her best when facing opposition. At a meeting in Jaipur she was faced with Swatantra adherents, supporters of the Maharani who was a rival candidate, trying to break up the meeting. She lost her temper, to electrifying effect: "I am not going to be cowed down. I know who is behind these demonstrations, and I know how to make myself heard. I am going to do some plain speaking today. Go and ask the Maharajas how many wells they dug for their people in their states when they ruled them, how many roads they constructed, what they did to fight the slavery of the British while they lived in luxury at the cost of the people."[15]

In Bhuvaneshwar in Orissa, a brick thrown from the crowd hit Indira on the face, fracturing her nose. Blood poured down her face, but she covered it with her sari and refused to leave the platform, telling the crowd, "This is an insult not to myself but to the country, because as the Prime Minister of India I represent the country."[16] She described her appearance to Dorothy Norman: "I looked like a boxer—I was a terrible sight in the mirror. My nose, the left side, looked completely crooked. As it was, I tried to put it right myself and heard a little 'tik' sound. The left lip had swollen to the size of a big egg. Most of my face was also discolored and I bled for quite a while through the nose."[17] Back in Delhi, her nose was operated on and she playfully said afterwards that the doctors had failed to take the opportunity of improving her looks by shortening her nose.[18] In fact, she was serious, as she wrote to Dorothy Norman, ". . . ever since plastic surgery was heard of I have been wanting to get something done to my nose. I even started putting money by for it."[19] She went on with her tour to Calcutta, though she must have been in extreme pain.

When the election results came in, it was a miserable time for Congress. They lost 83 seats, retaining only a 25-seat majority in the

Lok Sabha, and lost power to opposition coalitions in eight states. Some of the Syndicate leaders, including Kamaraj, had been defeated. While Indira was an easy scapegoat for the failure, the problems that resulted in electoral discontent, such as drought, devaluation and the cost of the war, had been forced on her or were out of her control. The underlying change in India was the way in which a one-party state was being transformed into a multi-party state now the controlling force of Jawaharlal was no more. Paradoxically, a weakened Congress, particularly one with some of the party bosses out of action, strengthened Indira as a visible center of power.

She had also won a large majority in her own constituency, as had Morarji Desai, who again aspired to the leadership. As a compromise, he became deputy prime minister and finance minister, not the appointment he desired, but Indira had held out against his getting the Home Ministry, where his sectarian approach could have done real damage.

Morarji Desai was a self-righteous, humorless man, who was said to have all the fads of Gandhi with none of his virtues. He propounded teetotalism with a religious vigor, and abstained from all sources of pleasure except the pursuit of political power. He did not smoke, eat meat, eggs or fish, or drink coffee or tea: he stopped having sex when he was twenty-seven, and drank a glass of his own urine every day. As governor of Bombay he campaigned against the use of cosmetics, female figures in advertising, popular music and public dancing by unmarried couples. When there were riots in Bombay over the language issue, Desai attempted to stop them with a Gandhi-style fast, at which the mob rioted with redoubled vigor in the hope they would be rid of him. He abandoned the fast.

No friend to false modesty, Desai asserted to journalists that he was "better suited and better qualified to lead the Congress and the country"[20] than Indira, but still she was confirmed as prime minister on March 12, 1967, with a cabinet team chosen by herself, of more or less loyal supporters. She abandoned the system of ranking cabinet members by number indicating seniority, and now had them (after Desai, as second in command) listed in alphabetical order.

Desai made no attempt to hide his contempt for Indira. At a meeting of the Planning Commission early in 1967 he used the familiar *Indiraben*, meaning "sister Indira." He interrupted her as soon as she started speaking: "Indiraben, you don't understand this matter. Let me deal with it."[21] She was seething, but let him go on. It was her usual style: she retained anger and reserved the right to later retaliation. Another reason for her silence was that this was his territory; economic planning was not her forte, and when she attacked she wanted it to be from a position of strength.

The term of the national president was nearing an end and, although the current incumbent Radhakrishnan wanted another term, Indira was against it. He was kindly, but he had patronized her and lectured her on what she should do, rather than finding out what she wanted to do and helping her to achieve it. Against the wishes of the Syndicate and Desai, now working as allies, she succeeded in having a Muslim, Dr. Zakir Hussain, elected president of India. It was a considerable achievement, because his membership of the minority community gave reassurance to minorities at a time when communal violence was still a major force. It was also daring: if too many Congress parliamentarians had voted along communal lines, and Hussain had been defeated, Indira as his main sponsor would have felt it necessary to resign.

One MP's disappointed hopes of preferment continued to test her patience. This was her aunt Vijaya, who was returned for Jawaharlal's seat of Phulpur. Vijaya felt others were "telling tales" about her to Indira, and remarked, "Indira easily believes tales of anything said against her and does not take criticism well."[22] Vijaya was unable to discuss her differences with her niece, she protested, because Indira simply did not respond. She wrote to her daughter just before the election campaign, "I went yesterday evening by appointment to see Indi. We sat in stony silence for fifteen minutes after which I came home. Most frustrating. I don't know what to do to make a breakthrough."[23] A short time later Indira called Vijaya in to discuss with her an informal suggestion from the Wilson government in Britain that, as relations between the two countries were strained, perhaps Vijaya could be sent again as High Commissioner, having been successful and popular in that role before. Indira sat doodling while Vijaya waited, then eventually told her about the suggestion from the UK. "Well," asked Vijaya after a long silence, "what do you think about it?" Indira was silent again, then in a very soft voice said, "Well, Puphi [aunt], I don't really trust you." Vijaya recalled, "I had lived with pretense so long that what she said actually came as a relief. I walked round the table to where she sat and, kissing the top of her head, I said, 'Thank you, Indu, for telling me the truth.'"[24]

This moment of candor did nothing to heal relations between them: Vijaya was neither given any government post, nor invited to the Prime Minister's parties, nor included in any committee at home, nor delegation going abroad. She was burning with resentment at the despised Kamala's daughter treating her thus. She once called on Indira for permission to be abroad when the vote on Zakir Hussain's presidency came up. Indira refused as they needed all the votes they could get, and whatever negative feeling she might have about Vijaya, she could certainly rely on her to support the Nehru principle of a secular state. "She then said she wanted to say something personal," Vijaya wrote to her daughter, "her eyes filled with tears and she was obviously distressed. She said she knew I was being wasted. She wanted to use my talents. She kept thinking what she could do for me. But she kept hearing things which shook her trust in me. I told her there was nothing I could do to prove my real affection for her and my desire that she should succeed in the task she had undertaken. Trust, I said, was something intangible. It was there or it was not . . . I would have been satisfied if I could have been associated in a small way with either the government or the Congress. What was mortifying for me was to be left out in the cold year after year when so many things required to be done intelligently and honestly." She said she was thinking of resigning her seat, which at last shook Indira into a response, "You can't resign—I wouldn't let you. We can't keep Phulpur without you," she said.[25] So now Vijaya knew what to do to hurt Indira: in 1968 she resigned and forced a by-election. Congress held the seat.

When Indira donated Anand Bhavan to the nation in 1970 as a memorial, she refused Vijaya's request to stay for one last night in the house, although Jawaharlal's will specifically said it must always be open to the family. Indira stayed alone to remember with bitterness the humiliations of her mother and the pain she had suffered there.

Indira's other aunt, Krishna, had always adored her and was working on an adulatory biography of her niece called *Dear to Behold*, after the meaning of Indira's middle name, Priyadarshini. The book had to be finished by her husband, Raja, for in 1967 she had a heart attack and died alone in a London hotel room, just short of her sixtieth birthday. The suddenness of Krishna's death shocked the whole family, but particularly Indira, who was always close to her aunt.

As prime minister, Indira missed her former freedom of movement, much as her father had done. She regretted not being able to go to the cinema when she wanted. In other ways, life was surprisingly unchanged: she still oversaw domestic matters, such as checking the menus, supervising the welfare and training of servants, and keeping an eye on flower arrangements. She remarked that she did not like flowers, so much as arranging flowers; and at times of political weariness she would often say she would rather have been an interior designer. She chose her clothes with care, wearing elegant saris and Kashmiri shawls, and made visits to her hairdresser a priority. Barbara Cartland, who often visited Indira, recalled the prime minister's delight in face cream or vitamins she brought, and remembered how she kept the colored paper and ribbons in which Cartland had wrapped her gifts to use again.[26]

Number 1 Safdarjung Road was much too small for Indira's needs, particularly as Rajiv and Sanjay were to return from England soon and would live with her. She hoped there would be a popular call for her to return to Teen Murti House, now earmarked as the Nehru Museum and Library, but no such call came, so her house was enlarged, and the bungalow next door converted into a private office.

Rajiv and Sanjay, in the words of Jawaharlal's secretary, M. O. Mathai, with whom they were frequently left, "grew up as rather self-centered boys with little thought or consideration for others. They grew up in an atmosphere which instilled in them the wrong idea that the rest of the world was meant for them. To say 'thank you' did not come naturally to them."[27] Sanjay liked to win. Once, when he and Rajiv were taken fishing, Rajiv caught a fish but he did not, so he persuaded Mathai to buy him a slightly bigger fish than Rajiv's from a fishmonger so that he could boast about his "catch."

Rajiv, and later Sanjay, went to the Doon School in the Himalayan foothills, in keeping with Congress policy to educate children in India. The Doon School, however, was like an English public school, right down to the Spartan conditions and awful food. Neither brother was very academic, though Rajiv was always willing to get on and do school work. Sanjay was the one most obviously bright, with enormous energy, and was later said by his teachers to be always getting into fights. He was said to be sullen, negligent of his academic work and resentful of authority. He had no interest in games, something of an impediment to progress in that public school atmosphere, but he enjoyed the school workshop, showing an early aptitude for mechanics: he was obsessed with cars and airplanes. On feast nights, when parents would drive to the school to be with their sons, Sanjay and his friends would tour the grounds looking for cars with keys left in the ignition and take them for quick joyrides, returning them before they were missed. Sanjay should have stayed on for two years after Rajiv, but it was clear he was too restless for the place, so he was withdrawn. Back in Delhi he attended St. Columbus School, without distinction, and busied himself buying old cars and making them work; to the alarm of his friends, his method of testing the brakes was to drive a vehicle down a steep hill, then try to stop it. He was also said to be involved in a spate of car thefts in Delhi, where a group of teenagers took cars for joyrides before abandoning them.

The writer Marie Seton said of the teenage Sanjay, "He had developed an aloofness which was almost formidable."[28] In 1964 he went to the Rolls Royce factory in Coventry, England, as an apprentice, and got on well with the young men with whom he shared a hostel. One of his supervisors, Chris Ladley, said, "He had a Jaguar and would get into scrapes with the police for speeding. He loved parties, was terribly attractive to women, but loved most of all to talk about Indian politics; he would deride British politics. He used to say Britain would become weak and India would develop into a leading industrial nation." He knew politics and had strong views with which it was hard to argue. Ladley said, "He was a born leader, he would obviously end up as something big, partially due to family tradition which he was very conscious of."[29]

Sanjay could be very charming, visiting colleagues in other departments, asking if they were married and had children. He could also show the Nehru temper. Once, when called to account for a mistake he had made, he told his supervisor, "Look, the British have fucked up India for centuries, and I've now come to fuck up Britain."[30]

Rajiv had a milder disposition altogether. Both boys were spoiled, having been brought up in privilege and seclusion: Jawaharlal even bought them their own racing car to drive around the grounds of Teen

Murti House. Rajiv, however, was far more sensitive than Sanjay to the suffering of others. When the veteran Congress leader and family friend Govind Pant was ill in 1961, seventeen-year-old Rajiv often visited, and was there on the morning of the Home Minister's death, where Indira found him when she came to pay her respects. She wrote to her father, "After a while I saw his face crumpling up and sent him home on the excuse that it was getting chilly . . . throughout Pantji's illness he had been most concerned. Probably, this had reminded him of Feroze."[31] Indira steered Rajiv towards his grandfather's Alma Mater, Trinity College, Cambridge. The Master of Trinity exempted Rajiv from the Advanced Level examinations and the college entrance exam, but demanded over 60 percent in the qualifying examination required of all students wishing to take the Mechanical Sciences Tripos. Rajiv stayed in London to prepare for the exam and presumably passed, as he was admitted. Like his predecessors, Rajiv was never allowed to forget that he was the embodiment of the nation. Indira wrote to him, "One has to be extra careful about one's manners and behavior, otherwise one brings discredit not only to the family but to the country as well."[32]

He duplicated the patchy academic performance of his mother and Motilal. Jawaharlal was the only Nehru who had genuine academic ability. At Trinity Rajiv felt that he was letting the family down by his poor performance. He was unable to keep up with the course and was eventually sent down, ending up at Imperial College, London, where he studied engineering. He was clearly not going to be a scientist, which had been an interim ambition, and went back to his first love—aircraft.

Rajiv was known as a gentle, unpretentious student, not inclined to play up his relationship with the Prime Minister of India. He is once said to have denied being related to Mahatma Gandhi without enlightening the inquirer further. His time at Cambridge was most remarkable for meeting Sonia Maino, an Italian industrialist's daughter, whom he met when she was attending an advanced English language course. Rajiv spotted her in The Varsity, a Greek restaurant he often visited, and asked the owner, Charles Antoni, to seat him near her, and asked another friend to introduce them. Sonia later said, "As our eyes met for the first time, I could feel my heart pounding. We greeted each other and, as far as I was concerned, it was love at first sight."[33] It was for Rajiv too; Sonia was his first and only girlfriend. He said, "The first time I saw her, I knew she was the girl for me. Then we fell in love."[34]

Rajiv proposed and she accepted, but with some trepidation, for she had only a vague notion of India "with its snakes, elephants and jungles, but exactly where it was and what it was really all about, I was not sure."[35] She was eighteen when she met Rajiv. Her father tried to keep them apart until she was older, but he did allow her to meet Indira Gandhi during her trip to London in 1965, after Rajiv had written respectfully requesting permission.

Notwithstanding this meeting, her father enforced their separation from July 1966, when she returned to Italy. Rajiv, however, did visit Italy to see her and meet her family late in 1966, having worked as a laborer on a building site to raise money for the trip. He left Imperial College without completing his degree and, true to his childhood ambition, became a pilot in England. On returning to India, he trained as a commercial pilot and was soon working with Indian Airways. It was not until January 1968 that Sonia, now twenty-one, arrived in India to marry Rajiv. She said, "The moment I saw him, I was filled with a tremendous sense of relief. I was at his side now and nothing and nobody was ever going to separate us again."[36]

Sonia stayed with Harivansh Rai Bachchan and his family, old friends of the Nehrus. At first she found Indian clothes awkward and uncomfortable and Indian food not to her taste, but she persevered with the unaccustomed lifestyle. She started learning Hindi and such skills as how to tie a sari and some Indian cooking.

Rajiv and Sonia were married on February 25, 1968 in a civil ceremony at 1 Safdarjung Road. Sonia, dark-haired and extremely beautiful, wore a pink sari made of the fine handspun cloth Jawaharlal had made in prison. Sonia's mother and some Italian relations came, but not her father, who did not approve of his daughter marrying outside the Catholic faith.

The young couple moved in with Indira, and Sonia quickly began to assume the task of running the household. She soon became indispensable to the Prime Minister, the daughter Indira never had, and she even took to calling her "mummy." Indira wrote to Dorothy Norman, "Apart from being beautiful, Sonia is a really nice girl, wholesome and straightforward."[37] The family always tried to eat together, and at these times Sonia found Indira "a delightful conversational-ist—quick in her observation, clear in her descriptions." The naturally reserved young bride found it frightening, however, to be "a new member of a family that had lived for years in the public eye. Everything they did and said, as well as what they didn't say or didn't do, was analyzed and judged. How was it possible to live like this!"[38]

By December 15, 1969 Indira was excitedly telling Dorothy Norman that Sonia was expecting a baby. Rahul was born in the summer of 1970, and Priyanka the following year. Indira delighted in her grandchildren, to the extent that she would not take lunchtime meetings so that she could get home to play with them. She took to inviting visiting dignitaries to her home for a family dinner, where she would serve them herself, rather than hosting state banquets.

Sanjay was also living at his mother's house on his return to India. His performance as an apprentice in England had been unsatisfactory and he publicly declared that there was nothing more Rolls Royce could teach him. M. O. Mathai said that Sanjay had read a book about Henry Ford and longed to emulate him, so he set up a small outfit in Old Delhi. He could throw together a car from old parts, but did not realize that organizing a modern assembly line was another matter. This did not prevent him, in 1970, from winning the coveted license to set up a factory producing small popular cars for the Indian market. This development caused Indira considerable embarrassment, though she told parliament she had no hand in granting the license and that Sanjay should not be prevented from obtaining it "merely because he was the prime minister's son."[39]

Indira's warmth towards her close family and friends did not extend to people she met in an official capacity. She told her aides to do away with introductions and plunge straight into the subject whenever they had anything to report. She was always punctual, and always allowed each interview exactly its allotted time but no more. She always listened, but sometimes had very little to say. Even people who favored her often found talking to her very hard work. For most people, she considered that to be available was enough—she felt no urge to make herself likable. The writer Dom Moraes, who was a real fan of Indira, found interviewing her very hard work. He wrote, "She answered my questions more or less monosyllabically. She never smiled. Indeed, she appeared to become very tired of the whole interview about sixty seconds after it began." This was when he made his first mistake, of asking if Jawaharlal had had a great influence on her policies. "She looked at me for the first and only time during this ill-fated interview, frightening me with her eyes, and said, 'Does everybody who interviews me have to ask the same question?' Moraes went away dejected: "I had liked her and I had been of no interest to her: she had done what was expected of her and then shelved me in her memory."[40]

Moraes was the son of Frank Moraes, the celebrated journalist and biographer of Jawaharlal, which doubtless helped him to get the interview. Indira's behavior was nothing to do with his comparative obscurity, however: even James Callaghan, sometime British prime minister and foreign secretary, had a very unhappy breakfast with her: "She was cross and I was stubborn and both of us sat for ten long minutes without speaking or looking at each other."[41] Indira actually boasted of her extreme silences. When U.S. Ambassador Chester Bowles criticized Indira's foreign policy for being pro-Arab and anti-Israeli, she said, "He lectured me and did not give me a chance to say what was in my mind. He did not want to know. So I refused to speak, was cordial, wished him a pleasant trip, but kept silent—and that was that."[42]

Two reverses were to affect Indira towards the middle of her term of office, which obliged her to reassert the upper hand over opponents in her own party—these were over the Congress presidency and the national presidency. Indira succeeded in having Kamaraj stand down from the Congress presidency, though he wanted a further term. She did not, however, take the position herself, which had been her intention, or get her own nominee into the post. The right-wing candidate, Nijalingappa, was elected, and never worked easily with Indira. He played a crucial role in the selection of the new national president, which became a showdown issue between Indira and the Syndicate.

Zakir Hussain died in office two years after becoming president, in April 1969, necessitating another standoff battle between Indira and the Syndicate for the post. Indira favored Jagjivan Ram, a loyalist who was also an untouchable, as his elevation to the presidency would have immense symbolic importance among the poor of India whom Indira considered her true constituency. At a Congress committee meeting in Bangalore in July 1969 the Syndicate succeeded in effecting the nomination of Sanjiva Reddy, former chief minister of

Andhra Pradesh, because a minister thought to be an Indira loyalist, Y. B. Chavan, changed his vote at the last minute. Indira lost by one vote, "an assault on my office and attitudes" she is reported to have said, in extreme anger.[43] Her personality, long since associated with India as a whole, was now being seen as identical with the government—an assault on one was an assault on both. "She has been taught a lesson now," wrote Nijalingappa, but, "I feel she will do something nasty in a huff. She is so very much angry and upset about Chavan and then Morarji; she expected that being her cabinet colleagues they should go with her in whatever she does. Wrong approach. Let us see what she may do."[44]

Pupul Jayakar described how Indira confronted a crisis: "As the assault against her increased in velocity, she instinctively avoided any reflexive reaction or confrontation, waited till the energy of the attack had abated and her opponents felt a false sense of security . . . out of this conservation of her resources, when the time was right, she struck when it was least expected."[45]

She aimed to hit back in the area of domestic policy where the Congress right wing were particularly vulnerable. In May 1967, in the wake of the election in which the left had made gains among the young and the poor at the expense of Congress, the Congress Working Committee thought it necessary for the party to adopt a left-wing ten-point program involving nationalization, increased state control, land reform and the abolition of princely privileges. Such statements were frequently made with no sincerity, and certainly Morarji Desai had said banks would never be nationalized while he was finance minister. Indira gave no support to this measure and it was watered down to become "social control" of banks at a later meeting.

Four days after the vote over Jagjivan Ram's candidature, on July 16, 1969, she sacked Morarji Desai as finance minister, saying it would be unfair to burden him with the responsibility of implementing an economic policy with which he disagreed. Indira took the portfolio herself and offered to allow him to stay as deputy prime minister. This he angrily rejected. Three days following his sacking, Indira nationalized India's fourteen national banks by presidential ordinance signed by the acting president, former vice-president V. V. Giri.

It was a bold move for many reasons, not least because Indira hardly knew what she was doing. Shortly after the nationalization, she told her economic affairs secretary with somewhat startling candor, "Morarji Desai knew something about finance, I know nothing. I have taken this portfolio because the prime minister of India should understand the economic problems of the country and also know how to comprehend the budget."[46] It is not remarkable for ministers to know little about the subject of their portfolio—politicians are supposedly successful because of their general judgment, not their specialist knowledge—but it is unusual for ministers to be quite so honest about their ignorance. It shows Indira's confidence that once she had set her mind to understand a subject that did not come naturally to her, she would do so, and had no fear about her eventual facility.

The nationalization of the banks was a wild political success, being represented in the country as taking India's financial resources from the capitalists and giving them to the people. There were street celebrations with dancing crowds praising Indira, many of them people who had never even been in a bank. Huge crowds gathered at Indira's house to fete her. Farmers, small traders and businessmen were also enthusiastic at the prospect of receiving credit on better terms from the nationalized banks, and the left-wing parties lined up solidly behind Indira.

From this summit of popularity, she could move against her opponents, who had already backed down from publicly censuring her for sacking Desai. Events moved in her direction. Luckily for Indira, Vice-President V. V. Giri, a trade union leader, had decided to run as an independent for the post of national president, otherwise she would have had to accept Reddy's elevation as a *fait accompli*. Giri's candidature was quite in order, as Indira said: "So far all the vice-presidents had become presidents and although it didn't mean that we should always stick by this precedent, there was no reason to bypass Giri."[47] Nijalingappa was so unsure of the outcome now an election was to take place that he began canvassing for support for Reddy among opposition parties. This bargaining for votes with reactionary communalist parties was a betrayal of Congress policies, Indira claimed, and she argued in favor of a free vote among parliamentarians for the presidential post. "Vote according to your conscience," she advised. Indira considered this vote a make-or-break issue, a test of strength between herself and the Syndicate: she even said she might have to resign if Giri lost the vote. After a tense two counts, however, on August 20,

1968, V. V. Giri was elected president. "The crisis has only now begun," Indira told Pupul Jayakar on first hearing the news.[48]

The old guard and the right wing now insisted that Indira be disciplined for her attack on the Congress presidential candidate. The center and left wing of Congress, however, and the left-wing parties (both communist parties and the socialists) backed Indira. She was not displaying mere paranoia in her fears—there was a Syndicate plot to oust her, with Desai becoming prime minister, while the duplicitous Chavan would be paid off for his support with the post of deputy prime minister and the promise of the premiership after the 1972 election. The only comfort was that no one with any sense would trust people who were prepared to make such a deal. Chavan felt his best interests would be served by staying with Indira, so he switched sides again and now backed her.

The conflict in Congress continued, with Indira and Nijalingappa trying to exert influence over each other, until the time came for a clear trial of strength between the two factions, who were equally divided on the Congress Working Committee. Nijalingappa, displaying his indifferent skill as a strategist, attempted to redress this balance by dismissing two supporters of Indira, Fakhruddin Ahmed and C. Subramaniam. This crude gesture was intended to reduce her supporters to a minority, but of course Indira was far too clever to simply walk into a meeting in which she had already been rendered impotent. She herself called a "requisition" meeting of the Congress Working Committee to commence at the same time as that called by the Congress president. Now the members must decide between them.

On November 1, 1969, therefore, to the fascination of the media, two Congress Working Committee meetings took place, one at the Congress offices and the other at 1 Safdarjung Road. Ten members of the twenty-one member committee attended each meeting. The twenty-first, A. C. Abraham, briefly attended both. Abraham excepted, all the delegates at the meeting in the Congress offices were spat at and roughed up by the crowd of Indira supporters who waited outside. "These were for the most part old men, incapable of violence, who were being threatened in such a cowardly fashion," a journalist who observed it reported.[49] No one would suggest such behavior took place at Indira's behest, but her failure to discourage rowdy supporters implied her connivance.

Nijalingappa then announced Indira's expulsion from the Congress Party "for her deliberate action of defiance." It accused her of dividing Congress members into those who were her supporters and those who were not, "her peculiar attitude to questions of discipline, her basic and overriding desire to concentrate all power in her hands, so that her colleagues are nominees in any office they might occupy."[50] The expulsion notice added that as she was not a member, she could not lead the Congress Party in parliament and they must elect a new leader. Indira could not have had a better gift than this clumsy action, for it left her as prime minister unencumbered by party discipline. She asked those members of her Cabinet who could not give her whole-hearted support to resign, and went on to the next battle. This was for the election of the Congress parliamentary leader.

Lobbying took place all night over the vote for Congress leader. The major question was not really who should lead the Congress. MPs have a strong sense of self-preservation, and there were real fears of losing their seats if an election were called, so they felt constrained to vote for a figure of stability, and for one who was an election winner. Of the 429 Congress members of both houses of parliament, about 310 attended a meeting Indira had called. She therefore had a majority of the members of Congress, but was in a minority in parliament as a whole. This was of no consequence, as the left-wing parties were prepared to support her, and even to swell the huge supportive demonstrations outside her house, which she addressed in terms of defiance, denouncing the party bosses who would not back her campaign for the poor and exploited.

The Syndicate's side of the split became known as Congress (O) meaning Organization. Indira's was called Congress (R) for Requisitionist, but was more generally known as Congress Indira. Each side of Congress claimed to be the true inheritor of the Congress mantle, but as Jawaharlal's daughter, Indira clearly had the superior claim in the eyes of the people.

At a meeting of the All India Congress Committee on November 22, 1969, Indira held 446 of the total 705 members. For the first time she broke down in public, crying on the platform at the thought that party bosses should have expelled her from the Congress to which her family had given so much. How genuine these tears were in a woman famously given to reserve is a matter of question. Perhaps it simply had to look harder for Indira to split the Congress than it actually was. After personalizing the issue, she turned to the matter of policy, which solidified her grasp on the radical wing of Congress, and the masses outside: "I want to assure you quite categorically that we shall not take a single step backward in implementing the economic program. We want to go forward more speedily, and I hope with your help we shall be able to fight the battle against poverty more effectively."[51]

Her cousin, Nayantara Sahgal, with excusable severity, considered Indira personally responsible for the decline of political standards in India. She said, "The campaign of street arousal introduced a throbbing undercurrent of exaggeration, excess and violence, waiting like electricity to be switched on."[52]

It was this battle, the fight to the finish for control of Congress, that made Indira Gandhi as the world was to know her. She was a confident and commanding personality, no more cowed by the jibes of the Opposition or by the complexities of government. She had become calculating and ruthless. However, her blossoming as a politician brought a concomitant increase in her isolation and paranoia, some of which may have been justified. She was, for example, convinced that a military coup was imminent, but so were many others in the big cities of India, where such gossip was rife. It reached the ears of Indira herself, who called the Chief of Army Staff Sam Manekshaw to her office. With few preliminaries she said, "Everybody says you're going to take over from me." Manekshaw recalled, "That shook me for a little while, not very long, three seconds. I walked across to her. She had a long nose, and I've got a long nose, and I put mine next to her and I said, 'What do you think, Prime Minister?' And she said, 'You can't.' And I said, 'Oh, do you think I'm so incompetent?' She said, 'I didn't mean that, I meant you wouldn't.' And I said, 'You're quite right, Prime Minister . . . I don't interfere in the political world . . .' I came back in the car thinking to myself, 'She's a very clever girl. She's just made a point: Sam, if you're thinking of doing anything, I know all about it.'"[53]

As Indira became more personally successful and eliminated her opponents from the political scene, replacing them in the Cabinet with yes-men, she became increasingly reliant on her coterie of "advisers" who operated as a "kitchen cabinet." Fearful of crossing her, ministers would pass decisions on to Indira via her secretariat, which thus had far-reaching powers in deciding which measures would go to the Prime Minister and which would be held up. Her supporters were able to get away with gross corruption with impunity. Jagjivan Ram, whom she had proposed as national president, had for ten years failed to pay taxes on his considerable income. Indira treated it lightly—he was a busy man and had "obviously forgotten" to send in his tax returns.[54]

One secret of Indira's success was her instinctive knowledge of what would please her supporters, and her ruthlessness in ensuring that she could deliver. Following the arrangements reached for the handover of the princely states by Sardar Patel, hundreds of Indian royal families enjoyed 40 million rupees a year in "privy purse" payments from the nation in perpetuity, guaranteed by the constitution. The princes had not gained in popularity, or usefulness, in the years since independence. Dangerously, in terms of their own preservation, they had developed political aspirations, forming the Swatantra Party with other disaffected sections of society, and contesting the 1967 election with some success.

Congress had a policy of abolishing the privy purses and privileges of the princes since the "radical" All India Congress Committee meeting of 1967 held in the wake of the election, but it was treated as one of the policies which would never be enacted. With her finely tuned political instinct, Indira realized it was an area where she could gain popularity at little cost. She said, "What irritated people most was not the privy purse but the rest of it, the fact that princes didn't pay water and electricity rates. The poor man had to pay but the prince did not."[55] Indira made it a personal crusade, and in August 1970 introduced a measure in parliament to change the constitution. She had it passed with the necessary two-thirds majority in the lower house, the Lok Sabha, but in the upper house, the Rajya Sabha, the measure failed to be passed by one vote.

Parliament was only a means to an end for Indira, and if she could not achieve her end by parliamentary means, she would go by another route. On the evening of the Rajya Sabha vote, she held an emergency cabinet meeting and then obtained a proclamation from the President she had worked so hard to have elected "derecognizing" the princes. In a "derecognized" state they could enjoy no privileges under the constitution, so the measure was achieved.

The princes took the matter to the Supreme Court and were successful in invalidating the presidential proclamation. It was Indira's
second major conflict with the Supreme Court. The first had been
over bank nationalization, when her order nationalizing the banks
was declared invalid and she had to nationalize more slowly by taking
over the management of the banks and enacting a law which overcame the Supreme Court's decisions. Still, she was not prepared to be
frustrated on every one of her populist measures. On December 27,
1970 she drove to the presidential palace and asked Giri to dissolve
parliament. That evening she spoke in a radio broadcast to the nation
about the need for a fresh mandate after measures of the government's
policy had been obstructed by "vested interests" and "reactionary
forces."[56]

The Opposition used the slogan *Indira Hatao* ("Remove Indira")
for the election, which Indira's supporters transformed to *Garibi Hatao*
("Remove Poverty"), something the poor found very easy to vote for.
Indira's supporters emphasized the connection between their leader
and the entire nation with the slogan, "Indira is you." Unlike the
Opposition, she made it clear that she was not interested in national
coalitions with other parties; she wanted a majority so that she could
rule with a mandate. At each election she seemed to be striving to
beat the records of previous campaigns, driving herself onwards with
flashing eyes, hardly stopping to sleep or eat. She addressed 13 million
people and another 7 million stood, by the road often for hours, to
catch a glimpse of her. In forty-three days she addressed more than
300 meetings, traveling over 36,000 miles. "It was wonderful to see
the light in their eyes," said Indira, only really happy as the center of
attention in a crowd.[57] She inspired the poor, the untouchables and
the Muslims, who had all been politically apathetic, to believe that
the nation cared for them, while also convincing the middle class that
a stable government, which only she could provide, would permit the
conditions for the creation of wealth.

Indira won majestically with a two-thirds majority, 352 out of 518
seats, sufficient to amend the constitution as she required. To recover
her strength, she went to The Retreat in Mashobra in the Simla Hills,
where Mountbatten had taken Jawaharlal. Now it belonged to the
President, but no one had used it since the Mountbattens left. There
she wrote a letter to Dorothy Norman explaining the atmosphere in

which she had won in a campaign with all the moneyed interests against her, where her workers had the least resources, their funds made up of donations from small and middle industrialists and the general public.

"What has been extraordinary and exhilarating is that the elections became a sort of movement—a people's movement. Thus, from village after village we got news that when our sympathizers went to campaign, they were stopped at the entrance and asked for whom they stood. If they took my name, they were welcomed—often with brass bands and sweets! or told that the village vote was solid for us and therefore they need not waste their time. Taxi drivers and scooter rickshaw drivers not only offered the use of their vehicles free but themselves paid for the gasoline. These are only a few examples. The peasant, the worker and, above all, the youth cut across all caste, religious and other barriers to make this their own campaign with tremendous enthusiasm. In Delhi, large numbers of people who had regular jobs, and who worked in offices, factories or elsewhere in the daytime, came to our office afterwards and worked until two and three in the morning for nearly a month on a purely voluntary basis."[58]

Her greatest boast was that in all these travels, except in some districts and in some untouchable tribes, "nowhere did I see the sort of poverty which was so prevalent twenty years ago. Whether they had proper shelter and clothing or not, almost everywhere the children were healthy and bright-eyed."[59] The problem of how to feed the people had become a problem of where to store the surpluses. It was Indira's India and she was very proud.

# TWELVE

# INDIRA RIDES A TIGER

The next stage in Indira's progress towards deification happened not in India but in East Pakistan. When India was divided in 1947 along poorly conceived communal lines, Pakistan was created out of two quite separate entities divided by 1000 miles. There was no unity between these nations: the Urdu-speaking West Pakistanis were tall, lightish-skinned people, descendants of the original conquerors of India; the Bengali-speaking East Pakistanis were short and dark, descendants of the conquered. The only thing they had in common was Islam, which they shared with many millions of others: it was no basis for nationhood.

The smaller but more populous and poorer East Pakistan was starved of resources by West Pakistan, which kept control of the military and political centers. The liberal Awami Party, led by Sheikh Mujib-ur Rehman, pointed out the massive disparity in resources granted to them by the central government for such services as health, education and power. He argued for representation on the basis of population (which would give East Pakistan a majority) and regional autonomy. Pakistan was under a military dictator, General Yahya Khan, but he held the first free and fair elections in Pakistan's history in December 1970. The results gave Rehman an overall majority in the national assembly. The West Pakistanis had given Zulfiqar Ali Bhutto a majority in their region. He was, like so many rulers of the subcontinent, a Western-educated lawyer, who had gone into politics on returning to his home country. He promoted a brand of "Islamic socialism," which combined economic radicalism and anti-Indian nationalism. Although the majority won by Rehman in Bengal made him the overall victor, Bhutto had no intention of allowing that country to take political power, and he refused to allow the national assembly to meet until an agreement had been reached on the future power structure in Pakistan as a whole.

With democracy having produced an undesired result, General Yahya, on March 25, 1971, ordered the arrest of Rehman and the repression of East Pakistan in a brutal clampdown unseen since the days of partition. The army, in obviously preplanned raids, targeted university teachers, writers, student leaders and anyone who might be described as a leader or an intellectual, dragged them out of their beds and killed them. What Bengali contingents there were in the police and the army revolted, declared independence, and the civil war in East Pakistan became a war of liberation for Bangladesh.

The attack on East Pakistan came just eight days after Indira was elected leader of the Congress Parliamentary Party. The slaughter and mass rape led to a huge refugee problem, with eventually 9 or 10 million people flowing across the border into Bengal, which was already very heavily populated. They had to be given shelter, food and protection from epidemics. As atrocities increased and the refugees put more pressure on India's resources, there was a public outcry in India for the army to be sent in. Indira knew the great danger of such a step: India would be accused of stimulating the secessionist movement in East Pakistan, which would be discredited if it were seen as an instrument of Indian policy. Pakistani propaganda already said that the independence movement was a conspiracy by Hindu India against Islam. Indira was, however, prepared to equip and train the guerrilla bands who were sheltering on the Indian side of the border.

Chief of Army Staff, Sam Manekshaw, had doubts about the fighting prowess of these guerrillas. He said, "They were small Bengali people. They came up against these big, hefty, Punjabi Muslims and when they saw them they ran like hell. They did do a certain amount of things, but they were no match for the Pakistan armed forces who were really good fighting soldiers."[1]

Indira held firm, maintaining caution while the cost of keeping the refugees threatened to ruin the economy. Her experience with refugee camps at the time of partition had taught her that panic or despair were the wrong responses. Instead, fighting was carried on by the indigenous guerrillas, while secret military preparations were under way for the Indian forces to be able to strike when necessary. Even if it were politically desirable, it would be impracticable to wage war at an early stage—the monsoons were about to break, which would hamper troop movements, and passes over the Himalayas would soon be open, allowing the Chinese to move in easily to support Pakistan.

Indira turned most of her attention to the field of foreign relations. The United States had been seeking *rapprochement* with China, and

Indira had been told that they would not help if the Chinese attacked. However much Indira could lay claim to the moral high ground, the wider ambitions of the superpowers threatened to inter-vene. Pakistan had maintained close relations with China, for much the same reason that India had with the Soviets. Indira had unwit-tingly disturbed a cherished strategy of the Nixon/Kissinger adminis-tration—to use Pakistan as a conduit for the U.S. opening to China. However lamentable Pakistan's record in East Bengal, Kissinger believed that "we can't allow a friend of ours and China's to get screwed by a conflict with a friend of Russia's."[2] There was therefore a risk in moving still closer to the Soviets, but Indira nevertheless aban-doned her previous restraint and signed a twenty-year "Treaty of Peace, Friendship and Cooperation" in August 1971. Now India had considerable access to Soviet weapons. Indira was warmly received on a visit to Moscow in September 1971, while her diplomats set about stimulating support for India with the second-rank powers. She wished to garner a harvest of international outrage at a time when the man who should have been prime minister of Pakistan, Sheikh Mujib-ur Rehman, was being tried in camera by a military court, and West Pakistani troops were still conducting what seemed more like geno-cide than war.

In order to stimulate political support, Indira went on a three-week tour of European capitals, ensuring massive publicity as the Western media continued to cover stories of atrocities in East Pakistan. In Britain, Belgium, Austria, France, West Germany and finally the United States, Indira stated her position: the refugee situation was intolerable, the problem was not of India's making, but if necessary India would take action. She raged at a British interviewer, "When Hitler was on the rampage, why didn't you say, 'Let's keep quiet and let's have peace with Germany and the Jews die, or let Belgium die, let France die'?" Asked why she refused to have talks with Pakistan she said, "Talks with whom—and about what? Up to now President Yahya Khan is telling everybody . . . that the situation in Bangladesh is absolutely normal. Now, either he doesn't know what is happening, or he is telling a deliberate untruth."[3]

With some daring, while in the United States, Indira used a strat-egy of appealing to the people over the heads of the politicians. She knew she would get a frosty reception from Nixon, who was notoriously favorable to Pakistan, which effectively meant West Pakistan. "I am haunted by the tormented faces in our overcrowded refugee camps," said Indira in answer to Nixon's welcoming speech in which he had not mentioned the war. "I have come here looking for a deeper understanding of the situation in our part of the world."[4]

She met her old friend Dorothy Norman, who found that Indira was besieged by queries about what the United States could do to help: her strategy was working. Press and public opinion were turning against Nixon for his support of the gruesome leaders of Pakistan. Norman noticed that the strain of traveling, of maintaining restraint and reasonableness in the face of provocation, were beginning to show in Indira. They attended a performance of the New York Philharmonic Orchestra together, and Norman later bought tickets for the New York City Ballet performing a work by Stravinsky. "At the last moment, Indira said she could not join me. I showed my surprise; she looked unnerved and sad. I could not understand what had happened . . . Indira commented only, 'I can't go. It will be too wonderful. I won't be able to bear it.' She was on the verge of tears. In the morning she regained her equilibrium."[5]

Her steadiness held when she returned home, fully aware now of the possible repercussions of an all-out war, although she did not know that the apparent unity of Indian opinion behind her was breached by her former deputy Morarji Desai, who was alleged by American writer Seymour M. Hersh to be an informer for the CIA. Bangladeshi guerrillas continued to raid Pakistani positions and there were border incidents when the Pakistanis followed them. Pakistanis were also shelling Indian towns on the border. An all-out war was inevitable, but still Indira waited. An attack was to be launched on December 4, 1971, but to her great relief the Pakistani dictator preempted it. On December 3 he launched an ineffectual airstrike on eight Indian airfields, thus allowing India's response to be a defensive action. This was not part of a Machiavellian plan by Indira; she was in Calcutta at the time and it took two hours to locate her. She immediately flew back to Delhi, despite the danger of attack from enemy aircraft, and went straight to a briefing on the Pakistani attack. That night she held a meeting of the Cabinet, followed by a meeting with Opposition leaders, who assured her of their support.

Now the guerrillas infiltrated deep into Bangladesh, followed by the Indian Army, which was welcomed by villagers as an army of liberation. Pakistan launched a massive attack over the western Indian border, but India held the line, maintaining a defensive action in the west while concentrating on a well-prepared plan for the conquest of Bangladesh in fifteen days. Within twenty-four hours the Pakistani Air Force had been virtually put out of action in the east, and there were no reinforcements. Yahya Khan had strained his friendships to the limit: to his dismay, neither China nor the United States came to his aid. The most the U.S. did was to send the Seventh Fleet to the Bay of Bengal, probably in an attempt to divert Indian attention; but Indira was not deflected from her objective, and in response sent D. P. Dhar, the chairman of her Foreign Policy Planning Committee, to Moscow. He returned with a promise of Russian support if China entered the war, and a Soviet fleet sailed towards the Bay of Bengal from Vladivostock. In the United Nations Security Council two American motions calling for a ceasefire were vetoed, while Britain and France abstained.

With staff from the naval headquarters, Indira diverted the Indian Army to the Bay of Bengal where they were able to occupy the ports and take the surrender of the Pakistani troops defending them before the U.S. Seventh Fleet arrived. If the United States did intend an invasion in support of Pakistan, it would now be difficult, to the point of impossibility.

Indira's defiance in the face of a U.S. threat was overwhelmingly supported by the nation. American action, which was largely President Nixon's decision unsupported by his colleagues, stimulated a surge of anti-American feeling in India, and in the U.S. itself there was fear that Nixon's clumsy approach had propelled India towards the Soviets.

Under American diplomatic pressure, Indira wrote an open letter to Nixon, remarking that war "could have been avoided if the power, influence and authority of all the states and above all of the United States had got Sheikh Mujib-ur Rehman released . . . Lip-service was paid to the need for a political solution, but not a single worthwhile step was taken to bring this about . . . with all the knowledge and deep understanding of human affairs you, as President of the United States and reflecting the will, the aspirations and idealism of the great American people, will at least let me know where precisely we have gone wrong before your representatives or spokesmen deal with us with such harshness of language."⁶ One can see why Nixon so disliked her.

Soon diplomacy was superfluous anyway: on December 16, after a two-week war, over 93,000 Pakistani troops in Bangladesh laid down their arms. Indira was waiting in her office to hear that the surrender had been signed (the Pakistanis had been offering to surrender for days), while honoring a commitment to a long-booked Swedish television crew. The interviewer was more concerned with Indira's childhood and preference in clothes than the war, and the interview came to an abrupt end when her Commander-in-Chief phoned to say that the surrender had been signed. She went straight to parliament and announced to the expectant MPs, "Dacca is now the free capital of a free country . . ." but the rest of her statement was lost in cheering.⁷ Indira ordered a ceasefire on the western front, where her troops occupied nearly 5000 square miles of West Pakistan. She could have gone on to further victories, but it was a mature decision to end the war unilaterally at the point of victory. Stopping as soon as her objectives had been reached gave no chance for China and the United States to take action.

She had led the nation rather than directing the war: that she had left to her Commander-in-Chief, Sam Manekshaw, who was promoted to the rank of field marshal after the war, the first in India's history. She had been briefed by him daily, but had restricted her role to addressing the nation with stirring speeches, sympathizing with the refugees whose camps she frequently visited, and encouraging the troops, to whom she spoke with maternal warmth.

In delivering a decisive military victory, she had restored the national pride of India, so damaged by the 1962 Indo-Chinese debacle. The President awarded her the highest Indian honor, the Bharat Ratna. She was likened to Durga, the goddess of war who rode on a tiger, defeating the demons in battle after they had ousted the gods from heaven, and restoring the gods to their rightful place. In some villages, women began worshipping Indira as a goddess. She herself, she told Pupul Jayakar, had some intimations of supernatural powers: "Throughout the war and even previous to it I had strange experiences—an extended vision I had known at times in my youth. The color red suffused me throughout the war. On occasions I found myself speaking, saw things behind me which I could never have seen. The intensity disappeared immediately after the war ended and so have the experiences."[8]

A lasting peace with Pakistan was now possible and necessary. Bhutto had become President of Pakistan following the collapse of the military government, and Mujib-ur Rehman was released to become President of Bangladesh. He had been sentenced to death, so India's action had literally saved his life. Indira was eager to use the war as a means of achieving a settlement over Kashmir, and re-entered negotiations with Jawaharlal's old friend Sheikh Abdullah, the Kashmiri leader who, until now, had been under political restrictions. Bhutto had a tenuous grip on power, something he communicated to Indira at the Simla peace conference in the summer of 1972. He was unable, he said, to return to Pakistan with a humiliating peace, implying that if this happened he might be replaced by more reckless and militant leaders who would pose a greater long-term threat to India. Indira wanted a complete solution to the Kashmir problem, but Bhutto could not give up all claims to the territory. An agreement was finally reached in which Pakistan renounced the use of force to settle the Kashmir dispute, and both sides resolved to settle the matter between them without involving the UN. This at last redressed the error Jawaharlal had made in bringing UN observers into the dispute. The existing line of control in Kashmir was accepted. It was not a solution, but it was closer to one than anyone else had achieved, and Bhutto came out of the negotiations with considerably more respect for Indira than he had when he entered them. He had previously made scornful remarks about her poor academic performance, additionally remarking that her position was entirely due to her parentage. He left the conference full of admiration for her statesmanship, saying that she was "a lady with a great sense of discipline in her approach to matters . . . she makes up her mind and tenaciously pursues her objectives."[9]

The Green Revolution had filled the grain stocks and relative economic stability had enriched the exchequer, but the war had depleted both. Stored grain had been used to feed the refugees and military costs had emptied the national coffers. When the rains failed again in 1972, grain was scarce so the price rose to levels the peasants could not afford. Indira's election promise to remove poverty now had a hollow ring; sour wits said she was doing her best to remove the poor.

With widespread national distress, Indira needed to revitalize her radical image, so she agreed to nationalization of the wholesale grain trade in April 1973. This was designed to ameliorate the situation, but in fact made it worse, as panic buying caused shortages and shortages caused food riots with raids on food trucks. The nationalization of coal mining and general insurance (as opposed to life insurance) were an earlier nod to radicalism, which did not impress the international banking community.

The already huge problems of government were not eased by an explosion of corruption, directly attributable to Indira's style of government. State planning and centralization of authority led to corruption, as the control and finance of such matters as government contracts were concentrated in just a few hands. As power in the Congress Party, and therefore political and financial power, came ultimately from the membership, unscrupulous party bosses proceeded to inflate their membership figures with fictitious members who could be relied upon for their votes. The "record membership" of 10 million claimed for Congress in 1972 was estimated to contain 6 million bogus members. Thus Congress became hollowed out, empty of any real contact with the masses, an organization of rich party bosses and greasy party stooges doing their bidding in return for handouts.

Indira contributed to the murky atmosphere by banning political donations from joint stock companies. This was born of a fear that big business would fund attacks on her, but the result was not a cessation of donations so much as a growth in secret deals, where money would be given to political parties for favors and would not be even cursorily recorded. Indira also, in direct contradiction to her father's practice, insisted that the collection and distribution of all party funds should be in her hands. Rumors abounded of suitcases full of notes being delivered to the Prime Minister's house.

The most strange and outrageous case of dubious financial transactions was the Nagarwala affair. This began on May 24, 1971, when Ved Prakash Malhotra, chief cashier of the State Bank of India, received a telephone call from Indira instructing him to withdraw 6 million rupees and deliver them to a person waiting on a road who would identify himself as a "man from Bangladesh." Malhotra took the money in a taxi and handed it to a man who gave the appropriate password. Malhotra then proceeded to Indira's house to announce he had achieved his mission and to ask for a receipt.

There, the Prime Minister's private secretary, P. N. Haksar, told him that Indira had made no such call and advised him to go to the police. After a swift investigation, the money and the perpetrator of the scam were recovered the same day. The villain was a sometime intelligence officer and army captain, Rustom Sohrab Nagarwala, who had imitated Indira's voice to obtain the money. Within the remarkably short period of three days, he was tried and sentenced to four years' imprisonment. He later died of a heart attack in jail and the investigating officer died in a car crash, so no further disclosures were likely. Nagarwala had links with the CIA and it may well have been that the whole plan was a setup to discredit Indira at a time when her outspoken position on Bangladesh was undermining the Nixon administration's policy on Pakistan.

None of this was satisfactory to the Opposition, however, who even if they were prepared to accept that this was just a criminal or an espionage conspiracy, still needed to know how Malhotra fell for it. Was he in the habit of receiving verbal instructions from the Prime Minister telling him to withdraw cash and give it to an unknown man in the street? How could a cashier have access to large sums of money with nothing but a verbal request? Whose money was it? Indira imperiously refused to answer questions about the grubby affair, but she had clearly laid herself open to rumormongers.

With her enhanced majority from the 1971 re-election, Indira felt it was time to take on the courts. Despite her father and grandfather having been lawyers, most of Indira's experience of the legal system had been of its injustice, not least the imprisonment of members of her family and Congress workers. One of her earliest memories was of sitting in court on Motilal's knee while a travesty of justice was played out in front of them. She simply had no respect for the legal system. This attitude was intensified when the Supreme Court blocked her radical and popular measures to nationalize banks and deprive the princes of their privy purses. Eventually, achieving these objectives was not enough for Indira; she wanted to cow the courts and irrevocably assert the power of the nation's elected leader over the judiciary. She wanted to show them who was boss. The showdown arrived in the shape of a law allowing parliament unrestricted rights to amend the constitution. It was challenged in the Supreme Court and became the subject of a thirteen-man commission of judges headed by the Chief Justice, S. M. Sikri. Unfortunately for Indira, six judges voted with her, six against, and Sikri's casting vote found in her favor only to a limited degree: it was interpreted as a defeat for Indira and she felt it as such.

She was incensed: these vested interests, having failed at the polls, were seeking to impede the will of the people by other means. Sikri was due to retire, so in her indignation Indira flouted the convention of appointing the next most senior judge to the top position, and went shopping for a judge who could be relied upon to support her. The offended judges who had been leap-frogged resigned amid widespread criticism of Indira, even among those who had not previously been opponents, for attempting to suborn the judiciary. She was building up enemies for herself, and a fresh confrontation with the judges was inevitable.

Indira had won this round, at some cost to her reputation; but an unforeseen legal maneuver which was grinding its way through the courts would eventually trip her up. This was a case brought by Raj Narain, the socialist candidate who ran against Indira at Rae Bareli in 1971. While Narain was thought of as something of a buffoon and was referred to as the "Clown Prince of India," his flamboyant behavior concealed high political skill and tenacity. Narain challenged Indira's election on the basis of "corrupt electoral practices," but with the usual speed of the court system in India, it would take years.

From 1972 to 1975 the drought continued and subsequent bad harvests cursed many parts of the nation. At the very end of 1973 Arab oil producers, in pique at having lost the Arab-Israeli war, quadrupled the price of crude oil. The move had a shocking effect on world economies and particularly damaged developing countries. Inflation in India was soon running at 25 percent. Even before this, however, Indira had felt obliged to swallow her pride and go to the World Bank and International Monetary Fund, who gave help on condition that Indira backtracked on public spending. However resentfully, she did so. It was another example of her ability to grit her teeth and make unpalatable decisions, so long as the result was that she remained in power.

Within herself Indira felt increasingly isolated. Her morbid introspection was intensified after an air accident in May 1973 when some of her friends and acquaintances died. She wrote to Dorothy Norman, "Aren't we presumptuous in equating ourselves with the world? Does it really matter if the human race as we know it ceases to exist? The earth will continue and probably another species evolve . . . I am feeling imprisoned—by the security people who think they can hide their utter incompetence by sheer numbers and a tighter closing in, but also and perhaps more so by the realization that I have come to an end, that there's no further growing in this direction. One has friends at school and at various stages of life but comes a time when one outpaces them and leaves them behind. There can be talk and meeting but no longer the sharing. This is what I feel."[10]

Unlike her positive relationship with Sonia, Indira had no such comforting rapport with Sanjay's consort. At the age of twenty-seven, Sanjay had met a pretty seventeen-year-old Sikh girl called Maneka Anand at a cocktail party given by her uncle, Major-General Kapur, to celebrate his son's forthcoming wedding. She was a student, who was also working as a journalist and a model, though when marriage to Sanjay was in the offing, advertising posters featuring her were quickly taken down. Sanjay had inherited his father's taste for women, but Maneka Anand seems to have been the first girl he loved. After their first meeting they saw each other every day, normally in each other's homes, as Sanjay did not favor restaurants or the cinema.

Indira had hoped Sanjay would marry a Kashmiri girl, but he was determined to marry Maneka, the daughter of an army colonel. With Sanjay's customary haste, the engagement was announced on July 29, 1974, and the wedding followed on September 23. It was a small, private ceremony in the home of a family friend, Mohammed Yunus Khan. Vijaya was not invited. For the son of a Hindu and a Parsi to marry a Sikh in the home of a Muslim was a potent demonstration of the secular India represented by the Nehru clan.

Like Sonia, Maneka moved into the Prime Minister's house, but she was a more difficult inhabitant, being an energetic and demanding young woman who needed more attention than the busy and rather sober home of her mother-in-law could provide. Sanjay at twenty-seven was prematurely balding, like his grandfather, and eager to make his mark on Indian society. Maneka at this time was pretty and girlish, coquettish in some pictures, sulky in others. She described her experiences in the household: "Marriage was not all roses; I was young, immature and easily bored. I didn't know any housework and did not want to learn cooking."[11] She found the family reserved compared to her own: in Indira's house nobody smoked or drank or used bad language. Maneka was considered foul-mouthed because she swore, but she explained, "In my own home we are utterly informal and often brash in our dealings with each other. The Gandhis observe decorum in their dealings with each other."[12]

She often felt neglected by Sanjay, and wrote him rhymes to attract his attention. One of them ran, "Sanjay Gandhi, ferocious being/Who never looks without seeing./Whose facts are almost always right./Whose judgments almost always bite./Who's so totally work-oriented,/That he's driven his wife demented . . ."[13]

Sanjay had developed his Maruti project for the "people's car" in two garages and now wanted to expand it into a factory capable of full production. The chief minister of Haryana state, Bansi Lal, helped Sanjay to obtain land, in contravention of planning regulations and to the loss of the peasants who were cultivating the land. This behavior was typical of Bansi Lal, a powerful farmer-landlord and smooth political operator who typified the new type of congressman Sanjay was encouraging.

Everyone who dared to give Indira advice, like her principal secretary P. N. Haksar, advised that Sanjay did not have the experience to carry through a major industrial project. When Haksar was dropped from his post in 1973, the Maruti story became murkier. The problem was not only Sanjay's lack of ability in running a car plant, but his overbearing attitude, which insisted that every aspect of the car's design, from the engine to the color scheme, had to be his own decision. This megalomania also extended to the selection of personnel. Sanjay was skeptical of people with "too many degrees," having doubtless learned that anyone who knew what they were doing would realize the errors of his methods.[14]

Sanjay was backed by businessmen who knew the failings of his approach but supported him financially because they wanted political favors, and by the nationalized Indian banks which loaned him large sums.[15] A mildly critical report of the project in the *Hindustani Times* made Sanjay vindictively manipulate the dismissal of the editor. The inefficiency and wastefulness of the project attracted parliamentary Opposition attacks, particularly as no cars were produced from the well-funded factory. Indira finally had her finance minister, C. Subramaniam, look into Maruti. He asked for a project report but was told there could not be one until the project was under way. When he protested that a complex operation like a car plant had to have a report showing how each component would be produced, the unit cost and so on, Sanjay said these were old methods of operating and not necessary for him.[16] In 1972 he unveiled the prototype Maruti with the news that it would be on the road by April 1973.

The fiercely loyal Maneka defended Sanjay. "When he answered questions in a straightforward manner, they attributed it to his being uncouth and lacking in sophistication, his inability to comprehend politics, understand politicians or because of his "inborn arrogance." As a matter of fact Sanjay understood people and situations only too well. He regarded life as a game which he had to win. Life's problems were obstacles which had to be overcome before one could reach the winning post."[17]

Sanjay's love of speed led him to take up flying, and he began going in for aerial acrobatics, which his flying companions found so dangerous that they would not go up with him. Maneka became his only passenger. His weakness for faster and more dangerous devices was coupled with an overwhelming confidence in his own abilities. The Western media characterization of him as a "playboy" was entirely inaccurate: Sanjay did not drink, use drugs or lead a life of leisure. In fact, he worked ferociously hard, becoming more involved in business and political life than many people liked.

The corruption, riots, strikes, lockouts and general disorganization in some states were unrelenting. Up to 20,000 political prisoners were being held in West Bengal, where a Naxalite or China-orientated Marxist uprising had long been taking place. Accusations of ill treatment, including torture, of political prisoners were commonplace. Between April and December 1974 there were thirty-eight major strikes in Bihar, where student protests over education reform had already escalated into rioting and arson. There was also violent unrest in Gujarat, where ships were looted and government property burned over a ten-week period, after a Congress Party boss allowed cooking oil prices to rise without limit in return for political donations by the oil manufacturers.

Indira fought with boldness and even brutality against what she saw as the encroaching anarchy. She used methods of ruthless repression to crush a national railway strike in May 1974, declaring the strike illegal, arresting the railway workers' leader and rounding up all local railway union officials. The strike began with a million workers out, of whom 60,000 were arrested in the first few days. The army, the navy and all other apparatus of the State were used, and Indira reportedly boasted that if this strike were crushed, there would not be another for fifty years.[18] In three weeks, after massive use of force, the strike was defeated.

Indira's socialism, such as it was, was ideological and bypassed trade unionism altogether. She had the temerity to tell a trade union conference, "In a country where there are millions of unemployed and underemployed, what is needed is a fair distribution of opportunities for gainful employment. In this sense the employed, particularly in the organized sector, who enjoy a measure of social security, should recognize that in our country to be employed is in itself a privilege."[19]

She had scored a victory over the railway unions, but it resulted in no great jubilation. The sorry end of the episode was the assassination of the railway minister, Lalit Narayan Mishra, in early 1975. Indira seemed to have lost her touch for populist measures, or to have run out of tricks. The explosion of a nuclear device in Rajasthan in 1974, making India the world's sixth nuclear power, resulted in self-congratulation but no mass sense of achievement. The annexation of neighboring Sikkim was a similar crowd-pleaser, but did not divert attention from economic ills for long. Indira would make speeches and be greeted by crowds waving black flags, calling for food. Increasingly isolated from the people, and pampered by her aides, Indira saw popular reaction to the country's distress as evidence of a powerful conspiracy backed by hostile foreign powers. Her feelings of paranoia had been exacerbated by the ousting and assassination of the democratically elected socialist president of Chile, Salvador Allende, in a CIA-backed coup in September 1973.

The overall distress of the country brought a hero of the nationalist movement, Jayaprakash (J.P.) Narayan, back into the political fray. He was an old Gandhian socialist who called on youth to regenerate parliamentary democracy using non-violent mass resistance. It was ironic for Indira to be confronted by Congress methods from the early days. His movement began with student agitation in Bihar, which he hoped would be the basis of a nationwide moral regeneration. Unfortunately, it quickly lost its non-violent character and was controlled only by repressive measures involving a large number of police.

J.P. was elderly and frail and his movement stated only what it was against: Congress corruption. What it stood for, none could say, though an alliance with the Hindu chauvinist Jana Sangh Party indicated its likely future direction. Rather more important than what J.P.'s movement did or said, was the fact that he had seized the initiative: previously Indira had acted and others had been obliged to react; now she was in the reactive position. Increasingly isolated and mistrustful of former colleagues, she relied more and more on Sanjay's advice, inexperienced though he was in parliamentary politics. He came to be the only one she really trusted.

Four years after it was lodged, the case brought by Raj Narain against Indira over alleged election irregularities was finally heard in the Allahabad High Court, where Motilal had seen his greatest professional moments. Indira was charged with technical and minor electoral irregularities which deserved a fine: government offices and engineers had erected rostrums at her election meetings and there had been an overlap of time when her (government-paid) private secretary was also her election agent. Slight though these offenses were, the court was out to get her. On June 12, 1975 it invalidated her election of 1971 and disbarred her from office for six years. The judgment had been widely leaked, so Indira, and her opponents, had a good idea of what was coming. Rajiv was the first of her family to hear officially the judgment had gone against her, and went to tell Indira himself. She received the news calmly and was considering resignation by the time Sanjay arrived. He angrily told her he would not let her do so, and ordered her staff to deny even a temporary resignation of office. This, as it turned out, was a turning point that rendered subsequent events virtually inevitable.

As the family dealt with the shock, more information came via the teleprinter: the execution of the sentence was deferred for twenty days to give the government time to appoint a new prime minister, and would, as usual, be subject to appeal in the Supreme Court. This gave a breathing space for Indira to gather her forces and for Sanjay to arrange demonstrations outside her house, with activists commandeering buses from the public bus service to ferry in supporters from villages outside the city. Indira addressed the crowds standing on a stepladder.

J.P.'s supporters arranged counter-demonstrations at the presidential palace. They were in buoyant mood, having already enjoyed their first election victory. On the same day the High Court judgment against Indira was announced, the results came through of an election called in Gujarat in the wake of violent disturbances (and the habitual fast-to-the-death by Morarji Desai). It was an overwhelming victory for Desai's coalition and a defeat for Indira's Congress.

Sanjay urged his mother that all the trouble was being caused by around fifty opposition leaders and some sections of the press; if they could be curbed, the problems would be over. She defiantly addressed a massive gathering of 100,000 people on June 20 at the Boat Club in Delhi, where, for the first time, she was flanked by her sons and their wives.

Four days later another judge ruled that Indira could stay as prime minister till her appeal was heard by the Supreme Court. This staved off the immediate threat of her cabinet colleagues edging in to take her position on a "temporary" basis. The mood now escalated into a confident, united opposition to Indira, and J.P. upped the stakes by calling on the police and army not to obey orders he deemed "unlawful" and organizing a week-long protest outside Indira's house, due to start on June 29, 1975. Morarji Desai told the press, "We intend to overthrow her, to force her to resign . . . This lady won't survive our movement . . . Thousands of us will surround her house to prevent her going out . . . We shall camp there night and day."[20]

This was a *gherao*, an intimidation aimed at stopping the subject from carrying out any normal activities. On the day it was announced, June 25, Indira called on the President of India, Fakhruddin Ali Ahmed, who had replaced Giri on the latter's retirement, to ensure he would stay on call when she needed him. She went back to her own offices and met her advisers, who assured her that she needed no meeting of the Cabinet to declare a state of emergency: the emergency order could be promulgated and ratified retrospectively by Cabinet. That same day a proclamation was drafted for the President, in which he declared "that a grave emergency exists whereby the security of India is threatened by internal disturbances." He signed it just before midnight. At the same time power was cut to Bahadurshah

Zafar Marg, the street in Delhi where most newspapers were printed, ensuring there would be no coverage the following day. J.P. and Morarji Desai were arrested that night and held in a house near Delhi. Six hundred other opposition leaders were also arrested, including Raj Narain, who had brought the troublesome election petition against Indira. Some opposition leaders for whom Indira had friendship or respect, such as Kamaraj, were not arrested.

Members of Indira's cabinet were also awakened that night to be told that they must attend a meeting at 6 A.M. the following morning. Indira explained simply that an emergency had been declared and the opposition leaders imprisoned. They were all stunned, but swiftly realized their best interests lay in silence. Only the Defense Minister Swaran Singh asked why a state of emergency was necessary.

Well he might ask. Indira spoke of a "deep and widespread conspiracy . . . forces of disintegration in full play." In a message to the nation on the night of June 27 she said, "A climate of violence and hatred had been created which resulted in the assassination of a cabinet minister and an attempt on the life of a chief justice. The opposition parties had chalked out a program of countrywide *gheraos*, agitation, disruption and incitement to industrial workers, police and defense forces in an attempt to paralyze totally the central government."[21] The armed forces were being incited not to obey orders they considered wrong, the press had "deliberately distorted news and made malicious and provocative comments." She urged that "the entire purpose is to bring about a situation of calmness and stability." As well as mass arrests, the emergency saw the general election postponed, then canceled; there was a ban on strikes, demonstrations and any meeting of more than five people without permission; a wage freeze and press censorship were imposed. It was press censorship that required a state of emergency: most of the other emergency restrictions could have been accomplished under the Maintenance of Internal Security Act of 1971, popularly known as the Maintenance of Indira and Sanjay Act. This repressive legislation was a direct inheritance of British rule and a reminder, for those old enough to remember, of the Rowlatt Acts of 1919, which had such a galvanizing effect on the independence movement.

The declaration of states of emergency was not so remarkable in the volatile 1970s, at a time when constitutions were threatening to break under the strain of world problems. It was not merely the developing countries, like those in Latin America, which felt it necessary to declare an emergency: in Britain Edward Heath's government called five brief states of emergency in the four years of its existence. In Australia, another Commonwealth country, the Governor-General dismissed the Prime Minister and government in 1975, but then called a general election. In India there had been states of emergency declared during wartime in 1962 and 1971; and this latter state of "external" emergency, called for the Bangladeshi war, had never been repealed. Some states such as Assam, Kerala, Bihar and Punjab had been ruled under presidential decree for extended periods.

Still, the question remained: why call a state of emergency in India in summer 1975? The emergency, in fact, related more to Indira's psyche than to political events. Unrest in individual states could be dealt with by presidential decree in those states: there was serious opposition to the government, but it was not a national crisis. Years later the Shah Report on the emergency found that there was no evidence of a threat to the constitution or to law and order.

What had happened was that Indira, insulated from reality by her handpicked advisers and sycophants, had projected her own fears and insecurities on to the nation. It was no secret that she saw herself as a beleaguered child struggling against a hostile world; she would tell friends, conferences, the press, anyone who was prepared to listen. "The whole of my life has been meeting tests and transcending them," she said to Marie Seton.[22] "I go to difficulties head on. Since I was a child I have been able to proceed only in this way," she told a planning conference.[23] "I doubt that you could find anyone who has led as hard a life as I have from infancy," she told the press.[24] She had never stopped being that neglected child.

A book of Indira's speeches and reminiscences was published in 1975, called simply *India*. (Interestingly, it is copyrighted to Indira Nehru Gandhi.) She wrote a preface emphasizing her duty to "preserve the life-giving and creative diversity of India" as if she herself were the holy river sustaining the life of the nation.[25] It was not that India was "in peril from both internal and external enemies," as she protested, but Indira was, and she so closely identified her fate with that of the nation that she was unable to distinguish that a threat to one was not necessarily a threat to both.

# THIRTEEN

# SANJAY ALSO RISES

The first morning of the emergency, and the following mornings, were greeted with an astonishing calm. There were no demonstrations or spontaneous outbursts against Indira. Most people were glad the strikes and disturbances had stopped, and peace descended on India. Crime, including the disturbing increase in sexual crime, was reduced so it was safe to walk the streets again; smugglers and tax defaulters were imprisoned; government officials, aware of a new atmosphere of severity, started working with diligence; the trains ran on time. M. F. Husain, an acclaimed modern Indian artist, painted a huge triptych of Indira as the goddess Durga, riding through fire on a tiger and vanquishing her foes. If the emergency was a gamble, it had paid off.

The emergency could have been a great success for Indira, were it not for Sanjay, whose lack of position in the government or the Congress Party did not deter him from taking an active part in public life. The decision to cut power from the newspapers on the first night of the emergency was probably his, as was an order to lock the doors of all the high courts the same morning—a decision Indira countermanded.[1]

Later on the first day of the emergency a cabinet committee ordered press censorship. When the minister of information and broadcasting, Inder Kumar Gujral, came out of the meeting he found Sanjay waiting outside "as if he had taken over." Sanjay asked the education minister to compile a list of university lecturers with opposition sympathies, then turned to Gujral and asked for copies of all news bulletins before they were broadcast. Gujral explained that this was not possible, as they were confidential documents. Indira overheard and said an individual could be assigned to bring them to the home of the Prime Minister. Later, Sanjay upset Gujral by saying he had not been doing his job, as Indira's Delhi Boat Club rally had not been broadcast live on television. Sanjay assumed control over the media in a way the minister could not because Gujral preferred to work with journalists rather than against them. He told Sanjay he had better learn to be courteous: "You are younger than my son and I owe you no explanations."[2] Indira subsequently removed Gujral from the information and broadcasting ministry and gave it to V. C. Shukla, who imposed tough censorship laws, even banning newspapers from quoting Gandhi and Jawaharlal in favor of freedom of expression. Swaran Singh, who had questioned the necessity for a state of emergency, was sacked and replaced by the peasant leader Bansi Lal, who had been so helpful to Sanjay in setting up the Maruti project when he was chief minister of Haryana. Sanjay was on his way to becoming the most powerful man in India.

The press censorship was worse than anything the British had imposed during the independence movement, as the eighty-year-old Morarji Desai reflected in the state hotel room where he was being held. Under British rule, at least newspapers could publish the names of those arrested and the jails in which they were held. Currently, there were only whispers of his detention and that of other opposition leaders.[3] Probably 100,000 people were imprisoned without trial during the whole of the emergency, though many of these were not opposition leaders but criminals for whom the due process of law was too cumbersome for an administration in a hurry.

Indira was correct about the pusillanimous nature of the press, or at least the majority of the press. It was said by L. K. Advani, the first post-emergency broadcasting and information minister, that they "crawled when they were merely asked to bend,"[4] so Indira did not simply receive a good or bland press—she was the subject of adulation for the period of the emergency.

A presidential ordinance of July 18 forbade those held under the Maintenance of Internal Security Act to claim their right to personal liberty by virtue of natural or common law; in effect it was a suspension of habeas corpus. Later in July and the following month the Lok Sabha gave the Prime Minister the same immunity from criminal proceedings as enjoyed by the President and state governors, and retrospectively absolved Indira from any election offenses.

Indira had a very selective view of democracy, as she told the Lok Sabha "the very summoning of parliament is proof that democracy is functioning in India. The large number of opposition members present is evidence that not every one of them is behind bars or in detention," though those on the benches opposite doubtless had a keen awareness of such a possibility.[5] The Constitutional Amendment Bill, virtually a new constitution which was introduced on August 30, consolidated the centralization of power in the hands of ministers at the expense of the courts and parliament.

Indira wanted the emergency to achieve something, so she announced a twenty-point program on July 1, 1975. Much of it had long since been Congress policy, but little had been done about such things as land reform and stabilizing prices. Two of the points were new and radical: to make bonded labor illegal and to cancel the debts of the rural poor to village moneylenders. The "cult of personality" surrounding Indira at this time seems more a contribution of zealous supporters than a prime ministerial ordinance. For example, posters proclaiming her as the savior of law and order appeared in streets throughout the country; shops were obliged to display her picture, together with a pledge supporting the twenty-point program.

Few foreigners found much to admire in the emergency. Dorothy Norman and seventy-nine other friends of India sent Indira a letter saying, in part, "We deplore these events, especially in India, because there democracy was established after a long struggle for freedom led by some of the greatest contemporary exponents of human rights, and also because the respect of democratic India for these human rights was for so many years a beacon light for all newly independent and developing countries."[6]

Indira found it impossible to accept criticism: she saw intellectuals who questioned the emergency as dupes of hostile foreign powers, and saw herself as a heroine who had prevented the Opposition from carrying out its plan to paralyze the nation: "There would have been a serious breakdown. The same foreign newspapers which shed tears over our firm steps would then have gloated over our weakness. After all, let us not forget the support and admiration they have for regimes which get results but do not even claim to have democracy."[7] It was difficult for Indira now to travel the globe with a superior air. In October 1975 she visited Mauritius, Tanzania and Zambia, where she proclaimed India's solidarity with South African Liberation Movements, the irony of the situation presumably escaping her. The only country where she was still very welcome was the Soviet Union, which she visited with both sons in August 1976.

Indira planned to call an end to the state of emergency in her Independence Day speech on August 15, 1975, after less than two months. On her way to the platform at the Red Fort in Delhi, however, she heard some shocking news: Sheikh Mujib-ur Rehman, whom she had established in his rightful position as President of Bangladesh, had been assassinated in an army coup. The full story was even worse than that: Rehman's wife, three sons, two daughters-in-law and two nephews were also killed. His assassins were trying to make very sure there would be no Rehman dynasty. The massacre of the entire family shocked Indira to the core of her being: "Rahul is about the same age as Mujib's son," she said, "it could be him tomorrow. They would like to destroy me and my family."[8] Her speech pondered on generalities, and the emergency stayed in place.

The British Labor leader Michael Foot went to see Indira during the emergency, though many urged him not to, saying it would give legitimacy to the regime. He was even warned by the British High Commissioner when he got off the plane in Delhi that he should not see Indira, but he did, and over a long conversation raised the expulsion of a British journalist and the imprisonment of a socialist leader. "Especially of course," he said, "I raised the question of whether she was going to have another election. 'Of course I'm going to have another election,' she said, 'but I don't want to suffer the fate of Allende.' Of course, just a few months ago Allende had been assassinated by the CIA."[9]

Indira's fears were not mere paranoia. Denied the legitimacy of normal trade union activity because of government repression, railway leader George Fernandes launched an underground resistance movement, blowing up bridges, derailing trains and burning government property. The assassination of Indira was plotted, as she knew from secret reports obtained by the security services, but Fernandes' opposition was ended when he and the other conspirators were captured in May and June 1976 and put on trial—the only emergency prisoners to be tried. Some prisoners were tortured during interrogation over this conspiracy, but many more suffered physical privations to the point of death from bad conditions in the prisons.

Pupul Jayakar said that from the time of Rehman's assassination "it became difficult to enter into a dialogue with Indira. She continued to meet me but her eyes were shadowed and she was wary of what she said."[10] Indira turned increasingly to Sanjay, as Rajiv and his friends were openly critical of the emergency. Rajiv and Sonia even considered leaving for Italy. Indira's bedroom and Sanjay's were separated by a small enclosed passage. After the assassination, the door which connected her room with the passage was always kept open.

It may have been that Sanjay was particularly concerned to save Indira's rule because the game was up with Maruti: as early as 1972 he had signed on nearly seventy-five dealers of Maruti and charged up to 300,000 rupees each as deposits, with the cars due to arrive in six months. He told them to build showrooms for displaying the cars, and many did, borrowing the money and pledging their property against the loans. He also asked dealers to collect deposits from potential customers. No cars were ever received, and two dealers reckless enough to ask for the return of their deposits were jailed during the emergency. Sanjay soon ran out of sources of money: he had realized by the end of 1974 that Maruti had no chance of producing small cars and was selling off some of the factory's steel ration.

Sanjay now had to build up his personal power base. For this, he and Indira chose the Youth Congress, an organization that was semi-moribund in most states, largely a cheerleading body for the grownup Congress. Sanjay was elevated to the general council in December 1975 and thenceforth operated as leader of the Youth Congress, traveling the country and enjoying the competition between chief ministers of states to produce glorious receptions for the young hero. Newspapers and television covered his activities in fawning detail. "His image shines in its own light," one enthused, "firmly established in the hearts of the people."[11]

Sanjay had to effect his progress via the party machinery, for he had no oratorical powers. His speechmaking was pedestrian, though this was not unusual for a Nehru; Jawaharlal was always ponderous and conversational in his speeches, and Indira did not become a compelling public speaker until some time after she became prime minister. Sanjay had a clutch of loyal supporters, *chamchas* or "spoons," as sycophants were called in India. They were flashy, coarse types, smart rather than intellectual, with no knowledge of politics except that it could help them to "get rich quick" if they proved their loyalty to Sanjay.

The emergency did not abolish the normal democratic procedures, it just suspended them, so in January 1976 the Lok Sabha elections were postponed for a year. January also saw Sanjay make his contribution to policy-making, with a four-point program which he added to his mother's twenty points. He called on the Indian people to beautify the country; to eradicate illiteracy by teaching someone to read (each one teach one); to abolish the caste and dowry systems; and to practice family planning. Later, "beautification" was divided into slum clearance and tree planting, so four points became five. While these were estimable objectives which would have improved the nation and earned lasting respect for their instigator, they needed a more thoughtful man than Sanjay Gandhi to ensure their success. Sanjay was always described as a "young man in a hurry," a verdict with which he did not demur, his personal slogan being "Less talk, more work." It was the brutal impatience of Sanjay and his supporters that discredited him, the emergency and, by association, Indira.

Most importantly, a valuable attempt to reduce India's burgeoning population turned into a grotesque carnival of abduction, mutilation and disease. Population had been one of Jawaharlal's failures of imagination. He had thought India was not overpopulated, was in fact underpopulated in some areas, and that industrialization would produce the wealth to feed India's millions. To some extent the population problems were caused by the success of health programs, which had increased life expectancy from twenty-seven to forty-five and reduced infant mortality. There were simply more people living more reproductive years. Agricultural improvements could hardly keep step with the increase in numbers; education was advancing but so was illiteracy; wealth was increasing but so was poverty. As Sanjay said, "No amount of progress will be of any use if the population explosion is not checked. Today, even if a million jobs are created, there are 10 million looking for these jobs. Industrial development, increased agricultural production and a developmental infrastructure are no use if the population continues to grow at the present rate."[12]

As a permanent, low-cost birth control option, sterilization was chosen as the method most suited to India, and sterilization programs were supported by large influxes of Western money. As the male operation is easier to perform, the campaign was aimed at men. Unfortunately, Sanjay's lack of insight prevented him from understanding that the peasant population equated sterilization with castration.

Nonetheless, sterilization teams took to the country seizing people in areas where there were insufficient volunteers, and set about operating on the young, the old, the newly married, the long widowed, those with children and the childless, and those who had already been sterilized—including at least one recorded case of a man who had been sterilized three times.[13] As the program offered no counseling or aftercare, there was a serious danger of the wounds turning septic and of the patient, having no access to medical facilities, being maimed or killed by infection.

In the middle of 1976 sterilization targets were set for every state and district, with no concern paid to the shortage of facilities or medical personnel. People were taken off buses or from movie queues to be sterilized. Now the nation was aware of the abuses, sterilization vans were stoned when they approached villages, and police were called to quell the disturbances, often opening fire. There were stories of whole villages surrounded by the police at night in pursuit of sterilization victims.

The family planning drive began to endanger health programs in general as people feared going near medical personnel in case they grabbed them to be sterilized. Myth and rumor were promoted by village storytellers, who expounded tales of heroic actions against the cruel government vans, and of Indira, not now the mother of the nation but a powerful, savage, female castrator: still divine, but now an incarnation of cruelty.

State governments were free to introduce their own incentives and disincentives, and to apply the programs in their own way, so there were regional variations in the application of the sterilization program. In general, on the incentive side, a patient would receive 10-15 rupees, a prompter or motivator 10 rupees, and a doctor 3 or 5 rupees per patient. On the disincentive side, no promotion or ration card, or even licenses or loans would be granted without sterilization certificates.

On March 7, 1976 the Uttar Pradesh government announced that salaries would be paid only to government employees who "motivated" two people to be sterilized by the end of the month. The Delhi administration made the March salary payment of its teachers conditional on their bringing in five people to be sterilized. Using such methods, more than 10 million people were said to have been sterilized by the end of the emergency.

Another part of Sanjay's program was slum clearance. He was determined to clean up India, starting with the Turkman Gate area of Old Delhi, near the mosque of Jama Masjid. It was a Muslim area, one of those which had been protected by Indira during the partition riots, inhabited by people who had been told by Jawaharlal that they would be protected and need not flee to Pakistan.

The Delhi Development Authority started to clear the area on April 14. Demolition gangs protected by armed police began demolishing good buildings along with shacks, forcibly transporting the new homeless by truck to vacant lots where there was no drinking water, sanitation, electricity or transport. Within a few days the demolition teams were joined by the sterilization squads, who made "suburban relocation" dependent on sterilization. Spontaneous demonstrations turned to violence as the crowd grew to 3000, and the police used *lathis*, tear gas and eventually guns to break it up. In hours of fighting, some police were killed, as were nearly 100 residents. An estimated 10,000 people were forcibly evicted.

Sheikh Abdullah, who was in Delhi at the time, and President Fakhruddin Ali Ahmed protested to Indira about this treatment of their co-religionists, but she was not prepared to hear criticism of Sanjay. Sheikh Abdullah was one politician who retained dignity throughout the emergency. Sanjay once walked into a room where some eminent Congress leaders were in a discussion. They all got to their feet on his entry and greeted him, excepting Abdullah. Sanjay asked, "Who are you?" to which Abdullah said, "Well, pup, go and ask your mummy who I am." Sanjay had Congress withdraw its support from Abdullah during the Kashmiri election.[14]

"Slum clearance," including the clearance of slum-dwellers, cleared land all over the country for property developers. After the emergency, Justice J. C. Shah described Sanjay: "Here was a young man who literally amused himself with demolishing the residential, commercial and industrial buildings in locality after locality without having the slightest realization of the miseries he was heaping on the helpless population."[15]

At the time, only wild praise was heard for the heir apparent: "Sanjay Gandhi is a man of uncommon intelligence and unfailing courage . . . the ablest and the most effective young administrator that the country has produced so far."[16] "Sanjay Gandhi's rise to power came to us as history's own answer to our prayers. Here at last was a young man uncontaminated by the political inhibitions and spiritual decadence of the past."[17] He was compared to the great leaders and philosophers of history, and inevitably that he was Jawaharlal reborn.

With a transparent lack of nobility on public display in the later months of the emergency, Indira relied much on her noble lineage. A book was produced in May 1976 on the 115th anniversary of Motilal's birth, perhaps an unusual anniversary to celebrate, but one which did Indira some good. It was introduced with three uplifting quotes, from Motilal, Jawaharlal and Indira, the last singularly lacking in paeans to democracy.

While atrocities were being committed in the name of family planning, Indira became feted among some for being Sanjay's mother:

> To the World's greatest woman,
> Goddess of the downtrodden
> The savior of the poor
> The mother of the "do-er"
> She's Indu—the moon
> She's the cosmic boon . . .[18]

Indira said extravagant praise was "perhaps a form of oriental excess, to which I pay no attention."[19] There were opportunities for her to discourage such behavior, which she failed to take, such as at the annual Congress meeting in December 1975 when the national anthem was followed by a new song, "Indira Hindustan Ban Gai" (Indira has become India).

In the sixth month of the emergency, the Congress president, Dev Kanta Barooah, announced that Indira had "made democracy stable and viable in this country" and noted that her deeds would be "inscribed in the history books of the future, in letters of stone, not of gold because these don't last."[20] It was Barooah who coined the slogan "Indira is India, and India is Indira," which was seen all over the country, most strikingly in huge letters stretched right around Connaught Circus in Delhi. The editor of *Blitz* magazine went even further by ascribing actual divinity to Indira: "The gods rest within us; it is for us to incarnate them. Can Indira Gandhi have incarnated at least some of them? I see no other explanation."[21]

She may even have believed her own propaganda. All the information she received was siphoned through her supporters, so she, as much as everyone else, was a victim of press censorship. In a rare moment of loquacity on the subject, Indira later commented to Dom Moraes, "My secretariat from top to bottom was full of people who kept visitors away from me. Not only that, but when I wanted to meet people, editors, people from the press, my staff would say it wasn't— what was their usual phrase?—'necessary.'"[22]

Her close relationship with her advisers, and their protective behavior towards her, led to gossip about her personal life. In earlier years it was suggested she was having an affair with her father's secretary M. O. Mathai, and after the emergency he encouraged this belief. She was also said to be linked romantically with Dinesh Singh, a leading member of her "kitchen cabinet," with her guru Brahmachari, and with others. In fact, Indira was never a particularly active woman sexually.

The area of her life that might have contained romance and physical closeness to another adult was curiously absent in Indira. She said, "Even with Feroze, it was not at all sex. I tried to explain to him that I wanted children and companionship." She showed a perhaps surprising self-knowledge when she discussed this with Pupul, saying "I do not behave like a woman. The lack of sex in me partly explains this."[23]

Her lack of desire for adult relationships left an aching need in Indira which was filled with the love of her youngest son. Sanjay was both her support and her tormentor: he would give her strength to bear the attacks on her, and would take actions which justified the attacks. He would feed her paranoia with tales of enemies all around her, and calm her fears with encouraging and defiant words. Whenever any brave soul had the temerity to question her about the abuses for which Sanjay was responsible, she would hear nothing of it, and say, "Those who attack Sanjay attack me."[24] Apart from obvious maternal affection, it may be that the aspect of Sanjay's personality which was most offensive to others—his refusal to consider the consequences of his actions—was precisely what Indira admired most about her son. "He isn't a thinker. He's a doer," she enthused to Dom Moraes, "I mean, cent percent a doer. When he wants something doing, he gets it done."[25] With her long experience of Jawaharlal's contemplative indecision, what she saw as Sanjay's decisiveness was a welcome trait. Some have conjectured that Indira suffered all her life from guilt that she had taken their beloved father away from the boys, and Sanjay in particular played on this to manipulate Indira. There is, however, no real evidence to support such a view.

In November 1976 Indira proposed releasing all political prisoners and calling an immediate election. She need not have done it at this point, particularly as the order suspending elections for a further year was passed in the same month. Her advisers, including Sanjay, suggested releasing the prisoners immediately but holding an election in a year's time. It was one of the rare times she did not bend to Sanjay's will. On January 18, 1977 she announced her decision to hold an election on March 19, and that the opposition leaders would be released. Asked why, she said that the country had now got over "instability and indiscipline."[26]

While it can reasonably be argued that the emergency need not have been declared, in the short term it did bring stability to the nation. The World Bank and the Reserve Bank of India pointed out economic and financial recovery which had taken place since the proclamation of the emergency. Indira said, "It was because we took rather severe measures that we were able to put the economy back on an even level. Our agricultural production, our industrial production, our exports, all these rose to an unprecedented level . . . For the first time our balance of payments was almost embarrassingly satisfactory."[27] The economy of the emergency also benefited from two good harvests.

Another unequivocal success was an agreement with the Naga people to end their insurrection. The Nagas were primitive tribes living on the border between India, Pakistan and Burma. They had refused to be integrated into the Empire and after independence had wished to secede. Their insurrection continued until 1975, when the state was put under the direct rule of Delhi. Later an agreement was signed with representatives of the Naga underground to end their rebellion. It was, like the victory over Pakistan, rather more than Indira's predecessors had managed.

On the negative side, the emergency had gone on far longer than necessary so that emergency powers, rather than being an occasional tool of democracy, had corroded the nature of democracy itself. The excessive power assumed by Sanjay, unelected as he was, was the worst aspect of the emergency, and ultimately the cause of Indira's fall from power. Without the abuses related to family planning Indira could have won the 1977 election, but she refused to recognize the damage Sanjay was doing. She called the election because she actually thought she would win.

The election began badly, with the Communist Party of India (CPI), the only other party which had backed Indira through the emergency, withdrawing its support. Again, the problem was not Indira, but Sanjay. The Communists were suspicious of his right-wing rhetoric and of the government's concessions to private industry. Nor had Sanjay endeared himself to his mother's allies by denouncing them as the richest and most corrupt of politicians.[28] The CPI supported Indira's twenty-point program for social reform, but not Sanjay's five-point program. The rival Communist Party in West Bengal, the CP(M), opposed the emergency throughout. J. P. Narayan, who had been released from detention early because of a kidney disorder, lumped together a coalition of the major parties: the Socialists, the Jana Sangh, the Akali Dal, the Bharatiya Lok Dal and the Old Congress, containing a number of different Congress members, to become the Janata or people's party. They aimed to defeat "the dictatorship of mother and boy."[29] Morarji Desai, freed after months of imprisonment, became the leading candidate to replace Indira as prime minister.

There were two unexpected blows: on February 1, President Fakhruddin Ali Ahmed died; he was one of Indira's firmest supporters from the days of the split in 1969. The following day Jagjivan Ram, the leader of 100 million untouchables and one of Indira's most important ministers, defected to create Congress for Democracy, which formed an alliance with Janata. In reply to his accusatory letter of resignation, Indira coldly said: "It is strange you should have remained silent all these months, but should make these baseless charges now."[30] She thought it was because he wanted to be prime minister and believed he would achieve his desire by breaking away.

Shortly afterwards Indira's aunt, Vijaya, who had been subjected to surveillance during the first months of the emergency, came out of retirement to campaign for the Janata and Congress for Democracy parties. Indira's friends were turning against her and her old enemies were coming to get her. Sanjay urged her to cancel the elections when he realized defeat was almost certain, but she refused. She toured the country relentlessly with her customary determination, sleeping only three hours each night. According to Pupul Jayakar, it was only on this tour that she realized the widespread misery caused by the family planning program, when villagers whom she expected to cheer were sullen and silent.

On March 21, 1977 the election results were announced. Janata and Congress for Democracy won 299 seats, Indira won 153. Raj Narain won in Indira's constituency of Rae Bareli with a lead of more than 20,000. Sanjay also failed to win his seat, Amethi, part of a catastrophic collapse in the state of Uttar Pradesh, where Congress did not win a single seat—a direct result of the ferociously applied family planning campaign. In the words of a wizened old Congress Party worker observing the election results coming into Delhi, "Look what that bastard has done."[31] It was the fall of the Nehru dynasty, and of Congress. For the first time since Independence, the Congress Party was not in power. Despite her part in the fall of her niece, Vijaya wept when she heard the Rae Bareli result.[32] Elsewhere there were scenes of festivity and merriment, fireworks and free sweets: Delhi had seen nothing like it since 1947. At last, at the age of eighty-one, Morarji Desai had his longed-for chance to be prime minister.

Indira was somewhat piqued that "everybody gave the credit for democracy to the Opposition whereas it was I who decided the elections and I accepted the defeat very gracefully."[33] In Indira's favor, she had restored democracy in a nation now stable and enjoying greater prosperity, in a free election. What subversion had taken place over the election was conducted by Janata sympathizers doing such things as stuffing the ballot boxes with extra votes after the count had closed, with the connivance of election officers. It was unnecessary, given the scale of the victory.

Pupul Jayakar was with Indira that night and later described her stoic face: ". . . a tightening of the lines accentuated its beauty and austerity . . . in her defeat she was endowed with grace."[34] At ten-thirty that night Indira ordered dinner and ate in silence with a tight-lipped Rajiv and weeping Sonia. As Pupul was leaving, Rajiv spoke to her with tears in his eyes: "I will never forgive Sanjay for having brought Mummy to this position. He is responsible. I had spoken to her about Sanjay and what people were saying on several occasions, but she refused to believe." Pupul commented that it was feared that if Congress had won, Sanjay would have become home minister.[35]

Sanjay was flying back in a private plane with Maneka from the constituency where he had run. He was not particularly downcast, according to his wife, and even took over the controls to land at Palam airport. "It was then that I realized the strength and character of the man I had married," wrote the adoring Maneka.[36]

After midnight Indira had a final cabinet meeting with her ministers, many of whom had lost their seats. They made their final act: a formal recommendation to the acting president that the emergency be lifted, which was done immediately. Indira then asked Rajiv and Sonia to leave, taking Rahul and Priyanka with them to a friend's house. She feared an assassination attempt. She was alone when Sanjay arrived, a meeting which doubtless strained her impressive capacity for meaningful silences.

Viewing the wreckage in the morning, there was only the consolation that Indira's vote had held up in the south. In the north, where the family planning campaign had been most brutal, Congress had been wiped out. Indira had been at the center of power for twenty-eight years. Sanjay had lived all his life in the Prime Minister's house. If they had ever faced a test of character, it was now, when mother and son were at their lowest—powerless and virtually homeless: the house was a courtesy residence which went with the job Indira was no longer doing. Her present lack of resources demonstrated that, whatever corruption had taken place under her rule, it had not profited her personally. Mohammed Yunus Khan, the family friend in whose home Sanjay and Maneka had been married, vacated his house at 12 Willingdon Crescent and Indira and family moved in, finding the accommodation rather more cramped than they were used to.

When Dom Moraes called to see Indira shortly after the election, he found her in the middle of domestic clutter; her possessions were all disorganized, furniture was being moved and small items being packed up. Moraes felt she looked terrible, the bags under her eyes were "black pouches, and she seemed physically to have shrunk," but she spoke lightly. "I feel as though an enormous weight has been lifted off my shoulders," she said.[37] An old colleague on the left, Aruna Asaf Ali, also went to see her and reported, "Her eyes filled with tears when I said that the people would come back to her. 'When,' she asked sadly, 'after I am dead?'"[38]

# FOURTEEN

# LEGEND IN A SARI

The new government, which took power on March 24, 1977, planned to restore civil liberties, reverse the changes which had been made to the constitution, and punish those guilty of crimes during the emergency. As a political program to unite five parties, those plans were lacking. Being against Indira was simply not enough. There were also deep divisions in the government arising from doctrinal and personality differences. Charan Singh and Jagjivan Ram were disappointed that Morarji Desai had been chosen as prime minister (by J. P. Narayan) in preference to themselves, though none of the three could command a majority of votes over the other two. Most of their members of parliament, moreover, had no previous experience of office. The Janata government itself was soon using the provisions of the emergency's 42nd amendment to the constitution to force elections for the state legislatures, most of which had previously been controlled by Congress.

Recriminations and reparations followed. The inhabitants of Turkman Gate returned in jubilation, threatening to sterilize Sanjay. Sanjiva Reddy, whose candidature as president of the republic had led Indira to split Congress in 1969, was elected to a post now vacated by Fakhruddin Ali Ahmed's death. George Fernandes, who had run as a candidate from prison and been elected, was released; the charges against him were dropped and he was made industry minister. His first ministerial action was the reinstatement of all railway workers sacked during the 1974 strike.

A number of commissions of inquiry were set in motion to investigate the various misdeeds of which Indira and Sanjay were accused. Sanjay also faced charges of fraud relating to Maruti and other business deals, of involvement in the murder of a criminal called Sunder, and of stealing and burning the negative and all the prints of a film called A Tale of a Chair, made by an MP called Amrit Nahata, which satirized him and his mother. The literal English translation of the film title does not give the full meaning, which conveys the sense of "the seat of power." Another inquiry was held into the Nagarwala affair involving the man who had imitated Indira's voice to have money handed over by the state bank.

Absurd stories were told about Indira's family, which detracted from the credibility of the genuine charges against them. Much political capital was made of a bank draft in Maneka's name from a Swiss bank, which was later admitted to be a forgery; there was suspicion when a woman who had allegedly supplied prostitutes for Sanjay and his cronies was found dead, but it turned out to be a case of murder by a former servant. More mysterious was the death of Maneka's father, who was found shot dead in a field near Delhi in June 1977. Given his history of depression and a previous attempt to take his own life, the death was recorded as suicide, but gossip said he had been silenced because he knew too much about Sanjay's business deals.

Indira continued to deny that Sanjay was unpopular with the people, and ascribed his unpopularity with ministers and the press to his being "blunt" and "direct."[1] The opposition to Sanjay and herself, and the charges against her, she considered to be a conspiracy of injustice by people who would stop at nothing, even her murder. She wrote to a friend, "I am the victim of a witch-hunt which probably has no parallel in history, for it is a culmination of a sustained and determined campaign by political opponents of my father and all that the Congress has stood and struggled for. . . . Neither my son nor I are suicide-committing types, so I hope you won't believe any such news."[2] She also feared that Sanjay would be imprisoned and tortured.

The problem of these accusations for the government and its supporters was that the Indian courts were slow and could not be relied upon to bring in guilty verdicts. Government opinion was divided between Morarji Desai, who supported due process, and Charan Singh, who wanted immediate retribution. Commissions were supposedly a means of bypassing the courts in a way which was public and fair. A former chief justice of the Supreme Court, Jayantilal C. Shah, was appointed to investigate "all complaints of excesses, malpractices and abuses of authority" during the emergency. Indira initially refused to appear before the Shah Commission, but Sanjay appeared, unrepentant and surrounded by his supporters. The inquiry spawned others, and brought further charges, so that soon there were half a dozen commissions of inquiry and more than forty criminal cases filed against Sanjay.

Very shortly after the election, Indira began to attract supporters again, people who would travel hundreds of miles in organized groups to see her, as if she had never been in disgrace. Nor could Indira stay long from the center of attention. The orthodox Hindu nature of the new administration created an atmosphere in which caste Hindus in some areas felt free to subjugate the untouchables. In July 1977 a particularly terrible atrocity occurred in Belchi, a remote village in Bihar, where the local landowners attacked a village of landless untouchables, raping women and massacring whole families, including children, and throwing their bodies into a fire. Morarji Desai, who considered the abolition of cow slaughter and the introduction of alcohol prohibition to be burning national issues, was complacent about this sort of event.

Indira knew immediately what she must do. While the government dithered, she set out across the bandit-ridden countryside of Bihar, a state in which her party had not won a single seat. She and a band of followers reached Bihar Sharif, the nearest town to the massacre site, and were warned to go no further: it was raining heavily and the Ganges was in flood—all paths to Belchi had been washed away. Indira pressed on by jeep, but it became bogged down and had to be towed by a tractor, which itself later became stuck in the mud. Indira and her now dwindling band of followers continued on foot through the rain and mud until they reached the bank of a river. The storm made crossing impossible and the boatmen would not go out. Local villagers begged her not to go forward, but seeing that she was determined to do so, they brought an elephant from a temple in a neighboring village. Indira mounted the elephant, joined now by only one follower, a Bihar Congress leader called Pratibha Singh, who held on in fear as the elephant waded across the swollen river.

It was dark by the time they arrived at the village where the survivors of the massacre had taken shelter together in a single building. Flaming torches were lit in the darkness and the terrified and despised untouchables came forward to throw themselves at Indira's feet. She could give nothing but her time, but for the frightened faces in the darkness it was enough to know that she cared. It was a miracle of presence.

When she later returned across the river, now navigable by boat, there was another miracle. The villagers from all around had heard of her visit and come out with food and flowers, and torches to light her way. The women sang songs in her praise and begged forgiveness for voting against her.

Indira had an instinctive appreciation of what must be her next move. After a stop in Delhi, she returned to Uttar Pradesh, proceeding as if in triumph over the state which had so comprehensively rejected her only four months before, receiving a rapturous welcome in her constituency.

Indira's return to strength infuriated government leaders who were incompetently struggling with a country that was again descending into lawlessness now that criminals imprisoned under the emergency had been released. There was no solace in the government's attempts to bring Indira and her supporters to book for the emergency. The inquiries quickly became bogged down in detail and in claims and counter-claims about the partiality of the individuals sitting on them. A range of people were arrested, including Bansi Lal and a number of other ministers. The newspapers were full of reports about crimes committed during the emergency, confirming that Indira continued to dominate national life, even though she had no position and no power.

Goaded into action, Charan Singh, the home minister, made the most important mistake of his life when he ordered the arrest of Indira on October 3, 1977. The charges were that she had allegedly coerced two companies into donating 114 jeeps for the Congress Party's use during the election campaign, and had then sold them to the army. She was also said to have awarded a government contract to a company which had tendered at a higher price than another, suggesting corruption. Told she was going to prison she said, "It will be a nice rest."[3]

When the police arrived at 12 Willingdon Crescent to arrest her, she asked to see their warrant and then demanded that they handcuff her. They begged her not to embarrass them, and she retired for several hours before finally deciding to go with them. Meanwhile, although the telephone line had been cut, her staff quickly rallied supporters, who soon mobbed the house. They were joined by numerous reporters. When she eventually left the house, she was showered with rose petals by the cheering crowd. She made a statement to the press, not complaining about her arrest, but regretting that it interfered with her public duties by preventing her from making a planned visit to tribal Gujarat.

The police car finally drove off, followed by a motorcade of press and Indira's supporters, led by Sanjay and the rest of her close family. Two weeping grandchildren were left in the care of the servants, history repeating itself again in the Nehru dynasty. Indira was not told where she was going, but as the car left Delhi and headed towards Haryana state, it was clear she would be outside the administrative jurisdiction of any warrant issued in Delhi. Consequently, when the police car stopped at a railway crossing, Indira got out and sat on the ground, surrounded by her lawyers. They advised her not to move and told the police that they were exceeding their authority. The attempt to disgrace and humiliate Indira had gone badly wrong; the motorcade turned back to Delhi, where Indira was lodged in the officers' mess at a police camp. She was composed and dignified as she said goodbye to her sons and daughters-in-law. The officer on duty, at a loss for the appropriate response, saluted her.

The following day she was taken to the magistrates' court on Parliament Street, where there were clashes between her own and Janata demonstrators. These were broken up by the police using *lathis* and tear gas, while the rival protesters shouted "Death to Indira Gandhi" and "Long Live Indira Gandhi." When the charges against Indira were argued in court, no evidence was produced to support them, so the magistrate ordered Indira's unconditional release. Sanjay ran from the court shouting, "Dismissed! Dismissed!," creating another explosion of enthusiasm among the crowds. The tear gas used to disperse them even entered the court room and affected Indira. She left in triumph and went on her tour of Gujarat, while embarrassed members of the government tried to explain away their actions to the foreign press. They had succeeded in making Indira appear a victim of an overbearing administration. Increasingly, public sympathy was with her, despite a blanket ban on positive images of her in the press, radio and television. Her reaction was to go directly to the public, touring the country by train and car, despite stone-throwing attacks from opponents, and gaining strength daily from the fulsome support of the poor who had always been her principal constituents. Her comfort was the unconditional love of the anonymous masses. She wrote, "All my life I have had welcoming crowds . . . When I am rushing past in

242

an open jeep in the midst of millions of men, women and children, seeing their eyes light up, my own often fill with tears."[4]

It was easier for her to feel close to "the people" in general than any people in particular. While she was entirely justified in fearing for the safety of herself and her family, Indira's morbidly suspicious nature came between her and even those who had proved themselves trustworthy by staying close to her in defeat. Dom Moraes, a true friend and supporter of Indira, who was writing a book about her, received a polite letter from her in 1978 which gave him a "dull shock" and left him hurt and confused: it broke off their relationship. "Barely a week ago," Moraes wrote, "my friendship for her and trust in her had been, apparently, mutual. Now, because of rumors of unspecified stories I had written about, brought to her by unnamed people, this period was at an end."[5] It was an experience many were to have, as Indira was all too ready to believe that friends were telling tales against her.

The accusations against Sanjay were more difficult to counter than those against Indira. Maruti, for example, had failed so conspicuously that nothing could excuse Sanjay. He argued that the project's lack of success was due to the steep rise in the cost of raw materials. But when the Janata government put the company into liquidation, they allowed journalists to examine the factory and reveal the extent of amateurism they found: a workshop where car bodies were hand-stitched and a foundry where melted ingots were hand-poured into a single set of engine molds. Two British reporters "found almost the entire Maruti car production—twenty finished models and twenty car bodies—abandoned like toys in the center of the indoor stadium that is the car assembly."[6]

According to Maneka, Sanjay was much more relaxed after his defeat at Amethi; their room was always full of friends while he discussed or worked on the cases brought against him. He had the easy optimism of someone who had never faced a setback from which he had not recovered. He cheerfully offered the secret service agents who were trailing him a ride in his van to save gasoline.

The most problematic case against him concerned the criminal charge of destroying the satirical film entitled *A Tale of a Chair*, so called because "chair" in many Indian languages has connotations of power. The censor would not give the film a certificate, presumably because of the political embarrassment it would cause rather than because it broke censorship rules. Amrit Nahata, who had made the film, therefore appealed to the Supreme Court to grant a certificate, and an order was made for the judge to be allowed to see it. It was then that Sanjay and V. C. Shukla, the former broadcasting and information minister, had the negative and prints destroyed, thus subverting the judicial process. Sanjay was sent to Tihar Jail on May 5, 1978 when his bail was canceled by the Supreme Court, allegedly to stop him from interfering with witnesses. Indira visited Sanjay that same day and said, "Be brave, this is your political rebirth, and do not worry. Remember that me, my father, all have spent life in prison."[7] Maneka brought him meals every day. She reveled in the adventure of the life they were living now, and warmed to a role where she was more necessary to her husband than she had been when he was surrounded by supporters. Bail was renewed after a month and Sanjay endured a long trial, showing defiance throughout. "I have no doubt," Maneka wrote, "that his fearlessness came from the conviction that what he was doing was right and his total disregard for the consequences of what he regarded as a righteous act."[8]

Indira gave the counsel of a lioness to her cub. On December 13, 1978 she wrote in a birthday message, "Remember, everything that strengthens, hurts. Some are crushed and crippled, a few become stronger. You have had to face a great deal from a very young age and I am proud of the dignified manner in which you have done so . . . be strong in mind and body, learn to tolerate and to try and win over rather than reciprocating aggressiveness and dislike. This I say from my own experience, for I used to react as you do, and found it only increases one's troubles."[9] Indira was terrified of the effect jail would have on Sanjay, and particularly feared that he would be physically attacked. She was always far more concerned for his physical security than her own.

Throughout this period of charges and trials, there was a grim reminder of what political retribution could mean in neighboring Pakistan, where the former prime minister Zulfiqar Ali Bhutto was tried and sentenced to death. He was confined in circumstances of sadistic humiliation, and despite pleas for clemency from many people, including Indira, he was hanged.

On February 26, 1979 Sanjay and V. C. Shukla were sentenced to two years' imprisonment, but both were released pending appeal. During 1979 Sanjay was imprisoned six times, spending five weeks in the jails of Delhi, Dehra Dun and Bareilly. As it had for his grandfather, jail brought out the best in Sanjay; he rounded up other inmates to play team games and clean the compound, and sat up nursing sick fellow prisoners. One two-week sentence was imposed for his part in organizing a rally in Delhi on May 1, 1979 against the proposed Special Courts which were to try him and Indira without benefit of appeal. The rally of 1500 people was attacked by the police with *lathis*, and he was arrested along with 302 others. It was just like the old days of the Congress, a comparison incessantly repeated.

While Sanjay fought out his battles in the courts and on the streets, Indira was mustering her forces for an onslaught on her tormentors. In this she was aided by disunity in the government and the increasing lawlessness of society. The end of the emergency had seen the release of many prisoners, most of whom were criminals the legal system was too slow or clumsy to deal with. They soon returned to crime, and the police were split by government decisions to investigate and prosecute those police officers who had been guilty of excessive zeal during the emergency: those accused of crimes were being investigated by those who were not. Meanwhile, the rains failed, prices rose, and attacks on the Muslim minority in various places further exacerbated communal tensions.

Scandal had tainted the air for a long time, but now the new leaders of India found they were not immune to it. Morarji Desai's son had long been accused of shady deals, but they came under more scrutiny as he now lived in the prime minister's residence; there were also charges against Charan Singh's wife and son-in-law. Most damagingly, Jagjivan Ram's son was featured in *Surya*, a magazine edited by Maneka, having sex outdoors with a woman other than his wife. In comparison, Sanjay seemed almost a victim of these tainted men.

Nevertheless, the Sanjay issue was the one which most disrupted the unity of Indira's supporters. They would follow her to the ends of the Earth, but not with him, whom they considered largely responsible for the 1977 election debacle. Matters were not helped by several former Congress ministers who had appeared before the Shah Commission and excused their actions during the emergency by saying they had been driven to them by Indira. Party unity could not be maintained in such an atmosphere, so Indira split Congress for a second time in a decade, forming Congress-Indira on January 2, 1978, with herself as its president. Its symbol of a hand raised in blessing was easily recognizable in a nation of mass illiteracy. Swaran Singh headed what remained of the former Congress, calling it Congress (S). The following month in state elections Congress (I) won in two southern states, Karnataka and Andhra Pradesh, and formed a coalition ministry in Maharashtra.

Now Indira had a new power base, and in a by-election on November 7, 1978 she was returned by a massive majority to the Lok Sabha for Chikmagalur, a constituency in Karnataka state, part of India where she had a consistent following. Soon after her return to parliament she left for Britain, to which she had been invited by several Indian associations. As well as addressing meetings of expatriates, she met Prime Minister James Callaghan and Margaret Thatcher, leader of the Opposition, who was already a firm friend despite their political differences. Thatcher said, "Mrs. Gandhi was a delight to deal with, and she always looked so lovely. I can understand that people think it strange that Mrs. Gandhi and I got on so well personally, because her political views were almost the other end of the political spectrum from mine . . . She had this combination of things, which sometimes male politicians find difficult, of being both very feminine and very understanding in the human way, but nevertheless capable of making very tough decisions."[10]

Events at home, however, had not been in Indira's favor. While away, she had been found guilty by the Privileges Committee of contempt of parliament in obstructing four officials who were collecting information for a parliamentary question on Maruti. She refused to apologize, and announced her refusal in a defiant speech, saying, "Every insult hurled against me will rebound. Every punishment inflicted on me will be a source of strength to me."[11] On December 19, 1978 she was sentenced by the Lok Sabha to be expelled from parliament and imprisoned.

The journalist Pran Chopra, who was in the press gallery, described the scene: "The resolution had been moved about expelling her, but instead of adopting it with proper dignity and solemnity of occasion, a number of Congress members began to deride her. As she was approaching the door through which she was going to exit, she turned around, threw up her hand and said, 'I will be back.'"[12] It was this gesture that gave Indira's party its symbol. Numerous statues of her were later made showing her in this defiant stance against her tormenters.

The hawks of Janata had finally got what they wanted—Indira behind bars—and in doing so had forfeited any last vestige of the moral superiority with which they had assumed power as the representatives of a wronged nation. Now *they* were the bullies who imprisoned without trial and subverted the expressed desires of the electorate. Sonia took home-cooked meals to Indira in Tihar Jail as she refused to eat or drink anything not provided by her family. She also took her daughter Priyanka, continuing the Nehru tradition of prison visits. Sonia feared the effects that constant upheavals in the household and incessant throngs of people around the house were having on her children.

The division between the Indira and Vijaya wings of the Nehru clan continued, with Nayantara Sahgal publishing a book, *Indira Gandhi's Emergence and Style* in 1978, which castigated Indira for both her political and personal shortcomings. Among the latter were matters of a petty, family nature, including the letter Jawaharlal wrote to his sister Vijaya from prison saying he felt the teenage Indira ignored him and did not write often enough.

Indira's own stay in prison lasted only a week. She was already testing the weakness of her opponents by making overtures to her enemies and exploiting their divisions. While in jail, she arranged for a bouquet of flowers to be sent to Charan Singh, the Janata leader, who had by now been sacked from the Cabinet by Morarji Desai and then reinstated in a lesser position. Desai had also removed Raj Narain, who became Charan Singh's chief lieutenant. Sanjay became the negotiator with his mother's old archenemy Narain, who had masterminded the court action which led to her declaring a state of emergency. Sanjay could promise to give Congress Indira backing to Charan Singh and Narain in ousting prime minister Desai so Charan Singh could take the job. These machiavellian maneuvers were based on mutual suspicion of different sets of enemies rather than any bonds of affection between allies.

With the support of Indira, Charan Singh and Raj Narain brought their own government down with a no-confidence motion. Indira supported Charan Singh's claim to be prime minister, but only in return for the withdrawal of the new Special Courts Act under which she and Sanjay were to be prosecuted without the usual legal protection. Charan Singh either could not or would not revoke the Act, so Indira withdrew her support and Charan Singh's government lasted just twenty-eight days, being brought down by a no-confidence motion instigated by defense minister Jagjivan Ram. The President asked Charan Singh to stay on as caretaker prime minister, and ordered elections for January 1980.

Sanjay had won his political spurs with his negotiations to oust Janata. With a little exaggeration a Gandhi supporter wrote, "Sanjay had literally demolished the artificial unity of the Janata government and they had to fight the elections as four different parties. And if there was one single party, it was the Indira Congress."[13] As a reward for his loyalty, Sanjay was allowed to pick some candidates, and a third of those who eventually ran were from his Youth Congress supporters. (The term "youth" had been much debased during the emergency, and those candidates were not necessarily young.) Sanjay's supporters took to calling him Raj Kumar, or Crown Prince.

In one of her punishing, whirlwind election tours, Indira again notched up record-breaking statistics. She and Sanjay had identified the areas where she could gain support, arranging for Youth Congress members to get rural supporters to the polling booths. Indira went out to the country, traveling 40,000 miles and addressing twenty-two meetings a day with a combined audience of 100 million. She was heard or seen by almost one in every four voters. *Newsweek* commented on the hapless government ministers, "At times it seemed they were running not so much against a diminutive sixty-two-year-old political candidate but a myth, a legend in a sari and dusty sandals."[14] She hardly referred to the emergency, but concentrated on urgent domestic issues: the price of kerosene, sugar and onions, which had escalated during the Janata government's period of office, and the breakdown of law and order over the same period. When a huge victory was assured, Indira left her house, entering the usual throng of supporters and press. A Scandinavian journalist asked her how it felt to be India's leader again. Indira responded ferociously, "I have always been India's leader."[15]

Of 524 seats in the Lok Sabha, Congress Indira won 351. Sanjay won Amethi, the seat he had lost ignominiously three years earlier. Indira had contested Rae Bareli in the north and Medak in the south (the constitution allowed a candidate to run in two constituencies). She won both and then withdrew from Rae Bareli, which she passed on, wanting to keep the constituency in the family, to Arun Nehru, the son of her cousin, Anand Nehru. Soon Indira and her close family moved back to 1 Safdarjung Road.

Indira would not be sworn in until January 14, 1980, which her astrologers told her was the most auspicious day for the ceremony. She had shepherded India into the nuclear age with an atomic test in 1974, and was to see an Indian satellite in orbit in mid-1980, but her astrologer and her yogi were still very much part of her court. She had also become increasingly religious: where in 1966 she had affirmed the oath of office, in 1980 she swore to God. She had always enjoyed religion as part of the rich cultural tradition of India and had not allied herself closely with any one sect, but over 1979 she had started getting up at 3 A.M. for prayers, and worshipping again in the evening. In the first months of her new administration she seemed to exhibit a compulsion to visit shrines and temples, offering prayers and doing other obeisance, such as prostrating herself before images of deities.[16]

Home life, where there had been extreme tensions between Indira and Maneka and personality disagreements between Maneka and Sonia, was much softened by the announcement in autumn 1979 that Maneka was pregnant. Indira put aside their differences and fussed over Maneka, who gloried in the attention she was receiving. Maneka was terrified of physical pain, so Sanjay went with her whenever she had to have an injection and stayed with her throughout the delivery, the first man to have done so in her doctors' experience.[17] Feroze Varun, named after Sanjay's father, was born on March 13, 1980. Now the vivacious Maneka settled down to being a wife and mother; in June 1980 she even bought her first cookbook.

After his election, Sanjay again began to meddle in every aspect of Indian life, from flight paths into Delhi and congestion in hospitals, to animal welfare (this last at the behest of Maneka, for whom it was an abiding passion). Although he was a new backbench MP, the journalist Inder Malhotra observed, "Sanjay's power was at its zenith and practically irresistible. Ministers and top civil servants vied with each other to do his bidding, however arbitrary."[18] His acolytes ensured that any criticism of him or Indira in parliament was dealt with by jeering to such an extent that the Lok Sabha functioned on his terms or not at all. Sanjay was unanimously asked by the legislators of Uttar Pradesh to become chief minister in June 1980, but Indira refused to allow it. Instead, she promoted him to general secretary of Congress, a position his grandfather had held for two terms.

While there was still a high level of flattery and sycophancy around Sanjay, sober commentators began to reassess his position. On June 22 the *Times of India* opined, "Even his detractors are beginning to concede that he may, in fact, possess certain qualities the country needs in this difficult transition period. Sanjay's political acumen is widely recognized . . . he has enormous capacity for hard work and he can make tough and unpopular decisions. He has without a doubt a large support base among the youth which held up when Mrs. Gandhi was in deep trouble . . . What was unthinkable just six months ago has become thinkable. A lot of people are beginning to accept that Sanjay can be India's next prime minister."[19]

Something amazing was happening, though not quite so amazing if one thinks about the slow development of Jawaharlal and, to a more limited extent, of Motilal and Indira: they all took a long time to develop into adults, and did so only in response to great challenges. What Sanjay was encountering at the age of thirty-three was a simple, natural process: he was growing up. It is entirely conceivable that after a respectable political apprenticeship he was going to develop from callow youth in a hurry to energetic and visionary politician.

Rajiv and Sonia tried to maintain calm in their part of the house where they were bringing up Rahul and Priyanka. They kept their own circle of friends and were a very family-based couple. Rajiv still displayed some mementoes of his father—his ashtray, watch, pipe, gun and many photographs—and was always emotional when talking about his father; he knew the value of parental companionship, and did not want to deny this to his children. His leisure interests were homey: he maintained his father's old workshop, he enjoyed music and photography and was a radio ham.

While Rajiv was a pilot by profession, flying had always been Sanjay's passion. When in 1977 the government vindictively took away his pilot's license, he started making radio-controlled model aircraft. When he got back into government, he had his license restored and started looking for a challenging aircraft. He chose a new Pitts S-2A plane, despite the dangers of flying an acrobatic light aircraft. Sanjay, who cared nothing for physical danger, had attracted a reputation for performing dangerous stunts and been criticized for violating air safety regulations. He angrily denied this and the official responsible had been sent on compulsory leave.

At 7:30 A.M. on June 23, 1980 Sanjay left for Safdarjung airport to put the Pitts aircraft, owned by the Delhi Flying Club, through its paces. He arrived early and did not wait for the aviation minister, who was to be his companion that day, but invited a rather unwilling Captain Subhash Saxena, former chief instructor at the flying club, to join him. He flew over 1 Safdarjung Road and at a few minutes past eight started practicing loops. The aircraft went into a dive, perhaps to perform a loop, perhaps as part of an unsuccessful "stall turn" maneuver higher up, but did not pull out of it. The plane plummeted down, crashing into a wooded area. Both men died instantly.

Within minutes of the crash Indira was informed. She rushed out of her office, hair awry, and was driven at speed to the crash site. She arrived to find the almost unrecognizable wreckage of the tiny plane from which the fire brigade had extracted the crushed bodies of the two men. She cried out on seeing Sanjay's mutilated body, then immediately composed herself and took charge, ordering the bodies to be placed in the ambulance, where she joined them on the journey to Ram Hospital. Political leaders flocked to the hospital to find Indira standing immobile, dark glasses screening her emotions. She was a sentinel of grief, waiting while the doctors prepared Sanjay's body so it could be seen. This was a matter of compassion on their part—there was no medical work which could be done.

Maneka arrived at the hospital, seemingly out of her mind with anguish, refusing to accept that Sanjay was dead and trying to enter the room where the doctors were working. Indira comforted her and consoled the wife and mother of Captain Saxena. She returned to the crash site, where officials were conducting an investigation, and collected what remained of Sanjay's possessions. Back at the hospital the doctors worked on the body for more than three hours, then Indira spent some time alone with her son. At last, she went to tell Maneka he was dead. "Not Sanjay, not Sanjay, anyone but Sanjay," said the young widow, over and again.[20]

The hospital was swamped with crowds and politicians. As usual with the Nehru/Gandhi dynasty it was a private grief played out before crowds and cameras. The body was taken back to the house and displayed on a bier containing huge blocks of ice. Rajiv, Sonia and the children returned swiftly from abroad, and the wider family also closed ranks. Family bonds were more powerful than the disagreements which had divided them, and Vijaya rushed to Delhi to be with Indira as soon as she heard of Sanjay's death. "Indu's dignity and calm are amazing," she later wrote to her daughter, "and I am full of admiration for her courage . . . [She] met me with affection and took me inside—presently brought out the baby [Feroze] Varun and put him in my arms. Later Maneka was brought to me. Seeing the fat smiling baby moved me and I began to cry, whereupon Indu came up and said, 'Now, now Puphi [aunt], you know we don't cry.'"[21] Only the red-rimmed eyes gave any indication of tears shed in private.

The sense of foreboding with which Indira always regarded Sanjay suggested to her friend Pupul Jayakar that some astrologer had predicted an early and violent death for him. Her cousin Nayantara said her "extreme and awesome stoicism in her loss conveyed as nothing else could have done that she had perhaps lived through the possibility of just such a disaster many times in her imagination."[22]

When she remarked on it in public she said, "People come and go but the nation continues to live," as usual seeing a family tragedy in a national context.[23] He was cremated at Shantivana, close to where Jawaharlal had been cremated. The lavish funeral, at state expense, was in keeping with the style of Sanjay's supporters, who erected statues to him, had roads named after him and elicited promises of schools and hospitals to be built in his memory. All this was seen by cynical commentators as less a genuine outpouring of grief than a desperate attempt to maintain hold of political power and privileges by maintaining an association with Sanjay and therefore Indira. Not surprisingly, many felt Sanjay's death had been providential, and the nation had been spared the terrible fate of Sanjay as prime minister. Indira, however, never acknowledged any errors or wrongdoing on Sanjay's part. She wrote to Dorothy Norman on August 3, 1980, "Seldom has any person had to brave such hardship and such a sustained campaign of calumny. It is to Sanjay's credit that he retained his dignity and calmness of spirit and to the end was a help and a joy to have around the house."[24]

Indira wrote to Pupul Jayakar that sorrow "can be neither forgotten nor overcome. One has to learn to live with it, to absorb it into one's being, as a part of life."[25] She fasted for two days, and was back at her desk on June 27, four days after Sanjay's death, dealing with the affairs of state. "You've got to put away your personal sorrow," she said, "and you have to discharge your responsibility."[26] Despite her outward stoicism, she would wake in the night and go looking for Sanjay.

# FATAL INHERITANCE

# FIFTEEN

# THE FAMILY DIVIDED

Rajiv and Sonia had a marriage beyond the dreams of romance—it had survived separation, cultural difference and parental opposition. They had a close personal relationship, Rajiv enjoyed his job and Sonia her cultural activities, and they had two beautiful children. If Rajiv had worries, it was over such matters as how to tell Rahul, then at the Doon School, that one of the many family dogs had died. "Think of how you played with her, how much fun she had and we had when we took her out . . . you will learn to live with the fact that at some time we all have to die," he wrote, in gentle words of fatherly advice.[1] Their apparently perfect family life seemed too good to last.

Rajiv's family was not entirely untainted by the air of corruption that surrounded his brother, and which seemed to have become endemic in Indian politics. Sanjay had set up another company, associated with Maruti, called Maruti Technical Services (MTS) and had somehow talked Sonia into being a partner, and had even involved the children, Rahul and Priyanka. The company became known as a "family firm." Rajiv said Sanjay asked Sonia to sign papers for the firm while he was away from Delhi.[2] Sonia doubtless believed MTS was a genuine company and was never accused of any wrongdoing.

Sanjay's death, which occurred when Rajiv, Sonia and the children were on vacation in Italy, was a disaster far in excess of grief at losing a brother. It was immediately apparent that Rajiv would be called upon to take Sanjay's place at Indira's side. For the first time in the fifteen years they had known each other there was tension between Rajiv and Sonia. She wrote, "I fought like a tigress—for him, for us and our children, for the life we had made together, his flying which he loved, our uncomplicated, easy friendships, and, above all, for our freedom: that simple human right that we had so carefully and consistently preserved." They had seen politics at close quarters: the politicians who had backed Indira and then denounced her when her luck ran out; the people who had been intimidated by the vindictive campaign against her; the deliberate distortions of the truth; the intolerable burden of power.[3]

On the other hand, Rajiv was tormented by seeing his mother crushed and alone. How could he turn away when she most needed him? Sonia understood this emotionally, but was "angry and resentful towards a system which, as I saw it, demanded him as a sacrificial lamb. It would crush him and destroy him—of this I was certain."[4]

Indira's increasing reliance on Rajiv and his family was quite marked. The door leading from her bedroom to Sanjay's, now occupied by Maneka alone and previously kept open, was closed, and the door leading to Rajiv's room was opened. She took to sleeping with her grandson, Feroze Varun. Rajiv held out against co-option into politics, but was clearly under immense personal and public pressure. All the members of Congress (I) in parliament signed a petition in August 1980 calling him to take up Sanjay's work.

It was not only Indira who saw a role for Rajiv. T. N. Kaul, a former diplomat and a family friend, said, "Mrs. Gandhi was shocked, she felt very lonely. The shock was so great that she tried to suppress it, and she never shed a tear in public. But that had its reaction on her, and she felt more insecure and lonely than ever before. I asked her, 'Why don't you ask Rajiv to stand by your side, not to join the government, but to join the party and hold your hand, just as you held your father's hand when he was lonely?' She said, 'I will not influence Rajiv's judgment, he should do what he likes. If you wish to speak to him, you may.'"[5]

Kaul did so, reminding Rajiv of the family history of sacrifice for the nation, how Indira had sacrificed her personal and domestic life for service to her father. Indira was a woman, Rajiv a man, he must support her.

Sonia later wrote that she remembered the year after Sanjay's death as being "one of complete helplessness, with every minute drawing us closer to the abyss. I kept hoping for a miracle, a solution which would be acceptable and fair to all of us. Finally I realized that I could no longer bear to watch Rajiv being torn apart. He was my Rajiv, we loved each other, and if he felt that he ought to offer his help to his mother, then I would bow to those forces which were now beyond me to fight, and I would go with him wherever they took him."[6] This sense of resignation came about only after much anguish. *India Today* later reported that Sonia had "retreated to her room and cried for four days. She appeared haggard, lost weight, and refused to dress in her customary elegant manner."[7]

Rajiv had ultimately agreed to go into politics, after four meetings with Kaul and hours of discussion, only on condition that he did not have to join the government. Kaul accepted this and reminded Rajiv that Indira had not joined the government when she had supported Jawaharlal. Rajiv was prepared to work within the party because, "I felt that there was a void and I couldn't see anyone else filling it; there was in a sense an inevitability about it."[8] At a huge meeting organized by the Youth Congress on December 14, 1980 to commemorate Sanjay's birth, Rajiv pledged to complete the tasks left unfinished by Sanjay.

Rajiv's lack of aptitude for his new role was not his only worry. He had a wife and children to support and, unlike the frugal Sanjay, enjoyed a middle-class lifestyle. He could not simply give up work and become a voluntary Congress (I) supporter. He was also doing a job he loved and making steady progress. "The airline was very cushy," he said later. "I enjoyed the work, it wasn't like working, it was like a hobby, and it gave us a lot of time to do what we liked. We had a little family and we were all very happy."[9] In December 1980 he was to fulfill a long-held ambition by taking his Boeing command test which would allow him to pilot jets. Six months after doing so he resigned from Indian Airlines and successfully ran for the Amethi constituency which Sanjay had represented. He could not combine his career and politics, so he made politics his career. He was also appointed a general secretary of Congress (I). Indira had said to reporters that Rajiv "is a serious, sincere and deeply dedicated young man . . . nobody can take Sanjay's place." Asked if he would make a successful politician, she said, "He has the qualities to make a success of anything he does. But there is no question that he will take Sanjay's place . . . They are two entirely different types of person."[10] Rajiv ingenuously confessed to reporters that he "[didn't] know much about politics. The way I see it is that Mummy had to be helped somehow."[11]

Rajiv's political naïveté could be disconcerting to outsiders. Around the time that he was entering politics he was introduced to a political scientist, James Manor, who later said, "He said he was so pleased to meet me because he was going into politics and he wanted to get to know the science of it. Could I tell him what the principles were and perhaps recommend a few books. I explained that politics was not credible as a science, like physics or chemistry, and he was very disappointed in me for not being a real scientist."[12]

Many other observers were disconcerted at the nepotism behind Rajiv's move into politics. Nayantara Sahgal, Indira's cousin, said that when Sanjay died "many people felt that here was a chance for the party to throw up its own leader. But by then Mrs. Gandhi had so isolated herself that she could only rely on her kith and kin, her direct bloodline."[13]

It was not that Rajiv lacked public qualities. He was a candid and agreeable individual, a natural conciliator with the ability to appear judicious to everyone. He had the strength of appearing courteous, firm but controlled, and he had the great advantage of being a Nehru-Gandhi so there was an expectation in others of his success. Rajiv accepted the burdens of political life without complaint, though his life and that of his family were transformed. Previously, according to Sonia, there had been days of concentrated activity and long spans of leisure; now it was the reverse. "Before it was an intimate, recognizable world. Now his life was crowded with people, hundreds of them every day, politicians, party workers, Amethi constituents, pressing him with their urgent problems and demands. His time was no longer flexible and each hour he could spend with us became all the more precious."[14] Rahul went away to the Doon school in 1982 and Priyanka went to the sister school, Welham, in 1983, but then fears of a terrorist attack intensified and they were admitted to schools in Delhi in the spring of 1984.

Rajiv was given responsibility for the Asian Games, billed as the most spectacular sporting event ever to be held in India. He oversaw the building of several modern stadiums to international standards in the space of twenty-two months and later said, "The Asian Games was a window for the world to see what India is capable of doing when we really mean business."[15]

The games, however, are better remembered for the scandals surrounding the building work than for displays of sporting prowess. There were many contracts to build arenas, roads and hotels, but while these monuments to wealth (and corruption) were created, the bonded laborers who worked in the quarries to produce the required stone lived under conditions of virtual slavery. It is an indication of how little he was like his mother or grandfather that Rajiv was either ignorant of or complacent about the labor conditions on the project for which he was responsible. It took a Supreme Court judgment against the government, brought on the workers' behalf by a social activist, to ameliorate the laborers' working conditions and return the bonded laborers (who had effectively been kidnapped) back to their home provinces. This scandal is not so much a reflection on Rajiv, who had never set himself up as a guardian of the poor, as evidence that Indira was losing her grip.

Rajiv's partner in making the Asian Games a sporting success was his cousin Arun Nehru. They worked increasingly together under Indira and, as Arun said, by 1983 "we had the last say on most things. At one point, she hauled me into her office and chastised me for working so closely with Rajiv. She said she would stop consulting us at all if we continued to do that. She said she needed us to be two sep-arate power centers which she could rely on separately. She was very switched on politically, she knew how to manipulate the system very well."[16] She also knew what made Arun Nehru tick, and in telling him this gave him a sense of his own importance, while also maintaining "power centers" which in fact drew their power from their relation-ship with her.

There had been no honeymoon period for Indira's second term of office after the election of 1980. There were immediate problems in the northeastern state of Assam where unemployment had led to a vio-lent campaign against immigrant labor from Bangladesh, which was largely Muslim. The militant Hindu group, the RSS, two of whose supporters had been responsible for Mahatma Gandhi's death, was undergoing a resurgence. Their extremist supporters were also attracted to political groupings such as the Bharatiya Janata Party, for-merly called the Jana Sangh. The law and order issues, on which Indira was always strong, began to misfire on the government when the police in some areas lost all sense of responsibility and started to behave in the most grotesque fashion. On the day Indira was sworn in, the police went on a rampage of torture, rape and killing in Narainpur, Uttar Pradesh, her political heartland. In West Bengal, nine villages of the Islampur area were set ablaze by the police; and in the worst inci-dent, police in the Bihar town of Bhagalpur were found to be routinely blinding suspected criminals with acid. These ghastly occurrences had resulted from constant political interference in the work of the police and the courts. There was no longer any *esprit de corps* in the police: factions within the force stood violently opposed to each other and used their position to promote their own or communal interests. Land-lords were left free to treat their local villagers as they wished, which frequently meant in a fashion of brutal exploitation. The "bandit queen" Phoolan Devi flourished during this period, gaining a reputa-tion as a heroine for insurgency against privilege.

Hindu-Muslim violence also flared up again, typified by events at Moradabad in Uttar Pradesh, where a pig wandering into a mosque led to a month of conflict and more than 100 deaths. Indira's collapse of morale following Sanjay's death was most obvious over this inci-dent, for despite Moradabad's proximity to Delhi and her lifelong habit of flying to scenes of communal violence to bestow comfort like a secular saint, this time she did not go until it was too late and the Muslims thought she had abandoned them. She was tired of violence, tired of giving comfort, tired of being Mother Indira when her own son was dead. Sonia said that Indira "for all her courage and compo-sure was broken in spirit."[17]

She was also responsible, in a wider sense, for the decline in stan-dards in public life. The old Congress Party, for all its faults, had attempted a national consensus which, to some extent, transcended personal requirements. Now the key to political success was loyalty to Indira Gandhi, and once that was given, personal or communal ends could be followed. The 1983 Congress held in Calcutta seemed to observers as no more than a collection of people who had come for an all-expenses-paid good time, so long as they were prepared to cheer Indira and Rajiv Gandhi. Indira was so embarrassed about their behavior that she urged them in Hindi (so their guest could not understand) to remain seated while the speaker from the Soviet Union addressed them; she then introduced him in English. As he walked towards the microphone, the arena emptied, to Indira's impo-tent anger.[18]

She turned, as her father had in times of internal tension, to the international scene, where she could stride the stage with the confi-dence of a survivor at Commonwealth and nonaligned meetings. As journalist Vir Sanghvi said, "Mrs. Gandhi was very conscious of the fact that by 1982 and 1983 she was about the most senior world leader there was. How many other people were there in office who had been prime minister in 1966? She had outlasted all her contemporaries."[19]

The Soviet invasion of Afghanistan in 1980 took place in the interregnum between Charan Singh's caretaker government and Indira's government, so Indian reaction was muted at the time. She was reluctant to condemn the Soviet Union, particularly as the Soviet invasion led to increased U.S. support for Pakistan, thus strengthening a nation on India's borders which had shown itself to be unfriendly. More support from the Soviets might soon be required therefore, so it would be unwise to alienate them. The heightening of international tension fed Indira's paranoia as prime minister.

She was always quick to see a conspiracy in unwelcome events, began to see a "foreign hand" even behind such internally explicable events as the continuing unrest in Assam, and the mistrust with which she was held by India's intelligentsia.[20] She brought much of this abuse on her own head with high-handed autocratic moves, such as having the governor of Jammu and Kashmir, her cousin B. K. Nehru, moved to become governor of Gujarat because he refused to dismiss his previous government when it displeased her. Similarly, she compelled the governor of Andhra Pradesh to dismiss the government of that state.

Indira's home life was hardly less turbulent than the political life of the nation. Maneka was eager to assume the mantle of Sanjay. She had developed from a teenage bride into a politically astute woman, who disdained Rajiv for his lack of political skill and cultivated Sanjay's acolytes who knew their interests were better served by her than by Rajiv. Arun Nehru blames the breakdown of relations between Indira and Maneka on the younger woman's impatience. He said, "Maneka was very young. If she had waited for a few months, things would have come naturally, but the party was not going to accept Maneka in Sanjay's position overnight. Sanjay had paid his dues for five or six years, and Maneka would have had to go though the same thing . . . But you can't demand a position."[21] Indira had never liked her daughter-in-law; Maneka's fiery temperament was anathema to a woman who was marked by a taciturn humor and long-held resentments. She also may have feared that, under the appropriate conditions, Maneka could develop into a threat to her.

Nor did Maneka and Sonia get on well. Sonia, obviously the favored daughter, was considered much the most Indian of the two, wearing saris and having a life centered on the home and children. Maneka, who often wore Western clothes, was a career woman with her own plans and designs. When Indira proposed taking on Maneka as her political secretary, presumably in an attempt to defuse the young woman's political potential by making it subservient to her own interests, Sonia protested and Indira withdrew the offer. Both Rajiv and Sonia may have thought that if Maneka were to assume the role of heir apparent, she would be the dominant representative of the younger generation in the household, and they were reluctant to relinquish this position to her. Indira tried to involve her daughters-in-law in her public life on an equal basis, taking them both on an official visit to France in November 1981, for example; but no impression of a happy family could be manufactured. Sonia's compliant and restrained manner was a constant reproach to Maneka.

The first intimation that a household disagreement would move into the public sphere was when Khushwant Singh, a distant relative of Maneka, promoted Maneka's claim to inherit Sanjay's place in politics. Khushwant, a well-respected author and journalist, compounded this offense by pointing out in print the simple truth that Rajiv had no interest in politics and would make a poor substitute for Sanjay. By comparison, Maneka was "like her late husband, utterly fearless when aroused, the very reincarnation of Durga astride a tiger."[22] This was a serious failure of tact; only Indira had been compared to Durga and, as Pupul Jayakar said, "there could not be two Durgas riding tigers under one roof."[23] True to form, Indira did not explode at Maneka, but instead cut Khushwant Singh out of her circle, despite the fact that he had remained loyal to her even after the emergency. Indira now told everyone Khushwant had been "our enemy all along."[24] Khushwant's few visits to the Prime Minister's house were on Maneka's side, where he saw a graphic reversal of fortune: "I used to see long queues outside the Sanjay part of the house when he was alive, but there was hardly anyone on that side after he died. Those same long queues were outside Rajiv Gandhi's part of the house."[25] The influence and patronage distributed by Rajiv's cronies, however, were far from the vulgarity and aggressiveness that had characterized those of Sanjay. In a barely concealed attack on the Sanjay-Maneka faction of Congress, Rajiv said in an interview that he wanted to "attract a new breed of person to politics—intelligent, Westernized young men with non-feudal, non-criminal ideas, who want to make India prosper rather than merely themselves."[26]

Maneka knew her position in the household was precarious, and as her mentor Sanjay had taught her, she planned her strategy four steps ahead. She established her hegemony over Sanjay's memory with a book of photographs of him for which Indira was going to write the text; Indira later refused to do so, then had the publication of the book held up because she was not happy with some of the text and captions. The conflict between Indira and Maneka, bridging the personal and the political, became, as one commentator put it, "a real-life soap opera" with gossip of the latest door-slamming row between mother-in-law and daughter-in-law of the nation's first family eagerly awaited.[27]

A clear signal that the personal antagonism was going to result in political opposition came over *Surya*, the magazine Maneka edited, which Sanjay had set up for her and which was owned by her mother (no friend of Indira). Early in 1982, the magazine was sold to a supporter of the extreme right-wing Hindu Rashtriya Swayamsevak Sangh (RSS) and other major political opponents of Indira. She was furious, but in characteristic fashion she contained her anger and bided her time.

Sanjay's old group of supporters, who now had political positions but no leader, were feeling increasingly isolated from the wellsprings of power. They planned a convention of Sanjay loyalists at Lucknow at the end of March 1982. While Indira was away in London opening the Festival of India, Maneka sent her a message saying she planned to address the convention. Indira replied that if she went to Lucknow, she need not return to 1 Safdarjung Road. Maneka ignored the warning. She and the conference organizers made an ostentatious display of loyalty to Indira. The convention hall was hung with pictures of Indira, Sanjay and Maneka and slogans such as "Long Live Mrs. Gandhi!" and "Sanjay Is Immortal!" Maneka urged loyalty to the Prime Minister and affirmed her own continuity with the family tradition, saying, "I shall always honor the discipline and reputation of the great Nehru-Gandhi family I belong to."[28]

Indira was not mollified by this disingenuous display. On her return from England, she summoned Maneka and ordered her out of the house in terms, according to her daughter-in-law, which were virtually incomprehensible through her rage. Maneka begged a couple of days' grace to get packed, but Indira said, "You're not taking anything out of this house, apart from your clothes." Maneka had anticipated this and over the days when Indira was abroad had moved out all the things she needed. Khushwant Singh said, "She wasn't interested in things like saris and jewelry; there were files and other things."[29]

Maneka called on her sister, Ambika, to support her, and Indira foolishly became involved in a shouting match with the two young women which, according to Khushwant Singh, left Indira in hysterical tears.[30] Rajiv and Arun Nehru tried to take over, asking the security officer to throw the sisters out, but he asked for the order in writing and no one wanted to commit himself.

As Maneka's luggage was being taken out, two men of Indira's court, her private secretary R. K. Dhawan and her yogi Brahmachari, stopped the servants in order to search the bags. Maneka protested, Indira insisted, but ultimately the bags left unsearched. Maneka also triumphed by leaving in the full glare of publicity, despite her mother-in-law's staff having cut off her telephone to prevent journalists being notified. When Khushwant Singh arrived, he found "The entire foreign press had been informed and were at the gates . . . Maneka scored the first round completely."[31] She had learned Indira's lesson well, to her mother-in-law's impotent rage; whatever your enemies want to do to you, let them do it as publicly as possible to show them in the worst possible light.

With uncharacteristic impetuousness born of overwhelming anger, Indira now wrote a letter to Maneka accusing her of rudeness and impertinence and compounding her insults with a jibe against Maneka's family: "Although you came from a different background, we accepted you because of Sanjay, but now we see you cannot adjust," she must therefore leave the household.[32] The comment on Maneka's family was ill-advised; at best it was snobbish, at worst it was anti-Sikh. The letter was leaked to the press, as was Maneka's reply, written that night before she left the house and addressed to "Mummy": "As soon as Sanjay died, you started literally torturing me in every conceivable way. I have borne it for a long time because of Sanjay and because I am your *bahu* [daughter-in-law]. If I had wanted to be against you I would not have fought so bitterly for you in the Janata years—a fact you seem to have conveniently forgotten—when the rest of your family was packed and ready to go abroad."[33]

Indira's worst mistake in a disaster-prone night was in attempting to keep her grandson, two-year-old Feroze Varun. He was with Indira when the servants came to collect him for his mother, but she refused to let him go. Maneka said if she could not take her son she would sit outside the house in civil disobedience until he was handed over. Maneka may not have had much of Mahatma Gandhi about her, but she had certainly learned the value of the well-placed moral protest. Indira's staff spent several hours talking with the police and lawyers to find a way in which Indira could keep Feroze Varun, but there was none. If Indira kept the child, Maneka could file a complaint and the police would be legally bound to restore him to his mother. Finally, Maneka left with her son and her maid, waving to journalists from the car.

Shortly after this family fiasco, Maneka called a press conference in order to present herself as a loyal daughter-in-law, cruelly mistreated by Indira: "I feel it is alien to Indian culture to first kick your daughter-in-law out and then write an invective against her and release it to the press." On the jibe about her family, which was most damaging to Indira, Maneka took the moral high ground, above talk of background and class: "I have always treated human beings as human beings."[34]

Indira's subtlety completely failed her when it came to dealing with Maneka; she even maligned Maneka and Sanjay's relationship, saying, "Sanjay spoke to me and others of his deep unhappiness" in his marriage.[35] About Feroze Varun, she was the venomous grandmother: "I am sad that the little boy is not getting the care that is his due, nor is he in surroundings which could help to build his character and inculcate virtues."[36]

It is not difficult to appreciate why the mature Indira dealt so badly with the twenty-four-year-old Maneka. That she had not recovered emotionally from the blow of Sanjay's death is certain, but there was more to it than that. Marie Seton, who was to visit Indira for several months soon after, said of Maneka: "She has done more damage to Indira than anyone else . . . that awful woman got under Indira's skin."[37] The reason seems to be that despite their obvious difference in temperament, that Maneka was voluble and Indira was taciturn, they were actually very similar individuals. Sanjay had picked a wife who was a younger version of his mother, a not uncommon occurrence. Maneka was already a woman in competition with Indira for the attention of her son, a usual cause of friction between mothers and daughters-in-law, but when she began to move into the political sphere and astute commentators actually compared her with Indira, the pressure on the older woman was too great: Maneka had to go.

Maneka continued to show a spirit true to the family she had married into, and began touring the country promoting Sanjay's ideas, talking in the sort of simple language that Indira had made her trademark. When she was excluded from the functions organized to commemorate the second anniversary of Sanjay's death in 1982, she marked the day by calling rallies of widows and distributing clothes to them. Hers was a slow and steady progress, using all the political guile and relentless energy which was normally associated with Indira. On August 25, 1982 she announced at a press conference that because of "the non-functioning of the government" (again a phrase Indira had used against her enemies) she was changing the apolitical Sanjay Forum into a political party. This was formally organized in March 1983 as the Rashtriya Sanjay Manch (National Sanjay Organization) with a claimed membership of 800,000. Maneka said she would be contesting Rajiv's Amethi seat (formerly Sanjay's) at the next election, which was taking the fight right into enemy territory—an astute political move.

Maneka started appearing in Amethi, stimulating rather more visits from Rajiv and Sonia than there had been previously. Maneka presented herself as the wronged widow, cast out of the family home with her infant son by her cruel mother-in-law, and left to fend for herself by her husband's elder brother and foreign wife. This may not have been the strict truth, but it was the stuff of which soap operas are made—simple domestic tales of family jealousy and injustice. Her very appearance in Amethi was presented as a triumph of courage. She told meetings, "When I began in politics I was told, 'Don't go to Amethi, go around the whole country, but don't go to Amethi. There are important people there, they will eat you up.' I said, 'This is the land Sanjay dedicated himself to. Because I am Sanjay's wife, it is my in-laws' home. It is my duty to come here and work here, for it is my home.'"[38] The legal questions concerning Maneka's share of Sanjay's estate and Indira's right to see Feroze Varun kept the family feud alive and in the public eye.

Dirty tricks abounded. Three of Maneka's close supporters were arrested on a murder charge, which was unceremoniously thrown out of court as soon as they appeared there. Everything Indira did seemed to be wrong; she was ruling with a small cabal, a "personalized dicta-torship" which did not even have the merit of efficiency; Rajiv was not making headway with the public while Maneka was the darling of the press. Indira called elections in two states, Andhra Pradesh and Karnataka, for January 1983. Maneka was greeted warmly by the pub-lic when she went campaigning; Rajiv, who was organizing the elec-tion for Congress (I) with Arun Nehru, was not. Congress (I) lost in both states, and Maneka's party won four out of the five seats it con-tested. This was quite a blow to Indira because it was in an area tra-ditionally loyal to her. Maneka's inexorable progress continued as her party won a by-election for the Lok Sabha seat of Malliahabad in Indira's home state of Uttar Pradesh early in 1984. If Indira had not been so bitterly opposed for personal reasons, she would have admired her daughter-in-law.

It was over the question of a separate Sikh state that Indira met her nemesis, rather appropriately, as she had granted a separate Punjabi-speaking state in 1966, something Jawaharlal had always resisted. Sikh separatists had used this issue as a door-opener to a fully inde-pendent state, which had long been their aim. The Sikhs had proved themselves so militarily valuable to the British that the Raj had encouraged them to consider themselves separate from (and superior to) other Indians.

The Akali Dal was the political wing of the group that controlled the holy shrines of Sikhism. While not all of the Akali Dal were agi-tating for a separate Sikh nation, it was a significant strand in their thinking. Indira wanted to break the Akali Dal's hold on Punjabi pol-itics, so Sanjay and the then Punjabi home minister, Giani Zail Singh, a Congress member, decided to promote an alternative Sikh leader in order to split Sikh nationalist support. They picked on Jarnail Singh Bhindranwale, who had a reputation as an itinerant village preacher promoting orthodox Sikhism. He was drawn into politics and given Congress support for promoting some candidates in local elections. Splitting the nationalist Sikh vote succeeded, in that Congress (I) took the Punjab in the 1980 election. As Bhindranwale developed a taste for politics, however, he realized he could gain more by being anti-Indira, anti-Congress and anti-Hindu, so he was wooed over to the Akali Dal, who felt their purposes would be best served by supporting him. He, of course, was no passive stooge in all this, seeing that *his* best interests lay in using the Akali Dal to further his own ends.

Bhindranwale was arrested in 1981 for the murder of a newspaper editor, but abruptly freed when the Akali Dal demanded his immediate and unconditional release, and Indira, unaccountably, conceded. Too late, Indira realized the danger from Bhindranwale and tried to re-establish an agreement with Akali Dal, but always backed down from agreeing to their demands. Aware of his political isolation, Bhindranwale realized that his best hope lay in a violent assertion of his position. To this end he moved into a hostel for pilgrims, part of a complex of buildings around the Golden Temple, the holiest shrine of Sikhism. From this vantage point he now openly called for secession from India and the creation of Khalistan, a separate Sikh state.

Giani Zail Singh became President of India in 1982 at Indira's behest, and though having a Sikh president should have made negotiations over Punjab easier, it did not do so. In fact, the President, the government of Punjab, and Indira were not able to agree what course of action to follow. This loss of control and decisiveness reflected badly on Indira, who was accused on the one hand of not crushing Sikh extremism, and on the other of artificially stimulating a crisis in order to unify the Hindu vote behind Congress (I). Even the Communists began to oppose her, despite her petitioning Soviet leaders to use their good offices with the CPI.

From his position in the Golden Temple complex, Bhindranwale directed gangs of killers, who drove around the countryside on motorcycles shooting people at will. The police found it difficult to deal with Bhindranwale as convention prevented them entering the Golden Temple. General lawlessness in the country had also much reduced police morale.

Violence had been escalating throughout 1982, with Akali campaigns often leading to violence and stimulating police action against (innocent) Sikhs in other states. This only served to heighten the Sikh sense of grievance. While the situation in Punjab continued to deteriorate, there was also violence in state elections in Kashmir and Assam, which intensified the impression of a nation plunging into chaos. Nothing demonstrated this more clearly than the murder of a senior police officer, Deputy Inspector-General A. S. Atwal, who had been worshipping at the Golden Temple on April 23, 1983. He was shot by Bhindranwale's armed supporters from inside the temple complex and his body lay for hours in front of the shrine until the safety of those removing it could be ensured.

This was the point at which Indira could, with the support of public opinion (including the Sikhs, who were appalled by the desecration of the temple), have either moved in with the army to oust Bhindranwale, or laid siege to the complex and starve out the terrorists. No such action was taken, perhaps for fear of being swamped by Sikhs from all over Punjab coming to support the nationalists. The Punjabi chief minister, Darbara Singh, wanted to go in at this time but was dissuaded by Indira, who may well have been listening to advice from Zail Singh. Other politicians, such as Indira's home minister, assured the Sikhs that the government would not retake the shrine by force. Four fruitless attempts were made to settle the matter by talks with the Akali leaders, while bombings, looting and murder continued. Akali demands, including the transfer of the city of Chandigarh to Punjab and control over the rivers flowing through the state, were seen by secessionists as transitional demands working towards an independent Sikh nation. The Akalis would gain concessions in negotiation, then any deal short of full Sikh autonomy would be vetoed by Bhindranwale. Members of the Akali Dal who tended to moderation, it should be said, became targets for Bhindranwale's assassination squads.

Emboldened by the government's failure to do anything about the murder of Atwal and other killings around the Golden Temple, Bhindranwale and his supporters moved from the pilgrims' hostel to Akal Takht, the second most sacred part of the temple. He began massive fortification of his stronghold and bought sophisticated armaments, paid for by supporters who had settled in Britain and other countries outside India. Government plans to retake the temple did not begin until January 1984, more than two years after the terrorists had first moved in. Even at this late stage, the assault on the Golden Temple could have been avoided if the Akali leadership had taken action against Bhindranwale or even distanced themselves from him. However, they inflamed the situation by announcing that they would stop shipments of grain to the rest of India and cut electric power lines, unless their demands were granted.

Indira asked General K. Sundarji, her army Commander-in-Chief, if he could take the Golden Temple without damage. In response, he produced aerial pictures taken the previous day showing that all windows, doors and other orifices were barricaded with bricks or sandbags. Sundarji warned her that the chances of grievous damage were very high.

Finally, it was decided to go in with as much military force as necessary, a decision probably made without the knowledge of President Zail Singh—a source of considerable anger to him after the event. On June 2, 1984 Indira addressed the nation, saying, "This is not the time for anger. Too much blood has been shed" but innocents had been killed, and there was arson, looting and sabotage. "A systematic campaign is spreading bitterness and hatred between Hindus and Sikhs. And worst of all, the unity and integrity of our motherland is being openly challenged by a few who find refuge in holy shrines . . ."[39] She appealed to the Akalis to call off their sabotage without making a specific threat.

Sundarji's forces besieged the Golden Temple in Operation Blue Star on June 5, calling on the terrorists to surrender. Bhindranwale and his supporters were well entrenched in a maze of tunnels behind strong fortifications and were equipped with sophisticated weapons. It took twenty-four hours of hard fighting, involving the death of ninety soldiers and 712 Sikh extremists, including Bhindranwale, before there was calm. In order to minimize damage to the Golden Temple, Sundarji delayed using tanks until the early hours of the morning, when the army forces had already taken many casualties. Operation Blue Star did, however, result in the complete destruction of the second holiest shrine, the Akal Takht, and some damage to the holiest, the Harmandir Sahib.

President Zail Singh visited on June 8, when there was still sporadic gunfire, and wept to see the destruction. "The complex looked like it was bombed from an airplane," said one of his aides.[40] The President and the most senior Sikh minister in Indira's cabinet, Buta Singh, were excommunicated by Sikh high priests. Khushwant Singh, an MP and long-time Indira supporter, told her in parliament, "You made a mistake for which the country will pay the price for centuries to come. I am not blaming you of any communal prejudice. But it was an enormous error of judgment."[41] He felt that while the terrorists were wrong to take shelter in their shrines, the government was wrong to break the convention of not interfering with these holy places. The only way to have won on this issue was to have gone in earlier, before the Golden Temple was reinforced. Although the country was generally positive that, at long last, the terrorists had finally been beaten in their stronghold, no one was under any illusion that Sikh unrest was at an end. The political atmosphere was heavy with foreboding.

Sikh extremists, including those based in Britain and the United States, made blood-curdling threats against Indira and her family. A mutiny of mainly newly recruited and untrained Sikhs in the army (where they made up a far greater proportion than Sikhs did in the population as a whole) was quickly put down. There was a proposal that Sikhs should be removed from Indira's security guard, but when it was passed to Indira she wrote, "Aren't we secular?" on the file, meaning that she could not allow government appointments to be made on the grounds of religion.

Marie Seton was in India from March to June 1984, and observed that Indira was exhausted. She said Indira told her "that she could no longer respond to a challenge—always her strongest point. This she could always do. She could always improvise. Now she was retreating from communication. She has always had moods like this. She would describe it as being stinking. She would say, 'I am stinking now, right all the way through.'"[42] All Indira's last letters show an encircling despair: "The situation here is a disturbing one . . . the terrible period we are going through here. I am truly depressed."[43]

Death was much in her mind. She wrote, "If I die a violent death, as some fear and a few are plotting, I know the violence will be in the thought and the action of the assassin, not in my dying—for no hate is dark enough to overshadow the extent of my love for my people and my country, no force is strong enough to divert me from my purpose and my endeavor to take this country forward."[44] In a newspaper interview she said, "India has lived a long, long time—thousands of years—and my sixty-six years hardly count. India will survive . . ."[45]

Vishnu Mathur, a producer making a film about Rajiv, felt himself lucky to obtain a brief interview with Indira in the rose garden of her house. In the event, he found her voluble and relaxed, prepared to make time to talk about her family. He said, "I was hoping for ten minutes but she spent two or two and a half hours with me, as if she had to talk compulsively. She talked about Rajiv, she talked about Sanjay, about her husband Feroze—I was running out of film."[46]

When she last saw Pupul Jayakar, Indira said she was going to Kashmir, as she had never seen the Chinar leaves turn brilliant red and orange in the autumn. It seemed for her time to return to the ancient homeland. She said, "Papu used to love rivers, but I am the daughter of the mountains, and my heart is free of care. I have told my sons [sic] that when I die, to scatter my ashes over the Himalayas."[47] She had already spoken to Rajiv and Sonia about the arrangements for her funeral, and spoke to fourteen-year-old Rahul, telling him "to be brave when the time came: she had lived her life and done all she had to do and could do; he was not to cry for her."[48]

On October 30, at a meeting in Bhuvaneshwar in Orissa state, Indira gave her last great public pronouncement of defiance: "It does not matter to me whether I live or die. As long as I draw breath I will carry on serving. And when I die, every drop of my blood will nourish and strengthen my free and undivided country."[49] That night, P. C. Alexander, her principal secretary, found her looking all of her sixty-seven years. He said, "For the first time in my experience I found her to be very, very tired. She didn't like to be told she looked tired but I told her she was, so I'd just take a couple of minutes and come back tomorrow, but she said, 'No, no, no, no, you sit down, let us talk,'" which he did.[50]

The following morning the children came to say goodbye before going off to school. She kissed Priyanka and hugged her very tightly. She called Rahul back to remind him of what she had said earlier about being brave when the time came for her to die. Indira then went out into the sunshine in her bright orange sari. She was going to be interviewed by Peter Ustinov for a television program, so she did not have a bulky bulletproof vest on under the light fabric, making her slight figure more evident. She walked down the path separating the family's living quarters from her office, walking towards one her bodyguards, Sub-Inspector Beant Singh. She smiled at him and gave the namaste greeting with both hands pressed together. He drew his pistol and shot her in the stomach at point blank range five times. As she collapsed, there was a pause while Beant Singh urged another Sikh bodyguard, Constable Satwant Singh, to play his part. Others who might have helped (for Indira was probably not yet fatally wounded) seemed frozen to the spot. No one stopped Satwant Singh as he fired twenty-five bullets from his Sten gun into the supine body of Indira Gandhi.

There was pandemonium as officials and guards ran for cover. The assassins dropped their weapons on the grass in a gesture of surrender. Beant Singh calmly raised his arms and said, "I have done what I had to do. Now you do what you like." Guards responsible for the outer security of the compound marched off the assassins and, allegedly during an attempt to escape, they were both shot. Beant Singh died, but Satwant Singh survived, to be later executed for murder.

Sonia was running a bath when she heard what she thought was a burst of firecrackers—not unusual given that the festival of Diwali had recently taken place. She called out to the children's nanny to see what was happening, then the air was filled with screams. It had to be danger. She ran out, still in her housecoat, calling "Mummy! Mummy!" The doctor on duty was trying to give Indira artificial respiration. A duty ambulance was at the Prime Minister's residence, but not the driver, who was on his tea break. Indira was moved by Sonia and Indira's staff to the back of her Ambassador car. Sonia knelt by the body with Indira's blood seeping through her housecoat. It was a nightmarish drive to the hospital through heavy traffic while Sonia held the body, hoping against hope that Indira was unconscious and could be brought round.

The All India Institute of Medical Sciences, almost three miles away, had not been alerted to the emergency, so Indira's car was met only by the junior doctors on duty, who were overawed by the sudden responsibility. Indira was put on the heart-lung machine and operated on to remove the bullets. Continuous blood transfusions were set up, though more for the sake of appearances than any expectation of the patient's survival. Her internal organs, with the exception of her heart, had been destroyed in the hail of bullets: Indira had died in the attack.

Arun Nehru arrived at the hospital within minutes of Indira's body. He found Sonia hysterical about the safety of her children, fearing the same fate for them that Indira had feared after the assassination of Mujib-ur Rehman: the destruction of the entire family to the third generation. Arun Nehru was dispatched to their house where he found, "There was not a security guard. Anybody could have walked in off the road."[51] He arranged security to protect Rahul and Priyanka, who had been brought from school and were being looked after by a family friend.

P. C. Alexander rushed from the meeting in Bombay and arrived at the All India Medical Institute to find turmoil. He had no official position now, as his authority had died with Indira, but he said, "I was aware that I was there as nobody, but I decided to take charge of the situation because all the senior ministers were away out of the country."[52] He ordered the police to clear the area and talked to the few ministers who were on the veranda outside the room where Indira's body was lying. According to the constitution, someone could be appointed as acting prime minister as soon as the Prime Minister was dead. But, with the President abroad, the machinery for filling the post was not in place, so Alexander delayed making the official announcement of Indira's death. She was thus constitutionally alive until the arrival of Zail Singh to appoint an interim successor.

Rajiv was in Calcutta addressing a public meeting when he received a message that his mother had been taken to the hospital. He wound up the meeting and started the journey back, learning on the plane that his mother was in fact dead. The finance minister, Pranab Mukherjee, who was on the plane, approached Rajiv, who had gone to sit by himself after hearing the grim news, and told him to take over. Rajiv said, "I have no interest at all, Pranab, don't bother me with this."[53]

Arun Nehru had meanwhile been making plans for the succession, talking to Congress leaders on the telephone. He went to the airport to meet Rajiv, armed with the information that everyone was unanimous in wanting him to be prime minister. "I hadn't even discussed the matter with Rajiv," he said. "I only informed him when I went to pick him up at the airport. I must say he was very calm and collected."[54]

P. C. Alexander said Rajiv was "the very picture of coolness and courage. In a situation like this anybody would have really broken down, but he arrived with great self-composure and confidence. He went and saw the dead body and immediately came back to where Soniaji was standing and crying; she was in utter grief."[55] Rajiv was still surrounded by his entourage. Sonia felt a longing to be left alone with him for a moment and eventually they went into a separate room. There he told her they had already asked him to become party leader, and he was going to be sworn in as prime minister. Sonia begged him not to let them do it. "I pleaded with him, and others around him too," she later recalled. "He held my hands, hugged me, tried to soothe my desperation."[56] P. C. Alexander went in to the couple and found Sonia in tears in "a poignant and tragic scene . . . she was persuading her husband not to accept the prime ministership. They were hugging each other and he was kissing her forehead and telling her, 'It's my duty. I have to do it.'"[57] Sonia said he would be killed. He had no choice, he said, he would be killed anyway.[58] Rajiv was facing his own tryst with destiny. P. C. Alexander tapped him on the shoulder and they withdrew to an adjoining bathroom, where Rajiv agreed he must wait for the President. Some had been urging that the swearing-in ceremony should take place with the Vice-President, even in a bathroom of the All India Medical Institute itself with Indira's body lying in the next room. Good taste and constitutional propriety finally prevailed.

President Zail Singh was on an official tour of Yemen when he received the news and set off immediately for Delhi, reading on the plane the copy of the Indian constitution which he always carried with him. He made a decision not to appoint an interim prime minister, which he was not obliged to do constitutionally, though he could have chosen to do so.

Arun Nehru went to meet the President at the airport. In his position as a general secretary of Congress, he told Zail Singh the party had taken a decision and Rajiv would be prime minister. Zail Singh did not demur. His later contention was that he had already decided only Rajiv could command a majority of the Congress Party in the Lok Sabha. Indeed, Indira had not encouraged any successors to her rule except Rajiv. As Arun Shourie, editor of the English-language daily *Indian Express*, said, "By that time the Congress Party had been decimated. There were no internal processes by which another more competent or sagacious or more experienced leader could be selected. In retrospect it seems as if India as a whole went for Rajiv Gandhi because of some affection for a dynasty, or because royalty still matters in India."[59] It was a just comment: Rajiv was not even a minister, let alone a cabinet minister, and had had few great responsibilities save being the Prime Minister's son.

Arun and Zail Singh drove to the hospital, and people milling outside stoned the car, an early indication of the violence which was to
overwhelm all Sikhs, however exalted their position. Zail Singh told
Rajiv to come to the presidential palace immediately. At 6 P.M. the
official announcement of Indira's death was made, nearly nine hours
after she had been shot, and long after the BBC World Service had
announced the news. At 6:20 Rajiv was sworn in. After three years in
parliament, with no cabinet or even junior ministerial experience,
Rajiv Gandhi became prime minister of the world's largest democracy.

State television broadcast that Rajiv would make an announcement at 10:30 P.M. It was actually broadcast, pre-recorded, shortly
before midnight. Arun Nehru and others who had helped him wrote
the address in English, then translated it into Hindi. Rajiv found the
English easy but stumbled over the Hindi and had to do several
retakes. He nonetheless passed this first challenge with great dignity
and restraint. He said, "Indira Gandhi has been assassinated. She was
mother not only to me but to the whole nation. She served the Indian
people to her last drop of blood."[60] It was not a valediction to a great
politician, or even a great leader; it was as if part of the nation itself
had died. He continued, "Indira Gandhi is dead. India is living.
India's soul is living." It was as near as one could approach in a democracy to saying "The queen is dead, long live the king."

Indira's body was taken to lie in state at Teen Murti House, where
she had lived with Jawaharlal. Crowds waiting outside for a last
chance to see her chanted "blood for blood." The city was plunged
into anti-Sikh riots immediately the official announcement of Indira's
death was made. Sikhs were pulled out of their cars and homes and
killed; their shops were looted and burned. Armed gangs roamed
around Delhi looking for Sikhs who, with their distinctive turbans
covering long hair, could not easily disguise themselves. Mobs often
carried gasoline cans to burn Sikh shops while the police looked the
other way. Khushwant Singh, who with his wife took refuge in the
Swedish embassy, said, "What the mobs were after was Sikh property,
television sets and refrigerators, because we are more prosperous than
others. Killing and burning people alive was just fun and games."[61]

As always in these events, some Hindus sheltered endangered
Sikhs, but for the most part, those who did not take part did nothing
to prevent the outrages in which almost 2500 died, many burned

alive. Now there were no such courageous Congress members as Jawaharlal and Indira to go out into the streets to quell the rioters. Congress leaders were more likely to be found in the leadership of the mob. Rajiv Gandhi had assumed the mantle of the Nehru dynasty in a city where the flickering flames of burning homes and shops illuminated the blood spilled on the streets.

SIXTEEN

# THE RELUCTANT PRIME MINISTER

In the bloody aftermath of Indira's assassination Zail Singh struggled to contact members of the government but failed to obtain any action to stop the rape, arson and slaughter. Pupul Jayakar went in desperation to Rajiv's house. Later she talked of begging Rajiv to call out the army and make a television appearance calling for calm on the evening after the assassination. She said, "Look, I can't tell the Prime Minister what to do, but I'll tell you what your mother would have done. She would have gone on television with all the strength and energy she has and she would have told the people of Delhi, 'You will not touch a single Sikh. I will see to it that no further violence takes place. It has to end.'"[1] Pupul Jayakar had even the cadences of Indira's speech right, as Rajiv recognized when he said, "You write it out for me," which she did. For the first but by no means the last time Rajiv was being brought face to face with the difference between himself and his mother. The passion that guided her, steered by finely honed political skill, was simply lacking in Rajiv. He did not make a broadcast that evening; instead, Narasimha Rao, the home minister, went on television and appealed for calm. Questioned on the widespread anarchy arising on his mother's death, Rajiv later said, "When a giant tree falls, the earth shakes,"[2] an insensitive remark doubtless made under the stress of new office and personal grief.

Indira's body was kept for three days—an unusually long time before a Hindu funeral—and no curfew was imposed. The violence had kept crowds away from her funeral, so by Nehru-Gandhi standards there were not many mourners, though this still meant tens of thousands. Among the foreign dignitaries present was British premier Margaret Thatcher, for whom Indira's death had a special poignancy: they had enjoyed a close relationship, and only weeks earlier Thatcher herself had been the target of a bomb attack at a party conference. She survived unscathed, but the bomb killed a number of delegates, and Thatcher later received a letter from Indira urging resolve against terrorism. Mrs. (later Baroness) Thatcher said, "It's not very often that you known a person in life and that you see them in death,

280

except with your own family. She looked so small . . . I saw in Rajiv the same kind of self-control that I had seen in Mrs. Gandhi earlier, in his having to take over in that way . . . Sonia was absolutely grief-stricken. Had anyone painted that scene, her grief alone would have communicated itself to other people."³ By general agreement, Rajiv's steely self-control in these times endeared him to the nation, and to political colleagues who wondered whether he had the mettle to hold the premiership.

Indira was cremated in the same place as Jawaharlal and Sanjay, on land next to Shantivana, on November 3. Rajiv, Sonia, Rahul and Priyanka made a picture of family grief. Journalist Vir Sanghvi described Rajiv at the funeral: "There was chaos all around him, but he projected confidence, he seemed to be in control. You had the setting sun behind him, you had his mother's funeral pyre in the foreground, and you had him holding his son, who was clearly devastated. I don't think there was a single dry eye in the country."⁴ Some days later, flying in an Indian Air Force transport plane, Rajiv scattered the ashes over the Himalayas.

Soon after the cremation Rajiv finally took control of the situation in Delhi and made a public appearance denouncing the rioters. He said, "While hundreds of millions of Indians are mourning the tragic loss of their beloved leader, some people are casting a slur on her memory by indulging in acts of hatred and violence. Disgraceful incidents of arson, looting and murder have taken place and must stop forthwith."⁵ He called out the army, who quickly assumed command of the situation. Rajiv also visited the refugee camp where some of the 25,000 Sikhs left homeless by the Delhi riots were staying. It was a significant gesture of reconciliation that he, the son of the murdered woman, publicly sympathized with Sikhs rather than blaming them. The government refused for months, however, to investigate who was behind the riots, stimulating Sikh suspicion that they had been organized and coordinated by Congress activists after the initial spontaneous acts of violence.

The political scientist James Manor felt that Rajiv harbored a scarcely contained resentment against Sikhs. He recalled a public meeting in early December 1984 at which the Sikh mayor of Delhi was present when Rajiv used deliberately inflammatory language. "He said, 'We will take our vengeance in our own way at our own time.'" Manor also investigated a case in which Rajiv had government officials withhold evidence from the courts about the Congress members alleged to have been responsible for the attacks on Sikhs. He said, "Rajiv was a good man in most things, but over the Sikh issue he was not."[6]

Nonetheless, regardless of grief and resentment, politics continued. An election would have to be held soon, as Indira's government had almost completed its five-year term when she was killed. Congress leaders also saw the benefits to be gained from the sympathy vote. Rajiv did not demur: Vishnu Mathur, the producer who had been making a film about Rajiv before Indira's assassination, approached him shortly after with some trepidation, feeling that the new Prime Minister would have much better things to do than to talk to him. In fact, Rajiv was delighted to see him and watch the finished film, which showed how he had stimulated funds for schools in his Amethi constituency, and for industry and training projects to stop the exodus of young men from the rural area in a search for jobs. At the request of Congress leaders, Mathur made 5000 video copies of the film, which they took to villages around India in special vans containing viewing equipment. Villagers were thus given the impression that what Rajiv had achieved in his own constituency, he would do in the rest of India.[7]

In an immensely expensive election, with party coffers presumably swelled with money donated after Indira's death, there was widespread poster and newspaper advertising, with millions of audio cassettes, booklets and party flags distributed. When the votes came in at the end of December 1984, Rajiv had gained a national landslide, with 415 out of 543 seats, the largest mandate in Indian history, and a better result than either Indira or Jawaharlal had received. Journalist Vir Sanghvi asked Rajiv why he had won and found no illusions in his answer: "Mainly because of my mother's death. . . . Nobody knew anything about me, so they'd projected on to me. I became the symbol of their hopes."[8] He promised "efficient, clean government," which, in the event, he found easier to offer than to deliver.[9]

One of the many losers in the 1984 elections was Maneka, who had campaigned ferociously in Amethi, often seen on the hustings cradling Feroze Varun in her arms; but whatever support she might have garnered was swept away in the wave of sympathy for Rajiv. Her prospects were not improved by Congress activists who disgracefully made use of her Sikh background and presented a vote for Maneka as a vote for Sikh separatism.

Family life now took the full toll of political success. Rajiv no longer had any privacy and had little time for his family. He even dropped his hobby of taking photographs, which he had been doing since he was a child, achieving a professional standard of work; his pictures of his wife and children were particularly striking.[10] Now he had to put everything into politics. He had the Nehru capacity for punishingly hard work, which he tried to encourage in his son. He wrote to Rahul, "When you have to do something you must remember that it must be done in the best way possible. There should not be a halfway point where you say it is good enough. You must always do your very best and then try a little harder. If it is just a race that you are running . . . you must put in that extra bit, that might make you feel that you are about to burst, only then can you get ahead . . . You must try and work till you get perfection. It is all the little details that make the difference."[11]

Rajiv now adopted a rigorous schedule which allowed him only four or five hours sleep. The family managed to eat meals together on most days, and would wait up for him until three or four in the morning; he would be back at his work by nine. As soon as Rajiv was sworn in, the security forces surrounded the family, putting an end to what remained of their privacy and freedom. The day of Indira's death was the last day Rahul and Priyanka ever attended school. In March 1985 they left 1 Safdarjung Road for a house on Race Course Road designated as the Prime Minister's official residence. The children remained at home for the next five years in what was virtually a prison. Sonia said, "The only space outside our four walls where we could step without a cordon of security was our garden."[12] Margaret Thatcher, who visited the family at this time, reported, "They were living in a small, rather cramped house . . . My abiding impression was of the tight security which surrounded [them]."[13]

The dynastic nature of the government was reinforced by Arun Nehru, Rajiv's exact contemporary, who was initially minister for power, then, in 1985, minister for internal security, police, rehabilitation and law and order. Arun was descended from Motilal's elder brother Nandlal, whose branch of the family had also played a large part in the independence movement. Arun's grandfather Shamlal and his grandmother Uma Nehru were both imprisoned for the movement, and Uma was later an MP for three terms. B. K. Nehru was their nephew. Arun said, "I would go campaigning with my grandmother from the age of eight. I had seen power come and go in the family, so when my time came, I wore power very easily."[14] By 1985 Arun Nehru was also a general secretary of Congress while Rajiv was president, continuing the tradition, established by Indira, of the prime minister also being president of the party. Arun suffered a heart attack in Kashmir in May 1986, which happened to coincide with the end of Rajiv's "honeymoon" period as prime minister: the leader who at first could do no wrong, could now do no right.

Rajiv brought some friends into politics, including the former industrialist Arun Singh and a former airline pilot Satish Sharma. Sharma looked after Rajiv's Amethi seat and ensured Rajiv knew when his pilot's license was up for renewal so that he could put in the necessary flying hours to retain it: he was determined to remain a competent pilot. Sharma said, "Rajiv's weak point was that he was not a politician, as I am not a politician. We are professionals. We are not used to all this conniving. He was a visionary who wanted the country to be a modern India in the 21st century, and in that he was absolutely sincere."[15]

Rajiv liked taking executive decisions as if he were a company chairman. He was not used to sharing decisions or working towards a consensus, a source of conflict between him and President Zail Singh, who complained that the government was not giving him full information which was his constitutional right. A letter of complaint from the President was leaked to the press, and Rajiv made the situation worse by ordering a raid on the offices of the *Indian Express*, looking for evidence of a conspiracy between them. This alienated the press and did nothing to repair the rift with Zail Singh.

Asked what he disliked about politics, Rajiv said, "The time people take to tell you something very simple. People seldom get to the point, they go round and round trying to hint at what they have to say. I find it very irritating."[16] Rajiv started his political career as a somewhat pedantic and pedestrian public speaker; although he never became thrilling, he did become effective. He also learned how to endear himself to crowds, doing such things as taking water offered by villagers—at some risk to his health. He never had a full mastery of

Hindi, often choosing the wrong word or pronouncing words incorrectly; and he had a poor grasp of history, mixing up events in India's past or commenting that the Opposition wanted to take India back to the Middle Ages—a figure of speech from European rather than Indian history.

Rajiv did, however, have the advantages of youth, charm and aristocratic bearing, while his freedom from religious or regional ties made him appear to be everyone's prime minister. As evidence of this he made a *rapprochement* with his aunt Vijaya, now in her eighties and long estranged from Indira's side of the family. Rajiv pledged himself to follow the approach and principles of Jawaharlal and Indira, but in fact his natural inclinations veered sharply away from their socialistic models of government. One thing he knew from his own conversations was that businessmen always complained how government controls hampered their efficiency. He therefore relaxed controls. He also appreciated the material requirements of the rising middle class, so he liberalized import policies, allowing people to buy imported TVs, radios and watches which had previously been available only at high prices or from smugglers.

During his first year of office he made frequent foreign trips on a Boeing 747, dubbed the "caviar express," and consequently became known as India's first non-resident prime minister. Questions were asked in parliament about the cost of his foreign trips, which involved two Boeings being taken out of Air India service (one as a reserve) for each trip and entailed the cancellation of scheduled flights and a subsequent loss of revenue. Many Indians, however, were delighted to see their leader treading the world stage and mixing with statesmen in Washington, London, Moscow and Paris. "We finally had a prime minister who was one of us," said Vir Sanghvi, "who was educated, who could go to the West and stand up to them. He was not like some obscure Third World statesman, clinging to obscure beliefs; he was a man who knew his own mind and yet could hold his own."[17]

Overseas, Rajiv projected the image of a progressive, left-wing politician. On his first state visit to Moscow in May 1985 he enumerated his concerns: "The continued denial of the legitimate rights of Palestinians, the blatant practice of apartheid and aggression in South Africa against African peoples, the denial of the rights of the Namibians, the efforts to frustrate the functioning of governments in Latin

America and the continuing conflicts in southwest and southeast Asia."[18] There is a suspicion when reading this sort of pronouncement by Rajiv that he was saying what he was expected to say or what his advisers had told him to say rather than what he felt. His comments in praise of Japan, "the first Asian country to assimilate the new scientific knowledge," seem far more heartfelt. On this visit to Japan he lauded the achievements of India of which he genuinely seemed proud: "At Independence, India had to import food to feed 350 million people; today we are self-sufficient for a population of 750 million people. In 1947 we did not produce even lathes; today, we build our own fast breeder reactors and launch our own satellites."[19]

In an attempt to clean up Indian politics, Rajiv introduced the Anti-Defection Bill to expel from the house any member who changed his party. This was designed to prevent the disgraceful scenes of horse-trading party loyalty for personal gain, which had increasingly disfigured parliaments in recent years. He also attempted to clean up Congress, which celebrated its centenary at a huge meeting at Brabourne Stadium in Bombay in December 1985. The assumption was, of course, that Congress Indira had inherited the mantle of the Congress founded in 1885. The high point of the conference was Rajiv's address, which, rather than giving an anodyne reassurance to the faithful, suggested that things would change. He said, "Millions of ordinary Congress workers throughout the country are full of enthusiasm for the Congress policies and programs. But they are handicapped, for on their backs ride the brokers of power and influence, who dispense patronage to convert a mass movement into a feudal oligarchy . . . We talk of the high principles and lofty ideals needed to build a strong and prosperous India. But we obey no discipline, no rule, follow no principle of public morality, display no sense of social awareness, show no concern for the public weal. Corruption is not only tolerated but even regarded as the hallmark of leadership."[20] These were doubtless heartfelt thoughts even if stylistically they did not appear to have been written by Rajiv himself.

The Brabourne Stadium, which had recently been the arena for a different kind of tension, as the Indian test team battled out a close cricket series, was entirely enclosed for the occasion. It resembled some vast, tented caravanserai for a party on the move, but unsure in which direction. Rajiv, in spotless white, had bounded on to a stage decorated by a backdrop of the Congress heroes, Mahatma Gandhi, Jawaharlal Nehru and Indira Gandhi, emphasizing his blood links with greatness. Around the stadium, stalls groaned under the weight of Congress memorabilia to martyrs of the struggle, women of the freedom fight, and the founding fathers and mothers. Hagiography of Indira Gandhi, the recently martyred leader, here presented as the mother of the nation, abounded. But Rajiv's speech went down uneasily with the Congress wallahs, who sat, arranged in rows, in the main conclave. Their discipline told them they must applaud, so they clapped, kept their faces to the platform and their thoughts to themselves. The soft-spoken young hero completed his speech. Outside the stadium the great city—the "Bollywood of India"—went on as before. Deals were struck. Politicians made promises. The socioeconomic class most identified with Rajiv made its due obeisance to power. Nothing much changed.

Rajiv did not have the political experience to mobilize support behind a reform movement; the most important effect of the speech was to distance him from the corrupt old guard without endearing himself to Sanjay's followers. Career diplomat and family intimate T. N. Kaul said, "He had good intentions, he said he was going to get rid of the power brokers, and he brought in younger elements, but they were inexperienced. The old gang in the party got round him, and did not allow him really to come to grips with the people in the party."[21] Rajiv's favorite metaphor for government was that of piloting a nation, where "there is so much free play in the controls that you can almost shake them at one end and nothing happens at the other. The inertia is great."[22]

One of the major events of Rajiv's premiership had little to do with the government, except that it was a legacy of incautious industrialization. On December 3, 1984 a serious leak developed in a giant pesticide factory owned by Union Carbide in the Madhya Pradesh town of Bhopal. The leaking gas killed 3000 people and blinded tens of thousands. Rajiv knew what he must do: he flew to the disaster area immediately, but somehow the common touch, that instant link with suffering humanity which his mother and grandfather had in such full measure, was absent from Rajiv. He knew he should be there—he did not know what to say.

Rajiv had no natural association with the poor; he became identi-

The Dynasty

fied with the upwardly mobile prosperous middle class, the rising power in India. As Pran Chopra said, "By Rajiv's entire bearing, his lack of experience in politics, his not being a grass roots politician, his being born with a silver spoon, his whole image of being a modern-minded technocrat, all these things put a stamp on him as the Prime Minister of the better-off India."[23]

He toured extensively to all parts of the country, and in 1987 even went on a pilgrimage to rural India, trying to improve his image with the poor. Though state television showed every speck of dirt on Rajiv's feet from walking the dusty streets of India, he never did look like a man of the people. One of his favorite slogans was, "A computer in every village school by the twenty-first century," apparently oblivious to the fact that many village schools did not have electricity, or even a blackboard.[24] It was as if he were trying to replace the ox cart with the cellular phone.

Rajiv tried to solve the problem of Punjab, still under the President's rule. As a goodwill gesture, he released the Sikh extremists who had been imprisoned during the last months of his mother's rule, and announced some economic measures, such as the building of a new dam to alleviate the electricity shortage in the state. Terrorism continued nonetheless, including a number of small bombs in Delhi and neighboring states, and the bombing of a Boeing 747 on a flight from Canada to India in June 1985, which killed all 325 people on board. Responsibility for this last act was claimed by two Sikh extremist groups (and one Kashmiri faction), and circumstantial evidence does suggest Sikh activists as the most likely culprits.

Throughout all this Rajiv refused to be diverted into instant reactions. He continued with delicate negotiations and eventually came to an agreement with the president of the Akali Dal Party, Harchand Singh Longowal, on July 24, 1985. He conceded Punjab exclusive use of the state capital Chandigarh, which had formerly been shared with the neighboring state of Haryana, in return for a statement of loyalty. Then, acting contrary to advice, he called an election, for he was eager to restore responsibility for Punjab to an elected state government. On August 20, however, Longowal was assassinated by extremists. The result of the election five weeks later was inconclusive, Punjab again descended into violent chaos, and the Longowal agreement was never implemented. Rajiv said that as

288

his agreement hinged entirely on one man, "[his] death made it very difficult to complete it."[25]

In a renewed attempt to step up the tension, extremists re-entered the Golden Temple in 1986 and tore down the Akal Takht, which had been rebuilt after damage during Operation Blue Star. They considered the holy building had been defiled by such rebuilding, or at least claimed they did, one pretext for violence being as good as another for them. Once again, weapons were taken into the temple complex and violence against Hindus resumed with redoubled vehemence. Sikhs who were not considered sufficiently devout also came under attack, as did liquor and meat sellers and barbers.

The only way to get the extremists out was by another military action, a move which Rajiv must have viewed with deep trepidation, as the last time it had led to the murder of his mother and not even restored peace. Once again, a similar opportunity for action presented itself when a policeman was shot near the temple. Immediately following this, in April 1988, Rajiv launched Operation Black Thunder, which he directed throughout from Delhi. In a ten-day siege, the police and army did not enter the precincts of the temple, but starved the militants out. Eventually, nearly 200 surrendered, and they were further discredited by pictures showing how they had desecrated the temple and had even fought with each other on holy ground.

Rajiv deserves sympathy, as does anyone who had to deal with the problem of Punjab. Although he lacked experience, ruthlessness and any number of other qualities supposedly required for political success, it is questionable whether even an F. D. Roosevelt could have come out of Punjabi politics with merit. Rajiv's administration tried various measures to stimulate village democracy (later extended to the whole country), to discredit terrorism and to appease the extremists, but all to no avail. Finally, in 1989, appeasement having failed, coercion was tried. A new amendment to the national constitution was pushed through: the 59th amendment, which allowed for a state of emergency to be declared, and for various constitutional rights, including the right to life, to be suspended. V. P. Singh described this as "the gravest folly" of Rajiv's government, and proof of his "desperation over Punjab," which it was.[26]

The unrest in Punjab continued to threaten both Rajiv's and Sonia's personal safety. On October 2, 1986, at a ceremony to commemorate Mahatma Gandhi at his shrine, a shot was fired in their direction, but the security people said it was a scooter backfiring. Later, the gunman, a lone Sikh, opened fire again. The crowd scattered and the would-be assassin was captured. No one was injured, but it was a somber reminder that the strict security under which the couple and their two children had been living was all too necessary.

Other internal security measures were dealt with patiently and firmly. The Assam Accord, to placate those agitating against Bangladeshi immigrants, was agreed in August 1985. It provided for the expulsion of those Bangladeshis who had arrived in Assam after March 25, 1971, the day the state of Bangladesh was proclaimed, and for the erection of a fence or wall along the border with Bangladesh. In fact, neither the expulsions nor the building of a border barrier were ever carried out, probably because the threat to do so was enough to quell the unrest of agitators. In addition, an election was held which (while being a defeat for the Congress Party) channeled the energies of the former student-led agitators into parliamentary politics. Rajiv also tried to come to peace with the tribal people in the northeast of the country, the Bodos, Gurkhas and Mizos, in a series of agreements which were more or less successful in bringing secessionist violence to a halt, though their provisions were rarely, if ever, implemented. Another agreement, which was more of a political deal, was concluded about Kashmir in November 1986, when Congress agreed to share power with Farooq Abdullah's National Conference. Not everyone applauded these measures. Arun Nehru, who had become increasingly estranged from Rajiv, said, "He meant extremely well, but it came about that every week he must do something new, even if it was totally impractical and everyone opposed it."[27]

Internationally, Rajiv looked stronger and more impressive than he did at home. At the Commonwealth Heads of Government Conference in Nassau in October 1985 Rajiv was chosen to take the lead in proposing full, mandatory economic sanctions against South Africa in an attempt to bring concerted pressure on the regime to introduce democracy. Mahatma Gandhi began his career fighting for justice in South Africa, which made it an issue on which Indian leaders were honor bound to intervene. Apartheid was an area of personal concern for Rajiv, both in terms of human justice and of Indian history.

The Commonwealth nations were largely united on the matter of sanctions, but had to persuade Britain, where premier Margaret Thatcher argued that to impose sanctions would damage Britain's trade with the rebel nation and therefore cause unemployment in Britain and in South Africa itself. As an old friend of his mother and an occasional family guest, Rajiv had gotten along with Margaret Thatcher well enough, but on this issue their differences became evident. Vir Sanghvi said, "I think he really disliked Mrs. Thatcher, not just because she was obnoxious and arrogant, but because he associated or saw in her opposition to sanctions traces of traditional British racism."[28]

Margaret Thatcher reflected on the situation at the Commonwealth Heads of Government meeting: "They were demanding sanctions against South Africa—sanctions, sanctions, sanctions. It became a parrot cry: sanctions! And they were thinking wouldn't it be good, boys, if we put sanctions on South Africa. And I said, 'Have you worked out what sanctions are? Don't you know if they work in South Africa, all the expansion of business will stop? You will throw hundreds of thousands and millions of people out of work.'"[29]

The conference stalled, and they adjourned for the weekend to Lyford Cay, one of the most luxurious places in the world. Negotiations resumed, but Thatcher was still inflexible and no progress could be made. Rajiv was sent to her with a compromise list of sanctions which they hoped she would be prepared to accept. "He was very tough," Thatcher said, but she would not agree to compromise. "I said, 'No, I'm not prepared to agree to those. If you want sanctions, I'm only prepared to have something which is a sort of visible sign, a small thing.'"[30]

Thatcher was then summoned to a meeting chaired by Rajiv, where other Commonwealth leaders berated her for intransigence. "Mr. Chairman," Thatcher said, "I'm not prepared to listen to this. I've never heard so many insults in my life as I've heard from the people assembled here, in spite of the fact that we are helping so very many of them with their problems, and I'm not going to stand for it." She was particularly incensed at Ugandan delegates accusing her of racial discrimination, when Uganda itself had expelled its Indian population, which subsequently came to Britain: "and very good people they are . . . they have brought great prosperity."[31]

Rajiv steered the meeting away from personal attacks towards the areas where he had already privately agreed with Thatcher that she would concede some points. "So I trotted out my little list," she later explained, and the conference agreed, "Yes, we'll have those." The atmosphere changed; instead of being the world's ogre, Thatcher was suddenly a statesman-like prime minister. She later made her famous television appearance saying she had conceded "just a tiny little bit," including a ban on the import of krugerrands and a prohibition on trade missions to South Africa. In a lame explanation to the media, Rajiv said, "We have come with a package that is the most effective package the Commonwealth could have come out with."[32]

Vir Sanghvi articulated the thoughts of many members of the Indian elite when he said, "As politicians went, Mrs. Thatcher was infinitely superior to Rajiv Gandhi. She could run circles around him: she was more aggressive, she was more stubborn, she was shrewder. I think Rajiv was probably prepared to put up with that. But at the end of the day he sensed that in the long run apartheid had to go. So it didn't matter whether Mrs. Thatcher won one skirmish or the other, it wasn't important to win, it was more important to be right."[33]

The sanctions issue continued to be controversial, and Rajiv played a key part in keeping it alive at the following year's Commonwealth meeting in London and the 1987 meeting in Vancouver. The cumulative pressure on South Africa finally paid off, and democracy was established following the release of Nelson Mandela, whom Rajiv was able to greet by telephone soon after Rajiv left office.

Rajiv ensured that India took a leading role in opposing nuclear weapons, working within the "six-nation five-continent initiative" which Indira had set in motion in the last months of her life, bringing together the heads of government of Argentina, Greece, India, Mexico, Sweden and Tanzania. Rajiv told their summit at Ixtapa in Mexico in 1986, "It is . . . our duty as non-nuclear weapon states to exert unremitting pressure on the nuclear weapon powers to negotiate and disarm."[34] India qualified as a non-nuclear weapon state, it was claimed, because it had only a "device" which had been exploded in Rajasthan in 1974 and never developed into a proper bomb. This is very much open to doubt, but as it falls within military state secrecy, hard facts are in short supply.

Rajiv visited Pakistan three times and got on well with Benazir Bhutto, who had been elected prime minister in the first free election since her father Zulfiqar Ali Bhutto was deposed in 1977. They were both young (she was nine years younger than Rajiv), both came from privileged, political families and both were educated in England. Although they signed important agreements about not bombing each other's nuclear installations and abiding by the Simla Accord which their parents had signed in 1972, neither had been ratified by the time Rajiv left office.

A resumption of border tension with China occurred in 1986, when China was believed to be constructing a helipad in an area claimed as Indian territory. In an attempt to defuse the highly sensitive situation, in December 1988, Rajiv became the first Indian prime minister to visit China since Jawaharlal in 1954. It was a historic meeting, but did not resolve the border territory dispute, and may have left Rajiv over-sensitive to Chinese sensibilities, as India was one of the few countries not to condemn the Tiananmen Square massacre of pro-democracy demonstrators in 1989.

It was in Sri Lanka that Rajiv's foreign policy began to go badly wrong, though it was Indira's policy rather than his. As Vir Sanghvi said, "I don't think you can look at Rajiv Gandhi's Sri Lanka policy without looking at his mother's. If you take the line that we should never have got involved in Lanka, I think that's reasonable, but the truth is we were already involved, his mother had got us involved. She'd picked insurgent groups, she'd arranged training for them, she'd sent our secret service in to interfere. Rajiv's job was really to clean up the mess his mother had left behind."[35]

In Sri Lanka (formerly Ceylon) the Tamil minority of 2.5 million, who were concentrated in the north of the island, had strong racial and linguistic links with the 55 million Tamil people in the Indian state of Tamil Nadu. When the Sri Lankan Tamils started fighting for independence from the Sinhalese majority, the chief minister of Tamil Nadu, M. G. Ramachandaran, gave the terrorist "Tamil Tigers" arms, money and refuge. He was almost certainly backed by Indira, who needed the support of this populist former film star as he was her only political ally in the south. It was another of Indira's late mistakes which she would not have made prior to 1980.

Refugees flooded into Tamil Nadu from Sri Lanka after the Sri Lankan government decided to win the guerrilla war launched by the Tamil Tigers. It was felt necessary to promote stability in Sri Lanka or discontent would spill over to the southern Indian state of Tamil Nadu. There was also a real danger that military pressure on the Tamils in Sri Lanka would lead to a flood of Tamil refugees into India, creating a situation analogous to that of the refugees from East Pakistan in 1971. Rajiv's plan, therefore, was to give potential refugees no urgent reason to move, so when the Sri Lankan army blockaded the Tamil-dominated Jaffna peninsula, he determined it was essential to supply the beleaguered Tamils. Relief supplies were sent in a convoy of fishing vessels, but they were turned back by the Sri Lankan Navy. Rajiv then ordered the contingency plan, which came to be called the "rice-bombing" of Jaffna. A series of transport planes escorted by fighters took off from Bangalore on June 4, 1987 and dropped 30–40 tons of supplies. The gesture was well conceived in that it had clear humanitarian implications, while also being an assertion of India's supremacy over a small neighboring power. It was also evidence that the tradition of creative, non-violent action was not dead in India.

Under such pressure, Sri Lanka could resist no more, and on July 29, 1987 Rajiv and President Junius Jayawardene signed the Indo-Sri Lanka Agreement. This declared that the Sri Lankan government agreed to a merger of the north and east of their island, and would call it the Tamil homeland. They would guarantee devolution of financial power and control of the land and establish a provisional government, and they would provide proportional representation for Tamils in public employment. The terms of the agreement led to rioting by the Sinhalese majority, fearful lest their privileges be eroded. Rajiv went to Colombo for the ratification of the agreement and proceeded to take the salute of the guard of honor, against the advice of his civil servants. He said to them, "What, do you expect the prime minister of India to show that he's afraid of a critical situation in a foreign country? Here we are signing an agreement guaranteeing their safety and security and you're going to tell them that I'm afraid to take the guard of honor?"[36]

As Rajiv was inspecting the guard, one of the naval ratings swung a heavy rifle butt at his head. He saw the attack coming and ducked just in time to take the blow on his shoulder. Rajiv continued with his task and stood for the national anthem. He then gave instructions that there should be no statement criticizing the military discipline of the Sri Lankan government. The Indian high commissioner for Sri Lanka,

J.N. "Mani" Dixit, said, "The man had a great sense of balance about not letting this explode into something major."[37] Rajiv's attacker was one of the Sinhalese angered by the extent to which India had forced Sri Lanka to make concessions to the Tamils.

Within hours of signing the agreement, an Indian Peace-Keeping Force, ultimately numbering 70,000, was sent to Sri Lanka. The Indian troops soon found that, far from bringing peace to Sri Lanka, they simply assumed the role of the Sri Lankan Army in attempting to control the guerrillas. The belligerents turned against the Indian troops, who were obliged to defend themselves and thus became inextricably embroiled in the conflict. The crucial point came early in October 1987, when seventeen Tamil Tigers, believed to be on a terrorist mission, were captured at sea by the Sri Lankan Navy. They, and their colleagues outside, were alarmed that they should be in Sri Lankan custody; the Indian forces had some responsibility to take them, but there was no Indian official empowered to make a decision—or bold enough to do so. The Chief of Army Staff, General K. Sundarji, said of the group coordinating operations, "It was not even a debating society, it was as effective as a mothers' sewing circle. We talked, wasted a lot of each other's time, got nowhere, no minutes were kept, there was no followup action."[38] Rajiv was out of the country and had left no clear command structure to deal with such problems. When the Sri Lankan security forces tried to move the captured Tamil Tigers to Colombo, they took their personal cyanide capsules. The Tamil Tigers felt not enough had been done by the Indians to take the captured men away from the Sri Lankans, but took their anger one stage further by attacking the Indian Peace-Keeping Force. Indian neutrality in Sri Lanka was effectively at an end. Growing parliamentary opposition started attacking Rajiv Gandhi for getting India embroiled there.

Rajiv blamed the Tamil Tigers, saying to parliament that they "went back on every commitment they had given us. They deliberately set out to wreck the agreement because they were unwilling or unable to make the transition from militancy to the democratic process."[39] Rajiv had put his own life on the line and the Tamil terrorists were unwilling to follow the democratic process. They were already planning to liquidate Rajiv himself.

# SEVENTEEN

# RAJIV'S TRYST WITH DESTINY

As Rajiv settled into the prime ministership, he began to exclude his old colleagues Arun Singh and Arun Nehru, and to seek new counsel. "I began to disagree with the way Rajiv was doing things," Arun Nehru said. "He began to leave us out of the decision-making. We were not sent papers, we were not told the truth—we were being sidelined."[1] Arun Nehru felt that Rajiv lacked the political sophistication to avoid the blandishments of sycophants whose loyalty was to the power of the movement rather than any deeper principle, or even to friendship. Nehru said, "To get into the inner circle and into the Prime Minister's confidence, you think the way he is thinking and urge him on. He may succeed or he may fail, but the good sycophant is not bothered about success or failure, he just wants to tout the boss's version."[2]

With such views, it is unsurprising that Arun Nehru was excluded. "Publicly he supported my work, but privately he made it difficult and we feuded," said Nehru, who believed that Rajiv took seriously the talk of competition between himself and his cousin. Arun Nehru resigned three times over Rajiv's treatment of him, but Rajiv refused to accept his resignation. In October 1986, however, Rajiv sacked him from his ministerial post, and Arun Nehru went into a general opposition, which became overt after he and some other former Rajiv confidantes were expelled from the Congress Party for disloyalty. *India Today* journalist Dilip Bobb wrote, "Trusted friends had gradually been discarded . . . sidelined in favor of sycophants and self-seekers, men of petty minds and shrunken stature."[3]

The foreign secretary, A. P. Venkateswaran, was effectively sacked at a televised news conference in January 1987, when, in answer to a question, Rajiv said, "You will talk with the new foreign secretary soon." The unfortunate bureaucrat had no idea until this moment that he was about to be sacked, and immediately tendered his resignation. Rajiv denied any intention of humiliating the man. "I didn't intend it that way, it just happened," he excused himself.[4]

The finance minister, V. P. Singh, had attempted to make businesses pay their taxes, a source of conflict with Rajiv, who seemed to view it as an unacceptable constraint on business. Rajiv moved Singh from finance to defense in January 1987, but they were soon at odds again, over a defense contract. Singh had received a telex from the Indian ambassador in Germany, which said a 7 percent "agent's fee" was being paid on a submarine deal. When Singh made this public and ordered an inquiry, Rajiv summoned him to his office: "That's the first time I'd seen Rajiv really angry, red in the face," said Singh, who was shocked to find him defending the company which had paid bribes. "That was the point of parting between us," said Singh, who resigned, was expelled from the Congress Party three months later, and thereafter became Rajiv's implacable opponent and the new "Mr. Clean" of Indian politics.[5] He thus became Rajiv's main accuser in the Bofors scandal, which broke only days after he had left office.

The Bofors deal was brought about by Rajiv's sensible policy of equipping India's armed services well and defending the country's borders. He was eager to establish India's superiority over its neighbors and around its long coastline—a further example of the way in which his India bore no relation to the non-violent, village ideal envisioned by Gandhi. On land, India's forces relied largely on home-produced weapons, the manufacture of which made India the largest producer of arms in the Third World and one of the world's leading producers of intermediate-range missiles. Some arms still had to be bought from abroad, however, and it was India's negotiations for the purchase of a long-range field gun which became the Bofors scandal. Three countries, Britain, France and Sweden, were bidding to supply India with a new field gun. The decision to purchase was made because Pakistan had been sold a U.S. ground radar system which allowed operators to pinpoint the location of field artillery as soon as a shell had been fired. It was therefore essential for India to have a powerful, maneuverable gun in order to fire it and move it away before detection.

A Swedish armaments company, Bofors, offered the most appropriate weapon and received a contract in March 1986 to supply 410 of the guns for $1.3 billion. In April 1987, however, Swedish radio broadcast a report in which it was asserted that Bofors had obtained the contract by bribing top Indian politicians and defense officials. *Indian Express* editor Arun Shourie picked up the story from an agency and made it a small item on the front page. The government immediately denied the story, calling it "one more link in the chain of denigration, and destabilization of our political system."[6] Shourie said, "I was struck by the ferocity with which Rajiv Gandhi's government came down on that little item. There were all sorts of denials, and motives being attributed, claims of CIA plots. If it was such a small allegation, what was the problem?"[7] One of the things the Bofors scandal showed was Rajiv's total inexperience at damage limitation.

The Opposition smelled fear, and by a set of circumstances fortunate for them, there was soon to be a debate occasioned by V. P. Singh's resignation as defense minister over the issue of payments for defense contracts. An added complication was that Rajiv himself was handling the defense portfolio at the time the Bofors contract was signed. Rajiv's friend and defense minister Arun Singh told parliament on April 21 that nothing had been paid for the deal. Three days later, however, the Bofors company gave details of payments made to various "middlemen," and further revelations from the Swedish Audit Bureau increased the Indian government's embarrassment.

President Zail Singh, already at daggers drawn with Rajiv because of the way the Prime Minister restricted his access to information, demanded an explanation. He was then plotting to remove Rajiv (though no charges were ever proved) because he felt he had not been treated with the political consideration he deserved, and because Rajiv was determined not to give him a second term in office (his current term would end in July 1987). The President's post was not held at the Prime Minister's pleasure, but Indira had established the principle that no president could be appointed without the agreement of the Prime Minister. For his part, it was constitutionally possible for Zail Singh to dismiss the Prime Minister, but to do so when he had such a large majority as Rajiv would be improper, particularly in circumstances short of a national emergency.

Whether by dismissal or forced resignation, Rajiv was not expected to survive June 1987 politically. Zail Singh reached the point of drafting a letter of dismissal, but did not send it. He could not count on his supporters; and perhaps he simply lacked the stomach for a bruising constitutional battle. Another factor in the situation was that V. P. Singh, the only alternative prime ministerial figure, was not prepared to run. His display of loyalty (or, more correctly, absence of disloyalty) was not rewarded, for on June 18, 1987 Rajiv expelled him from the

Congress Party, thus foolishly ensuring that he had no further reason to be loyal to the government. His ostensible offense was asking for an inquiry into the way one of Rajiv's friends and supporters had obtained a flat in Geneva. Now Singh was no longer a Congress man, he felt obliged to resign and formed the *Jan Morcha* or People's Front Party. He was soon back in parliament after winning a by-election in the Nehru heartland of Allahabad, a particularly galling defeat for Rajiv considering his family's long relationship with the city.

Soon after V. P. Singh's expulsion from Congress, on July 18, Arun Singh resigned as minister of state for defense, giving no reason. He has always remained silent, but commentators then and now have always taken his silence to indicate that there was something truly rotten about the administration.

Rajiv believed that the forces moving against him were part of an organized conspiracy in which Zail Singh was a leading character, but Zail Singh's disappearance from the scene at the end of his term of office did not alleviate Rajiv's problems. Rajiv was not yet free of his tormentors in parliament, and he compounded suspicions by denying something of which he had never been accused. He told the Lok Sabha in August, "I categorically declare in this highest forum of democracy that neither I nor any member of my family has received any consideration in these [Bofors] transactions," and added, "that is the truth," for good measure.

Disastrously, Rajiv even denied there were commissions paid over arms deals, or that any Indian had been given money in such deals. Arun Nehru articulated the disbelief with which this remark was received: "He said there are no commissions. Now, in Delhi every third person is a commission agent for some company or other. So he tied himself up in knots . . . Then somebody or other went on trying to hide the information and the press kept on getting the information, so it just went on and on. In these situations you don't look for judicial verdicts, you look for a public verdict, and the public verdict was that he'd got something to hide."[8] Insistence on this point led him to displays of bad temper. "Am I expected to reply to every dog that barks?" he said when asked why he had not replied to some charge made by the Opposition.[9]

The Chief of Army Staff, General K. Sundarji, recommended a simple expedient to the government: that they threaten to cancel the contract with the Swedes unless they revealed the recipients of the slush fund. He said, "I found there was not much enthusiasm on the part of the government to pursue this course of action."[10]

There was more than a suspicion that, if Rajiv Gandhi were not involved in the corruption, he was involved in a coverup of the corruption. As Arun Shourie said, "Like everybody in India, I have wished him well, but I am forced to conclude that he is falling into the ways of his mother in that he does not distinguish between truth and falsehood. The convenience of the moment seems to be everything to him. These small controversies could have been so easily handled with candor and truth."[11] Using the full machinery of government against the press was precisely the wrong approach, but it was the one Rajiv's administration adopted, with the Directorate of Revenue Intelligence launching simultaneous raids on the *Express'* eleven offices around the country. Another ill-advised move was a bill Rajiv introduced in 1988, supposedly to protect the individual from defamatory press comments. After an outcry from the press, plus strikes and demonstrations, the bill was withdrawn.

Years later, out of office, when Rajiv was able to reflect on the whole affair he said, "We didn't handle the Bofors issue at all well. We lost credibility right at the beginning and what we felt so helpless about was that here we thought we were on good ground, we had done a very good contract, had got it at a low rate and so we opened up and said we'll have an inquiry and we were quite frank. But the more frank we were, the more of a mess we got into."[12]

The many questions surrounding the Bofors deal were never adequately answered, and there may well have been much less mystery than Rajiv's detractors insinuated, for they infused every letter, document and remembered conversation pertaining to Bofors with suspicious meaning. Maybe this was just another example of Rajiv being a decent man in an indecent business. Faced with a problem of wrongdoing, he knew what he must do: he must stand by his friends, as his public school background dictated. In politics, however, the correct approach was to create a scapegoat and then distance yourself from him. Bofors could have been tidied away in this time-honored fashion, but Rajiv had no idea how to operate at this political level. As he wrote to Priyanka at one time, "The real world is quite a jungle, but even the laws of the jungle don't hold when you are in public life."[13]

As usual in India, there were large-scale problems the government could not control, but simply had to manage. The management of the 1987–88 drought, which affected 258 million people and their cattle, was described by Rajiv as the major challenge of his prime ministership. The crisis was successfully overcome, with no recourse to imported food grain, and for the first time the nation emerged from a drought with a positive rate of growth. Rajiv said, "There have been only two droughts as bad as this in recorded history. But nobody has died, nobody has starved, and we have not had to go running for grain from other countries."[14]

Near the end of 1988 a number of opposition parties, including V. P. Singh's Jan Morcha, came together to form the Janata Dal, its name a reminder of the Janata Party of 1977–79 which had ousted Indira. The new party hoped to repeat the trick on Rajiv under V. P. Singh, who now became the principal opposition leader and made exposure of corruption his main platform.

The departure of such close colleagues as Arun Nehru, Arun Singh and V. P. Singh from the Prime Minister's political circle by no means indicated a change in Rajiv's general style. He was constantly reshuffling his Cabinet, making almost thirty changes in five years, which meant ministers never had an opportunity to settle into a portfolio. Hiring and firing ministers was a rather crude demonstration of political power, which a more experienced leader would have used in the last instance, not the first. Under the pressure of office, the Nehru trait of bad temper began to show in Rajiv: he sometimes publicly rebuked ministers, and once removed a security officer who told him not to drive too fast because he was outpacing his security escort.

In another field, that of inter-communal conflict, what was described as Rajiv's "rule of error" had been continuing with potentially disastrous results in response to the Shah Bano case. In this civil action the Supreme Court had sanctioned a maintenance payment to a divorced Muslim woman beyond the period specified by Muslim law. This brought Rajiv's government right up against the fault line in Indian civic life: the point at which civil law and religious law touched. Muslims had their own personal law (*shariat*, in this case) for matters of religion and family, which applied to Muslims alone. Orthodox Muslims argued that civil law should not interfere (and certainly could not take precedence over) the law of God. A complication of the Shah Bano case was that some progressive Muslims argued that the Supreme Court decision—to award the seventy-three-year-old divorcee a sum of 500 rupees a month from her former husband—was entirely in accordance with the *shariah*. Thus there was a conflict between orthodox and progressive Muslims within their own community, and a further conflict with secular Muslims who considered that the Supreme Court of India should be the final arbitrator.

This situation resurrected an old problem—that India, under her constitution, was supposed to develop a common civil code. It fell to Rajiv's unpracticed hands to mold a workable compromise from such an uninviting confusion of values. Initially, he opposed any change in the law, but then, after consultation with prominent Muslim leaders, backed the Muslim Women (Protection of Rights on Divorce) Bill to exclude Muslim women from the provisions of Indian law under which the Shah Bano award had been made. This had been introduced as a private member's bill in February 1986 and was then adopted by the government. Thus, in supposedly secular India, a section of the population was being denied the protection of the law solely because of its religion. This prompted the departure of Rajiv's Muslim minister of state, Arif Mohammed Khan, who was angry at the appeasement of fundamentalist Muslims and at the Prime Minister's about-face; he later joined the Janata Dal.

Rajiv may have wanted to halt Congress's declining electoral fortunes by solidifying the Muslim vote which was traditionally pro-Congress. If this was so, it was the most shortsighted and foolish of all his actions. By abrogating the principle of equality before the law and making concessions to a religious minority, he left the stage wide open for every other religious body to demand separate treatment. This was most important in dealing with the volatile Hindu majority, some members of which were now agitating with renewed militancy for a return to the Rama Raj, the legendary Hindu golden age. This fabled time, celebrated in the *Ramayana*, was ruled by the god Ram, whose birthplace was said to be in the town of Ayodhya in Uttar Pradesh.

It was said (in a claim disputed by Muslims) that the Mogul emperor Babur had demolished the temple which stood on Ram's birthplace to erect a mosque in 1528. The Ayodhya mosque was closed by the courts in 1949, soon after partition, amid disturbances caused by Hindus who wished to repossess the building as a place of worship. Now, at the same time as the Muslim Women Bill was being considered, the smoldering Ayodhya dispute flared up again. In February 1986 a Hindu petition was granted to have the shrine reopened. In response to this, Muslims joined forces nationally to recover control of the mosque, and in March 1987 organized a demonstration of some 300,000 co-religionists in New Delhi. The Hindus wanting to take possession of Ayodhya themselves now started having larger and larger prayer meetings in the region, which soon became politicized by Hindu chauvinist leaders.

Rajiv was monitoring these religious events from their early stages. According to some, Congress Party bosses had targeted Ayodhya as a concession to the Hindus in recompense for the Muslim Women Bill, which had been a concession to the Muslims. This way, it was believed, the level of Hindu and Muslim votes could be maintained. Rajiv certainly changed his position on Muslim women: at first he was not in favor of a change in the law, but later he was. Arun Nehru, internal security minister at the time the dispute flared up, said: "He just reversed his stand. He left everybody in the lurch. When the matter was discussed in Cabinet, all the senior members, not knowing the Prime Minister's mind, just kept quiet. I kept saying, 'We have to take a decision either way.' As internal security minister my concern was not whether it was right or wrong, but what was happening on the streets in India. But not a single minister would give an opinion. They all blamed Rajiv for it but they all had an opportunity and nobody expressed an opinion."[15] There was evidently some murky plotting going on, but Arun Nehru was soon to lose his ministerial responsibility, so he did not preside over the Ayodhya dispute's progression into open violence.

The legalistic religious disputes seemed to trigger off apparently unrelated incidents of inter-communal violence. The most serious of these, early in 1987, took place in Meerut, north of Delhi, where a land dispute led to arson and killings. The Provincial Armed Constabulary were sent in, and were said to have been themselves responsible for further massacres. Rajiv visited the city, but did not insist that the guilty were brought to justice, thus conveying the impression (as it had been over the massacre of Sikhs following Indira's death) that Hindus could riot against religious minorities with impunity.

This inter-communal violence was accompanied by an explosive growth of the Bharatiya Janata Party (the Indian People's Party, always called the BJP), a Hindu right-wing extremist party which had been formed from the ruins of earlier parties which had broken up in squabbling prior to Indira's return to power. Now with a credible leadership, it was eroding Rajiv's electoral support from the right, just as the Janata Dal was doing from the left.

Short of ideas to appeal to the electorate, Rajiv had staked his fortunes on the *panchayati raj* proposals which he had toured the country promoting. Effectively, this would create a lower tier of government at village level (another proposal did something similar for towns). He explained that this proposal was a means of increasing representation, where currently in both houses of parliament and all the state legislatures some 6000 people represented a population of nearly 800 million. As a result, he said, "The gap has been occupied by the power brokers, the middlemen, the vested interests. For the minutest municipal function, the people have had to run around finding persons with the right connections who would intercede for them with the distant sources of power."[16] This problem, he promised, would be resolved by *panchayat* legislation. In parliament, however, enthusiasm for the plan was limited. The legislation sailed through the Lok Sabha, where the Opposition were boycotting the proceedings, but failed in the Rajya Sabha by three votes. Rajiv decided to call an election for the end of November, when he would have completed all but seven weeks of his five-year term.

Within days of the elections being announced, horrific violence returned on a scale not seen since partition: more than 1000 Muslims were killed and 25,000 left homeless in frenzied communal rioting of sickening ferocity in the Bhagalpur district of Bihar. Shops were looted and burned, women raped, mosques desecrated, whole families hacked to death and their bodies thrown down wells. The authorities were unable, or perhaps unwilling, to reassert control, but eventually, after days of mounting violence, the army was sent in to restore order—no easy task. In one well-recorded incident, the army entrusted 100 Muslim survivors to the local police while they went for supplies. When the army returned the next morning, every one of them had been butchered.[17]

How did such terrible things happen in a democracy with a good communications network? The pattern of these events is that the killings would start sporadically and perhaps in isolated places, the state hoping that the local police could deal with the problem and that it would die down. Some senior local figure should have taken the initiative, but in India the state governor cannot act without the state's chief minister, and the chief minister is unwilling to act without the agreement of the national Prime Minister, who in this case was busy on the campaign trail and may not have had the explosive nature of the events explained to him adequately in the first dispatches.

It was also said that Rajiv would not act sooner because he would alienate the Hindus by taking action, and frightening the Muslims would lead them to stay with their natural protector, the Congress Party, so inaction kept the votes of both. V. P. Singh certainly blamed Rajiv's government for the scale of the Bhagalpur atrocities, for failing to send in the troops soon enough and for stimulating the Ayodhya dispute to appease the Hindu vote. This last charge was one which had some merit: in a move to heighten the dispute, every village in India was invited by Ayodhya campaigners to send a consecrated brick to Ayodhya to be used to build the new temple to Ram. The Uttar Pradesh High Court had ruled against the building of a new temple on the disputed ground currently occupied by the mosque, but late in the election campaign the government had allowed five foundation bricks to be laid. This happened with great ceremony and celebration on the Hindu side and with grief among the Muslims. The intensifying dispute was blamed for the renewal of inter-communal violence such as that at Bhagalpur. Whether or not V. P. Singh was justified in blaming Rajiv, the Opposition leader would soon find out what it was like to rule divided, sectarian India.

The election campaign ground relentlessly on, with Rajiv, often accompanied by Rahul, appearing to crowd after crowd. Rajiv was no longer the raw politician of five years before, embarrassed by the chanting and the praise: now he was irritated, if anything, with the incessant pressure of decision-making and the need to get to the next location. Observers noted that he was moody and impatient, constantly on the brink of losing his temper. One compared the Rajiv of 1984 with the man of 1989: "The open, handsome face was now creased with age and worry, the gait was slower, the voice less firm."[18]

By contrast, Maneka Gandhi was storming through the neighboring constituency of Philibhit, addressing more than 100 meetings a week. She had become a general secretary of Janata Dal and, as a prolific newspaper columnist, had become a forceful advocate of environmental issues. *India Today* described her campaigning style as "the real Maneka: mature, confident, a tireless campaigner who knows exactly how to reach the rural heart. Her saris are in her party colors of green and saffron and her head is constantly covered; the perfect image of a demure but determined widow."[19] Her slogan was on every wall and mud hut: "The storm of the revolution: Maneka Gandhi." Some slogans were even more dramatic: "Indira's brave daughter-in-law will give her blood for the nation"; so being a daughter-in-law of the Nehru dynasty automatically gave her status as a prospective martyr.

Congress also took full advantage of their leader's dynastic pedigree, playing up the fact that the centenary of Jawaharlal's birth and the seventy-second anniversary of Indira's fell within the campaigning period. It was to no avail; Rajiv knew he would lose hundreds of Congress seats and could do nothing about it. No sacrifice would produce a better result; the die was cast.

Polling was on November 22 and 24, 1989, with the results announced four days later. Rajiv was re-elected in Amethi, and Congress won 197 out of 517 seats, making it the largest single party. The next largest was V. P. Singh's Janata Dal, with 144 seats; the BJP had eighty-six and the left-wing parties fifty-one. This meant Singh could command a majority only if he went into government backed by the Hindu chauvinists. In the event, he was prepared to rule with the government, supported by the left and the BJP from outside.

As leader of the party with the largest number of seats, Rajiv had a right to attempt to form a government, but he gave up his claim: he knew he did not have enough support in the minority parties to do so. It would be better for him to stay outside while the governing coalition fell apart and he worked on rejuvenating Congress. He was not unhappy to let V. P. Singh "do the worrying for a while," as he put it.[20] Rajiv resigned on November 29, 1989, saying, "In all humility we accept the people's verdict. We pledge to offer constructive support to the new government."[21] In a later broadcast he said, "I wish to thank the people of India for the affection they have showered upon me in such abundance,"[22] thus echoing the words of his grandfather's last will and testament—"the affection of all classes of the Indian people has come to me in such abundant measure that I have been overwhelmed by it."[23] It was more valedictory than he thought, for Rajiv's own tryst with destiny approached.

V. P. Singh had a far from easy passage. He was opposed for the top post by Chandra Shekhar, formerly president of the Janata Party, which had ruled in the 1977–79 period after the emergency. Arun Nehru performed his role as kingmaker again, and engineered V. P. Singh's triumph, but Chandra Shekhar never accepted V. P. Singh as leader. Several members of V. P. Singh's government had already played a part in the story of the Nehru dynasty: Arun Nehru, who became minister for commerce and tourism; George Fernandes, the railway workers' leader who had been such an opponent of Indira, became minister for railways; and Maneka Gandhi, who became minister of the environment and forests: her persistence had paid off.

Rajiv was re-elected leader of the Congress Party in parliament and took up the unaccustomed role of leader of the Opposition. Sonia had by now reconciled herself to his political work, though right up to November 1990 a journalist thought it proper to ask Rajiv, "Have you finally accepted politics as a full-time profession?" Rajiv answered in good humor, "Yes, only sometimes I feel like taking a break. That, I guess, is only human."[24]

Rajiv made light of the incessant security and constant threats to his life: "Living under terrorist threat or threat of death has never really bothered me; I've not let it interfere with my functioning or my thinking or put any pressure on me. Yes, it has caused inconvenience because of the security arrangements and other problems . . . but if it comes to having to die for what you believe in—I don't hesitate."[25]

Sonia and Priyanka had largely looked after the Amethi constituency, Sonia wearing a sari and speaking Hindi, "a daughter of Italy but a daughter-in-law of Amethi," while Rajiv had toured the country, often with Rahul. Now they were all happy to have their father home again. Rahul had been at St. Stephen's College in Delhi and, in 1990, would leave for Harvard, Massachusetts; after three generations of Nehrus attending Oxford or Cambridge, the family was now looking to the United States, the current world power, to educate its children. Priyanka was studying psychology at Jesus and Mary College in Delhi. Rajiv very much regretted the isolated conditions in which the children had been obliged to live. "This is the period in your life when you should have been getting about, meeting others your age, finding out

307

about the world as it really is," he lamented in a letter to them both.[26] The workload as leader of the Opposition was lighter than he had become used to and he would try to keep the afternoons free as "family time." He started to enjoy family life again, rediscovering the pleasures of having uninterrupted meals, watching video movies and listening to music. In early February the family moved out of the residence Rajiv had as prime minister, to a house at 10 Janpath.

Rajiv and Sonia remained romantically in love. Rajiv wrote to Sonia on her birthday in December 1990 "[To Sonia] who time never changes, who is even lovelier today than when I first saw her sitting back in the corner upstairs in the Varsity—on that beautiful day . . ."[27] They spent their wedding anniversary, February 25, 1991, in Tehran, Iran, where Sonia accompanied him on an official visit. She remembered fondly that they dined out at a restaurant, something they had not been able to do for many years. Rajiv had written asking her to come on this trip: "I feel like . . . [being] with you, only you and I, the two of us alone, without two hundred people always about us."[28]

Meanwhile, in the halls of government, V. P. Singh found he had no magic solutions to the problems with which Rajiv had grappled. When V. P. Singh took power, the Indian Peace-Keeping Force was withdrawn from Sri Lanka. Soon secessionist forces in Tamil Nadu, Kashmir, Punjab and Assam were gaining the upper hand. In Ayodhya, an already difficult situation was becoming disastrous, and far from calming the situation, the government added further fuel to the fire. This came in the form of a report by the Mandal Commission, which had been set up more than ten years previously by the old Janata Party. The Commission had attempted to deal with the problem of discrimination based on caste, which meant that people from lower castes or outside caste were always discriminated against in education and employment. Quotas had been set up by Jawaharlal in the 1950s, and the Mandal Commission had recommended extending these, but no action was taken by Indira or Rajiv. The problem was that what had been achievable in the idealistic, progressive India of Jawaharlal Nehru was no longer feasible in the increasingly turbulent nation of the 1980s and 1990s. There were demonstrations at the proposal to implement the Mandal Commission Report, where feelings ran so high that a number of upper-caste people immolated themselves in protest, some of them on the contested land of Ayodhya.

The BJP needed a spectacular response to this, so they launched a procession across the nation to galvanize Hindu chauvinist passions. This was a *rath yatra*, literally a chariot journey, where the images of deities would be carried by chariot, surrounded by celebratory crowds. In a deliberately confrontational move, they launched their procession from a temple in Gujarat, declaring their aim to march to Ayodhya and start building a temple next to the mosque.

The *rath yatra* raised the temperature of communal passions to boiling point and obliged the government to take action. V. P. Singh had the *rath yatra* interrupted in Bihar, before it reached its destination. In retaliation, on October 30, 1990 thousands of "volunteers" from the BJP stormed the Ayodhya mosque and twelve died in clashes with the police and army. The BJP now withdrew support from V. P. Singh's government, leaving parliament in roughly the situation it had been in the previous year: Congress was the largest party, but a government could be formed only via coalitions with other parties. Rajiv was now back in the driving seat. Chandra Shekhar, formerly V. P. Singh's rival for the premiership, made a visit to Rajiv at home on November 6, 1990, and after talking for forty minutes announced to reporters that they had agreed to work together. Rajiv did not want another election: Congress was not ready for it and would probably do no better than it had in 1989.

Only the day before, V. P. Singh had expelled thirty-five rebels from Janata Dal, but it was too late. On November 7, his government was defeated in a vote of confidence motion. His resignation letter to the President that night was closely followed by Chandra Shekhar's letter offering to form a government. Rajiv said Congress would support Chandra Shekhar from outside, which effectively gave him control over the government without having to take responsibility for it. Shekhar still had responsibility for his Cabinet, however, and he retained Maneka as a minister, despite Rajiv's disapproval. Throughout Chandra Shekhar's prime ministership, Rajiv sent him written comments on his performance, which Shekhar found less than helpful.

When the final split came, it was over intrusions into Rajiv's precious family space. He had a small farm in Haryana, not far from Delhi, where he would relax with Sonia and the children. It was discovered that two constables of the Haryana government were keeping Rajiv's residence under surveillance. Rajiv called Chandra Shekhar

309

and demanded not only the removal of the surveillance team, but the dismissal of the Haryana chief minister, the home minister and the party functionary, Om Prakash Chautala, who was apparently responsible for posting the surveillance officers.

Shekhar sympathized, but promised only an inquiry into the matter. Rajiv was angry and demanded immediate action against the men responsible "for the outrage." He later explained, "The question was trust. We put our faith in Mr. Chandra Shekhar. And we supported his government. . . . We found that we are not trusted and two constables are put to watch on us. When we tried to find out what is going on, we were told that the constables were posted by Mr. Om Prakash Chautala and that is why I asked Mr. Chandra Shekhar that he should take some action."[29]

There was no right course for Chandra Shekhar. He would foment disunity in his own party if he sacked functionaries or serving ministers at the behest of the leader of Congress; on the other hand, he would lose his ability to control parliament if Rajiv withdrew his support. Rajiv denied he had ever withdrawn support, though a non-negotiable demand that Chandra Shekhar drop some of his supporters does seem a *de facto* withdrawal of support. Rather than go into open opposition, Rajiv declared that Congress would boycott parliament, at which Shekhar tendered his resignation to the President, after four months as prime minister.

Chandra Shekhar stayed on as head of a caretaker government while the election commission selected polling dates, which were to be May 20, 23 and 26. Rajiv pinpointed the BJP as his major electoral enemy, given that the Janata Dal had been split and that the left never received more than a limited number of seats.

The country was in poor shape, the sort of condition which beckoned for an opposition party to take over: the economy was ailing, partly because the impending Gulf War had pushed up the price of oil; secessionist violence and law and order problems had continued unabated. Rajiv proposed a program based on government stability, law and order and economic reform, including privatization and the relaxing of controls on industry.

Regarding the mismanagement of affairs in Congress, T. N. Kaul said he asked Rajiv if he were going to fulfill the promises he made at the 1985 Bombay Congress and get rid of the power brokers. "He said to me,

'Uncle, I assure you that if I am returned to power I will do so this time, I have learned from my mistakes.'"[30] Rajiv also made up with Arun Nehru after their disagreements. His cousin remembered, "He said that we were both young and both wanted to go full steam ahead and neither of us wanted to back off." They did not become political allies again, but agreed not to fight between themselves. "For all his faults, I loved Rajiv Gandhi," said Nehru. "He was family and I couldn't stand for anyone else to say things about him."[31] Journalist Inder Malhotra also detected changes in Rajiv. He said, "The difference between Indira Gandhi's second coming and what looked to be Rajiv's second coming was that Rajiv had spent those years out of power in very genuine introspection and in discussion. Mrs. Gandhi didn't talk very much, didn't ask her friends, 'Where did I go wrong?' She just said that everybody else was wrong and she was right, and that she was being maligned. Whereas Rajiv knew that he had goofed. He was trying to correct himself and do things in a way that would redeem him."[32]

Rajiv started electioneering on May 1, 1991 with a visit to Amethi in the company of Sonia, descending from the sky in a small propeller aircraft which he piloted himself. In the campaign Rajiv was to travel to 600 national and state constituencies by plane, helicopter and car. Despite his position as a target for terrorists, his specially trained security guards had been withdrawn by the new government and replaced by forces not specially trained. Sonia said that every day brought new examples of how lightly Rajiv's security was viewed and how carelessly it was handled. Sonia and Priyanka would see him off on a tour accompanied by just one security officer. The security officer would be on a roster, but one of his regular officers, Sub-inspector Pradip Gupta, said, "If something happens to Rajivji, it will only be over my dead body."[33] Rahul was so concerned that he insisted on returning from Harvard at the end of March 1991 for his Easter break and accompanying his father on a tour to Bihar. He was appalled at the lack of elementary security, and told Sonia if something was not done, he would soon be back for his father's funeral.[34]

Lack of government support for higher level security was not the only problem, however: Rajiv had been told he had lost the last election because he failed to maintain contact with the people. It was imperative he put across the image of an accessible politician. His success in doing so was noted by the BBC reporter Brian Baron, who followed Rajiv on the campaign trail: "The former prime minister has a new, relaxed image, forgoing heavy security, projecting himself as a man of the people."[35] *India Today*, not generally a Rajiv supporter, remarked, "The image of the happy warrior plunging through the crowds, aware that he had lost touch with them and was now eagerly striving to show them he still greatly cared, was once again in clear evidence."[36] Ironically, Rajiv never seemed happier or more confident as a politician, electioneering, receiving garlands and meeting the people, than he did on this last trip.

Rajiv would try to see to it that the crowds could get to him, and even engaged in a pantomime with the police, which happened so often it was obviously an intentional piece of show. He would arrive at a location and crowds would mob his jeep; the police would push them back and Rajiv would become angry that the police were keeping the people from him and would assail them with blows while the crowd would clap and cheer. There were times when he had no security personnel at all with him in his car, as his personal security officers were busy taking part in the show and chasing away local policemen. Asked about the risks he was taking in campaigning, Rajiv said, "I can't distrust the common man. How long can I keep worrying about these things? I have to live life."[37]

On April 28 Sonia went canvassing in Amethi, where Priyanka later joined her. Rajiv sent her a rose with a message of love; it was going to be the longest stretch of time away from each other in twenty-three years. Sonia and Priyanka returned home on May 17 and waited for Rajiv to join them the following day. When he did, Sonia was shocked to see him: "He was exhausted. He could barely walk or speak. He had not slept or eaten properly for weeks. He had been campaigning an average of twenty to twenty-two hours a day. His hands and arms were badly scratched and swollen. His body was bruised and aching. Hundreds and thousands of well-wishers wanted to touch him, to shake his hands, to give him a brotherly hug or an affectionate thump on his back. It broke my heart to see him in that state."[38]

They chatted about their own experiences campaigning, and Rajiv had the rare luxury of five hours' sleep, leaving early the next morning for Bhopal. He returned that night, dead tired but relieved the campaign was drawing to a close. They were looking forward to all being together again when Rahul came home for his summer break on May 23.

On the morning of May 20, Rajiv and Sonia drove to the polling booth at 7:30 A.M. to cast their votes. He laughed when she told him she nearly panicked when she at first failed to find the Congress Party symbol on the huge ballot paper and he had been in danger of losing her vote. That afternoon, when his helicopter touched down for him to change transport and board a plane for Orissa, he took the opportunity to rush home for a few more moments with Sonia. He spoke briefly on the telephone to Rahul in the United States, said goodbye to Priyanka, and left promising to be back in two days. Sonia watched him, peeping from behind a curtain until he disappeared from view.

The last pictures show him standing up in his white Land Rover amid a sea of outstretched hands, or being helped through the throng by Pradip Gupta, his lone security officer. Rajiv spent the day of May 2, electioneering in Orissa, Andhra Pradesh and Tamil Nadu. His last engagement was to be at a small town between Madras and Kanchipuram, called Sriperumbudur. He almost failed to make it because the airport at his location in Andhra Pradesh did not have night flight facilities and visibility was becoming a problem. Plans were changed for Rajiv to fly to Madras, the capital of Tamil Nadu, the following morning and address the Sriperumbudur meeting the following afternoon, or perhaps cancel the engagement altogether. As they were driving back, however, a call came to say that visibility had improved and it was safe to take off, so Rajiv and his aides took the plane. They landed in Madras at 8:30 P.M., only an hour late (which was early, in terms of campaign time), and Rajiv gave a press conference at the airport. At 9 P.M. his motorcade started out to the quiet temple town of Sriperumbudur.

The crowd was good-naturedly watching a Tamil Nadu film music troupe, the sort of entertainment political organizers staged to make rallies colorful, entertaining events because important speakers almost never arrived on time. Firecrackers heralded Rajiv's arrival, as he garlanded a statue of Indira and stepped through the crowd on a red carpet laid over the mud track. His campaigning style, now he was at home with the crowds, was described by a journalist: "Rajiv the Indefatigable, the man who received his energy—and his power—from the people. Throughout his tortuous campaign—sleeping barely a couple of hours a day—Rajiv was like a man reborn. Laughing and joking with the crowds, playfully throwing garlands at women, scolding his security for keeping the crowds at bay, Rajiv seemed to have rediscovered his place in the sun . . . Shorn of the sycophants and the cliques and the courtiers, Rajiv was a man transformed. A man of the people."[39]

One of the people was a short, dark, bespectacled woman in her mid-thirties called Dhanu. She was wearing an orange "punjabi suit" consisting of a long shirt with trousers, rather unusual for a southern Indian woman, though some had taken to wearing such northern dress instead of a sari. She looked stout, or perhaps pregnant. No one would have suspected that her girth was made up of a denim vest, a nine-volt battery, a detonating switch and a series of six grenades with steel pellets molded into the plastic explosive.

As Rajiv started walking towards the dais where he was to speak, admirers embraced him, patted him and placed shawls around him. He put his hand affectionately on the shoulder of a fifteen-year-old girl, Kokila, the daughter of a party functionary, who recited a poem written in his honor. Dhanu, who was holding a garland, squeezed behind Kokila. When the girl finished her poem, the assassin moved towards Rajiv with her garland, but a woman police officer, Anusuya, put her hand up to stop her progress. Rajiv smiled at the policewoman. "Let everyone have a turn," he said. "Don't worry, relax." Anusuya moved back, in a gesture which saved her life, and Dhanu moved forward to place a 65-rupee garland of sandalwood shavings shaped into flowers around Rajiv's neck. He smiled as he took it off to hand it to a Congress worker beside him, and Dhanu stooped to touch his feet. He bent slightly, leaning over to lift her up. As he did so, her hand slipped to her waist and she pressed a toggle switch on her deadly belt.

Suman Dubey, Rajiv's aide, described the scene that followed: "Suddenly it looked like crackers were being burst where Rajiv was. When I turned I saw people fall apart in slow motion."[40] Barbara Crossette, a New York Times journalist who had been following Rajiv, said, "There was a very intense explosion . . . a sort of burst of air and people falling around in a circle like the petals falling off a flower. I remember people's panicked fear all around me as the larger crowd from outside the center circle began to move in to see what had happened, and there was a hole where Rajiv Gandhi had apparently been."[41] The cruel fragments of the bomb had torn through the assassin, through Rajiv and through the pressing crowd, killing eighteen in all and wounding many others.

Everyone scattered in terror, including the police, expecting that this was one of a number of bombs. When the dust and smoke of the blast cleared, there was a peculiar scene of carnage: the dais, the welcoming banners and the fence were still standing as they should be; it was just the people who were blown to pieces.

Dubey recovered himself and rushed towards the dais: "I was looking for white, as Rajiv wears white," he said. "Most of what I saw was black, charred stuff, and I kept searching." Other Congress workers approached. They found Pradip Gupta, Rajiv's security officer, still alive, lying on his back with his eyes open. Jayanti Natarajan, a Congress MP, asked him, "Are you all right?" and felt stupid because he so obviously was not. He died in seconds, as she watched. She saw a head on his knee and looked closer to see Rajiv's bald patch. He was bent over at an unnatural angle, still with some white clothes on, though others had been blown into rags; the familiar Lotto trainers were still on his feet. A Tamil Nadu Congress chief, G. K. Moopanar, tried to turn the body over "but I could not get a grip . . . my hand just went in."[42]

Rajiv had been literally eviscerated by the blast: his liver, kidneys and intestines had been blown out, his skull had been broken and his brain blown out. He had died instantly. As more people returned to the scene, help was given to the wounded, and what remained of Rajiv's body was picked up and placed in a police van which took it to the general hospital at Madras, where it was sutured into shape.

Within fifteen minutes of the blast, at 10:30 P.M., officials at Rajiv's home in Delhi were telephoned about the bomb explosion, but at that stage there was no confirmation of his death. Vincent George, Rajiv's secretary, told Sonia about the blast and she waited for further news. Soon after, to her stunned horror, she learned of Rajiv's death. Nineteen-year-old Priyanka immediately took control of the situation and refused everyone access to Sonia's room. She asked her father's old flying friend Satish Sharma and other aides who were present to make arrangements to fly her and her mother to Madras: they were going to be by the side of their beloved father and husband.

# EIGHTEEN

# SIFTING THROUGH
# THE FRAGMENTS

Events following Rajiv's assassination were to be different from those following his mother's. This time there would be no mas-sacres: around midnight a decision was taken to call in the army to maintain order, particularly in and around Delhi where the worst riots had taken place following Indira's death. As Sonia and Priyanka were boarding an Indian Air Force plane for Madras, a mob was already gathering outside the family home shouting slogans against V. P. Singh, Chandra Shekhar, the BJP and others. Photographers were attacked and the President's car was stoned, but the prompt action to bring in the security forces meant that the mood remained largely shocked dismay rather than riotous anger. Some damage to public property and that of political rivals took place, but deaths were kept to single figures.

A post-mortem was conducted on Rajiv's body, which was then sutured into some kind of shape at the Government General Hospital at Madras. It was taken to Meenambakkam airport in a wooden pack-ing case, but moved to a proper coffin before Sonia flew in from Delhi. She and Priyanka arrived in the early morning, clinging to each other, to be met by family friend Suman Dubey, who had been present at the blast and whose clothes were still smeared with Rajiv's blood. Sonia wept inconsolably as she lay a garland on Rajiv's coffin, and the plane took off for Delhi as the first rays of dawn broke over Madras. On the plane Priyanka, till then restrained in her grief, hugged her father's coffin and cried. During the flight Sonia noticed that Pradip Gupta's coffin, on the same flight, was bare, so she took some of the flowers from her husband's coffin and laid them on that of his bodyguard.

The plane was met in Delhi by the President and his wife, who laid wreaths on the coffin, which was taken by ambulance to the All India Institute of Medical Sciences. There doctors tried to reconstruct Rajiv's face with the help of plaster of Paris, but finally left it padded with cotton wool and bandages. Maneka arrived at the hospital with Feroze Varun, and tearfully said some words of condolence. From there the body went to 10 Janpath, where friends and family filed past, and finally to Teen Murti House, Rajiv's home as a child. His body lay in state here for two days, wrapped in the Indian flag, as the long line of mourners passed by. Journalist Vir Sanghvi summed up the general view when he said, "There was a great deal of sadness because even his political opponents could see that at the end of the day he was a decent human being."[1]

Sonia sat beside Rajiv's body, wincing each time the sheets were lifted to pack more ice around it: "She seemed to find peace only while sitting near the body," wrote an observer.[2] She did not eat for four days, and Priyanka took charge of arrangements, including meeting Rahul on his plane from the United States and overseeing the funeral plans until he was able to take over.

The tears of Congress party men dried quickly while they considered their future. The needed a leader who could win, who could capitalize on the inevitable sympathy vote for their dead leader. Operation Draft Sonia began within twenty-four hours of Rajiv's death. The Congress Working Committee met on the afternoon of May 22 and decided to call upon Sonia to become president of Congress, despite some reservations about such blatant "dynasticism." Congress workers gathered outside 10 Janpath and chanted "Save the country! Bring in Sonia Gandhi!" The party spokesman Pranab Mukherjee (the first man to approach Rajiv about taking over the premiership after his mother's death) was asked if Sonia had been consulted. "There is no question of her refusing," he said. "She is a party member and the decision will be communicated to her in due course."[3]

Sonia had always tried to distance herself from politics, despite her campaigning in the Amethi constituency. On May 23 she issued a letter saying she was "deeply touched" by the trust they had in her, but "The tragedy that has befallen my children and myself does not make it possible for me to accept the presidentship of the Congress Party."[4]

On May 24, three days after Rajiv's death, the cortège wound through Delhi's millions of mourners, past walls still covered with his smiling election posters, towards the cremation ground where the world's dignitaries waited. Sonia wore sunglasses to hide her tears, Priyanka's arms protectively encircling her. A helicopter flew low over the area, scattering rose petals while priests chanted Vedic mantras. Rahul poured oil on the body hidden within a mound of sandalwood logs, walked around it seven times and lit the pyre. As the flames leapt up, he stepped back to take his mother's hand.

The ashes were collected in an urn and taken in a white, open train carriage, accompanied by Sonia, Rahul and Priyanka, passing slowly through crowds of mourners on the journey to Allahabad. The urn was taken to Anand Bhavan, and then on to the confluence of the Ganges, the Yamuna and the mythical Saraswati, where Rahul performed the final rite of immersing the ashes.

Meanwhile police investigations continued and some of the more minor conspirators were arrested and interrogated. Now it was possible to piece the plot together and to understand the meticulous planning which had gone into Rajiv's assassination. The plan had been hatched deep in the jungles of northeast Sri Lanka, by V. Pirabhakaran, head of the LTTE or Tamil Tigers. He had summoned lieutenants skilled in subterfuge and bomb-making, and they had recruited Tamil activists in Madras—local Tamils were needed as the accents of Sri Lankans would give them away. There was the usual conspirators' network of knowledge, uncertainty and coercion: those running the safe houses knew only that they were working for the Tamil cause; others closer to the center knew their mission was to assassinate a politician "hostile to the LTTE cause"; only those at the center of the conspiracy knew Rajiv was the target.

The planning took in three rehearsals so that everyone knew his or her role: one in Madras, where Rajiv spoke on April 18; one on May 8, when V. P. Singh was used as a stand-in for the target; and a third, again with V. P. Singh, when the assassin garlanded him and touched his feet just as she would Rajiv's nine days later.

The motive for the assassination was largely revenge against Indian involvement in Sri Lankan peace-keeping, which had eventually become a measure of containment against the Tamil Tigers. The success of the plot indicated the reach and abilities of the Tigers, creating the dynamic image necessary for a successful terrorist group. In practical terms the removal of Rajiv also ruled out his returning to power, which Pirabhakaran feared would mean a return to direct Indian military involvement in Sri Lanka to the detriment of the Tamil Tigers. Within a few years, most of those involved in the murder were captured and awaiting trial, or had killed themselves at the point of capture, in time-honored Tamil tradition. Pirabhakaran, however, continued to evade capture in the jungles of northern Sri Lanka. Sonia felt that Pirabhakaran's continued liberty was evidence that the quest for Rajiv's killers was not being taken seriously enough. Political scientist James Manor called on Sonia some two years after Rajiv's death and found her still "fragile and vulnerable" and very naïve politically. Learning that Professor Manor was a Sri Lankan specialist, she asked why the government did not just go in and arrest Pirabhakaran: "It was surprising to her to learn from me that Pirabhakaran is rather a difficult fellow to catch."[5] The image of Sonia believing that a major terrorist could be arrested, as if the police could march into a terrorist organization's head office and read the man his rights is sad, but also indicates the sort of people she had around her, who played on her fears to ensure their own continued access to her. As well as genuine friends, Sonia retained the services and advice of numerous second-raters, whose principal merit was loyalty to the family.

Even when Rajiv was alive, Sonia had resisted calls to run for a seat in parliament. She was now urged to run for Amethi, and the seat was held vacant in the expectation that she might. It was not an outlandish suggestion: she had a genuine and long-lasting love of Amethi's people. She had spent many long days helping the local women and children and providing medicines for them; she knew many of them by name (everyone comments on Sonia's excellent memory). To Congress Party Leaders, moreover, there was the indubitable advantage that she would win the seat and thus continue the noble tradition of linking the Nehru-Gandhi name with the party.

Sonia continued to receive political visitors after Rajiv's death. Initially they called to give condolences. As an *India Today* reporter remarked, "Barely had Sonia reached home after the funeral when people started following her there, and the heads of states started calling her saying they wanted to pay their condolences in person . . . Ironically, it is the visitors who invariably break down while recounting their memories of Rajiv Gandhi. Sonia, however, is stoic."[6] She wrote many letters of thanks for the thousands of condolence messages in her own hand.

Sonia remained keeper of the Nehru-Gandhi flame—and the archive. In 1989 she had published her edited version of a first volume of letters between Jawaharlal and Indira spanning 1922 to 1939, entitled *Freedom's Daughter*. A second volume, *Two Alone, Two*

*Together,* covering the years 1940 to 1964, was published in 1992. She published a pictorial biography of her husband, called simply *Rajiv,* in 1992, and a compilation of his pictures, called *Rajiv's Eye,* in 1995. With probably conscious symbolism, while Maneka's pictorial biography of Sanjay had been bound in black, Sonia's of Rajiv was bound in pure white.

Sonia has been eager to preserve the memory of Rajiv, to give herself a worthwhile occupation which relates to her dead husband and to preserve her own center of power which leaves the Congress Party indebted to her. One reason for this is that she and her children still require a massive level of security. Home at 10 Janpath is like a fortress: only the resources of the state could maintain such a high level of protection. Rajiv's chair in his study is left untouched, but draped in the Indian flag which had been used to cover his body before cremation.

Anand Bhavan in Allahabad is a museum to Motilal and the Nehru dynasty in general. Teen Murti House, Jawaharlal's home as prime minister, is a museum to him, and 1 Safdarjung Road is a museum to Indira, displaying personal possessions, including the bloody sari from her assassination. The rooms Rajiv formerly occupied have been given over to a museum in his memory.

The most grandiose of the monuments to Rajiv, the Rajiv Gandhi Foundation, was set up in June 1991, exactly one month after his death, its objective being to promote the economic and social ideas he and Sonia shared. A grant of 100 million rupees was given by the government in August 1991, but voluntary donations, particularly from big business organizations eager to stay in with Congress, have immensely swelled the coffers and given Sonia enormous powers of patronage. The foundation helps mainly women and children in India and is involved in literacy, health, science and technology programs. Another organization, the Rajiv Gandhi Institute for Contemporary Studies, founded in 1992, has a more international flavor, hosting conferences and seminars involving visitors from around the world. Sonia also exerts influence through many other bodies, such as the Indira Gandhi Memorial Trust and the Jawaharlal Nehru Memorial Fund.

Initially Sonia would listen but not speak to callers who made appointments to talk about non-political subjects, but only on two days a week. As the years passed, she was prepared to see people every day, and eventually to discuss every subject: people would talk to her about problems in the country and the party, and ask her help in getting nomination to political office. By 1995 she was reported as asking questions of these callers, questions which showed she was well informed about political and party issues. Sonia could enter the political fray with immense success, but she would open herself up to questions from the Opposition, probably about such scandals as Bofors, which were never entirely forgotten on the Indian political scene. As the wise widow in command of the Nehru-Gandhi name and resources, she has unassailable power which she has learned to use with discretion. "The Sonia Factor" is a potent force in Indian politics. Particularly as the years have passed, Sonia has been prepared to attend essentially political meetings organized by Congress (I) but designed to keep Rajiv's memory alive. She only rarely speaks in public, and has never given a media interview. Her mere presence on the dais, however, lends support to the Congress faction, which in its turn promotes her interests.

Sonia's mission as priestess of the Nehru–Gandhi dynasty is a contradiction of her detestation of the politics which took away the people she loved: for the dynasty existed only as a political force. They were politicians or they were nothing. With the exception of Motilal, who was a superlative lawyer, and Rajiv, who was an accomplished pilot, the Nehru-Gandhis had no skill at anything except politics and could not have earned a living any other way.

Without active members of the family, Indian politics have continued in rather a dry fashion. The former home minister Narasimha Rao took over after the election, in which a sympathy vote guaranteed a Congress win. He maintained a few of the more able "family loyalists" but quietly dropped most of the second-raters who had surrounded Indira then Rajiv.

The only Gandhi still in the running was Maneka, but for the second time in her political career she failed to win an election on the wave of sympathy for a Gandhi assassinated just before the polls. True to form, she stayed in the race, continuing to publish books and articles on animal rights issues and to campaign for such things as the closure of a Delhi slaughter house, which was said to be both inhumane and insanitary. In the 1996 elections she was back, and was again made a minister of state for the environment, but political pressure from her enemies on the weak minority government which was ruling only with the consent of Congress forced the Prime Minister to drop her days after her appointment. She remains in the Lok Sabha as an extremely vocal backbench MP. She is the only prominent member of the Nehru-Gandhi dynasty still in parliament and still ambitious for office.

Priyanka Gandhi was the member of the younger generation always tipped for a political career. "Priyanka is strong-willed, like my mother," said Rajiv.[7] Once, when she was a small child, he ordered her to stand in the corner until she had modified her behavior. She stood there for two hours until he relented and let her go. Even as a teenager, it was remarked that Priyanka had developed fine political instincts, and those who saw her campaigning in Amethi for her father "spotted in her shades of the young Indira Gandhi."[8] In February 1997 Priyanka married Punjabi costume jeweler Robert Vadra. She wore the same pale pink cotton sari woven from cloth spun by Jawaharlal in prison, a sari worn by Indira and Sonia on their wedding days.

As yet Priyanka, twenty-five at the time of her wedding, has shown no explicit intention of entering politics. However, being a "late starter" in politics is not unusual for a Nehru-Gandhi: Motilal was twenty-seven before he attended his first Congress Meeting; Jawaharlal was thirty when he committed himself politically; Indira was forty-two when she first became Congress president in 1959; and Rajiv was thirty-six when he was ushered into politics at Sanjay's death. Sanjay had meddled in politics for years but did not run for election until 1980, when he was thirty-four.

Speculation on the future of the young Gandhis had best remain the preserve of gossip columnists. Rahul, Priyanka and Feroze Varun Gandhi have never sought publicity and deserve to be left to live in peace until they do.

It could reasonably be asked how much continuity there was in the Nehru-Gandhi dynasty. Indira certainly did not maintain her father's policies, in relation either to the economy of the country or the running of the Congress Party. There was greater, but hardly all-encompassing, continuity between Rajiv and his mother.

A long view shows not only how remarkable the family was, but also how true to form: Motilal had the bumptious confidence of a self-made man; Jawaharlal the effortless superiority of an only son who never wanted for anything; Indira the lifelong insecurity of a disturbed childhood and the emotional immaturity mixed with social concern common in an only child. Sanjay was the spoiled younger son, Rajiv the steadfast family man.

Observing the family through this troubled century shows not only how exceptional they are as a family, but how typical: Indira Gandhi's long-standing resentment of the aunt who treated her mother shabbily; Jawaharlal's hostility towards his daughter's husband; Indira's hatred of the woman her favorite son married: these are not the stuff of greatness but of the commonplace, and therefore one of the appealing aspects of the Nehru-Gandhi dynasty. Such family dramas are played out in every home, but the Nehru-Gandhis also played them out on the world stage among people who held the destiny of the largest democracy ever seen.

While terrible things happened to the family, they were in a literally tragic sense the architects of their own downfall. Their personalities and sense of destiny before the nation compelled them onwards into disaster. Jawaharlal's urbane, trusting nature led him to the conceit of believing in the Chinese who he had wooed, and to putting his friendship for Krishna Menon before the welfare of the nation. Sanjay's arrogance and recklessness caused both his political downfall and his death in an accident which would have been avoided in a more cautious man. Indira's political machinations to promote Sikh nationalism for the short-term benefit of Congress created a monster which destroyed her in a hail of bullets. Her similar activities to promote Sri Lankan guerrillas eventually led to her first son's death. Rajiv's death was in many ways the most tragic of all because of his youth and his transparent decency and because he should never have been in the firing line. If only he had not gone into politics, if only Rajiv and Sonia had let Maneka take the leading role, he would never have had to leave flying or become prime minister . . . In their own way, and in full sight of the nation, they all fashioned their own tryst with destiny.

# GLOSSARY OF INDIAN TERMS

**AICC** – All India Congress Committee, the executive committee of the Congress party.

**chamch** – literally "spear"; used to mean "sycophant."

**chief minister** – the leading elected politician in the legislative assembly of each of India's states.

**communal** – relating to the religious communities in India, hence "inter-communal violence" (cf. "sectarian").

**darshan** – the act of seeing an exalted person.

**governor** – nominated head of the government in a state.

**Hindi** – northern Indian language, the national language of India.

**Hindustani** – a mixture of Urdu and Hindi, a more literary and cultivated language than Hindi.

**-ji** – a suffix denoting respect, e.g. Gandhiji, meaning "respected Gandhi."

**khadi** – homespun cotton.

**khilafat** – literally "caliphate," a movement of Muslims for unity around the person of the caliph or guardian of the holy places of Islam.

**lathi** – baton used by Indian police for crowd control.

**Lok Sabha** – "people's assembly," the lower house of parliament elected by common suffrage every five years.

**panchayat** – the ruling body in a village.

**Panchayati raj** – government by village rule.

**panchsheel** – co-existence.

**president** – the national head of state.

**prime minister** – the leading politician in the national parliament

**Rajya Sabha** – "states' assembly," an upper house consisting of politicians nominated by the states and by the president.

**Rama Raj** – the mythical Hindu golden age when Lord Rama ruled India.

**sadhu** – mendicant holy man.

**satyagraha** – "desire for truth." Gandhi's technique of passive resistance, which he translated as "soul force."

**swaraj** – literally "self-rule."

**Urdu** – the language of the Muslim conquerors of India, rooted in Persian.

# NOTES

CHAPTER ONE: GENESIS OF A RULING FAMILY

1 Nehru, Jawaharlal, *An Autobiography*, London, 1953, p. 4.
2 Nanda, B. R., *The Nehrus: Motilal and Jawaharlal*, London, 1962, p. 24.
3 Nehru, op. cit., p. 5.
4 Nanda, op. cit., p. 69.
5 Gujral, Sheila, *Dada Nehru*, Delhi, 1980, p. 100. Whether this anecdote is literally true is less important than the fact that people believed it to be true, and that it was being reported as late as 1980 in a children's book on Motilal.
6 Gopal, Sarvepalli, *Jawaharlal Nehru: A Biography*, Vol. I, London, 1975, p. 16.
7 Pandit, Vijaya Lakshmi, *The Scope of Happiness: A Personal Memoir*, London, 1979, p. 39.
8 Nehru, op. cit., p. 13.
9 Diwaker, S. C., "Wit and Wisdom of Panditji" in *Pandit Motilal Nehru: A Great Patriot*, Delhi, 1976, p. 85.
10 Nayantara Sahgal interviewed by Brook Associates, May 2, 1996.
11 Pandit, op. cit., p. 45.
12 Hutheesing, Krishna Nehru and Hatch, Alden, *We Nehrus*, New York, 1967, p. 3.
13 Nehru, op. cit., p. 7.
14 Ibid., p. 7.
15 Ibid., p. 15.
16 Ibid., p. 16.
17 Ibid., p. 5. Jawaharlal often uses "English" to mean the same as "British," something many English people also do. In this case, however, the meaning is clear: it was an *English* private education Motilal required for his son.
18 Nanda, op. cit., p. 68.
19 Nehru, op. cit., p. 17.
20 Nanda, op. cit., p. 80.
21 Ibid., p. 71.
22 Ibid., p. 96.
23 Nehru, op. cit., p. 20.
24 Ibid.
25 Nanda, op. cit., p. 120.
26 Ibid., p. 90.
27 Nehru, op. cit., p. 25.
28 Nanda, op. cit., p. 121.
29 Nehru, op. cit., p. 26.
30 Moraes, Frank R., *Jawaharlal Nehru: A Biography*, Bombay, 1959.

CHAPTER TWO: WAITING FOR DESTINY

1 Hutheesing, Krishna Nehru, *Nehru's Letters to His Sister*, London, 1963, p. 7.

325

2 B. K. Nehru interviewed by Brook Associates, April 22, 1996.
3 Kalhan, Promilla, *Kamala Nehru: An Intimate Biography*, Delhi, 1973, p. 4.
4 Ibid., p. 6.
5 Gopal, Sarvepalli, *Jawaharlal Nehru: A Biography*, Vol. I, London, 1975, p. 30.
6 B. K. Nehru interviewed by Brook Associates, April 22, 1996.
7 Kalhan, op. cit., p. 7.
8 Ibid., p. 7.
9 Ibid., p. 8.
10 Gopal, op cit., p. 30.
11 Nehru, Jawaharlal, *An Autobiography*, London, 1953, p. 28.
12 Nanda, B. R., *The Nehrus: Motilal and Jawaharlal*, London, 1962, p. 86.
13 Ibid., p. 60.
14 Ibid., p. 92.
15 Ibid., p. 109.
16 Butler, Lord, *The Art of Memory*, London, 1981, p. 62.
17 Nanda, op. cit., p. 106.
18 Nehru, op. cit., p. 27.
19 Gopal, op. cit., p. 33.
20 Hutheesing, op. cit., p. 10.
21 B. K. Nehru interviewed by Brook Associates, April 22, 1996.
22 Kalhan, op. cit., pp. 13–14.
23 Sahgal, Nayantara, *Indira Gandhi: Her Road to Power*, London, 1978, p. 27.
24 Ali, Aruna Asaf, in Parthasarathi, G. and Sharada Prasad, H. Y. (eds), *Indira Gandhi: Statesmen, Scholars, Scientists and Friends Remember*, Delhi, 1985, p. 41.
25 Kalhan, op. cit., p. 16.
26 Malhotra, Inder, *Indira Gandhi: A Personal and Political Biography*, London, 1989, p. 26.

### CHAPTER THREE: A SON COMES OF AGE

1 Nehru, Jawaharlal, *An Autobiography*, London, 1953, p. 35.
2 B. K. Nehru interviewed by Brook Associates, April 22, 1996.
3 Nehru, op. cit. p. 41.
4 Pandit, Vijaya Lakshmi, *The Scope of Happiness: A Personal Memoir*, London, 1979, p. 63.
5 Ibid., p. 66.
6 Nehru, op. cit., p. 42.
7 Bipan Chandra interviewed by Brook Associates, September 26, 1996.
8 Nehru, op.cit., pp. 43–4.
9 Nehru, Jawaharlal, *India and the World*, London, 1936, p. 147. Quoted in Gopal, Sarvepalli, *Jawaharlal Nehru: A Biography*. Vol. 1, London, 1975.
10 Nehru, op. cit., 1953, p. 46.
11 Prasad, R. in *Pandit Motilal Nehru: A Great Patriot*, New Delhi, 1976, p. 29.
12 Nanda, R. B., *The Nehrus: Motilal and Jawaharlal*, London, 1962, p. 178.
13 Nehru, op.cit., p. 52.
14 Ibid., p. 57.

15 Chaudhuri, Nirad C., *Thy Hand Great Anarch!*, London, 1987, pp. 452–3.
16 Hutheesing, Krishna Nehru, *Nehru's Letters to His Sister*, London, 1963, p. 10.
17 Pandit, op. cit., p. 26.
18 Fischer, Louis, *The Life of Mahatma Gandhi*, London, 1951, p. 253.
19 Ibid.
20 Pandit, op. cit., p. 73.
21 B. K. Nehru interviewed by Brook Associates, April 22, 1996.
22 Motilal to Jawaharlal, September 16, 1920, quoted in Gopal, op.cit., p. 39.
23 Hutheesing, Krishna Nehru, and Hatch, Alden, *We Nehrus*, New York, 1967, p. 8.
24 Nanda, op. cit., p. 185.
25 Chandralekha Mehta interviewed by Brook Associates, May 3, 1996.
26 The *Leader*, February 18, 1931, quoted in Nanda, op. cit.
27 Gandhi, Indira, *India: The Speeches and Reminiscences of Indira Gandhi*, London, 1975, p. 13 (reprinted from an original text of 1957).
28 Gandhi, ibid., p. 14.
29 Khushwant Singh interviewed by Brook Associates, March 4, 1996.
30 Motilal to Jawaharlal, June 27, 1921, quoted in Gopal, op. cit.
31 Nehru, op.cit., 1953, p. 77.
32 Ibid., p. 68.
33 Fischer, op. cit., p. 215.
34 Ibid.
35 Nehru, op.cit., p. 77.
36 Ibid., p. 72.
37 Ibid., p. 80.
38 B. K. Nehru interviewed by Brook Associates, April 22, 1996.
39 Ziegler, Philip, *Mountbatten*, London, 1985, p. 61.
40 Nanda, op. cit., p. 196.
41 B. K. Nehru interviewed by Brook Associates, April 22, 1996.
42 Nehru, *An Autobiography*, op.cit., p. 80.
43 Ibid., p. 82.

CHAPTER FOUR: FATHER, SON AND HOLY GHOST

1 Gandhi to Jawaharlal, February 19, 1922, quoted in Nehru, Jawaharlal, *A Bunch of Old Letters*, Bombay, 1958, p. 24. While it is outside the scope of this book to discuss the matter in detail, it is a valid point that, had non-cooperation continued regardless, Indian independence might have been won with less overall violence than was the case twenty-five years later. Around 1921 was the one period when Hindu-Muslim unity was holding.
2 Motilal to Jawaharlal, May 24, 1922, quoted in Gopal, Sarvepalli, *Jawaharlal Nehru: A Biography*, Vol. I, London, 1975, p. 67.
3 Nanda, B. R., *The Nehrus: Motilal and Jawaharlal*, London, 1962, p. 203.
4 Ali, Asaf, "A Fascinating Figure," in *Pandit Motilal Nehru: A Great Patriot*, New Delhi, 1976, p. 42.
5 Gandhi, I., "The Story of Swaraj Bhavan," ibid., p. 88.
6 Hutheesing, Krishna Nehru and Hatch, Alden, *We Nehrus*, New York, 1967, pp. 54–5.

7 Malhotra, Inder, *Indira Gandhi: A Personal and Political Biography*, London, 1990, p. 38.

8 Pandit, Vijaya Lakshmi, *The Scope of Happiness: A Personal Memoir*, London, 1979, p. 21.

9 Malhotra, op. cit., p. 37. Malhotra was well known to Indira and her husband, and these personal comments can be taken as being derived from private conversation.

10 Kalhan, Promilla, *Kamala Nehru: An Intimate Biography*, Delhi, 1973, p. 141.

11 Ibid., p. 130.

12 Ibid., p. 137.

13 Gandhi, I., op. cit., p. 88.

14 Jawaharlal to Indira, October 17, 1922, quoted in Nanda, op. cit., p. 214.

15 Motilal to Jawaharlal, September 28, 1923, in Nehru, *A Bunch of Old Letters*, op. cit., p. 28.

16 Jawaharlal to Motilal, September 30, 1923, quoted in Gopal, op. cit., p. 78.

17 Nehru, Jawaharlal, *An Autobiography*, London, 1953, p. 106.

18 Ibid., p. 178.

19 Gandhi to Jawaharlal, December 3, 1928, quoted in Nehru, *A Bunch of Old Letters*, op. cit., 1958, p. 68.

20 Motilal Nehru quoted in *Pandit Motilal Nehru: A Great Patriot*, op. cit., p. 166.

21 Bipan Chandra interviewed by Brook Associates, September 26, 1996.

22 Ali, Tariq, *The Nehrus and the Gandhis: An Indian Dynasty*, London, 1985, p. 136.

23 Nanda, op. cit., p. 303.

24 Pran Chopra interviewed by Brook Associates, May 7, 1996.

25 G. D. Khosla interviewed by Brook Associates, May 13, 1996.

26 Nehru, op. cit., p. 203.

27 Kalhan, op. cit., p. 45.

28 Nehru, op. cit., p. 214.

29 The exact words are lost in time. An alternative version is, "Everybody has gone to jail." There was no time at which Jawaharlal, Motilal and Kamala were all in jail, but Kamala could have been visiting.

30 Hutheesing and Hatch, op. cit., p. 87.

31 Nehru, Jawaharlal, *Glimpses of World History*, London, 1962, p. v.

32 Ibid., p. 3.

33 Wedgwood Benn to Irwin, August 15, 1930, quoted in Gopal, op. cit., p. 146.

34 Sahgal, Nayantara, *Prison and Chocolate Cake*, London, 1957, p. 129.

35 Chandralekha Mehta interviewed by Brook Associates, May 3, 1996.

36 Diwaker, S. C., "Wit and Wisdom of Panditji" in *Pandit Motilal Nehru: A Great Patriot*, op. cit., p. 86.

37 Nehru, *An Autobiography*, op. cit., p. 274.

38 Hutheesing and Hatch, op cit., p. 93.

39 Gopal, op. cit., p. 150.

CHAPTER FIVE: DEATH, WAR AND IMPRISONMENT

1 Jayakar, Pupul, *Indira Gandhi: A Biography*, New Delhi, 1992, p. 43.
2 Nehru, Jawaharlal, *An Autobiography*, London, 1953, p. 333.
3 Ibid., p. 335.
4 Gopal, Sarvepalli, *Jawaharlal Nehru: A Biography*, London, 1975, Vol. I, p. 173.
5 Nehru, op. cit., p. 562.
6 Prison diary, April 9, 1934, in Nehru, Jawaharlal, *Selected Works*, Vol. 6, Delhi, 1974, p. 247.
7 Hutheesing, Krishna Nehru, *Nehru's Letters to His Sister*, London, 1963, p. 13.
8 Sahgal, Nayantara, *Prison and Chocolate Cake*, London, 1957, p. 34.
9 Jayakar, op. cit., p. 44.
10 Ibid., p. 45.
11 Masani, Zareer, *Indira Gandhi: A Biography*, London, 1975, p. 33.
12 Prison diary, June 3, 1934, in Nehru, *Selected Works*, op. cit., p. 255; and Jawaharlal to Vijaya, undated but c. 1932, quoted in Sahgal, Nayantara, *Indira Gandhi: Her Road to Power*, New York, 1978, p. 21.
13 Akbar, M. J., *Nehru: The Making of India*, London, 1988, p. 239.
14 Indira to Jawaharlal, August 29, 1934, in Gandhi, Sonia (ed.), *Freedom's Daughter*, London, 1989, p. 124.
15 Gandhi, Indira, *India: The Speeches and Reminiscences of Indira Gandhi*, London, 1975, p. 15.
16 Jayakar, op. cit., p. 479.
17 Kalhan, Promilla, *Kamal Nehru: An Intimate Biography*, Delhi, 1973, p. 89.
18 Prison diary, February 1, 1935, in Nehru, *Selected Works*, op. cit., p. 312.
19 Hutheesing, Krishna Nehru, and Hatch, Alden, *We Nehrus*, New York, 1967, p. 117.
20 Mehta, Vinod, *The Sanjay Story*, Bombay, 1978, p. 7.
21 Nehru, Jawaharlal, *The Discovery of India*, London, 1956, p. 34.
22 Ibid., p. 30.
23 Kalhan, op. cit., p. 137.
24 Nehru, *An Autobiography*, op. cit., p. 603.
25 Hutheesing and Hatch, op. cit., p. 126.
26 Nehru *An Autobiography*, op. cit., p. 562.
27 Gopal, op. cit., p. 216.
28 Gandhi, Sonia, op. cit., p. 6.
29 Nehru, *An Autobiography*, op. cit., p. 599.
30 Gandhi to Motilal, September 2, 1924, quoted in Nanda, B. R., *The Nehrus: Motilal and Jawaharlal*, London, 1962, p. 247.
31 Chaudhuri, Nirad C., *Thy Hand Great Anarch!*, London, 1987, p. 452.
32 Gopal, op. cit., p. 195.
33 Nehru, *An Autobiography*, op. cit., p. 604.
34 Ibid., p. 605.
35 Michael Foot interviewed by Brook Associates, July 19, 1996.
36 Norman, Dorothy, *Indira Gandhi: Letters to a Friend, 1950–1984*, London, 1986, p. 77.

37 Mehta, op. cit., p. 9.
38 Hutheesing, Krishna Nehru, *Dear to Behold: An Intimate Portrait of Indira Gandhi*, London, 1969, p. 79.
39 Murdoch, Iris, in Parthasarathi, G. and Sharada Prasad, H. Y. (eds), *Indira Gandhi: Statesmen, Scholars, Scientists and Friends Remember*, Delhi, 1985, p. 308.
40 Hutheesing, *Dear to Behold: An Intimate Portrait of Indira Gandhi*, op. cit., p. 85.
41 Jawaharlal to Indira, July 9, 1941, in Nehru, Jawaharlal, *Selected Works*, Vol. 11, Delhi, 1978, pp. 464–6.
42 Hutheesing, *Dear to Behold: An Intimate Portrait of Indira Gandhi*, op. cit., p. 91.
43 Hutheesing and Hatch, op. cit., p. 144.
44 Mukhopadhyay, Tarun Kumar, *Feroze Gandhi: A Crusader in Parliament*, New Delhi, 1992, p. 8.
45 Hutheesing and Hatch, op cit., p. 145.
46 Gandhi, Sonia, *Rajiv*, Delhi, 1992, p. 20.
47 Nayantara Sahgal interviewed by Brook Associates, May 2, 1996.
48 Gandhi, Indira, "A Page from the Book of Memory," September 1963, quoted in Masani, op. cit., p. 70.
49 Sahgal, op. cit., p. 10.
50 Ibid., p. 14.
51 Jawaharlal to Krishna, August 29, 1944, in Hutheesing, Krishna Nehru, *Nehru's Letters to His Sister*, London, 1963, p. 12.
52 Gandhi, Sonia, *Rajiv*, Delhi, 1992, p. 23.
53 Jawaharlal to Indira, July 1, 1945, in Gandhi, Sonia (ed.), *Two Alone, Two Together*, London, 1992, p. 512.

### CHAPTER SIX: FREEDOM AND DISASTER

1 Sardar Patel to D. P. Mishra, July 29, 1946, quoted in Gopal, Sarvepalli, *Jawaharlal Nehru: A Biography*, Vol. I, London, 1975, p. 327.
2 Quenna Hunt interviewed by Brook Associates, December 8, 1996.
3 Singh, S. Jagat, *Sanjay Gandhi and Awakening of Youth Power*, Delhi, 1977, p. 51.
4 Akbar, M. K., *Nehru: The Making of India*, London, 1988, p. 384.
5 Lady Pamela Hicks interviewed by Brook Associates, July 18, 1996.
6 Campbell-Johnson, Alan, *Mission with Mountbatten*, London, 1985, pp. 44, 56, 67, 52.
7 Khare, N. B. in Zakaria, Rafiq (ed.), *A Study of Nehru*, Bombay, 1960, p. 215.
8 Morgan, Janet, *Edwina Mountbatten: A Life of Her Own*, London, 1991, p. 395.
9 Shaukat Hyat Khan interviewed by Brook Associates, May 27, 1996.
10 Lady Pamela Hicks interviewed by Brook Associates, July 18, 1996.
11 Mountbatten to Lord Ismay, May 11, 1947, quoted in Akbar, op. cit.
12 Countess Mountbatten of Burma interviewed by Brook Associates, June 11, 1996.

13 Alan Campbell-Johnson interviewed by Brook Associates, June 11, 1996.
14 Ibid.
15 Jawaharlal to Radhakrishnan, May 14, 1947, quoted in Gopal, op. cit., p. 352.
16 Campbell-Johnson, op. cit., p. 160.
17 Lady Pamela Hicks interviewed by Brook Associates, July 18, 1996.
18 Said in 1946 to Jacques Marcuse and repeated at other times. Quoted in Gopal, Sarvepalli, *Jawaharlal Nehru: A Biography*, Vol. II, London, 1979, p. 14.
19 Kuldip Nayar interviewed by Brook Associates, September 25, 1996.
20 Jawaharlal to Rajendra Prasad, September 19, 1947, quoted in Gopal, Vol. II, op. cit., p. 17.
21 Quenna Hunt interviewed by Brook Associates, December 8, 1996.
22 Sahgal, Nayantara, *From Fear Set Free*, London, 1962, p. 46.
23 Morgan, op. cit., p. 427.
24 Ali, Tariq, *The Nehrus and the Gandhis: An Indian Dynasty* London, 1985, p. 264.
25 Norman, Dorothy, *Indira Gandhi: Letters to a Friend, 1950–1984*, London, 1985, p. 18.
26 Jayakar, Pupul, *Indira Gandhi: A Biography*, Delhi, 1992, p. 140.
27 Gandhi, Indira, *India: The Speeches and Reminiscences of Indira Gandhi*, London, 1975, p. 41.
28 Campbell-Johnson, op. cit., p. 189.
29 Quoted in Gopal, Vol II, op. cit., p. 21.
30 Sam Manekshaw interviewed by Brook Associates, May 14, 1996.
31 Sahgal, Nayantara, *Prison and Chocolate Cake*, London, 1957, p. 219.
32 Pran Chopra interviewed by Brook Associates, May 7, 1996.

CHAPTER SEVEN: THE LAST ENGLISHMAN

1 Gopal, Sarvepalli, *Jawaharlal Nehru: A Biography*, Vol. II, London, 1979, p. 18.
2 Galbraith, J. K., *Ambassador's Journal: A Personal Account of the Kennedy Years*, London, 1969, p. 76. Galbraith was a long-term adviser to Jawaharlal, and this comment, though made in 1961, is clearly retrospective.
3 Manor, James, *Nehru to the Nineties: The Changing Office of Prime Minister in India*, London, 1994, p. 8. The dates noted are 1948, 1949, 1950, 1951, 1954, 1957 and 1958.
4 Seton, Marie, *Panditji: A Portrait of Jawaharlal Nehru*, London, 1967, p. 187.
5 Sahgal, Nayantara, *From Fear Set Free*, London, 1962, p. 30.
6 Ibid., p. 140.
7 Phillips Talbot interviewed by Brook Associates, September 8 , 1996.
8 Hangen, Welles, *After Nehru, Who?*, London, 1962, p. 171.
9 Galbraith, op. cit., p. 50.
10 T. N. Kaul interviewed by Brook Associates, April 23, 1996.
11 Gopal, Sarvepalli, *Jawaharlal Nehru: A Biography*, Vol. III, London, 1984, p. 111.
12 Hutheesing, Krishna Nehru, *We Nehrus*, Bombay, 1968, p. 285.

13 Galbraith, J. K., "A Man of Two Worlds" in *Jawaharlal Nehru Centenary Volume*, London, 1989, p. 233.

14 Gandhi, Indira, *India: The Speeches and Reminiscences of Indira Gandhi*, London, 1975, p. 38.

15 Jawaharlal statement to the press quoted in Akbar, M. J., *Nehru: The Making of India*, London, 1988, p. 461.

16 Jawaharlal to Edwina, March 12, 1957, quoted in Ziegler, Philip, *Mountbatten*, London, 1985, p. 473.

17 Morgan, Janet, *Edwina Mountbatten: A Life of Her Own*, London, 1991, p. 428.

18 Mountbatten to Patricia Mountbatten, June 12, 1948, quoted in Ziegler, op. cit., p. 473.

19 Morgan, op. cit., p. 335 and passim.

20 Countess Mountbatten interviewed by Brook Associates, July 18, 1996.

21 Morgan, op. cit. p. 429.

22 Ibid., p. 430.

23 Ibid., p. 435.

24 Ibid., p. 470.

25 Ibid., p. 473.

26 Lady Pamela Hicks interviewed by Brook Associates, July 18, 1996.

27 Edwina to Mountbatten, February 8, 1952, quoted in Ziegler, op. cit., p. 474.

28 Mountbatten to Edwina, February 1, 1953, quoted in ibid., p. 474.

29 Hutheesing, op. cit., p. 263.

30 Grigg, John, "The Genius of Nehru" in *Jawaharlal Nehru Centenary Volume*, op. cit., p. 254.

31 Gandhi, Indira, op. cit., p. 38.

32 Cartland, Barbara, *Indira Gandhi*, no date—typescript sent to Brook Associates by author.

33 Arun Shourie interviewed by Brook Associates, May 7, 1996.

34 Jawaharlal to Indira, August 30, 1934, in Gandhi, Sonia (ed.), *Freedom's Daughter*, London, 1989, p. 125.

35 Norman, Dorothy, *Indira Gandhi: Letters to a Friend 1950–1984*, London, 1986, p. 48.

36 Seton, op. cit., p. 253.

37 Address to Congress parliamentary party, May 29, 1956, quoted in Gopal, Vol. II, op. cit., p. 317.

38 *The Tribune*, Alabama, November 5, 1957, quoted in Masani, Zareer, *Indira Gandhi: A Biography*, London, 1975, p. 93.

39 Masani, ibid., p. 90.

40 Gandhi, op. cit., p. 42.

41 Seton, op. cit., p. 137, said to the artist Satish Gujural.

42 Gandhi, op. cit., p. 43.

43 Gandhi, Sonia, *Rajiv*, Delhi, 1992, p. 43.

44 Malhotra, Inder, *Indira Gandhi: A Personal and Political Biography*, London, 1989, p. 68.

45 Indira interview with Betty Friedan, in *Ladies' Home Journal*, May 1966.

Quoted in Hutheesing, Krishna Nehru, *Dear to Behold: An Intimate Portrait of Indira Gandhi*, London, 1969, p. 137.

46 Jayakur, Pupul, *Indira Gandhi: A Biography*, Delhi, 1992, p. 154.

47 Masani, op. cit., p. 90.

48 Hutheesing, *Dear to Behold: An Intimate Portrait of Indira Gandhi*, op. cit., p. 139.

49 Grigg, op. cit., p. 253.

50 Hutheesing, op. cit., pp. 294–5.

51 Edwardes, Michael, *Nehru: A Political Biography*, London, 1973, p. 259.

52 Seton, op. cit., p. 252.

CHAPTER EIGHT: JAWAHARLAL LECTURES THE WORLD

1 Seton, Marie, *Panditji: A Portrait of Jawaharlal Nehru*, London, 1967, p. 146.

2 Jawaharlal Nehru interviewed by the BBC, June 12, 1953.

3 *Ceylon Observer*, October 11, 1964, quoted in Gopal, Sarvepalli, *Jawaharlal Nehru: A Biography*, Vol. III, London, 1984, p. 271.

4 Edwardes, Michael, *Nehru: A Political Biography*, London, 1973, p. 275.

5 B. K. Nehru interviewed by Brook Associates, April 22, 1996.

6 Jawaharlal to Mountbatten, September 2, 1956, quoted in Ziegler, Philip, *Mountbatten*, London, 1985, p. 541.

7 Ibid., p. 542.

8 B. K. Nehru interviewed by Brook Associates, April 22, 1996.

9 J. K. Galbraith interviewed by Brook Associates, July 20, 1996.

10 B. K. Nehru interviewed by Brook Associates, April 22, 1996.

11 George McGhee interviewed by Brook Associates, September 11, 1996.

12 British Movietone News, December 1949.

13 Phillips Talbot interviewed by Brook Associates, September 8, 1996.

14 Norman, Dorothy, *Indira Gandhi: Letters to a Friend, 1950–1984*, London, 1986, p. xv.

15 Masani, Zareer, *Indira Gandhi: A Biography*, London, 1975, p. 102.

16 Gandhi, Indira, *India: The Speeches and Reminiscences of Indira Gandhi*, London, 1975, p. 41.

17 Jawaharlal to Vijaya, March 12, 1957, quoted in Gopal, Vol. III, op. cit., p. 67.

18 Norman, op. cit., p. 57.

19 Dennis Kux interviewed by Brook Associates, September 12, 1996.

20 Krishna Iyer interviewed by Brook Associates, May 13, 1996.

21 Indira to Jawaharlal, October 30, 1959, in Gandhi, Sonia (ed.), *Two Alone, Two Together*, London, 1992, p. 627.

22 Seton, op. cit., p. 284.

23 Norman, op. cit., p. 80.

24 Moraes, Dom, *Mrs. Gandhi*, London, 1980, p. 146.

25 Indira to Dorothy Norman, September 24, 1960, quoted in Norman, op. cit., p. 79.

26 Jayakar, Pupul, *Indira Gandhi: A Biography*, Delhi, 1992, p. 161.

27 Gandhi, Sonia, *Rajiv*, Delhi, 1992, p. 50.

28 Hutheesing, Krishna Nehru, *We Nehrus*, Bombay, 1968, p. 260. In a slightly

different form in Hutheesing, Krishna Nehru, *Dear to Behold: An Intimate Portrait of Indira Gandhi*, London, 1969, p. 140.

## CHAPTER NINE: THE LAND AND THE KING

1 Hutheesing, Krishna Nehru, *We Nehrus*, Bombay, 1968, p. 296.
2 B. K. Nehru interviewed by Brook Associates, April 22, 1996.
3 Sarvepalli Gopal interviewed by Brook Associates, October 6, 1996.
4 Phillips Talbot interviewed by Brook Associates, September 8, 1996.
5 J. K. Galbraith interviewed by Brook Associates, July 2, 1996.
6 Galbraith, J. K., *Ambassador's Journal: A Personal Account of the Kennedy Years*, London, 1969, p. 618.
7 Ibid., p. 89.
8 Malhotra, Inder, *Indira Gandhi: A Personal and Political Biography*, London, 1989, p. 61.
9 Jawaharlal to chief ministers, October 21, 1962, quoted in Gopal, Sarvepelli, *Jawaharlal Nehru: A Biography*, Vol. III, London, 1984, p. 221.
10 Galbraith, op. cit., p. 466.
11 Ibid., p. 478.
12 Hutheesing, op. cit., p. 299.
13 Jayakar, Pupul, *Indira Gandhi: A Biography*, Delhi, 1988, p. 164.
14 Galbraith, op. cit., p. 517.
15 Seton, Marie, *Panditji: A Portrait of Jawaharlal Nehru*, London, 1967, p. 354.
16 B. K. Nehru interviewed by Brook Associates, April 22, 1996.
17 Galbraith, op. cit., p. 175.
18 Norman, Dorothy, *Indira Gandhi: Letters to a Friend, 1950–1984*, London, 1985, pp. 96–7.
19 Ibid., p. 103.
20 Seton, op. cit., p. 404.
21 Hangen, Welles, *After Nehru, Who?*, London, 1963, p. 160.
22 Ibid.
23 Ibid., p. 181.
24 Akbar, M. J., *Nehru: The Making of India*, London, 1988, p. 563.
25 Edwardes, Michael, *Nehru: A Political Biography*, London, 1971, p. 328.
26 Seton, op. cit., p. 474.
27 Masani, Zareer, *Indira Gandhi: A Biography*, London, 1975, p. 135.
28 Hutheesing, Krishna Nehru, *Dear to Behold: An Intimate Portrait of Indira Gandhi*, London, 1969, p. 154.
29 Usha Bhagat interviewed by Brook Associates, April 29, 1996.

## CHAPTER TEN: PASSING THE TORCH

1 Ali, Tariq, *The Nehrus and the Gandhis: An Indian Dynasty*, London, 1985, p. 146.
2 Jawaharlal's will quoted in Mathai, M. O., *Reminiscences of the Nehru Age*, Delhi, 1978, p. 267.
3 Gandhi, Sonia, *Rajiv*, Delhi, 1992, p. 2.
4 Malhotra, Inder, *Indira Gandhi: A Personal and Political Biography*, London, 1985, p. 83.

5 Vijaya to Indira, December 6, 1965, in Sahgal, Nayantara, *Indira Gandhi: Her Road to Power*, London, 1978, p. 4.
6 Indira to Vijaya, December 7, 1965, in Sahgal, ibid., p. 5.
7 Jayakar, Pupul, *Indira Gandhi: A Biography*, Delhi, 1992, p. 177.
8 Ibid., p. 177. Jayakar was present.
9 Hutheesing, Krishna Nehru, *We Nehrus*, Bombay, 1968, p. 338.
10 Masani, Zareer, *Indira Gandhi: A Biography*, London, 1975, p. 139.
11 Hutheesing, *Dear to Behold: An Intimate Portrait of Indira Gandhi*, Toronto, 1969, p. 169. Krishna says Indira thought of this, which may be poetic license on Krishna's part, or Indira may have told her on that or subsequent days.
12 Hutheesing, *We Nehrus*, op. cit., p. 340.
13 Quoted in Sen, Ela, *Indira Gandhi: A Biography*, London, 1973, p. 5.
14 Usha Bhagat interviewed by Brook Associates, April 29, 1996.

CHAPTER ELEVEN: CALL ME "SIR"
1 *Look*, April 30, 1968, quoted in Hutheesing, Krishna Nehru, *Dear to Behold: An Intimate Portrait of Indira Gandhi*, Toronto, 1969, p. 178.
2 Masani, Zareer, *Indira Gandhi: A Biography*, London, 1975, p. 149.
3 Jayakar, Pupul, *Indira Gandhi: A Biography*, Delhi, 1992, p. 187.
4 Gandhi, Indira, *My Truth*, Delhi, 1980, p. 118.
5 B. K. Nehru interviewed by Brook Associates, May 1996.
6 Ibid.
7 Ibid., and Malhotra, Inder, *Indira Gandhi: A Personal and Political Biography*, London, 1989, p. 96.
8 Jayakar, op. cit., p. 195.
9 Seton, Marie, *Panditji: A Portrait of Jawaharlal Nehru*, London, 1967, p. 497.
10 Mansai, op. cit., p. 155.
11 Gandhi, op. cit., p. 119.
12 Malhotra, op. cit., p. 101.
13 Ibid., p. 98.
14 Masani, op. cit., p. 171.
15 Ibid., p. 169, and Hutheesing, op. cit., p. 196.
16 Hutheesing, op. cit., p. 195.
17 Indira to Norman, February 10, 1967, in Norman, Dorothy, *Indira Gandhi: Letters to a Friend, 1950–1984*, London, 1985, p. 118.
18 Hutheesing, op. cit., p. 196.
19 Norman, op. cit., p. 117.
20 Malhotra, op. cit., 105.
21 Ibid., p. 107.
22 Pandit, Vijaya Lakshmi, *The Scope of Happiness: A Personal Memoir*, London, 1979, p. 4.
23 Sahgal, Nayantara, *Indira Gandhi: Her Road to Power*, London, 1978, p. 10.
24 Pandit, op. cit., p. 5.
25 Sahgal, op. cit., p. 11.
26 Cartland, Barbara, *Indira Gandhi*, typescript, no date.
27 Mathai, M. O., *My Days with Nehru*, Delhi, 1979, p. 62.

28 Seton, op. cit., p. 368.
29 Chris Ladley interviewed by Brook Associates, July 1996.
30 Ibid.
31 Indira to Jawaharlal, March 9, 1961, in Gandhi, Sonia (ed.), *Two Alone, Two Together*, London, 1992, p. 660.
32 Gandhi, Sonia, ibid., p. 3.
33 Ibid., p. 1.
34 Nugent, Nicholas, *Rajiv Gandhi: Son of a Dynasty*, London, 1990, p. 39.
35 Gandhi, Sonia, op. cit., p. 1.
36 Ibid., p. 3.
37 Indira to Norman, May 26, 1969, in Norman, op. cit., p. 121.
38 Gandhi, Sonia, op. cit., p. 3.
39 Masani, op. cit., p. 217.
40 Moraes, Dom, *Mrs. Gandhi*, London, 1980, pp. 110–11.
41 Callaghan, James, "A Briton Remembers" in *Jawaharlal Nehru Centenary Volume*, London, 1989, p. 106.
42 Jayakar, op. cit., p. 203.
43 Ibid., p. 206.
44 Masani, op. cit., p. 199.
45 Jayakar, op. cit. p. 207.
46 Ibid., p. 208.
47 Gandhi, Indira, op. cit., p. 132.
48 Jayakar, op. cit., p. 211.
49 Rajinder Puri quoted in Sahgal, op. cit., p. 50.
50 Masani, op. cit., p. 210.
51 Ibid., p. 211.
52 Sahgal, op. cit., p. 48.
53 Sam Manekshaw interviewed by Brook Associates, May 14, 1996.
54 Malhotra, op. cit., p. 124.
55 Gandhi, Indira, op. cit., p. 147.
56 Masani, op. cit., p. 217.
57 Indira to Norman, April 23, 1971, in Norman, op. cit., p. 130.
58 Ibid., pp. 131–2.
59 Ibid.

### CHAPTER TWELVE: INDIRA RIDES A TIGER

1 Sam Manekshaw interviewed by Brook Associates, May 14, 1996.
2 Hersh, Seymour, *The Price of Power*, New York, 1987, p. 475.
3 BBC *Panorama* interview of November 1, 1971, quoted in Masani, Zareer, *Indira Gandhi: A Biography*, London, 1975, p. 241.
4 Masani, ibid., p. 241.
5 Norman, Dorothy, *Indira Gandhi: Letters to a Friend, 1950–1984*, London, 1985, p. 135.
6 Gandhi, Indira, *India: The Speeches and Reminiscences of Indira Gandhi*, London, 1975, pp. 172–4.
7 Ibid., p. 174.
8 Jayakar, Pupul, *Indira Gandhi: A Biography*, Delhi, 1992, p. 245.

9 Masani, op. cit., p. 253.

10 Indira to Norman, June 3, 1973 in Norman, op. cit., p. 145.

11 Gandhi, Maneka, *Sanjay Gandhi*, Bombay, 1980, no page numbers.

12 Ibid.

13 Ibid. It should be noted that the strongest word detractors of Maneka quote her as using is "bastard."

14 Mehta, Vinod, *The Sanjay Story*, Bombay, 1978, p. 71.

15 Mathai, M. O., *My Days with Nehru*, Delhi, 1979, p. 66.

16 Jayakar, op. cit., p. 253.

17 Gandhi, Maneka, op. cit.

18 Ali, Tariq, *The Nehrus and the Gandhis: An Indian Dynasty*, London, 1985, p. 181.

19 Speech to Conference of Trade Union Organizations, May 1971, quoted in Masani, op. cit., p. 283.

20 Malhotra, Inder, *Indira Gandhi: A Personal and Political Biography*, London, 1989, p. 168.

21 Gandhi, Indira, *My Truth*, Delhi, 1980, p. 161.

22 Seton, Marie, *Panditji: A Portrait of Jawaharlal Nehru*, London, 1967, p. 333.

23 Speech to Planning Commission, Delhi, July 12, 1966, quoted in Sahgal, Nayantara, *Indira Gandhi, Her Road to Power*, London, 1982, p. 13.

24 From a press report, quoted in Gandhi, Indira, *My Truth*, op. cit., p. 113.

25 Gandhi, Indira, *Indira: The Speeches and Reminiscences of Indira Gandhi*, op. cit., Preface.

### CHAPTER THIRTEEN: SANJAY ALSO RISES

1 Jayakar, Pupul, *Indira Gandhi: A Biography*, Delhi, 1992, p. 278.

2 Ibid., p. 280.

3 Desai, Morarji, *The Story of My Life*, Vol. III, Oxford, 1979, p. 133.

4 Mehta, Vinod, *The Sanjay Story*, Bombay, 1978, p. 141.

5 Selbourne, David, *An Eye to India: The Unmasking of a Tyranny*, London, 1977, p. 135.

6 Norman, Dorothy, *Indira Gandhi: Letters to a Friend, 1950–1984*, London, 1985, p. 149.

7 Gandhi, Indira, *My Truth*, Delhi, 1980, p. 169.

8 Jayakar, op. cit., p. 289.

9 Michael Foot interviewed by Brook Associates, July 19, 1996.

10 Jayakar, op. cit., p. 291.

11 Selbourne, op. cit., p. 308.

12 Gandhi, Maneka, *Sanjay Gandhi*, Bombay, 1980, no page numbers.

13 Selbourne, op. cit., p. 273.

14 Singh, Jagat and Deep, Netra, *The Rise and Fall of the Sanjay Empire*, Delhi, 1977, p. 163.

15 Mathai, M. O., *My Days with Nehru*, Delhi, 1979, p. 67.

16 Sharma, Piare Lal, *Sanjay Gandhi: The World's Wisest Wizard*, Delhi, 1977, p. 32.

17 Mehta, op. cit., pp. 146–7.

18 Sharma, op. cit., dedication.

19 Selbourne, op. cit., p. 96.
20 Ibid., p. 98.
21 Ibid.
22 Moraes, Dom, Mrs. *Gandhi*, London, 1980, p. 214. She was addressing the situation immediately before the emergency here, but the same situation applied during it.
23 Jayakar, op. cit., p. 479.
24 Ali, Tariq, *The Nehrus and the Gandhis: An Indian Dynasty*, London, 1985, p. 191.
25 Moraes, op. cit., p. 227.
26 Gandhi, Indira, op. cit., p. 166.
27 Ibid., p. 163.
28 Mehta, op. cit., p. 83.
29 Mehta, Ved, *A Family Affair: India Under Three Prime Ministers*, Oxford, 1982, p. 23.
30 Ibid., p. 23.
31 Mehta, Vinod, op. cit., p. ix.
32 Sahgal, Nayantara, *Indira Gandhi: Her Road to Power*, London, 1983, p. 193.
33 Gandhi, Indira, op. cit., p. 166.
34 Jayakar, op. cit., p. 320.
35 Ibid., p. 321.
36 Gandhi, Maneka, op. cit.
37 Moraes, op. cit., p. xiii.
38 Ali, Aruna Asaf in Parthasarathi, G. and Sharada Prasad, H. Y. (eds), *Indira Gandhi: Statesmen, Scholars, Scientists and Friends Remember*, Delhi, 1985, p. 41.

CHAPTER FOURTEEN: LEGEND IN A SARI

1 Moraes, Dom, Mrs. *Gandhi*, London, 1980, pp. 240–1.
2 Cousins, Norman in Parthasarathi, G. and Sharada Prasad, H. Y. (eds), *Indira Gandhi: Statesmen, Scholars, Scientists and Friends Remember*, Delhi, 1985, p. 144.
3 Cartland, Barbara in Parthasarathi and Sharada Prasad, ibid., p. 102.
4 Jayakar, Pupul, *Indira Gandhi: A Biography*, Delhi, 1992, p. 388.
5 Moraes, op. cit., p. 317.
6 Sargeant, Graham and Mascarenhas, Anthony for *The Sunday Times*, quoted in Mehta, Vinod, *The Sanjay Story*, Bombay, 1978, p. 63.
7 Mathai, M. O., *My Days with Nehru*, Delhi, 1979, p. 211.
8 Gandhi, Maneka, *Sanjay Gandhi*, Bombay, 1980, no page numbers.
9 Ibid.
10 Baroness Thatcher interviewed by Brook Associates, August 15, 1996.
11 Lok Sabha debate quoted in Jayakar, op. cit., pp. 370–1.
12 Pran Chopra interviewed by Brook Associates, May 7, 1996.
13 Siddiqui, Ali, *Son of India*, Delhi, 1982, p. 19.
14 *Newsweek*, January 31, 1980, quoted in Jayakar, op. cit., p. 323.
15 Manor, James, *Nehru to the Nineties: The Changing Office of Prime Minister in India*, London, 1994, p. 8.

16 Sahgal, Nayantara, *Indira Gandhi: Her Road to Power*, London, 1983, p. 228.
17 Gandhi, op. cit.
18 Malhotra, Inder, *Indira Gandhi: A Personal and Political Biography*, London, 1989, p. 177.
19 *The Times of India*, June 22, 1980.
20 Jayakar, op. cit., p. 413.
21 Sahgal, op. cit., p. 32.
22 Ibid., p. 229.
23 Vazeeruddin, M., *India without Sanjay*, Chandigargh, 1982, p. 88.
24 Norman, Dorothy, *Indira Gandhi: Letters to a Friend, 1950–1984*, London, 1985, p. 152.
25 Indira to Pupul Jayakar, July 7, 1981, quoted in Malhotra, op. cit., p. 225.
26 Arun Nehru interviewed by Brook Associates, September 25, 1996.

### CHAPTER FIFTEEN: THE FAMILY DIVIDED

1 Gandhi, Sonia, *Rajiv*, Delhi, 1992, p. 5.
2 Mehta, Vinod, *The Sanjay Story*, Bombay, 1978, p. 70.
3 Gandhi, op. cit., p. 6.
4 Ibid., p. 7.
5 T. N. Kaul interviewed by Brook Associates, April 23, 1996.
6 Gandhi, op. cit., p. 7.
7 *India Today*, June 15, 1991.
8 Nugent, Nicholas, *Rajiv Gandhi: Son of a Dynasty*, London, 1990, p. 48.
9 Rajiv Gandhi interviewed by Siga Arts International, April 11, 1989.
10 Vazeeruddin, M., *India without Sanjay*, Chandigargh, 1982, p. 100.
11 *India Today*, June 15, 1991.
12 James Manor interviewed by Brook Associates, December 9, 1996.
13 Nayantara Sahgal interviewed by Brook Associates, May 2, 1996.
14 Gandhi, op. cit., p. 7.
15 Ibid., p. 88.
16 Arun Nehru interviewed by Brook Associates, April 1, 1996.
17 Gandhi, op. cit., p. 6.
18 Ali, Tariq, *The Nehrus and the Gandhis: An Indian Dynasty*, London, 1985, p. 228.
19 Vir Sanghvi interviewed by Brook Associates, September 27, 1996.
20 Malhotra, Inder, *Indira Gandhi: A Personal and Political Biography*, London, 1989, p. 235.
21 Arun Nehru interviewed by Brook Associates, September 25, 1996.
22 *The Hindustan Times*, June 28, 1980.
23 Jayakar, Pupul, *Indira Gandhi: A Biography*, Delhi, 1992, p. 416.
24 Malhotra, op. cit., p. 237.
25 Khushwant Singh interviewed by Brook Associates, March 4, 1996.
26 Ali, op. cit., p. 289.
27 Malhotra, op. cit., p. 238.
28 Mehta, Ved, *Rajiv Gandhi and Rama's Kingdom*, London, 1994, p. 9.
29 Khushwant Singh interviewed by Brook Associates, March 4, 1996.
30 Singh, Khushwant, in *India Today*, October 31, 1995.

31 Khushwant Singh interviewed by Brook Associates, March 4, 1996.
32 Malhotra, op. cit., p. 241.
33 Mehta, Ved, op. cit., p. 10.
34 Ibid., pp. 13–14.
35 Siddiqui, Ali, *Son of India*, Delhi, 1982, p. 39.
36 Ibid., p. 41.
37 Seton, Marie, in *The Sunday Times*, November 4, 1984.
38 Translation of Maneka Gandhi speech, BBC *Newsnight*, February 23, 1984.
39 Quoted in Jayakar, op. cit., p. 465.
40 Tarlochan Singh interviewed by Brook Associates, April 30, 1996.
41 Khushwant Singh interviewed by Brook Associates, March 4, 1996.
42 Seton, Marie, in *The Sunday Times*, November 4, 1984.
43 Indira to Dorothy Norman, April 5, 1984 and April 17, 1984, in Norman, Dorothy, *Indira Gandhi: Letters to a Friend, 1950–1984*, London, 1985, p. 176.
44 Quoted in Norman, op. cit., p. 179.
45 *The Sunday Times*, June 6, 1984.
46 Vishnu Mathur interviewed by Brook Associates, November 7, 1996.
47 Jayakar, op. cit., p. 481.
48 Gandhi, op. cit, p. 8.
49 Ibid., p. 9.
50 P. C. Alexander interviewed by Brook Associates, October 1, 1996.
51 Arun Nehru interviewed by Brook Associates, September 25, 1996.
52 P. C. Alexander interviewed by Brook Associates, October 1, 1996.
53 Vir Sanghvi interviewed by Brook Associates, September 27, 1996.
54 Arun Nehru interviewed by Brook Associates, September 25, 1996.
55 P. C. Alexander interviewed by Brook Associates, October 1, 1996.
56 Gandhi, op. cit., p. 9.
57 P. C. Alexander interviewed by Brook Associates, October 1, 1996.
58 Gandhi, op. cit., p. 9.
59 Arun Shourie interviewed by Brook Associates, May 7, 1996.
60 Merchant, Minhaz, *Rajiv Gandhi: The End of a Dream*, Delhi, 1991, p. 148.
61 Khushwant Singh interviewed by Brook Associates, March 4, 1996.

CHAPTER SIXTEEN: THE RELUCTANT PRIME MINISTER
1 Pupul Jayakar interviewed by Brook Associates, October 2, 1996.
2 *India Today*, November 15, 1989.
3 Margaret Thatcher interviewed by Brook Associates, August 15, 1996.
4 Vir Sanghvi interviewed by Brook Associates, September 27, 1996.
5 Doordarshan broadcast, November 3, 1984.
6 James Manor interviewed by Brook Associates, December 9, 1996.
7 Vishnu Mathur interviewed by Brook Associates, November 7, 1996.
8 Vir Sanghvi interviewed by Brook Associates, September 27, 1996.
9 BBC *Newsnight*, December 31, 1984.
10 A published collection of Rajiv's photographs appears in Gandhi, Sonia, *Rajiv's World*, Delhi, 1994.
11 Gandhi, Sonia, *Rajiv*, Delhi, 1992, p. 7.

12 Ibid., p. 10.
13 Thatcher, Margaret, *The Downing Street Years*, London, 1993, p. 504.
14 Arun Nehru interviewed by Brook Associates, April 1, 1996.
15 Satish Sharma interviewed by Brook Associates, April 21, 1996.
16 Rajiv Gandhi interviewed by Siga Arts International, April 1, 1989.
17 Vir Sanghvi interviewed by Brook Associates, September 27, 1996.
18 Gandhi, Sonia, *Rajiv*, op. cit., p. 106.
19 Ibid., p. 109.
20 Mehta, Ved, *Rajiv Gandhi and Rama's Kingdom*, London, 1994, p. 76.
21 T. N. Kaul interviewed by Brook Associates, April 23, 1996.
22 BBC *Panorama* interview, broadcast January 18, 1988.
23 Pran Chopra interviewed by Brook Associates, May 7,1996.
24 Mehta, op. cit., p. 81.
25 Rajiv Gandhi interviewed by Siga Arts International, March 4, 1989.
26 Nugent, Nicholas, *Rajiv Gandhi: Son of a Dynasty*, London, 1990, p. 105.
27 Arun Nehru interviewed by Brook Associates, September 25, 1996.
28 Vir Sanghvi interviewed by Brook Associates, September 27, 1996.
29 Margaret Thatcher interviewed by Brook Associates, August 15, 1996.
30 Ibid.
31 Ibid.
32 BBC Television News, October 21, 1985.
33 Vir Sanghvi interviewed by Brook Associates, September 27, 1996.
34 Gandhi, Sonia, *Rajiv*, op. cit., p. 118.
35 Vir Sanghvi interviewed by Brook Associates, September 27, 1996.
36 Mani Dixit interviewed by Brook Associates, April 30, 1996.
37 Ibid.
38 General K. Sundarji interviewed by Brook Associates, May 14, 1996.
39 Quoted in Nugent, op. cit., p. 118.

### CHAPTER SEVENTEEN: RAJIV'S TRYST WITH DESTINY

1 Arun Nehru interviewed by Brook Associates, March 1, 1996.
2 Ibid.
3 *India Today*, June 15, 1991.
4 Nugent, Nicholas, *Rajiv Gandhi: Son of a Dynasty*, London, 1990, p. 122.
5 BBC *Panorama* interview, broadcast January 18, 1988.
6 Quoted in Nugent, op. cit., p. 152.
7 Arun Shourie interviewed by Brook Associates, May 7, 1996.
8 Arun Nehru interviewed by Brook Associates, September 25, 1996.
9 *India Today*, November 15, 1989.
10 General K. Sundarji interviewed by Brook Associates, May 14, 1996.
11 Arun Shourie interviewed by Sveriges Television, April 28, 1987.
12 Rajiv Gandhi interviewed by Siga Arts International, March 12, 1991.
13 Gandhi, Sonia, *Rajiv*, Delhi, 1992, p. 12.
14 BBC *Panorama* interview, broadcast January 18, 1988.
15 Arun Nehru interviewed by Brook Associates, September 25, 1996.
16 Gandhi, op. cit., p. 136.
17 David Sells' report on BBC *Newsnight*, November 15, 1989.

18 Merchant, Minhaz, *Rajiv Gandhi: The End of a Dream*, Delhi, 1991, p. 259.
19 *India Today*, November 29, 1989.
20 Merchant, op. cit., p. 263.
21 *India Today*, June 15, 1991.
22 Rajiv broadcast reported on BBC News, November 29, 1989.
23 Jawaharlal's last will and testament of June 21, 1954, quoted in Akbar, M. J., *Nehru: The Making of India*, London, 1988, p. 582.
24 *India Today*, November 15, 1990.
25 Rajiv Gandhi interviewed by Siga Arts International, April 1, 1989.
26 Gandhi, op. cit., p. 13.
27 Ibid., p. 56.
28 Ibid., p. 14.
29 Rajiv in *The Times of India*, March 10, 1991, quoted in Merchant, op. cit., p. 280.
30 T. N. Kaul interviewed by Brook Associates, April 23, 1996.
31 Arun Nehru interviewed by Brook Associates, March 1, 1996.
32 Inder Malhotra interviewed by Brook Associates, September 26, 1996.
33 *India Today*, June 15, 1991.
34 Gandhi, op. cit., p. 13.
35 BBC Television News, May 13, 1991.
36 *India Today*, June 15, 1991.
37 Ibid.
38 Gandhi, op. cit. p. 14.
39 *India Today*, June 15, 1991.
40 Ibid.
41 Barbara Crossette interviewed by Brook Associates, September 8, 1996.
42 Merchant, op. cit., p. 302.

### CHAPTER EIGHTEEN: SIFTING THROUGH THE FRAGMENTS

1 Vir Sanghvi interviewed by Brook Associates, September 27, 1996.
2 *India Today*, June 15, 1991.
3 Mehta, Ved, *Rajiv Gandhi and Rama's Kingdom*, London, 1994, p. 153.
4 Reported on Visnews tape, May 22 and 23, 1991.
5 James Manor interviewed by Brook Associates, December 9, 1996.
6 *India Today*, June 30, 1991.
7 Gandhi, Sonia, *Rajiv*, Delhi, 1992, p. 72.
8 Merchant, Minhaz, *Rajiv Gandhi: The End of a Dream*, Delhi, 1991, p. 283.

# INDEX

# ABOUT THE AUTHORS

**Jad Adams** is a television producer and writer who has won both Royal Television Society and British Press awards for his work. He was educated at Sussex and London Universities. He worked on national newspapers until 1982 when he joined the BBC's current affairs series "Panorama."

**Phillip Whitehead** is one of Britain's foremost television producers. He joined the BBC in 1961, and later produced ITV's *This Week*. He first met Jawaharlal Nehru and Mrs. Pandit when President of the Union at Oxford, and subsequently led delegations to India which enabled him to retain links with prime ministers, Indira and Rajiv Gandhi. He has been a director of Brook Associates for ten years, making "The Thatcher Factor," "The Kennedys," for which he won an Emmy award in 1993, "The Windsors," "The Churchills" and "The Last of the Tsars."